Financial and Cost Management for Libraries and Information Services

Second Edition

Financial and Cost Management for Libraries and Information Services

Second Edition

Stephen A. Roberts

BOWKER
SAUR

London · Melborne · Munich · New Providence, NJ

Library of Congress Cataloging-in-Publication Data
Roberts, Stephen A. (Stephen Andrew)
Financial and cost management for libraries and information services / Stephen Roberts. – 2nd ed.
p. cm.
Rev. ed. of: Cost management for library and information services. 1985.
Includes bibliographical references and index.
ISBN 1-85739-089-X (acid-free paper)
1. Libraries–Cost control. 2. Information services–Cost control. 3. Information services–Finance. 4. Library finance. 5. Libraries–Great Britain–Cost control. 6. Information services–Great Britain – Cost control. 7. Information services–Great Britain–Finance. 8. Library finance–Great Britain. I. Roberts, Stephen A. (Stephen Andrew) Cost management for library and information services. II. Title.
Z683.R58 1997.
025.1'1–dc21
97-30611
CIP

British Library Cataloguing in Publication Data
Roberts, Stephen A. (Stephen Andrew), 1946–
Financial cost management for libraries and information services. – 2nd ed.
1. Library finance 2. Library administration
I. Title II. Cost management for library and information services
025.1'1
ISBN 185739089X

First edition, Cost Management for Library and Information Services, published 1985 by Butterworth & Co

Published by Bowker-Saur
Maypole House, Maypole Road
East Grinstead, West Sussex RH19 1HU, UK
Tel: +44 (0) 1342 330100 Fax: +44 (0) 1342 330191
E-mail: lis@bowker-saur.com
Internet Website: http://www.bowker-saur.com/service/
Bowker-Saur is part of REED BUSINESS INFORMATION LIMITED
ISBN 1 85739 089 X

Cover design by Juan Hayward
Typeset by Florencetype Ltd, Stoodleigh, Devon
Figure artwork by Sally Priest
Printed on acid-free paper
Printed and bound in Great Britain by Antony Rowe Ltd, Chippenham

Contents

Preface to the first edition

This book has been written in the hope that it will fill a yawning gap in the literature of library management. The author quickly recognized the existence of that gap when, as a researcher, the time came to carry out practical cost studies of various library operations. The literature of librarianship was not totally devoid of material of some relevance, but it was clear that there were many fundamental questions of library and information service cost studies which had hardly been written about. Twenty years ago the first steps in library automation were being taken and systems analysis naturally led on to cost analysis. At the same time, at least in the UK, there was more than a stirring of interest in considering the application of management science to library and information operations; hitherto, a field of interest largely confined to the professional area in the United States.

To answer some of the fundamental questions in many cases needed no more than a step in the direction of the many books on business enterprise management, cost accounting and work measurement. But on reflection the approaches taken by such works did not always easily fit the context and circumstances of library management; terminologies differed suggesting to the author a conceptual variance between normal business enterprise and normal library enterprise (leaving the term 'normal' undefined!). Now, after a period of addressing oneself to the questions and problems originally identified it is probably true to say that some convergence between enterprise methods and library methods is beginning to emerge, as indeed the conditions and environment of both areas of activity have themselves changed over twenty years. But, for the author at least, the slow working out and realization of differences and similarities has been an essential part of the process of convergence; the filling of the yawning gap as it were, at least in the writer's own mind.

The text of this book has emerged over a period of five years; the author would be the first to regret the delay. Its roots go back to the latter days of the Library Management Research Unit in 1978 and a series of projects costing various aspects of inter-library lending. This work raised the fundamental questions sufficiently to set in hand during 1979 a slow progress to exploring and reviewing the literature. By 1980 the idea of producing a manual of costing for library managers had seized the writer's mind, and had become an element in the programme of the Centre for Library and Information Management, which by then the LMRU had become, following its move from Cambridge to Loughborough. By Autumn 1981 when the author had the good fortune to make a professional study tour to the United States as the Sir Evelyn Wrench Travelling Scholar for the English-Speaking Union a fairly extensive draft of the text had been prepared. Discussions with library managers and researchers in the United States, and the chance to reflect which the tour provided, made an important contribution to the subsequent history of the manuscript. By then the idea of a manual, in loose leaf and sectional form, was proving a practical problem. It was clear that insufficient consensus existed to provide a solid groundbase for a manual or handbook which would be of direct operational use to library managers. At the same time the pressures of short-term contract research at the Centre called for publication and dissemination. During much of 1982 the whole text was extensively rewritten and revised, and what is now published is essentially the result of that period of work. Certain fundamental ideas were clarified in the author's mind and the time came to crystallize the argument, even if later events and views may not prove to be so kind. It was hoped to produce the text initially as a report which would have been circulated to many interested people for consultation and comment; thus the author's crude and often untested arguments were to be refined. There were at one point to be several other texts dealing with related matters in the field of library economics, some written in collaboration and others perhaps to be commissioned. That initial report might have ultimately become this or another monograph.

However, early 1982 brought unassailable difficulties at CLAIM following a massive cut in the projected budget for the Centre, and indeed changes of viewpoint as to the future purpose and development of the Centre. With a contract deadline of February 1983, the writer had to modify many of the plans originally made by himself and others for work arising out of the costing programme. But, the author was committed to the project and is now glad to present his ideas to professional colleagues in the present form. Hopefully it will provide a beginning for a debate about an area of library management which is important yet relatively neglected.

Many previous authors and professional colleagues have provided an impetus and stimulus for this book, and happily the writer is still associated with many of them, as he would hope to continue this association in future. Some names, however, must be mentioned. Maurice Line and Michael Brittain from a previous research project on social science information at University of Bath played a very significant part in the author's development as a researcher and investigator. Colleagues at the Library Management Research Unit, and latterly the Centre for Library and Information Management have provided support and stimulated debate; particularly to be mentioned are Alan Cooper, Lesley Gilder, Marilyn Hart, Patricia Layzell Ward and Andrea Merry. A much wider circle of research colleagues and friends have been an invaluable source of ideas, interest and encouragement for this book; amongst these are Peter Taylor, Andy Exon, Geoff Ford, Tom Whitehall and Malcolm Smith. Australians, John Barclay and Earle Gow are also well within the circle. Continuous maternal encouragement for the whole project has come from Mrs Betty Roberts; whilst at a late stage, Daphne Redwell made a vital contribution to the final reading of the proofs. Yet, all those to whom I have talked about this project in Britain, the United States and West Germany must receive their share of my thanks, and must not take offence that they remain anonymous. Several typists have laboured mightily with repeated typings of drafts; Sandra Knight and Sheila Fox will know what I mean and are praised and thanked by me for all their efforts. However, for any final errors and omissions, I must remain solely responsible.

Stephen A. Roberts
1985

From May 1975 to December 1983 the author was employed by University of Cambridge (to August 1976) and Loughborough University of Technology on research grants awarded to those institutions by the British Library Research and Development Department. A significant amount of the time required to prepare this book was provided through employment funded by those research grants which, in addition, was supplemented by work undertaken in the author's own time.

Preface to the second edition

More than a decade has passed since the predecessor to the present book was written and published. *Cost management for library and information services* appeared in 1985 in the hope that it would help to fill a 'yawning gap' in the literature of library management. The original preface may be consulted in the preliminaries to the present work for those who wish to know the whys and wherefores of its gestation, and a little about the motivation for it and the creative processes which were explored to realize it. At least it became a book which 'sold out' and which suggested that after a decent interval of time the question of a revision or a new edition might arise. Selling out may not tell much about the worth of a book which seemed at the time to have few established competitors, but perhaps the curiosity of the professional public for whom it was intended was satisfied. The evidence of reviews which mostly gave praise and constructive criticism suggested a mix of need and potential value for the book; this can be added to the subjective assumption that it has fulfilled a purpose.

Around 1992 the publishers (who were now Bowker Saur, and who had absorbed the library and information list of Butterworth & Co, the original publishers) suggested that a new edition should be considered. Given the usual reasons for delay which some authors feign or plead, the serious task of starting to produce the new work was held back until around 1995. Several years before that date the author had been collaborating with a co-author on another project of similar vein for another UK publisher. With considerable regret that project failed to achieve its final publication. Nevertheless that activity provided the author with impetus for a new *Cost management for library and information services.*

Thus by 1996 the present work under the title of *Financial and cost management for libraries and information services* was beginning to take shape on the following lines. Although the central core of cost management was still a necessary component advisers sensed that the market required a more broadly developed text which took a wider span of financial management as its direction. This has been a confirmation of changes that were beginning in the mid-1980s and which have become more fully developed in the 1990s. Library and information services were developing in the public and private sector alike in a growing commercial and market orientated environment. The modern information economy was emerging within the growing reality of the promised information society, itself adapting from the increasing use of information and communication technologies.

The present work has expanded the boundaries of the earlier text not only by developing the financial management theme in a technical manner, but by addressing its context in the wider setting of the organization and its management. This has required a broader treatment of the business and environmental context. Having modernized the approach to meet the needs of readers and publishers alike it is the author's hope that a central commitment to library and information professionalism has not been lost. In looking at financial managerial matters the already familiar features of costing and budgeting have been developed and strengthened, and the links to management information, performance and evaluation studies further enhanced in a way that encompasses the paradigm in library and information management. With a familiar basis to build on, the extension of discussion into areas of market, commercial enterprise and business development is given a continuity of treatment which many practitioners will find familiar.

The text of the original work remains intact, since the message it conveyed is largely unchanged and still very necessary. The author must then hope that the new material, which constitutes as much as two thirds of the work, is not merely grafted on to the old, but is well integrated so as to demonstrate that together both parts form a unified and greater whole. The original referencing to sources has been left unchanged, but there has been expansion through reference to post-1985 sources to make the text as contemporary as possible. It seems that very little of the original work's key sources have been replicated by fresh work; this earlier corpus then continues to provide much of the principles with later work demonstrating applications, as well as new critical perspectives.

Personal acknowledgements need to be made for the new work, which can best be described simply as a second edition, but more accurately as a new work based on a revised and expanded first edition. Personal acknowledgements are still required to all those who inspired the first edition; many thanks to all of you for your contributions in continuity. In addition there are some new ones to make. Sheila Pantry proved a valuable co-author irrespective of our joint fate with the above mentioned project and publisher; her practitioner viewpoint and experience of management in major government libraries served to sharpen my ideas and informed many stimulating discussions. Several pages of the present text use material reflecting her contribution to the co-authored text, and I thank her for this and many other beneficial insights. Tony Olden at Thames Valley University has given much encouragement as a working colleague at our home institution; some students as much as other staff there have been unwittingly involved in helping to clarify and test out my ideas; thanks to all of them.

The era of the personal computer has helped to relegate acknowledgement for secretarial support; this time I did it all myself on an Apple Macintosh. But even so there have been helpers. I am without any doubt indebted to my wife Teresita, who has patiently allowed me time to work on the book through all its diverse stages; without her support many more delays might have ensued. Her colleague Val Svendsen at the University of Reading worked wonders when it came to scanning the original text and helping us in the mysteries of the conversion; many thanks. Along the way Teresita's former professional colleagues in La Habana, Cuba have given encouragement through taking an interest in my work. Andy Exon and Carmel Maguire in Australia have said many right words. And not least, I have enjoyed the support and encouragement of the editorial team at Bowker Saur in East Grinstead; how tolerant you have been of all the missed deadlines! To all these, family, friends and colleagues many many thanks; you have all helped to make the journey happen and to have made it worthwhile.

Stephen A. Roberts
October 1997

Acknowledgements

The author wishes to record acknowledgements to the following for permission to reproduce extracts from publications or documents.

To the editor of *Aslib Proceedings* and the author for parts of the article by D. W. G. Clements, 'The costing of library systems', *Aslib Proceedings*, 27, (3), 98–111 (1975), reproduced in Appendix 1.

To the Chief of the Publications Service at the International Labour Office for two diagrams taken from INTERNATIONAL LABOUR OFFICE, *Introduction to Work Study*, Geneva, International Labour Office (1958), reproduced in *Figures 5.4 and 5.5*.

To the Institute of Cost and Management Accountants for extracts from J. M. S. Risk, *The Classification and Coding of Accounts*, London, IMCA, 76–79 (1956), reproduced in Appendix 3.

To the editor of *LIBER Bulletin* for material from K. W. Humphreys, 'Costing in university libraries', *LIBER Bulletin*, (5/6), 8–32 (1974), reproduced in Appendix 2.

To the Massachusetts Institute of Technology Press for material from M. Hamburg *et al.*, *Library Planning and Decision making Systems*, Cambridge, MIT Press, 156–164 and 192–195 (1974), reproduced in Appendix 6.

To Taylor Graham Publishing for material extracted from Allen, L. (1989) Strategic planning for libraries: a convergence of library management theory and research. *International Journal of Information and Library Research*, 1(3), 197–212 and from Line, M.B. (1986) The survival of academic libraries in hard times: reaction to pressures, rational and irrational. *British Journal of Academic Librarianship*, 1(1) 1–12.

Tables

Figures

Chapter 1

Context

1.1 Libraries, information and the financial environment: definitions and purpose

This discussion of financial management is designed to meet the needs of those who would describe themselves as information and/or library professionals working usually in some formal organizational capacity and who thus play a significant part in the communication and transfer of information from its origins and sources to actual and potential users. The formal organizational setting of information and library activity defines a mediating and intermediary role in the broad process of communication and information transfer.

Given the variety, complexity and changing nature of the information domain, the framework and language used for the discussion has to be concrete and specific enough to meet technical requirements, but also capable of a more varied and even local interpretation and application. The intention is to contextualize financial management in its information and library professional setting.

Accordingly the discussion is relevant to libraries and library services of all kinds and to organizational units providing information and related services to users. In addition to handling documentary and bibliographic media, the sources acquired to service user needs are increasingly in multiple media and multimedia. Person to person communication and bodies of expertise, expert knowledge and intelligence are also standard media in this environment. In the last decade of this century electronic and computer technologies are producing fundamental changes of lasting significance. However, the underlying financial reality remains constant.

The formal organizations just mentioned are likely to be called libraries, information services, information centres, information units, learning resource centres, information resources departments, library and information systems and departments, information resource centres, information management departments and units, information systems departments and sometimes computer centres and data centres or services. These aspects are examined in more detail later in this chapter (see other papers by the author, Roberts, 1987; Roberts, 1996). In this book *library* and its related terms are used in a generic sense to include the above categories as a class. Where the terms *information* and *library* are used together the precedence of one term over another does not carry any special significance; if any significance is meant it will be evident from the context or will be specifically noted.

Library and information professional is a useful generic occupational descriptor, which can be broken down into a whole variety of job titles. Typical titles are librarian, information officer, documentalist, archivist, information manager, information systems specialist and similar. Other role titles such as computer specialist, programmer, publisher, publications officer, bookseller, public relations officer, advice worker, counsellor, intelligence officer, researcher, analyst and so on are not usually seen within the target audience for this discussion, but when they encompass core library and documentation tasks it is relevant to them.

Given the organizational and occupational background and the activity processes involved, it remains to define the *financial environment* which forms the substantive theme of this book. (See Chapter Three for further definitional discussion)

Financial relates to the sourcing, deployment and utilization of monetary resources in direct or surrogate form, specifically in the domain and formal organizational contexts outlined above: that is, informational and documentary sources mediated through library and information service processes, directed towards satisfying the actual and potential information needs of users specifically and people in general.

Financial management, in the sense used in this book, is a process involving the monetarized dimensions of real physical, material and intellectual resources. The specific components of resources and financial management are discussed in detail in Chapters Two and

Three against the general context of the problem which forms the basis of this chapter.

Within the overall financial context, the rationale for the book is developed around the focus of *cost concepts* and *cost measurement.* The justification for this is built up around the status of cost data as the essential measure of financial processes. Accurate measurement of the associated cost and monetary flows is the key to the elaboration of financial management.

This orientation is of practical significance too, because the present book is a development from its first edition *Cost management for library and information services* (Roberts, 1985) and a further development of themes treated in a previous collection of readings (Roberts, 1984). Indeed the first edition text forms the core of the present work, subsequently elaborated to take account of a further decade of professional evolution and practice (Chapter One provides a discussion of these changes specifically). The author's hope is that this elaboration is sufficient and no claim is made to a complete review of circumstances and development since the mid-1980s; the integrity of the original text has been largely maintained, and along with it the referencing to what might be perceived now as somewhat historical material. Reference to this older material has been justified by its part in the original discussion, the fact that it represents the development of the financial and costing speciality, and to some extent because of the absence of replacement material in the literature following the mid-1980s.

Thus, reasonably and practically, there are some limitations to this book about which the reader must be aware. The book does not attempt to be either a formal or comprehensive treatment about the whole of financial management in general, from the raising of funding, through planning, budgeting, budgetary control and financial and business accounting, to the impact and consequences of such strategies and their tactical implementation. For this perspective the reader must go to the formal literatures of business, management, finance and accounting. Such coverage is beyond the knowledge and competence of the author at any level of detail. However, the book attempts to be comprehensive as regards the special characteristics of the library and information field.

As the discussion across the chapters will show, the present book does have a clear and even large niche to occupy. It provides a broad conspectus of the financial management field in so far as it reflects the circumstances, experiences and needs of the library and information sector as defined. It follows a route of historical progression from library and information professionals' concern with the economic aspects of their activities, to the realization that cost measures could provide a basic key to further understanding.

The discourse therefore treats financial management broadly, from a specific cost-driven perspective. Given a mastery of cost management the manager is provided with a set of more inclusive keys to address a whole scale of financial managerial issues. Hopefully the reader will therefore leave the discussion with a greater technical mastery and conceptual understanding of cost management, and thus a strengthened capacity to acquire a mastery of the broader financial management field, via the stops identified along the way.

1.2 The financial managerial environment

Every library manager recognizes the significance of cost data in some form as an essential aspect of service management. This is such an indelible fact that it can be supported without further qualification. However, in the field of library costing and in the further realms of library economics, even a cursory review of current practices reveals that there is little else that can be taken for granted. The practice of costing library and information operations and the principles and techniques available to support the economic management of library and information services are one of the weakest areas in the repertoire of library management.

If the normal enterprise model of a typical business firm, or some type of former public sector enterprise (e.g. electricity supply, municipal transport undertaking) is examined, a distinctive machinery for financial and economic management is readily identifiable. There will be some form of stewardship accounting showing, according to conventional detail, the annual financial position (income and expenditure account, and balance sheet).

A scrutiny of enterprise personnel will show that there is a number of financial officers: this may include a finance manager and/or budget director, an accountancy position with a financial and/or managerial component, administrative positions to deal with financial, budget and accounting functions including purchasing, sales, account control, and internal efficiency, as well as support positions elsewhere in the organization concerned with the collection and monitoring of financial and other management data. Even the smallest firm may have one or two specialist posts with considerable financial and accounting responsibilities, whereas in medium sized and large enterprises the number of specialist positions may number tens and even hundreds. In business, commerce and industry the concern with costs and the possibility of costing procedures is very marked.

In most libraries (except perhaps the largest national, research or academic library organizations) the financial and accounting apparatus appears very much more diluted and attentuated. This will be true whether the system concerned is a public library serving an urban, rural or mixed area, an educational library, a research library or a special library and information unit. In most typical libraries, and even in some quite large library systems, the centre of financial responsibility is the librarian alone, or the librarian and one other officer, with or without some direct clerical support. Certain financial responsibilities may be delegated to other staff members, but these will generally be for the purpose of data collection, rather than accountability and responsibility. The host organization of the library may or may not have some influence and responsibility.

In addition the actual machinery (consisting of procedures, conventions, systems, forms and specifications) will be found to be relatively underdeveloped compared to the conventional business enterprise, whether it be industrial or commercial, public or private sector. For our working argument this can be taken as the basic state of affairs; it can be well documented by reference to the library literature: for instance as listed in Cooper (1980), Prentice (1983), Smith (1991), Aren, Webreck and Mark (1987), Kantor (1989), and Virgo (1985); see Section 7.5.5 for further readings, reviews and bibliography.

Quite naturally there are some exceptions to this general picture of practice. For example, some of the major American research libraries have a greater level of financial, accounting and cost control built into their operating methods and administrations, but even here the general view of experts in library financial matters is that there is still a long way to go before adequate systems become a frequent practice (see Roberts, 1982b) for a previous commentary).

What most would agree is that although the level of information on financial inputs may be quite good (for example, in fairly detailed line-item, or even programme budgets) the systems still do not provide the library manager with the throughput and output cost data needed for both control and performance evaluation. Professional thinking about these matters does appear to be more advanced in the USA than in the UK. A number of library scientists and others in West Germany have also considered these problems. A seminar organized by the Association of Research Libraries provided what was then a state of the art survey (Association of Research Libraries, 1981). More recently the Office of Arts and Libraries in the UK has codified similar thinking (1990) derived from the North American experience via King Associates.

What reasons might explain this relatively weak development of financial and management accounting systems in libraries as compared to the conventional business enterprise? One initial reason may be the fact that many libraries have never been, and are unlikely to become corporate independent legal entities. For instance, they have rarely had to comply with the legal provisions of various types of legislation that affect private and public companies. The typical library and information unit is part of a larger corporate organization (local authority, firm, educational institution), and thus for public or external purposes does not have to be subject to such searching financial and accounting discipline.

Of course this is not the same as saying that internal financial accounting is unnecessary, but there is considerably less motivation to provide it. A library and information unit which is no more than another cost focus in a larger corporate body can often meet accounting requirements with only minimal representation in the open financial machinery, or in the published accounts of the host organization. Nevertheless, the picture has begun to change in the 1990s with the growth of commercial 'or-for-profit' information services, based on new technology and operating in multidisciplinary areas. Changing political philosophies (e.g. in the UK and USA) and trends towards cost recovery and privatization in times of economic stress have altered and continue to influence the situation (see Sections 1.6–1.9 and Chapter Three).

Where the requirement for public accountability (for instance to shareholders, or to a public corporation board) is weak it is easy to appreciate how the lack of financial obligation leads to almost total lack of action or activity in areas of financial and management accountability. It can be said that the mimimum standard will often be regarded as quite sufficient.

A third reason may spring from the historical fact that a tradition of financial and managerial accountability has never grown up or been nurtured in libraries. Therefore only a limited number of techniques and procedures have been necessary to provide a minimum degree of managerial control. So in the typical library there will be a budget usually constructed for the library and information organization as a whole, rather than one broken down into detail on a programme by programme basis. At the end of the financial period some kind of revenue and expenditure statement may be given: see for example, the usual format of library annual reports.

In many libraries the major element of staff expenditure and appropriation is handled outside the library, so there may be only minimal cost accounting here; all staff payments will be handled elsewhere in the host institution. This usually leaves bookfund and miscellaneous material expenditures under direct control of the library manager. The handling of invoices and orders can be a substantial task but the accounting principles involved are very simple; for example, making the appropriate control of bookfund divisions and regulating the flow of orders and accounts between suppliers. However, the trend to financial devolution in organizations in the 1990s is changing the position away from minimal to greater data requirements.

But these three points – non-corporateness, lack of motivation to develop systems, and lack of a historical tradition related to limited control over limited resources – only give part of the picture. They provide no real justification for the incontrovertible fact that whether or not the library resources are externally controlled and however they might be financially regulated in a wider sense, the library manager is still responsible for the allocation and utilization of resources within the organization, for the setting of goals and objectives, for the regulation of performance, accountability over the flows of resources (not always in the financial sense) and internal economic management.

All these managerial economic responsibilities should suggest and require the development of as much financial and managerial accounting discipline as might be expected in a fully responsible independent corporate enterprise. With this kind of need in mind the three reasons given above are hardly relevant except from the point of view of an academic post hoc categorization. If the library or information unit is considered for the moment as an internal or closed system, without the external responsibilities of the normal corporate enterprise, it is quite clear that the needs of economic management must in the end be much the same as those of the corporate enterprise. This suggests that the need for financial and managerial accountability is just as great, subject to the difference that internal data may not immediately find their way into the corporate system of general accountability. And yet there is still resistance in the face of this powerful argument for managerial economic information relating to finance and costs.

A fourth reason could be the one some commentators have suggested: that libraries lack a definable product or final output. This view would at least allow that total final costs are important, even if they do not represent a very specific or visible product and however crude this idea might be. At the present time, there is usually only a visible identification of throughput costs, for instance as a cost of technical processing per bibliographic item handled. The costing of units of user and reader service (however defined) is much less common and more difficult. The definition of output is related closely to the question of library performance measures. If it has been difficult to agree on appropriate measures of performance defined functionally, then it has also been difficult to agree on appropriate measures of output across a wide range of library activities.

A fifth reason could be that there is an inherent barrier to objective measurement and management stemming from the way resources are applied by library managers to service, or more philosophically or 'mystically' from some abstract or some believed quality about 'libraries' and/or information. There are many different forms of input, which are dispersed and divided in many different ways across the service and the means of providing the service. These subjective points about inherent complexity strike some emotional chords with library managers, but it would be difficult to explore the reasons why this is so, precisely because of this subjective element. For many reasons, the library looks different from many conventional business and manufacturing enterprises which are the source and model for the repertoire of financial accounting practices in management and commerce. The business of making the apocryphal 'widget' or 'blodgett' seems to have a clinical purity about it no matter the scale of the undertaking, in terms of men and material resources involved or quantity of product.

But many librarians do not have this starkly materialistic view of their work. It may even be that the library profession has made, and prefers to keep the view of its business emotionally different and let this influence economic rationality. There is a clear case for the view that library managements have strongly defended a particular 'metaphorical' view of their responsibilities for reasons of social, cultural and professional esteem. After all dentists, doctors and solicitors do not, by and large, run their activities in factory or production line fashion (although increasingly the idea of doing so may become more attractive to such professionals even if the drive comes from managers, administrators and political fashion).

A sixth reason could be that as a professional, the librarian has always considered the functions and impact of the final delivery of service to the client as being of paramount importance; this is after all part of the ethos of professionalism. Provided this can be achieved within a final budgetary target the librarian and funder may be quite content (although, where there are so few controls on performance, no one really knows whether the resources are being best used). Internal processes of library work have been treated contentedly for many years by many managers as a convenient black box, to be looked into as infrequently as possible.

In the normal corporate enterprise, input price, expense distribution, cashflow, unit costs and profit are the most used economic measures both of enterprise activity and performance achieved. In the library and information unit this must be broadly analogous, even if the final definition of some of the measures differs – most notably the notion of profit, which may be replaced by measures of value, welfare and satisfaction. Economic performance is in large measure about financial performance and therefore cost measurement should play a central role. When costs can be measured, and where performance may range over a number of alternative strategies, the need for control of costs, and therefore for accounting and accountability is ever present, to signal to the manager the level of performance that is being achieved, and the possible need to seek alternative strategies.

Without cost data there can be no real regulation, or control, or indeed understanding of economic performance. If any of the six reasons given earlier are even partly valid in explaining the current state of library practice in financial and managerial accounting, then it is clear that existing methods and practices are not likely to provide the capability required for developing the managerial economic tools which library and information units require. Furthermore, if the basic tools of measurement of cost are absent, the many copious schemes and proposals which are to be found in the library literature for regulating and measuring the operational and economic performance of library and information units will all achieve very little. It is from this lowly base that appropriate structures must be built. The objective of this book is to suggest how this might be done in general, in ways appropriate to a wide variety of library and information services.

The standpoint of the present book can now be made clear. As a closed system subject to internal control the library and information unit should be treated as a normal corporate enterprise with respect to financial management, managerial accounting needs, and managerial economics. Although the library may not have direct financial control over all resources used (e.g. staffing), internal management needs dictate that surrogate control is excercised. That is, the manager must have full information and data on all resources (including staff costs), so that all decisions about allocation and those of an economic nature can be taken in the light of the fullest possible management information.

1.3 Economic and financial pressures faced by libraries

In the last twenty years the economic and financial pressures on most libraries have grown enormously. Inflation in prices and costs due to long-term changes in economic conditions worldwide has become the most serious pressure. Library managers need no reminder of this. The following list is typical and useful as an aide-mémoire, in defining the extent of the problems faced. Webster (1981) cites a number of sources of cost increase.

- Extraordinary increases in unit costs of published materials, magnified for research libraries by the need to purchase foreign materials at a time when currency exchange rates are very volatile.
- The continued but varied and complex forces of growth in the number of published documents of all kinds which form the potential pool of library acquisitions; this is well complemented by the steady increase in the price of all documents and of academic materials.
- Ever growing demands from faculty and students to have access to a wider range of materials, and generating greater loads on library staff and resources in order to satisfy these demands.

In addition the perennial problems of other pressures can be cited.

- Wage and salary increases, burdening the staff sector of the budget, almost always the largest segment of any budget.
- Fixed or contracting library budgets in real terms means that staff costs absorb a higher proportion of the budget if no reduction in

establishment levels can be made, or gains established in productivity and efficiency.

- Pressures to adopt new technology are becoming intense, and although justified in terms of long-term savings, the short-term demand on capital is often great, leading to a temporary (or even permanent) sacrifice on other spending.
- The semi-fixed cost of commitment to serials subscriptions has continued to be a major management and resource problem. It is not always possible or desirable to pare subscriptions down at a rate faster than the overall increase in subscription costs.
- Where new building and capital projects can be undertaken the burden of new construction costs is fearsomely high, even for basic accommodation. Some new construction of buildings is unavoidable even when steady state collection policies are implemented.
- Inter-library lending and other externally purchased services all show cost and price increases.
- Even where substitutes exist between programme content and resources, the costs of transferring resources, restructuring and retraining are often very high. Projects and redeployments of resources are often undertaken on the basis of imperfect knowledge of their full economic consequences.
- To some extent libraries are in competition (directly or indirectly) with other programmes in host institutions and agencies. For example, library and information unit share of institution budget remains at best constant, but often declines in proportion from an already low level.

A trenchant review of the possibilities has been offered by Line (1986) and is well worth substantial quotation, where he offers some general precepts:

On suggested principles for running a library: 'the following are suggested as sound and defensible principles on which an academic library might be run.'

> (1) *The library/information services required by the institution should be provided in the way that is most cost-effective for the institution.* Nothing should inhibit the optimal use of resources made available to the library (as charging for selected services would, and as departmental control

of the budget probably would). This implies that the institution (with the librarian's guidance) should work out precisely what facilities and services are required to support the work of the institution, and what resources are required to provide these facilities and services. A similar principle should apply to every academic service.

(2) *Within the library deployment of resources – of money, staff and accommodation – should be optimised.* This requires that the librarian should (a) explore alternative ways of giving each required service; (b) calculate the cost of alternative ways, including the existing one; (c) calculate the effectiveness of alternative ways. If the results of these exercises are to achieve full usefulness, the librarian must have the freedom to deploy his resources for optimal cost-effectiveness. This requires a budget structure quite different from the norm.

(3) *The valid use of library resources – stock, staff, equipment and accommodation – should be maximised.* This minimises unit cost per use and helps to provide a justification for the operation – or not, as the case may be, depending on how low minimal is. The same principle should of course be applied to other academic facilities.

(4) *Abuse of resources should be minimised.* Where this conflicts with the principles above, it should normally be subsidiary to them. For example, heavy penalties or deterrent charges may minimise abuse at the expense of reducing valid use.

(5) *Individual members of the institution should not pay for facilities or services that they need to fulfill their function in the institution.* This has been argued above under 'Earning money' [see the actual paper for the argument].

(6) *Whether the library should carry the cost of a facility or service or require departments to pay them should be determined according to cost-effectiveness.* As where the term is used elsewhere in this paper, 'cost-effectiveness' is to be interpreted broadly and in the longer term. This criterion seems the only sound one on which to select activities for charging of all elements in library expenditure to departments, but this is very unlikely to achieve optimal cost-effectiveness (principle 1 above).

(7) *The library should not transfer its costs to users.* (Although the library may not charge users directly, and although it may not even charge departments, the reduction or cancellation of some services (such as personal assistance with manual bibliographic searches) can make the user incur costs, if only in time, that he cannot recover from the institution.

Line then goes on to outline some solutions to economic pressures 'if the reasoning above is sound, the following are measures that might reasonably be taken to mitigate economic pressures.'

(1) *Services can be provided to external users, particularly industry, for payment.* This can range from allowing external users and institutions access to the stock, to the provision of specially tailored services which recover more than they cost. Pump-priming may be needed. This could be a highly attractive course, some industries (as noted below) are contracting out their library and information services, and there is no fundamental reason why academic institutions should not make a bid. The extent to which staff attitudes may need to be changed – in the direction of entrepreneurship and giving value for money – should not be underestimated.

(2) *Economies can be sought in fulfilling existing functions.* This requires a radical scrutiny of every function, an exploration of different ways of achieving it, and a choice of the least costly. All costs should be taken into account.

(3) *The use of the total budget should be optimised.* This requires: (a) an adequate costing system, which calculates regularly the cost of all activities and services, including unit cost; (b) a financial control system, to ensure that expenditure is properly controlled from month to month. These can be implemented with any budget structure, though they require, certainly initally, a good deal of effort. More fundamentally, optimisation requires: (c) a budget structured by function, cutting across staff, acquisitions, equipment and other recurrent expenditure (and possibly accommodation also). Virement between these expenditure heads would be necessary. The budget would be divided into: (i) Information services, including cataloguing, database searching, reference services, SDI etc.; (ii) Document provision, including acquisitions, inter-library document supply, electronic text access, etc.

Although virement may be hard if not impossible to achieve, a mere paper exercise along these lines will be very revealing: for example, if acquisitions and inter-library access are seen as part of the same budget, an optimal balance is much more likely to be attained.

(4) *What is required to provide the institution with the information it requires to fulfill its functions should be determined.* This is a longer term exercise, but it should put the library/information service on a far sounder footing than has been customary. A similar exercise should of course take place for every function and activity of the institution: the library should not be the only operation exposed to this kind of zero-based

budgeting. The exercise would include the development – and use – of performance indicators.

(5) *A forward plan should be constructed, taking account of the likely pressures, technical developments, changing needs etc., to try and ensure that appropriate future provision is made.*

Line concludes his paper in similar vein. Written a year or so after the first edition of this book, both views appear to converge on the same problem, which was truly being sensed in the 1980s. The present book is both theoretically a rationale and a technical discussion based on Line's agenda, and in Chapters Six, Seven and Eight tries to push towards the practical remedies he envisages. In fact in the 1990s the spirit of much of Line's agenda has been realized, even if practical techniques are still not widely enough disseminated and practised.

Line's advocacy of progamme budgets is significant, as is his insistence on the centrality of cost information, and the view that performance measures have a place in a wholly integrated budgetary and resource planning cycle.

1.4 The need for management information

Lynch and Eckard (1981) have identified reasons for collecting information about libraries. It is noticeable that most of these reasons relate to the general external environment in which libraries operate. Those who fund, govern and host library and information services would be very likely to call for information of these types. The information would also be very relevant to the internal management and planning of library and information services. Most management information serves a dual function of internal and external interest.

Lynch and Eckard list the following needs for information about libraries:

- determination of the health of library services
- drafting of legislation
- promotion of funding
- providing for the 'unmet' information needs of the population
- arguing for library support necessary for communities and educational institutions

- planning for satisfying future information needs of the population
- planning for resource sharing and networking
- performance measurement of library service at present levels of funding
- planning for improvement and future directions of library service
- policy development
- promotion of library service.

This is one important way of defining and looking at the problem of information for management. There are other ways which are much closer to the operational strategies which library managers have to cope with on a day-to-day basis; the provision of highly specific cost data is one of these.

Schwuchow (1977), discussing the economic analysis and evalution of information and documentation systems (including libraries), provides a similar list with a focus on costing.

> The ascertainment and analysis of costs forms the basis for determining the efficiency of I and D systems. Cost accounting should essentially accomplish the following tasks:
>
> (1) Specification of the cost structure, i.e. the way in which the total annual budget is composed of various types of costs (employment costs equipment costs, cost of materials etc.) and how it is distributed over the particular operational functions (acquisition, indexing and abstracting, storage, search service, SDI, administration etc.)
>
> (2) Supervision of the efficiency of individual operational functions and activities
>
> (3) Provision of material for the calculation of inter alia – the process of different kinds of services (retrospective searches, SDI services etc.)
>
> (4) Provision of decision-making aids for dealing with the question of whether to carry out certain operational functions and services within the system or whether to farm them out
>
> (5) Performance of comparative calculations among systems
>
> (6) Provision of material for forecasting costs in planning new or reorganizing existing systems

In addition Schwuchow observes that in the information and documentation systems existing in Germany in 1977 there is rarely a policy of continuous, detailed cost accounting. In the few cases where certain cost calculations are made, they are not based on uniform systems and methods, nor are detailed enough to come near to accomplishing the tasks mentioned. And this seems to be in spite of the fact that a number of highly detailed work measurement and library economic studies have been undertaken in that country at that time.

1.5 Library and information organizations: defining characteristics

Following the introductory remarks about the focus of this book, it is useful to elaborate the common characteristics of the *generic* library type: that is to say, any organization characterized by many or all of the following is a member of the class to which the discussion in this book is chiefly relevant.

Typically library and information service-providing organizations are characterized by the following:

1 An asset of acquisitions of conventional library and information materials (books and journals, bibliographical documentation and an increasing amount of multimedia published format).

2 Library and information materials organized in such ways to make them accessible for use and requiring a considerable level of technical infrastructure investment to maximize their value.

3 An assigned space in a location with an investment in a built environment, together with suitable furnishings and equipment (Still a very significant characteristic although challenged by the concepts of virtuality, hypermedia and cyberspace).

4 An establishment of personnel of suitable background, training and capability.

5 Specialised physical equipment, and computer-based technologies and telecommunications.

6 A development of resources to provide facilities for serving users directly and indirectly, e.g. specialized service departments.

7 Provision to users of services and products, based in whole or in part on the collections of library and information materials, e.g. consultation, loans.

8 Methods of delivering services and products to users, including means of supplementing these for the users from other remote locations, e.g. by inter-lending.

9 A relationship of some kind to other areas of the host organization and/or to other external organizations, environments and markets which it actually or potentially serves.

10 A degree of relationship to other organizations and/or resources, which has consequences for service capability and resource implications which may be financially significant, e.g. library co-operation and networking.

These organizational characteristics serve to define many of the financial aspects of library and information service provision. In addition, they vary according to the sectoral characteristics of library and information service provision. These sectoral groups have a cohesive identity, not least in terms of the financial and economic environment. The non-UK based reader is encouraged to illustrate these categories in depth and in application to the problems discussed in this text, from their own material and local examples.

1. Public libraries on a city, municipal or regional basis

These are general libraries for public use providing a broad range of services to all groups in the community. In the UK these libraries receive a mix of local and central grant funding. The public library is a substantial programme and organizational area within local government services generally (Murison, 1988; Usherwood, 1988; Midwinter and McVicar, 1994; Department of National Heritage, 1995). In the last decade the service has come under increasing funding constraint and pressure on resources. Responses have included greater attention to financial management, assessment of priorities, rationalization of services, and a concern with improving performance, cost-effectiveness and providing value for money.

2. National library facilities

This implies a focus on the library defined as the National Library and those libraries which have some national function, for example as providers of the last resort (Line and Line, 1987). These libraries benefit from legal deposit of publications and in the UK consist of the British Library, National Library of Wales and the National Library of Scotland. Although actively developing network functions of some kind, these do not have a differentiating effect on financial management practices.

3. Libraries in higher education

These are principally university libraries and those in university-related institutions (including former polytechnic libraries and those in the colleges and institutes sector). They are centrally funded through their institutions, via central funding councils. Similar pressures to those in public libraries have been encountered in the last decade or more in their financial and economic circumstances. Units of resource have been contracting, and most gains have come through greater efficiency and rationalization. These libraries have been caught up in sweeping institutional and organizational changes. One significant financial managerial innovation has been towards the creation of 'internal markets' to improve the allocation of resources and to make a more visible linkage between supply and consumption (Stirling, 1981; Thompson and Carr, 1987; Line, 1990; Thompson, 1991; Joint Funding Council, 1993; Poll, 1993).

4. Tertiary level institutions

Institutions at tertiary level offering vocational, technical and further education now form a more cohesive library sector, as a result of organizational reforms in the 16–19 age group provision, and other post-school non-advanced education, including adult education and training. Hitherto characterized by low levels of library provison and underresourced, these organizations are now leading exponents of the adaptation of library and information services to flexible learning. The exploitation of information technology will require a more advanced approach to resource management with significant financial implications (Pack and Pack, 1988).

5. School library provision

At primary and secondary level this is a significant sector although the per capita allocation of resource has always been low. Provision ranges across a very large number of service points in schools, usually supported by centralized school library service provision normally based on a public library system. Organizational changes in school education since the implementation of the Educational Reform Act (1987) have produced significant changes in the way school library service and provision might be handled in the future (Kinnell, 1992; Kinnell, 1993).

6. Special library and information services in private sector industrial and commercial organisations

These services have necessarily had to derive and absorb their organizational and resource characteristics from their host institutions. They have often led the way professionally in turning towards state of the art management and financing (Dossett, 1992; Webb, 1995).

7. Special library and information services in central government departments

These services have enough organization and resource characteristics in common to form a small but distinctive sector. Although sharing an organizational culture and financial environment, they are now becoming more diverse and innovative as the organizational culture of central government evolves towards a market orientation.

8. Special library and information services in public sector, quasi-public sector and voluntary sector organisations

These have many organizational and resource characteristics in common, although funding may come directly and/or indirectly from public funds and/or from non-public sources. Unlike other types of special library this sector is very heterogeneous both in composition and in practices employed.

In the UK (as well as elsewhere in Europe (e.g. Dudley *et al.*, 1991; Stroetmann, 1991; Von Busse and Ernestus, 1972), and in other parts of the world, especially in the developed economies) there is a very significant number of library and information services defined on the basis of the characteristics and sectors outlined above. These interface with many other organizational units and functions which are engaged in an ever widening range of information management and communication activities, involving some dependence and relationship with the bibliographic and documentation culture. Increasingly these diverse ranges of units and functions are beginning to interact through networking activities.

This present work is in the first place devoted to questions and practices of resource and financial management in the sectors noted above, but mindful of the strong evolutionary trends in the information world, which are not wedded to the weight of traditional practices and boundaries. In the last decade strong evolutionary tendencies and structural changes have taken place resulting especially from the application of new information technologies.

The significance of information as a manageable resource has led to the recognition of information management functions in enterprises and organizations of all types. Centres for the management of information now comprise computer services provision, management information functions, corporate information analysis centres, marketing departments, and so forth. Recognizing these developments, their impact on 'classic' library and information services, and the convergence of many types of information handling and documentation activity, this book outlines a programme for financial and resource management which is applicable across the different sectoral environments (Roberts, 1996).

1.6 The changing organizational environment

In the early 1990s library and information services (and associated activities) in these sectors have experienced changes in at least eight main areas:

1 In the area of professional philosophy and practice as a result of a continuous process of critical evaluation about the role, purpose, function and value of libraries for different purposes in society. This has resulted in impacts on goal identification which form part of the substructure of assumptions upon which financial and managerial changes and activities are based.

2 The structure of services offered has been subject to review and change on the supply and consumption sides respectively. Financial constraints have effected the services that can be provided. The search has continued to explore the relations between resources consumed and results achieved, and the nature of demand has been examined through the perspective of user study, performance and evaluation concepts.

3 There has been an ongoing debate about the capability of library and information services to maintain their traditional orientation,

and at the same time respond to new opportunities. Inevitably this highlights the need to acquire new assets and resources to further opportunities and innovations (Cronin and Gudim, 1987).

4 The trend towards increasing managerialism has continued, and this has lent force to the need to increase financial and economic competences.

5 The combination of these trends has to some extent been responsible for the need to develop a greater understanding of library and information activities in economic terms. This requires both a conceptual apparatus and skills in practice. This trend provides strong encouragment for the improvement of financial management capabilities generally.

6 The application of information and communication technologies is a focus of innovative activity in library and information provision, with financial, economic and service repercussions.

7 The traditional boundary between the private (commercial) and public (government financed) sectors has been breached and become a zone of dynamic transition and innovation. The idea of partnerships between and across sectors has become a part of policy. The library and information sector has followed the trend, albeit with a degree of reluctance, sometimes by compulsion, often as a response to a shortage of public finance, but increasingly with an eye to the opportunities and benefits that can result.

8 Partnership has often meant the acceptance of some of the tenets of the 'enterprise' culture by the public sector partner. This has ensured that the private sector can find common ground with public sector financed institutions. The stimulus of partnerships across the sectors has also made autonomous commercial activities such as income generation and merchandizing more acceptable to publicly funded bodies.

1.7 Contemporary public and organizational life

In the UK and the USA (and in Western Europe and the western economic world generally) during the 1980s, there was a concerted attempt by the governments of the day to bring about a change in public and organizational life which was met with challenges from other sectors of public life and opinion.

In the UK the Conservative government, which came to power in 1979 and governed until 1997, implemented some largely irreversible changes in economic and public policy, stemming from a wish to reduce public expenditure and taxation. An economic boom in the mid-1980s was a short lived result of some of these changes, stemming from financial reforms and an enlarged supply of industrial and consumer credit. This boom was a product of the world economic cycle, as well as a result of a release of domestic resources for consumption derived from a favourable balance of payments from North Sea oil revenues and financial liberalization. Nevertheless, there were problems of which rising inflation, rising imports and later rising unemployment were the result.

The metaphor used to describe these events was the 'Enterprise economy' characterized by a reliance on the market to stimulate and regulate the levels of economic activity. There was a progressive move to reduce levels of government intervention and support, in the belief that such a hands off approach was more efficient and would more readily create growth through a release of enterprise.

It was soon apparent that institutions themselves would need to adjust to new requirements and changes, and government policy sought deliberately to do this by major exercises in organizational reform, especially in the public sector. The economic changes implied radical changes in organizational, social and political culture. Not surprisingly this met with considerable levels of opposition from the institutions themselves and from a large body of public opinion, especially within the public sector. The Conservative government sustained a very large parliamentary majority throughout the 1980s, and was therefore able to implement these radical changes.

It is against this background that the impact of contemporary conditions has affected libraries, especially those in the public sector. Since these libraries were never in a position to enjoy the benefits of the enterprise culture, even when the boom was on, their main experience was to feel the reduction in public funds reflected in their budgets throughout the period. First of all a tightening was experienced by moves to eliminate waste and inefficiency (no bad thing in itself) but later on came the reduction in real spending power, often complicated further by inflation of raw material prices and higher labour costs as employees tried to maintain their position. Furthermore, publicly funded libraries were several steps away from the centre of the process, and so always felt a lack of options and little participation in the process. At the same time as undergoing a natural process of reform and modernization from the 1970s onwards, the reforms of the 1980s felt very much imposed. The radical nature of some of the changes was initially too much to absorb, but there seemed to be little alternative.

These changes re-emphasized the need to continue the process of managerial and organizational reform in libraries of all types, and not least in the area of resource and financial management.

The general economic problem of cost inflation had been present throughout the 1980s in the UK, although some relief was now apparent in the early 1990s. This reduction in inflation has been achieved at a very high price for the public sector, not least through succumbing to the organizational reforms detailed earlier. The result has been a kind of efficiency forced upon systems through a process of cutting, rather than achieved through a natural evolution of appropriate management practices. But the net result has been the same; that is to bring about a fuller understanding of the need to view efficient financial management as a natural part of good organizational management. The creation of positive attitudes to economic management is a very essential precursor to the agendas discussed in this work.

Another feature of the times is the idea of competition; competing for investment, competing for custom, and engaging in competive practices in order to gain market share. Competition brings about efficiency; efficiency results in lower costs; this was the message beamed out to the public sector in particular. Establishing a profile of the economic and financial health of the organization was ever more necessary, and from this has stemmed the drive for knowledge of costs, and for the effectiveness of budgetary decisions, based on clear goals, sound planning, and efficient technical management of resources for production. Cost management enabled cost knowledge and the ability to charge and price effectively if required to do so for the internal or the external market.

The market and enterprise culture also stressed the idea of providing value: extracting value from resources applied to production, embodying value in the product, and giving value to the consumer manifest either in terms of price, cost reduction, or in qualitative values such as the idea of service and satisfaction received. The transfer of these values to public sector organizations such as libraries is not just part of a mainstream economic application, but offers a complementary framework to the well established professional tradition of striving for measures of library performance and service evaluation. Rather than view these concepts as a threat, the best approach is to strive to absorb them into modern professional practice. This is where the agenda of this book finds a natural home.

1.8 New paradigms in organizational management

The market

Librarians have shown a strong interest in marketing for some twenty years (a trend popularized by Blaise Cronin in the UK) as an adjunct to service promotion and as an extension of user studies. Cronin (1994) gives references to commentaries over the period. A concern with the market as an economic strategic concept is more recent, and matches the general trends described in the previous section. This concept of 'market' embodies a strong sense of the nature of the relationships between supply and demand, and the implications for resource use when their management is carried out in a more exacting environment of regulation through cost and price information.

Organizations have to establish their productive capacities more precisely, and ensure that there is an effective return on investment, cost recovery and a surplus over expenditure. This also focuses attention on the nature of demand and levels of consumption, and raises questions about the sensitivity of consumption to price levels. Management of demand by pricing cannot of course be done without recourse to cost knowledge in a financially conscious organization.

The consumer

In terms of the market paradigm the emerging focus on the consumer reflects a shift from a supply side dominance to a demand side dominance (Roberts, 1987). Libraries should be concerned with providing what users require (self-evidently) and where they emphasize a supply side function this should be combined with a promotion and marketing perspective, to assist in the formation of new demands.

Effective managerial and financial capabilities provide the underpinning for library responses to demand; the library is thus in the best position to allocate its resources, on the basis of a thorough knowledge of its internal economy and in response to the external market conditions.

Libraries are steadily endeavouring to orientate their activities towards consumption and the consumer. Pragmatic, flexible and adaptive allocations of resources have to be made to establish a consumer and demand orientated equilibrium. Financially focused management provides mechanisms for adjusting resource allocations to these new equilibria, with financial quantification permitting regulation, control, accountability and adjustment.

Without a strong economic and financial mechanism there can be no realization of a consumer orientated library. The consumer and the customer are the catalyst in the new organizational order of professional library and information services. The concern with customer and consumer has been taken up and reinforced by the popularization of total quality management (TQM) applied to information and library services (Jurow and Barnard, 1993; Brophy and Coulling, 1996).

Diversity and flexibility

The strongest indicator of change in the library and information services community has been the serious reviewing of the roles, functions and direction of the profession. General patterns of change in society and economy coupled with the growing impact of information technology have influenced professional development as well as started a general process of convergence in information and communication activities.

These movements have accelerated the process of making libraries less book and print orientated in their sourcing and resourcing, and have shown the way to continued enhancement of their information function. Thus libraries no longer look to the exclusive sourcing of information from printed documents, but have been drawn to the exploitation of databases and other electronic sources, as these have developed; this maintains and reinforces a competitive position in information supply. As sourcing of information has changed, so the service concepts have evolved and the potential range of products has broadened.

The organizational impact of these changes has been to encourage diversity and flexibility, whether in forms of organizational structure and design as much as in range of services and products offered, and positioning within the expanding marketplace. The pressure for change has of course not only come through a renewal of professional dynamism and philosophy, but also because of a narrowing of options in the traditional environment, and financial, ideological and political pressure. The process has been a mixture of push and pull.

The viability of a profession comes not only from specialization and restraint or protectionism, but from evolutionary and adaptive strategies. Diversity and flexibility are two major conceptual elements in this process. When it comes to addressing financial management the strengths to be gained from a managerial and business approach draw very closely on flexibility and diversity. These are characterisitics of the managerial mindset and culture which enable a problem to be seen in terms of its components, the relativities between choices understood, and appropriate decisions taken in a play which is strong on uncertainty and unpredictability.

Economic decision making: tools and models

Economics is often claimed to be the study of choices; more specifically in situations where resources are scarce, alternatives compete, and courses of action have a range of consequences. When economic decisions are taken according to a monetary calculus a careful study of the economic nature of the problem is very desirable. If this is so the economic study and financial management of library and information services are very closely related; this relationship is then very functional.

The economic characteristics and nature of library and information services has long attracted study, but it is only recently that a more coherent body of knowledge is emerging. This knowledge is becoming better understood and reviewed, and the reader is referred to a number of reviews (King, Roderer and Olsen, 1983; Cummings, 1986; Roberts, 1993).

When economics turns from theory to practice the essential requirement is for tools which can be used in managerial practice. This book is focused on the range of financial management tools that are available and how to use them. And the use of these tools is consistent with the new paradigms that are now influential in the library and information community.

The tool focused approach is well enough known even in librarianship. Librarians have grown accustomed to the collection of data and statistics to use for management purposes, often descriptively but now increasingly for analytical and decision making purposes. The tools of financial planning and management form an intermediate stage between data and economic modelling. Specifically the planning approach and budgetary planning and control, together with costing studies are the essentials of the link.

It would be possible but not practically useful to construct economic models for library decision making at a conceptual and abstract level. The value of these models derives from their ability to be used within and calibrated from any given working organization.

The financial management capability provides the capacity and information to exploit the power of modelling for economic decision making. Budgets implement plans and provide the framework for monitoring resource allocations, generating cost data and controlling the economic processes of the organization.

The ability to use economic tools and models in library and information practice makes an absolute necessity of adopting a financial mangerial approach to resource management.

1.9 Impacts of contemporary change on the nature of professional practice

Impact on different library sectors

Traditionally different sectors of the library world have placed themselves in a pecking order, usually on the basis of very subjective perceptions. If not a ranking order, then the order has been of degrees of isolation. In the UK the higher education sector has not sustained a common identity with the numerically larger public library sector. Special libraries in government, industry and the professions have often claimed a good deal of common interest and identity, but there have been differences between subsectors. Often groups have seen justification for isolation or difference in functional or market segment terms, e.g. hospital and medical, law libraries, pharmaceutical industry etc.

If these differences were described by quantitative indicators then they could have some interest and even some validity; they could certainly be a basis for correlations and comparisons The statistical survey carried out by the Library and Information Statistics Unit (LISU) at Loughborough University provides some evidence (Sumsion *et al.*, 1993). More to the point for our topic is the possibility that there have always been some real differences in terms of economic, financial and general management which may be undergoing a real process of accentuation.

Those libraries closest to the private sector, i.e. special libraries in industry and commerce, have been subject to close financial management and discipline for longest, and can claim to be competent, although the variation between cases has no doubt been great. Here budgeting, cost accountability and the scope for cost recovery and income generation have been evident and well documented; furthermore professional attitudes have been significantly managerial.

Despite anecdotal evidence to the contrary, public libraries have also been significant exponents of managerial and financial disciplines. The drive stems from the nature of their host organizations; the municipal and county public authorities. Budgetary management, some corporate planning increasingly, and a variety of control related activities have been quite common. The downside of the picture has been the fact that public authorities have tended to be both bureaucratic and monolithic. The transition to a more financially conscious environment has been a difficult one in the UK and elsewhere, and has met with resistance because public services have often been seen to deteriorate. The move to commercial and market discipline has however started and the positive side is beginning to be seen, although not without some painful consequences.

One of the main difficulties lies in the the need to demonstrate the value of the library service convincingly (from a professional standpoint), especially to those charged with macroeconomic management, and at the same time to achieve proper economic management and financial discipline. The issue is further complicated by the facts of continued underfunding over a long period, which is very difficult to recover in the medium term. The build up cycle for a system could well be between five and ten years. Professional goals have to be reconciled with the idea of a rigourous (and helpful) business planning.

With the public and special library sectors in mind the environment of higher education and academic libraries can also be appreciated. The independent and corporate status of many university institutions, together with their characteristic goals, has often protected them from financial circumstances, at least within their own campuses.

University libraries have been institutions of prestige and reputation, and university leaders have tried to be both generous and protective, mindful of the future. While subject to a degree of proper financial discipline and accountability university librarians have had the longer run in view, and have spent on collections if not on services too. But rising materials prices, inflation in staffing costs, increasing crises in state funding, and expansion and rising expectations have conspired to push many over the financial edge. Events in the UK after the UGC report of 1975 (University Grants Committee, 1975) form the material for a classic case study of pressures and changes, and new approaches to policy making, which have also involved technology and co-operation. Again pressure of events has forced professional librarians to become managers and expert financial ones at that. While great changes in financial tooling have not been made, the focus of the economic debate has moved to performance and evaluation studies. Indeed, the literature of academic library micro- and macroeconomics has swollen enormously.

The process of change has now reached the point of convergence where the philosophies of peformance are merging with those of administrative reform, and bringing about cost centre management, cost recovery and income generation. Nothing can be achieved here without internal financial reform. The US academic library community experienced these changes some twenty years ago and so comparative studies are useful when looking at other environments.

Impact on management styles

The slow realization of financial and managerial necessities in library and information service management is producing a transformation in the nature of professional work. This has not only impacted on practice, but is also reflected in professional education programmes.

A librarian in a leading organizational position is no longer just a broad professional with some incidental or instinctual managerial competences. The proper development of leading organizational roles is a process of gathering formal knowledge and experience, and gaining an understanding of its application in an environment which owes as much to management and business as it does to library and information professionalism. The result is a new kind of professionalism.

The adaptation of business methods to professional practice

At a technical level many business methods are broadly compatible with the needs of library and information centres; sucessful adaptation and implementation can be made. However, problems still lie in the area of cultural and psychological adaptation and there are many sources of resistance. The best way forward is to face this situation as a creative challenge rather than as a threat. Regarding these changes as an opportunity will reduce tendencies to be defensive.

Radical changes to territories, business and products

The adoption of financial and economic reforms is a fundamental process, which will lead to changes in structures and characteristics of library and information centre activities. Markets and users may as likely expand as contract, business led innovations may in fact lead to improved internal organizational dynamics, and new consumer demands may be revealed giving opportunities to create new products. What has to be resisted is the initial assumption that change is always problematic and negative. However, management itself may have to make changes and adaptations to gain the confidence and co-operation of the workforce.

1.9.1 Further reading

Context, orientation and purpose

The following references are listed mainly for their historical interest for the development of cost management; more recent references are given in later chapters (for costing see especially Chapter Five).

Baggot, J. (1973) *Cost and management accounting made simple*. London: W. H. Allen

Batty, J. (1968) *Cost and management accounting for students*. London: Heinemann

Dougherty, R. M. (1969) Cost analysis studies in libraries: is there a basis for comparison? *Library Resources and Technical Services*, **13**(4), 136–141

Flowerdew, A. D. J. and Whitehead, C. M. E. (1974) *Cost-effectiveness and cost-benifit analysis in information science*. London: London School of Economics

Gross, M. (1972) *Financial and accounting guide for non-profit organisations*. New York: Ronald Press

Hanson, C. W. (1951) Costing information services. *Aslib Proceedings*, **3**(5), 85–88

Hayes, R. M. and Becker, J. (1970) Cost accounting in libraries. In R. M. Hayes and J. Becker (1970) *Handbook of data processing for libraries*. New York: Wiley-Becker-Hayes. pp. 85–103

Heinritz, F. J. (1970) Quantitative management in libraries. *College and Research Libraries*, **31**(4), 232–238

Leimkuhler, F. F. and Cooper, M. D. (1971) Analytical models for library planning. *Journal of the American Society for Information Science*, **22**(6), 390–398

Parker, R. H. and Price, P. P. (1963) (eds.) Aspects of the financial administration of libraries. *Library Trends*, **11**(4) (various papers)

Price, D. S. (1974) The cost of information: a prerequisite for other analyses. In R. S. Taylor (1974) *The economics of information dissemination*. Syracuse: Syracuse University Press

Roberts, S. A. (1984) (ed.) *Costing and the economics of library and information services*. London: Aslib (Aslib Reader Series No. 5)

Shaw, R. (1954) (ed.) Scientific management in libraries. *Library Trends*, **2**(2) (various papers)

Solomons, D. (1968) (ed.) *Studies in cost analysis*. London: Sweet and Maxwell

Taylor, L. (1961) Cost research on a library service. *Aslib Proceedings*, **13**(9), 238–248

Vickery, B. C. (1972) Research by Aslib on costing information services. *Aslib Proceedings*, **24**(6), 337–341

Chapter 2

Resource management: strategies and techniques

2.1 The nature of resource management in library and information services

> Resource management is the systematic process used by managers to underpin and expedite the business goals chosen for the organization.
>
> The management of information resources and the supply of information services are a universal formulation of business goals for library and information services broadly defined.

From these two statements a useful and general description of likely resource requirements can be developed; this then can be applied with a particular set of business or sectoral circumstances in mind (see Section 1.5).

The ultimate achievement of the goals chosen is the measure of the success or otherwise of the organization's *resource management*. The handling of all matters related to finance and its monetary measure form the financial management component of resource management.

There are three distinct but related components that categorize resources: information resources, primary physical resources and resources for production.

Information resources

Information resources implies the primary sources of information used by the user community and deliverable in some form of service or product. The primary sources could be data, archives, documents (published and semi-published), non-book media, imagery, intelligence and opinion etc.

Primary physical resources

The management of information resources can be meaningfully differentiated: on the one hand, the intellectual exploitation of the information resource revolves around the techniques of professional information management, information science and information retrieval; on the other hand this exploitation depends on logistical methods (acquisition, storage, retrieval) dependent on a base of primary physical resources (buildings, space, equipment and technology-based systems).

The initial resource analysis with respect to business goals and organizational circumstances concentrates on physical and human resources.

These primary physical resources (to be distinguished from primary information resources) are the constituents of the infrastructure for library and information provision; the physical infrastructure of buildings, accommodation, plant and equipment. For the purpose of financial management these form the capital resource and fixed plant of the organization. For budgeting and costing purposes it is usual to categorize these as overheads to be regarded as fixed costs.

Resources for production

These elements of capital and fixed plant are used to provide the basis or platform upon which production activities are based; that is the supply of products and services which constitute the output of the organization. The supply of product/service requires the deployment of additional units of the resources for production (in whatever physical or non-physical form: physical resources and human resources specifically).

The quantities required depend upon the level of output, the methods and techniques employed to produce and their relative work efficiencies and productivity.

The requirements for resources are expressed in budgets, and it is this process which forms one of the strategic functions of financial management. Resources are required in various forms and variable quantities according to what is to be produced and how this production is to be carried out.

One of the basic and most useful measures for regulating processes at this level is the quantification of total expenditures and the calculation of the variable costs of different aspects of the process. The following relation applies:

prices of input(s) acquired + composite costs(s) of process(es)
= total expenditure on whole process(es)

The ways in which business goals are achieved (or not) is reflected ultimately in the way in which expenditures are made and fixed and variable costs patterns are formed, developed and managed. In so far as a measurable objective criterion of achievement can be formed, this can be represented as costs, which have the added advantage of being a basis for analysis and subsequent manipulation of resources.

The boundary between fixed and variable identities in resources and costs may be clear or dependent upon judgement. A convergence of judgement may in fact be very helpful for operational use, particuarly where rules and procedures are required to allocate and identify elements of resource usage and resource costs.

An illustration may help. People as staff employed represent a capital asset, often referred to as human capital. But for many accounting and financial purposes staff are regarded as a variable factor of production, and are treated as variable cost. This measure may be called a variable fixed cost. The justification for this treatment is that the staffing budget has to be continually replenished, and this is a variable element (e.g. it might vary between years). The variable element of staffing cost is most clearly realized when the staff element is looked at in an activity context; that is where staff is an expenditure category and a cost element.

To summarize:

information resources

+

primary physical resources (fixed capital/scaled to potential or actual output)

+

resources for production (variable according to level of output and constituting additional physical resources (consumables) and human resources)

=

the basis for resourcing and managing library and information services

When measured in monetary terms there is an explicit economic dimension, which creates the basis for financial management.

2.2 The requirements of contemporary library and information management

A summary of emerging features of the financial element of the library and information landscape can be made. This preliminary discussion sets out the justification for financial management, and provides the agenda for deeper discussion in this book, developed in the remainder of this chapter.

Planning and programming

Appropriate structures are required (programmes) which reflect the purpose of the library and information centre. These develop the environment for the implementation of the planning process (a conceptual, logistical and managerial approach to resource management).

Delegation and devolution: business centres

Degrees of autonomy and independence are beneficial, and appear to provide the ambience for optimizing resources and effort. The characteristics of decision making lie at the heart of the business process; these need to be cultivated in ways appropriate to the goals of library and information centres. The manager optimizes choices within a financial framework, using the tools of financial and economic management.

Explicit budgets and budgeting

The budget provides a clear framework for managing the resourcing of the options chosen. The global sum of money and resources defines the boundaries of the situation to be managed.

Rich information bases for action and decision

The manager can regard the budgetary process as providing a core of stability for developing other resources to assist in management of library and information centres. Developing access to data, management information and intelligence is a positive support to financial and budgetary management. Information can reduce uncertainty and increase the likelihood of achieving goals.

Modelling and quantification

A rich information supply in itself is not sufficient to provide optimum decision making. Research and development in library and information science and management has explored methods to increase the usage of data in practice. A financial information system will give a capacity to explore the economic consequences of decisions.

Behavioural awareness

Every organization is a social system as much as a technical system, and the consequences of this are now well appreciated by managers, particularly those who can demonstrate success in achievement. There is always a tendency, however irrational, to introduce a degree of noise into actions involving explicit financial circumstances; this may be shown by a resistance to participation in cost studies, or a preference to approximate or generalize about financial consequences. Experience shows that positive steps should be taken to resist this, but this may mean changes in managerial and organizational practice which are sometimes resisted by managements themselves. Open systems and organizational cultures tend to give better results.

Costs and other decision tools

However difficult to collect in practice there can be no doubt of the value of cost measurement. Cost provides a uniform calculus for measurement; the dangers lie not in cost collection, but in poor interpretation of data and a lack of understanding of how the measures were generated.

2.3 Business strategy

There can be little doubt that there is an increasing convergence between the provision of library and information services, formal management and business culture; the common element being the need to achieve results from the use of scarce resources in the most economical way, generating product, wealth and value, and where possible yielding a surplus profit.

The realization of this process cannot be left to chance; on the contrary it requires systematic organization of a high order. The best way to achieve this is to provide an overarching encompassing framework in which to create conditions for realization. The highest order of the framework is the strategic concept, which is required in every successful organization, and which can certainly be instanced over the full range of library and activities (Hayes and Brown, 1994).

The successful financial management of an organization is thus founded on the creation of a suitable business strategy, which can be used to define the framework for all subsequent financial and budgetary activities. Of course, a business strategy alone does not lead to organizational success, but the more attention given to making an explicit statement of strategy, the greater the chances of ultimate success.

The kernel of a business strategy is quite likely initially to be some act of creative imagination or inspiration, but it could equally be derived from reflective analysis of events, or from some systematic evaluation of a wide range of knowledge and intelligence. It is most likely to receive its initial impetus from a blend of all three and probably more qualities.

The initial acts of determining business strategy are then likely to be focused intensively within the structure and activities of the formal organization. The nature of this process could be exclusive, or it could be widely based, open and consensual. The results of the process then become clarified and translated into statements of mission and goals for the organization. These can then be refined more specifically and operationally into aims related to different activities; the process continues in a progressive way to identify operational objectives. At each stage the need to and feasibility of casting the process in resource terms is evident; and when resources are discussed, so also are quantities which have to be procured, almost certainly using available sources of finance. These processes are represented graphically in Figure 2.1.

Business strategy is a reflection of the dominant characteristics of the organization. Any action of the organization can be traced back to a consistent theme: e.g. to be the leading information provider in a given market. The strategy gives the organization the power to survive and to succeed.

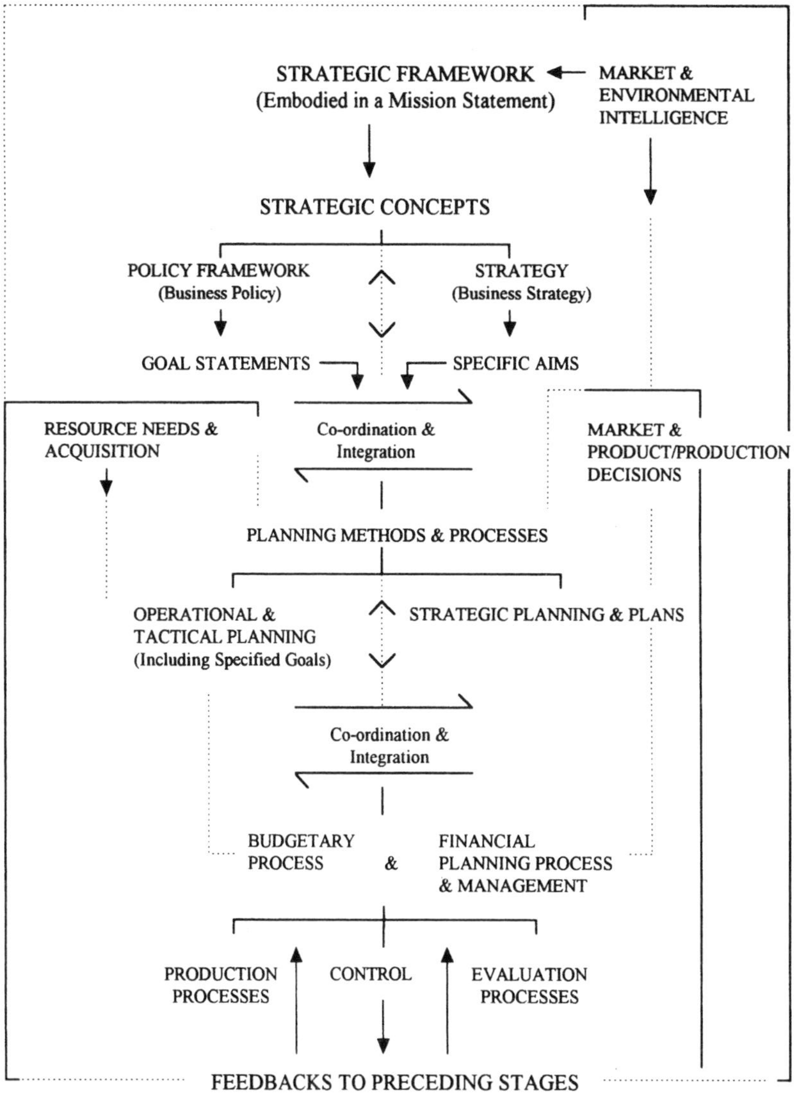

Figure 2.1. A business strategy framework: components and context

2.4 Business planning

Once the strategic framework has been established the real work of business planning can commence. The business plan is the operationalization of the strategic goals which will deliver the mission of the organization, subject to whatever constraints (time, money, product etc.) are identified.

Three factors are immediately apparent at this stage:

- in the majority of cases the strategic plan is formulated against the constraining background of an existing organization
- all plans are inherently or potentially weak in some respect or another
- the reality of organizations is a dynamic and changing one, necessitating monitoring and evaluation of the planning process as it progresses.

However, the process of planning and the articulation and documentation of a plan in concrete and explicit terms can and has to be done. The resulting plan will articulate the goals, make explicit structures to contain problems and events, and introduce ordering and prioritizing forces. The plan as the outcome of a process will correspond to both explicit programmes of activity, implicit resource concentrations, and financial plans contained in a formal budget process. This implicit and explicit relationship between plans, resources and activities is at the heart of the financial management process, the primary topic of this book.

Management theorists and many business practitioners place a lot of confidence in planning processes. West (1988) addressing the small business community makes planning a central solution. It will:

- identify business areas that are not completely under control, where inadequate attention has been given, and ones where action is essential
- provide a framework through which employees and others can be informed of the organization's future direction
- force management to consider the future strategy of the organization, and to weigh up strengths and weaknesses in an objective fashion
- demand that management information systems be improved, with consequent benefits for decision making
- identify key development areas for which the organization will need to enhance expertise

- provide a basis for analysing whether or not a new product or process will be a success, and feeding information into forecasts
- serve as a useful source of information on the prospects of the organization, especially when resources have to be obtained from funders.

Library and information service providers should nowadays have no difficulty identifying with the goals of planning. But a few cautionary words are also given by West.

- Planning is not a panacea; decisions are taken on the basis of planning, but only when equal weight is given to all other relevant factors (marketing, timing, political conditions, customer requirements etc.).
- Planning should not be seen as a rigid unbending answer to all the organization's problems.
- Planning is only as good as the people who carry it out and the use to which the plan is put.

With this understood a business plan can be drawn up. There is a number of steps to be followed. West has summarized these:

A historical/retrospective examination: where is the business now? In detail: a survey of products and services supplied; the organization within the wider industry; the role of marketing activity; methods of production; sources of finance and financial arrangements; personnel and human resources; the nature of administration and support services used.

Goals: where does the organization/business want to be?

Assumptions: are they correct? (For example, will the business service more or fewer clients in future; to what extent will present operations be influenced by technology; do we really understand our competitors; what makes our products and services attractive and competitive)?

Quantification: how can objectives be expressed in financial terms?

Resource allocation: how do we achieve objectives?

Checking: is the plan realistic?

Sensitivity analysis: is the plan flexible? This is a process of cross-checking by considering the effects of changes in the key assumptions on which the plan is based; in other words: how sensitive are the outcomes to these changes?

2.5 The strategy of library and information service businesses

Library and information services use information resources and other physical and intellectual resources to deliver library and information service as a product to clients. This could be regarded as the fundamental strategic objective, which clearly requires much further explication according to circumstances and conditions.

In practice the strategy can be explored quite conveniently by using library and information products and services as a starting point. Exploring back from this point will relate product and service to suitability of context, e.g. library sector. A public reference library could ask the 'zero-based' question: should we be doing this? The process will highlight the use of existing resources, or identify the potential resources which would be required to produce the good or service. This backstream exploration is supply orientated.

The downstream exploration is demand orientated, and among other things will explore the question: if we commit resources to this product or service, will there be a demand for it? If the product is being produced the performance achieved will provide significant information for planning and budgeting. The relationship between performance, planning and budgeting is absolutely crucial; the PPBS budgeting method is explicit acknowledgement of this.

Product related approaches to financial management are convenient and practical. There are alternative methods (such as function or departmental approaches), but this one has much to recommend itself, and will be used extensively in this book. The sourcing of products in the organization can be used to define programmes with contiguous resource requirements and common operational identities. This is a very pertinent approach to planning, and one which can be clearly nested within business strategy and directly related to budgeting and all other financial management activities.

The approach just outlined can be illustrated on a sector-by-sector basis for different types of library and information service. In the ten year strategic plan for the British Library (British Library, 1989) the marketing, human resources, service and collection foundations for the Document Supply Centre were clearly stated, and the financial implications identified. In the university sector the strategic impact of new information technologies for libraries in higher education has been considered in the Follett report; the logic of argument used is indicative of strategic analysis, and the report follows through to implementation strategies (Joint Funding Council, 1993). Strategic issues in both these sectors have been previously addressed by the Dainton (1969), Parry (1963) and Atkinson reports (University Grants Committee, 1975).

In retrospect it is possible to discern a developing strategic analysis in the sectors of UK librarianship (as well as in the USA, Europe and many countries which have also addressed policy issues); these have been reviewed by Hill (1994). The Library and Information Services Council (1988) and Department of Education and Science/OAL (1987) reports address the strategic issues, but in a way which is fragmented, gradual and insufficiently geared to implementation. The strategic approach in business must address not only the goals to be sought, but also the implementation and fulfilment of those goals. Library and information plans (LIPs) provide a strategic method for public libraries in the UK (Buckley, 1993; Kennington 1990). The National Health Service (NHS) has taken a strategic approach to the implementation of IT and training for IT use (Brittain and Abbott, 1993).

2.6 Planning the productive process: constructing the business plan

Having decided what is to be produced, attention can be turned to how it is to be produced and what resources and raw materials are going to be used. Although the design of the product or service is a distinctive issue in itself, the context in which production takes place is also significant. The business planning task can be visualized in terms of a concentric model, with product at the centre and segments of supporting activities: the nature and configuration of the organization; the market and the marketing process; the supply of resources for production; technology; human resources; financial and economic environment etc.

Business planning is a comprehensive application, which is dedicated to supporting the main productive purpose of the business, enterprise or organization. The business plans need to be expressed and communicated in a range of forms; for example as an overall statement of corporate and commercial policy; as a set of specific guidelines that can be used to support the budgetary planning process; as the basis for criteria to be used for monitoring and evaluation; as directives for setting up detailed operational and work plans; as specifications for developing a marketing policy. Although the business planning environment is a complex system characterized by complex systems of interaction, it can usefully be presented in rather simpler linear terms.

1 What specific products, goods and services are to be produced?
2 Who is going to consume the products?
3 How much product should be produced over a given period of time?
4 What resources are required to produce the product?
5 What is the relationship between production and consumption, especially in economic terms; this implies the establishment of a market position in the relationship between demand and supply.
6 What is the dominant commercial-economic orientation of the organization as a producer: e.g. a profit seeking and profit maximizing trading organization; a public sector organization offering goods and services free at the point of consumption; an organization with a mixed approach.
7 What measures/results indicate successful performance and goal achievement?

Allen (1989) provides an example of a corporate planning approach in the Library and Information Service of Western Australia. Her discussion (derived from pp.201–204) shows how programme management evolves from the corporate planning process. Strongly influenced by Checkland's soft systems methodology the mission statement was developed from the 'root definition', signified by CATWOE (Customers (of LISWA), Actors (staff of LISWA), Transformation (activities going on in LISWA), World View ('Weltanschauung'), the Owners, and the Environmental constraints).

The interim mission statement became: the Library and Information Service of Western Australia is a statutory authority established under the Library Board of Western Australia Act 1951–1083 which, in an equitable, effective and efficient manner, promotes and provides access to resources and services which meet the intellectual, economic, social and recreational information needs of the people of Western Australia by actively seeking, acquiring, organizing, preserving and distributing appropriate library and archival materials through co-operation and consultation where appropriate with local government, library and information based organizations worldwide, state funded organizations and relevant professional bodies.

Corporate objectives: these are the objectives which apply to the total organization and form the umbrella under which the separate objectives can be developed at programme level. They are considered to be long term objectives, reflecting the type of organization the service wishes to become. This has come from the Executive agreeing that these objectives are feasible, desirable and fit the mission of the organization. They are:

1. To acquire, organize and distribute library resources which equitably meet the requirements of public libraries and other approved bodies by the efficient management of the State government subsidy scheme.
2. To develop and maintain collections appropriate to the information and reference needs of the people of Western Australia.
3. To collect, conserve and preserve material which record the culture and heritage of Western Australia.
4. To provide responsive reference and information services.
5. To provide leadership, policy advice and consultancy services to state and local government and other organizations involved in information management in Western Australia.

Corporate strategies: From corporate objectives high level strategies can be developed. These are long term plans which can be turned into programmes within the context of corporate objectives. The strategies suggested to date are:

1. Participating co-operatively in relevant library, archival and information management networks, both manual and automated.
2. Augmenting the use of collections through maintaining an awareness of and expertise in Australian and overseas collections and databases.

3. Supporting and encouraging the activities of reading and creative writing in the community.
4. Adopting an entrepreneurial approach in the provision of new, targeted and value added and fee based services while protecting the free public library service.
5. Encouraging and facilitating mechanisms whereby appropriate catalogues and indexes which record the Western Australian heritage are developed and maintained.
6. Increasing the awareness of the Service's role and collections in the community.
7. Improving productivity and effective use of resources through staff development.
8. Participating in and initiating research activities whose result will benefit Western Australians' access to relevant information.

Programme Management: by focussing on the client, by producing conceptual models and arriving at the above definitions of the role of the Service, we can determine the major services which will be delivered (and are delivered) by the Service. This is not a focus on functions or organizational structure. It is a client oriented breakdown of the *raison d'être* of the organization. It is probably best described in general by outlining the six main programmes.

1. The provision of materials and services to public libraries.
2. The provision of reference and information services from the Alexander Building (HQ in Perth, WA).
3. The management of archival materials and services.
4. The marketing, promotion and generation of income.
5. Collection management.
6. Corporate policy, planning and management.

These high level functions are then translated into the sub-programmes and components of the whole organization, so that the whole organization's foci are modelled. Plans are then developed to support these activities. This may involve a matrix of plans. For example, the Information Technology plan will cover all programmes, whereas the Resources Provision plan for public libraries will cover only one programme.

Allen's account encapsulates very well the broad philosophy offered in this present discussion. The professional thrust of library service can clearly be structured in organizational and business oriented terms.

2.7 Programme basis and definition

The programme is the structural unit of the budget, and can be defined as follows: it is a coherent entity that represents an area of activity in an organisation; it is a recognizable focus for income and expenditure; it is amenable to planning and management, and therefore has operational validity; it serves as a centre of cost burden (cost centre); it has tangible resource implications (either directly or as overhead); and it can be related to outputs achieved (providing scope for performance measures).

Work plans are essentially statements of the content of programme areas; these two conceptual ideas help to define fully the nature of a budget.

The programme structure chosen by managers for financial and budgetary planning has to reflect the dominant and the particular characteristics of the library and information service/business engaged in. However, there are common elements in most of these businesses. This section examines these and also tries to draw together a consensus of types of programme area for the main types of library and information service.

In practice, the resolution of the problem is far from easy. Although library and information professionals share a common occupational culture, in general, when it comes to committing the facts to the record difficulties arise in definition, terminology, drawing boundaries and establishing relationships.

What can be seen and agreed is that the problem is typically that of defining an information system, because the capacity to handle and relate information is basic to the task of financial (and resource) management. The information is in many ways the mirror image of the system and its structures. The same information could be derived from different formulations of the structures within the system, but it would clearly be advantageous to converge on a homogenous view of the system and its structures. This would be logical, convenient and economical, and would enable managers in different organizations to benefit from a similar language for handling the problem; without affecting the individuality of any one organization the similarity would assist co-operation, co-ordination, and accountability, as well as education and training.

The eagerness of library managers to address questions of library statistical data and management information is a strong motivation for establishing a clear relationship between systems, structures and information.

While it would be ideal to have one acceptable and applicable scheme, in practice there will also be a tendency to introduce variation and localization. But there are sufficient general elements of principle that can be incorporated and reflected in any given scheme. This would make a clear distinction between internal and external and between technical service aspects and reader service aspects. And, furthermore, the reversibility between programme structures and their descriptive equivalent in the information structures selected has to be acknowledged and incorporated in any chosen scheme. Put simply, much of financial management has to do with the management of financial information: it is financial information management. This is the key property that has to be elaborated in any management system.

The manager has wide scope in defining a set of programmes within the organization for budgetary purposes. Broadly, the programmes will be of three types:

1 Ones which reflect the chosen organizational units (typically those on the organigram).

2 Programmes which reflect coherent functions, which may be concerned with input, throughput or output related activities separately, or in some combination. These programmes may coincide exactly with the organizational units, or they may cut across several.

3 There will be programmes which are common to all of type 1 and type 2; buildings and plant are one example, but there could be others such as postal and transport services which are shared. Type 3 programmes are similar to 'overhead', and are effectively treatable as such for later costing purposes.

In constructing the programme set, the manager has to ensure that there is no double counting, and that all areas of activity are ultimately allocable to a programme; there can be no loose ends. The programme set is a neat and effective way to divide up structures, functions and activities in a form hospitable to planning and budgeting, suitable for accounting and control, and meaningful enough to relate to output and performance measurement.

The programmes are the bedrock of the budget process. They are the most effective development of the once popular line-item approach to budgeting. A programme budget may of course have some line-item characteristics, but only within the superimposed structure determined by the real activities, services and products of the organization. The programmes provide a financial map of the territory, which can then be the basis for a real analysis; by analogy this could be demographic, statistical, cost and performance related.

2.8 Resource distribution and allocation

With the full range of programmes clearly mapped out, and with knowledge of the range of performance standards to hand the manager can distribute and allocate resources to programmes. When this process has been carried out the full summing of quantities and costs can be done, necessary overhead rates allocated, and a global money figure for each programme identified. Athough the first task is to complete the expenditure budget, it is at this point that the revenue budget can be drawn up. There may be no effective income from revenue generated; instead the grant allocation from the host organization budget is substituted. But if revenue is dependent upon sales, this is the point at which market intelligence and sales forecasts have to be included in the picture.

This process continues across each programme area. The end result means that there is a full and detailed picture of the forthcoming year's budget, backed up from an evaluation of previous budgetary performance. When this stage has been completed it may be useful to make a series of breakdowns back across the budget, by type of resource, staff level and so on. This analysis of the budgetary plans serves as a challenge and a double check. There is a chance to give some perspective and to ask critical questions again of the proposals. In reality this may be the ideal, but it would be honest to attempt, as many organizations do, a selective review of the budget areas on a rotating basis.

2.9 Budgetary planning

Budgetary planning comprises the whole process of establishing the structures (including programmes) methods and operative processes for managing the financial aspects of resources in an organization.

The remainder of this chapter is designed to provide a step-by-step guide to planning a budget for a library and information service. It has been written with the assumption that you might be setting out as a new organization or with a new product/project and have the freedom to translate the principles into practice. However, you may be in an organization with well established procedures; these may not be as efficient as you would like, or else may be in need of development; in which case the approach described here might provide you with a model to achieve reforms in practices and methods.

The main steps of the planning model can be identified as:

- formulating a budgetary policy (Section 2.10)
- determining a budgetary structure: business decisions and budgetary methods (Section 2.11)
- implementing a suitable budgetary structure; initiating a cycle of budgetary planning; budgetary management and monitoring (Section 2.12)

2.10 Budgetary policy and budgetary strategy

Ideally, you need a clear policy agreed at the outset about the kind of budgetary planning required. The policy should be determined before any budget creation is attempted, and most of all before any staff in the organization come together to participate in the process. The essence of budgetary strategy can be defined at two levels:

1 The policy which leads to the budgetary strategy chosen. The policy reflects the requirements that have to be satisfied, the resources required and that are available, the options addressed, and the decisions made about all factors up to the allocation and commitment of resources to eventual production goals.

   The budgetary strategy is consequent on the policy set: for example, the adoption of programme budgeting, with a clear establishment of cost centres, development of business plans, and a schedule of formal staff consultation and participation. Implementation of the budgetary strategy is facilitated by the use of suitable methods, techniques and procedures.

2 The methods, techniques and procedures that are going to be used to develop and implement a budget in the organization;

this acknowledges that a given level of simplicity or complexity is appropriate, requiring no more or no less elaboration than is justified by the task.

For example, the policy might be to rely entirely on a grant of income received from public funds, to make no charge to the end user for products and services supplied, and not to take any steps to generate income through charging or cost recovery. However, noting what has been said about the market environment at the present time such a basis for budgetary strategy would be unusual or restrictive. It would certainly have the effect of reducing the level of detail and complexity of budgetary procedures, since rigorous cost analysis might not be so urgent, even for internal purposes, although financial control and accountability would still have to be excercised (returning attention whatever the circumstances to the collection of some cost data).

2.11 Budgetary structures: the basis for planning

General categories
In circumstances where the budget is going to have to reflect the variety within a complex organization, a clear framework or structure is essential to direct discussion and planning to clear results and conclusions. This will also assist the task of compilation and documentation, and provide a clear summary of all the different elements. Such clarity and transparency is desirable on its own, but it also provides circumstances helpful for defending the proposals when they are scrutinized and challenged, as well as helping the ultimate processes of control and accountability. These considerations also play a part in ensuring the overall financial efficiency of the organization.

The choices available to structure a budget are generally according to class of expenditure, type of activity or, an extension of this, zero-based budget.

Structuring the budget according to classes of expenditure This is the line-item approach, and it will usually be elaborated according to departmental and organizational structures which are taken to represent likely concordances with normally undertaken activities. For example a line-item budget for a bibliographical services department might reasonably be taken as a statement of resources and spending on bibliographical services. The organizational unit probably closely represents the function and the product, so that unit costs and performance activity indicators may actually represent what they seem to.

Structuring the budget according to types of activity This is often to a very specific level or degree, and normally involves grouping together activities and functions as programmes. The manager has a wide choice over the formulation of programme areas using both organizational structural and functional criteria; the degree of representativeness (mentioned earlier) is therefore more deliberate and less coincidental. This closer profiling gives a stronger base for cost location, unit costing and performance activity indicator creation.

While the theory behind programme areas is seemingly strong the practice may also require a good deal of thought and judgement on the part of managers; the first attempt may not produce the best result, and some trial and error is to be expected. Although line-item budgets may provide the basis for good control over functions and activities, the programme approach gives a better likelihood. In reality it provides a more accurate mapping of the financial flows and resource utilization in the organization.

The zero-based budget (ZBB) In each budgetary round the proposals for allocation to each programme are justified positively, starting from zero monies allocated. In theory the zero-based model could be used with a line-item structure, but the structures are incongruent with the way in which functions and activities are realized in practice.

Budget creation and budget documentation While one year's budget is being spent (Year 0) the previous year's is being evaluated (Year -1), and the forthcoming year is being planned (Year +1). This encapsulates the cycle of budget creation working on three levels.

The annual financial calendar varies between countries, hemispheres, sectors and organizations. Variants include: April to March (UK business); January to December (full calendar year); August to July (higher education). Whatever period is chosen the pattern of events is likely to remain much the same. The following discussion builds on a 24 period cycle with a (-12) to (+12) notation.

In the period (-12) to (0) the performance of previous budgetary years is being evaluated between (-12) and (-9). Draft budgets for (Year +1) will usually be available from (-12) or even before, since departments will have a wish list of bids and proposals, which they are waiting to bring forward. Evaluation meetings and first round proposal discussions may take place simultaneously. The main work of drafting the new budgets will have taken place between (-12) and (-8).

Budget drafts are submitted to executive committees between (-8) and (-6). At this stage there is negotiation between departments through the executive committees. The executive is looking to see that general policy has been followed at departmental level drafting stages, and that the emerging overall organizational budget conforms to policy and strategy. After (-6) and certainly by (-3) the processes should be focusing on achieving a successful negotiation and resolution of claims. The fact that this does not always happen in reality is accepted but delay is not productive. There needs to be a period after (-6) when a clear picture can be drawn, and the budget disseminated for wider information and approval, before the appropriations are authorized.

This idealized picture of budget creation is subject to wider variations. The overall availability of funds may be generally known before (-12); in the public sector the global sums are known between (-36) and (-12) at ministerial level. In the private sector strategic financial planning also has a long run-in period. However, the immediate period of c. 12 months prior to the implementation of a new budget sees this typical concentration of activities at departmental and central level within the organization.

As the creation period progresses the documentation grows in quantity and detail. There is a range of documentation from evaluation reports to position papers and proposals as different interests compete; surveys, investigations and position statements are all part of the process. What is important is that this wider documentation is gradually focused into the common format of budgetary statements. Budget estimates are tabulations and matrices in which expenditures for programmes and activities are quantified and classified by type of spend. Where income generation is an activity revenue budgets require the same analytical treatment in the budgetary process.

The derivation of a proper format for organizational purposes is a task for every organization. Clarity is essential. Tabulations and commentaries can then be drawn together in a comprehensive document finally submitted for discussion and approval.

A key element in this process is a budgetary officer with a brief to co-ordinate all documentation, and to ensure that departments

run to the agreed timetable. This officer could be the secretary to the executive committee, and discharges an essential technical function. The quality of overview depends on good documentation; this helps to defuse any political confrontations which inevitably emerge as departments compete for limited funds.
Roberts (1985) attempted to show how the problem could be resolved by taking the views of a number of experts who had tackled the issue. The same appendices are reproduced here (Appendices 1–4) and identify specimen information file contents (after Clements, 1975), description of library systems (after Humphreys', 1974), industrial accounts classification (after Risk, 1956), summary task description listing (after Library Association, 1974 and other sources), specimen data recording forms, and a proposed library management information system (after Hamburg *et al.*, 1974).

Presenting a budget and justification of proposals The presentation of the budget marks a formal end to the process of evaluation and compilation, in which the negotiation between claims on resource predominates. On the one hand the presentation is an event; on the other it is a form of statement which can be read and discussed for eventual approval. To reach this stage there will already have been many justificatory steps. But the final presentation still requires an overall justification. It is important not just as a calculation but as a strategic statement reflecting the goals of the organization and the way in which resources are allocated to achieve those purposes in a structured, systematic and accountable way. The use of monies defines and limits powers and capabilities.

The hope is always that the budget will achieve recognition and acceptance throughout the organizational community. But there will inevitably be disappointments among some interests, not just because of inadequate justification but shortage of funding overall. A long-term sequence of budgetary reviews may help to get things into perspective, and there needs to be feedback to policy after each cycle, so that budgeting and planning are ever more strongly connected.

Appropriation and implementation of a budget Executive action on the budget proposals will lead to authorization of appropriation. Organizational units have their resources for the coming period confirmed. The implementation of the budget assures continuity in the first place of existing operations, and then signals the manoeuvring space for managers. Orders can be placed with confidence and the detailed financial control of spending is activated. Orders can be placed and invoices passed for payment. Each department of the organization is creditworthy.

Once implemented the priorities for the current period pass to budgetary management and control (discussed fully in the next section). At the heart of this process must be an information system for recording expenditures and payments, forecasting flows of expenditure and revenue, collecting performance indicators (especially units of work achieved and output), monitoring expenditure and output of service/product (as a basis for cost measurement), aggregating data (for establishing performance ratios), and generating arrays of data for review and and analysis (weekly, monthly or quarterly returns by department); these can be used for variance analysis of spending, costs and outputs.

These information functions have to be tied in to staff responsibility within and across programmes and activities. The budgetary officer can continue to discharge these functions (a deputy librarian may be the person to do this in a medium to large size library), and oversee the allocation of and responsibility for fulfilling these tasks amongst other staff. Staff with or without the use of supporting technologies that generate data expedite this function, aided by clear means of presentation, such as standard forms and tabulations. Suitable graphical presentation of budgetary control information is obviously beneficial.

Budgeting in practice The conceptual model of budgeting is a sequence of resource management activities which become increasingly focused and co-ordinated. Budgeting practice in the organization should therefore reflect this; the manager needs to work from a strong mental construct or 'mental map' of the organization to expedite the process.

While hands on experience is the best teacher, professional writing in this field is supportive. A choice of readings on this topic is provided in section 3.12.1 at the end of the chapter on financial management. Papers by Martin (1978), Koenig (1981) and Koenig and Stam (1986) provide a basis; Prentice (1985a; 1985b) and contributors to Drexel Library Quarterly add further dimensions. Ford (1991) and Baker (1992) contribute to the discussion from a British perspective, as do Midwinter and McVicar (1991). Clark (1985), Alley and Cargill (1986) and Khoo (1991) serve to emphasize practical aspects important for planning, as well as monitoring and control.

2.12 Budgetary management and monitoring

Overall management of the budget From the preceding discussion it is clear that the creation of a well constructed budget as part of the overall financial management of the organization is a process requiring a significant amount of time and effort. Therefore, once the framework has been developed and an annual budget created the proper management of the system and all its outcomes is of the utmost importance.

Budgetary management is the sum of methods, techniques and events which contribute to the final outcomes from the allocation of resources to library and information production notwithstanding the necessary complement of all other events and actions which make-up the professional task.

It is helpful to envisage budgetary management as a more or less sequence of stages:

- a budgetary control cycle with definite stages of activity
- the generation of budgetary variances
- an intelligent evaluation stage
- decision making on corrective actions
- a cycle of performance review. This will include budgetary review prior to initiation of the next budgetary cycle, justification of spending and discussion of forward planning issues.

The budgetary control cycle and its implications Budgetary control is a function of monitoring, regulating, evaluating, accounting for and taking corrective action where required throughout the defined cycle of a budget. Since the budget is a financial plan the locus of control is applied through checking and comparing financial data on income, revenue, and usage and expenditure in the appropriate programme, activity area or spending category.

The most basic control procedure checks the actual expenditures against the planned expenditures; this is a simple form of variance analysis. If the amounts are equal the budget is deemed to be in balance (there is nil variance). If there is a negative variance, further action is called for, although there may be an expectation that the deficit would normally be self-correcting. There may be a positive variance, which could be welcome or unwelcome; this might signify that a payment which was expected had not been made (and that the monies should be held in reserve, rather than assumed as surplus or diverted elsewhere); but it might be that resources have not been used, signifying a possible decline in activity that was not anticipated. Corrective actions (see later) would be maintaining the positive balance under that head (budget code), or considering re-allocation (if rules on virement between heads or codes was allowable).

There are many reasons which could explain the budgetary variance. The moral of these cases of variance is that no unwarranted assumption should be made, and that budgetary control procedures far from being seen as routine or trivial should be seen as potentially objective tests applied to circumstances at any point.

While the purpose and effects of budgetary control are clear the limitations of its financial orientation and dependency must be appreciated. Budgetary control using financial data is a quantitative method applied to circumstances which have a strong qualitative dimension. Behind the 'figures' lies a whole realm of organizational political, social and professional circumstances. These may not be controllable through the manipulation and interpretation of financial data alone. It is at this junction in the budgetary process that the surface and the depth of budgetary control interact with each other.

The financial aspect of budgetary control can be regarded as complete in itself at one level which is both crucial and inclusive. But the effectiveness of overall budgetary control is extended and enhanced by allowing for opportunities and mechanisms to correlate in the other circumstances and dimensions. This requirement is shown figuratively in Figure 2.2, and is used here as a basis for outlining practical guidance.

Budgetary control is clearly a significant component in the performance and evaluation regime, lying strategically between the decisions on resource allocation and production planning, and the steps necessary to measure performance actively and use those data for evaluation of outcomes and impact.

Budgetary variance and corrective action Budgetary variances provide quantitative signals about the state of the system, which should be acknowledged rather than ignored. These signals may be subject to the qualifications noted in the preceding paragraphs, and may require differing types of corrective action.

One of the first considerations should be to establish the frequency with which the signals are sampled. There can be no

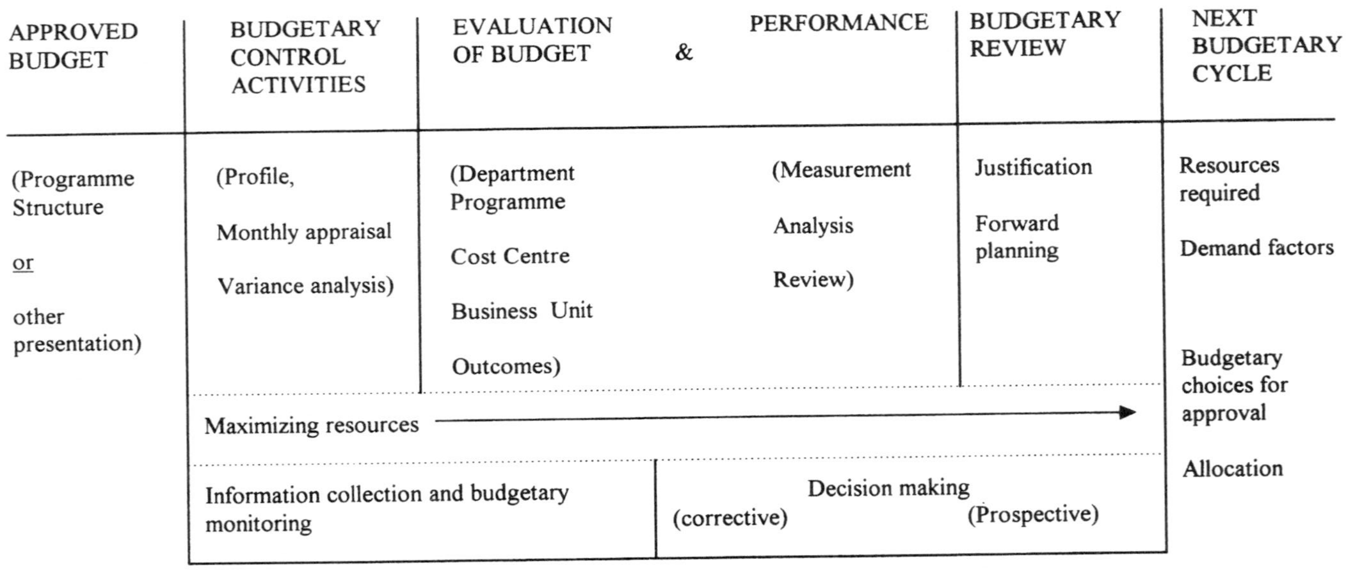
APPROVED BUDGET
BUDGETARY CONTROL ACTIVITIES
EVALUATION OF BUDGET
&
PERFORMANCE
BUDGETARY REVIEW
NEXT BUDGETARY CYCLE
(Programme Structure
or
other presentation)
(Profile,
Monthly appraisal
Variance analysis)
(Department
Programme
Cost Centre
Business Unit
Outcomes)
(Measurement
Analysis
Review)
Justification
Forward planning
Resources required
Demand factors
Budgetary choices for approval
Allocation
Maximizing resources
Information collection and budgetary monitoring
Decision making
(corrective)
(Prospective)

Figure 2.2. Budgetary control

hard and fast rules, but most organizations should try to determine a conventional pattern. Line managers and chief executives might find a regular weekly or monthly period sufficient, but size and complexity of organization and transaction volume will be the most significant factors. When the periods of business are more active, or the use of funds constrained and circumstances are critical, the frequency can be increased.

Whatever the periodicity chosen, it must be remembered that some indicators are 'lagging' where others are 'leading'. It is not good to be caught out by noting an indicator and then realizing that action was required two days ago; when payments, credits and interest are concerned such inattentions are not always welcome. One remedy is to step up the sampling of signals, but this could be seen as obsessive, and may also serve to distract from other significant tasks.

As in many things information technology has come to solve the problem. Computer databases of budgetary data give the option of online access. This might only serve to increase prurient interest and heighten neuroticism, which could be self-defeating. And furthermore online access may give the feeling of security that is not justified. The database still has to updated, and the sourcing of financial returns is both critical and may turn out to be the weak link in the chain. In this case managerial attention has to be turned as well to the sourcing of figures and the reliability of reporting.

This view of budgetary management and variance analysis makes a point that should not be lost. The whole exercise is not just about statistical data and failsafe technologies of reporting. Nor is it just a case of the figures being acquired and speaking for themselves. The signals are only indicators, not necessarily whole truths. Proper budgetary management and budgetary control is also an intuitive, creative and genuinely foresighted activity at its best. If it is not, then there is a danger that management of the budget is just another kind of organizational tyranny, where mistakes are made and only uncovered when it is too late. Above all the key quality sought is one of intelligence; intelligent budgetary management and intelligent decison making.

The intelligent evaluation stage: reviewing ongoing performance A wide choice of peformance signals and measures provides the basis for ongoing budgetary management. Budgetary variances provide financial signals and output and performance activity indicators provide professionally readable signals. In combination these provide a basis for budgetary mangement and monitoring, as well as for wider purposes. These two types of signal can be read to give a shorter or longer term perspective as required.

It is worth distinguishing between reviews of ongoing performance (part of the budgetary control cycle), and wider and deeper cycles of performance review (see later for discussion). The intelligent evaluation stage is part of ongoing review and day-to-day management; it is tactical rather than strategic. Earlier strategic planning will provide the basis for this tactical management. And later on the sum of tactical measures will provide the basis for continuing the strategic process, or for modifying it. A sum of negative tactical signals will encourage a review of strategic options and later a strategic redirection.

Decision making on corrective actions A reading of budgetary variances will provide the grounds for considering the need for corrective action. In line with developing a systematic regime of budgetary management a structure for deciding on the need for and nature of corrective action is required.

The structure should be consistent with the organizational structure, and with the pattern of line and executive responsibilities and lines of reporting.

1 There has to be a pattern for initiating a report from the system.
2 The report has to be reviewed, with appropriate participation from those responsible for the activity.
3 Evaluation and statement of outcomes are required.
4 Options for corrective or other action must be determined, reviewed and decided.
5 Decisions have to be reported and communicated elsewhere.
6 Further actions have to receive authorization internally or from elsewhere.

These steps could form the basis of a typical mechanism for action following the analysis of budgetary signals.

A cycle of performance review At the end of the financial year it will be clear how the actual achievements measure up to plans. This conclusion is best reached through formal mechanisms, of which the annual performance review will be the basic element. This should be staged over the whole organization, at significant levels of programme and activity within the organization, and wherever responsibilities lie for resource use and productive outcomes.

Systematic performance review is a logical outcome of programme type budgeting. In the last decade more and more organizations have been adopting this approach as integral to their organizational life. This adoption has paralleled the introduction of business and market cultures into library and information organizations. In this way budgetary management and budgetary control have started to weave themselves into organizational life and processes as part of a much wider change in methods, style and cultures. This is one of the most significant features of late 20th century management.

2.13 Resources: an overview of the main types

To complete this chapter a five part categorization of resources is presented to emphasize the range and richness of material, human and intellectual support which can contribute to library and information service. Choices about, decisions on and allocations of resources are a major underpinning of financial management responsibilities. Financial management must never be treated in abstraction from organizational and marketplace reality. The broad expenditure classification (capital/fixed or current/variable) is given (as a framework for budgetary planning and costing) as well as the typical funding source (relation to income).

The physical and institutional base

Comprising fixed buildings and accommodation space, furnishings and equipment these elements represent capital expenditures, with a current expenditure element on fixed plant for maintenance.

Capital funding may be derived from a host institution grant; if capital is obtained from market sources the usual treatment is as a capital project with full justification required, analysis of benefits and payback calculation.

Service utilities (electric power, gas, water and other environmental amenities) are enabling resources and are treated as current expenditures.

Consumable resources (e.g. for office administration, reprographics, publishing and dissemination activities) are also current expenditures.

This whole class of physical and institutional expenditures is a significant adjunct to variable costs (and a component that has to be absorbed by total costs); thus in planning these need to be related to production volumes and expected current income. However, they may equally be regarded as a part of overhead expenses, and this flexibility in allocation is advantageous for the financial management of resources.

The processes of programme budgeting help to see clearly what method is best to adopt. As a general rule, the clearer the end product and the greater the likelihood that costs have to be allocated to end users and/or through charges, the more important it is that expense burdens should be appropriately allocated. Publicly funded libraries which do not levy end user charges have a stronger case for consolidating costs to overhead, but they cannot escape the responsibility properly to identify all costs, and to control wasteful expenditure.

This category of resources covers all non-human/non-informational physical resources. They have an acquisition cost, and their acquisition also consumes resources (especially staff). Each category has a total annual cost to the organization which must be covered by sources of income.

Accommodation costs may be very diverse due to differences of regional location, position and demand. Properties can be freehold, leasehold or rented and a useful measure is price per square metre, which can then be multiplied by function and requirement to give a cost estimate (say, per annum). The UK Civil Service has standard allowances, which can be used in cost calculations: Director 20.9–27.9 sq m; Heads of Sections 16.3–20.9 sq m; Senior Librarian 12.5 sq m; Librarian 10.2 sq m; Assistant Librarian 7.7 sq m; Administrative Officer 5.6 sq m; Senior PS/Typist 4.7 sq m; these standards can be used to calculate space/accommodation costs for different posts.

Human resources

Staffing is funded from current income, with the expectation that the human resource will appreciate in value over time rather than deplete through staff mobility and turnover. In theory, long-serving staff can be regarded as assets and a kind of capital stock with an annual maintenance cost. And the relation between staffing and the power to realize the potential of the physical and institutional base is self-evident. Such human resource accounting is too often neglected in financial management practice.

The overall staffing budget of the organization is usually fixed in monetary terms depending on the establishment levels in operation. However, it may be possible to make adjustments in numbers across grades, although practically employer/trade union agreements reduce flexibility.

The manager will need to assess the staff skill requirements for services and products and the availability of these across different grades (thereby reflecting staff costs factors). Personnel policies within organizations are significant, but need prudently to reflect national agreements and guidelines.

Professional bodies (such as the Library Association) have long addressed the question of job content and grading at professional and non-professional levels. Trends towards flexible deployment, de-skilling and the impacts of technology have all been recognized and absorbed in a variety of ways. The UK Civil Service has paid much attention to personnel and staffing issues and its practices form one possible standard view.

By the same token the private sector has also led the way in innovations, and increasingly government policies seem to be taking a lead from the private sector under the guise of market conditions and competition. The move towards contractual reform is clearly being undertaken with financial managerial objectives in mind, evidently reducing employer commitment and shedding overheads.

The importance of effective management of staff in organizations is fully recognized through personnel managers in practice and through the expanding body of knowledge in human resources management. In fact staff resources have been the subject of greater managerial attention in the past than have other resources; a trend which should continue and be matched by the fully effective management of all resources, physical or financial. Grade and task relationships need proper investigation both for effective human resource management and for economic and financial management.

Quantifying staffing requirements is one of the most difficult tasks to perfect, in spite of the wealth of information coming from standards and operational experience. The motivation of staff to work and achieve results is critical to success, depending on many 'soft' and behavioural factors. Most managers have to work within the constraints of an existing arrangement or decision, but starting afresh may be no better guarantee of results. The resource effectiveness which produces the optimal cost performance has two components: first, a physical quantity of staff resource with a given cost, working on and with other resources; second, a resource value added which depends upon the interaction of the staff with other staff, resources, human factors, managerial skills and the organizational environment. The cost significance of the human resource factor in overall resource management must never be omitted from the overall financial equation.

In most library and information services staffing represents more than half the total expenditure. The organization's financial department is a source of salary data and staff costs. Average salaries can be computed or modal points on scales used to give a basic staff cost (the ready reckoner). The Library Association produces a useful series of pamphlets giving national salary scales, and surveys have been carried out by the Institute of Information Scientists.

Other components have then to be added to/included in the salary scale related costs. (These aspects are discussed further in sections 5.3.5 to 5.3.7).

- earnings related National Insurance contributions
- superannuation/pension fund contributions from employers
- special allowances (locally established, e.g. UK London allowances)
- common services costs

  Total staff costs should include a staffing overhead component if necessary; this could be made up from personnel department costs, training inhouse, accounting costs (e.g. salaries department), plus a wide range from which all staff generally benefit, e.g. typing, office services, messenger and delivery services, security and first aid, staff restaurant, registry and mailroom. While these departments may be substantial activity and cost centres on their own they are nevertheless common services to all staff.
- general adminstrative costs

  It may be appropriate to distinguish a further range of costs to add to staff costs e.g. stationery, printing and photocopying, telecommunications, postage and office sundries. If not added to staff costs these will be a separate resource/budget/cost heading.
- senior management and additional staffing costs

  In larger organizations there may be some advantage in adding supervisory and managerial costs to staff costs, as well as distinguishing them on their own.

- overtime

  Usually paid at an agreed rate, e.g. standard rates for Monday–Friday, time and a half for Saturday and double time for Sunday. Overtime should be a separate item on the staff budget and may be called upon to meet emergencies or staff absences.

- daily and hourly divisions

  When calculating staffing requirements it should be remembered that the annual costs will need to be divided into daily and hourly rates for costing jobs/tasks to be carried out. The following example shows how the year can be broken down to provide the number of working days, from which the daily and hourly rates can be derived: 365 days per year less 104 weekend days (261) less say 8 statutory holidays (253) less 25 days' holiday allowance gives 228 working days per year. The 228 working days may be divided into working hours. An average workday is 7.5 hours, giving 1710 effective working hours (these aspects are discussed in 5.7.3).

- staff travel and subsistence costs

  This may be a significant element if multisite operation is a normal requirement, and in addition travel to training events, meetings and other functions has to be covered.

- training

  A training budget is a financial expression by management that staff training is a policy requirement. Some organizations have an agreed percentage of payroll costs allocated to training. But it is difficult to have hard and fast rules on what is best. The demand for training will depend on the number of locations covered, the types of services offered, the age and experience of staff and staff turnover.

As regards this last point, the UK Local Government Training Board suggests 1.5–2.5 per cent of payroll costs be spent on training. There may be good grounds in the UK and elsewhere at present to allocate a higher proportion to cope with the needs of new technology and retraining due to structural adjustment. Travel and subsistence budgets will also have to increase in line (training overhead costs).

The training budget must meet the needs of all staff grades and should include induction, updating, retraining, preparation for promotion and even for retirement. As the training manager identifies individual needs costs can be assessed (e.g. from courses on offer). Training needs also have to be prioritized making a benefit evaluation as part of the resourcing process. The use of online services, for example, highlight the needs for training. Post-training follow up and appraisal is essential as part of the overall resourcing package.

The following factors can be considered useful in a training budget:

- training objectives
- cost of training sessions
- trainee support costs, including staff support
- staff replacement costs if required.

An important decision is whether training is resourced internally or externally. There may be payoffs to be gained from investing inhouse, but there will always be requirements which cannot be covered in this way. Proper appraisal of needs and provision is likely to be very cost-effective. Training budgets need to be monitored over time in much the same way as acquisition budgets.

Document and information resources

While the proportion of budget devoted to materials has tended to fall, the importance of adequate documentary and information materials as a vital component of service cannot be denied, and therefore the question of adequate funding is not to be avoided. This at least is the traditional standpoint of general, public and academic librarians. General principles are well reviewed in Gorman and Howes (1989) and Jenkins and Morley (1991 and 1993).

However, there is no doubt that electronic publishing will modify the picture as it is already starting to do. The cost per page of electronic information is falling, and is likely to become as cheap if not cheaper than print and bring with it corresponding advantages that are not available with print. This will not bring total comfort to traditionalists and it will not help to bring the value and virtue of printed materials to those who need them or prefer them and are denied them for lack of funds. But this is stated as a fact to get the issues into proportion.

Printed and electronic documents each have their role and purpose, and their costs. User requirements and information requirements are the two conditions that have to be satisfied by library managers, and, using rational business, economic and professional judgement, decisions about collection resources have to be taken. Price of materials, availability of funds, costs of alternatives, urgency of requirement and expected life are typical factors in the complex decision problems surrounding collection resources.

Structures and organization

The creation of an organizational system is a product of time, effort, intellectual energy and money. It should therefore be regarded as a significant secondary resource. The well constructed organization makes a significant contribution to efficient resource use overall. The last decade has seen organizational reform as a major topic, spurred along by the need to create among other things the conditions for the introduction of information technologies.

Information systems

While library and information services are dedicated to creating value from the information resource, they in turn need to ensure that they have good internal information systems. The professional community has taken strong steps to implement management information systems of the kind used in all other general organizations. In the first instance these systems were attractive mainly for developing performance measurement and evaluation techniques and took library statistics collection and use surveys as their basis (see Chapter Four).

But managerial reform has demonstrated the need to obtain proper management information to assist the integration of organizational systems and give a basis for control. This has opened the agenda for output and cost measurement, and latterly for addressing budgetary planning and resource management generally.

2.14 Resource management models and the process of resource management

A basic conceptualization of resource management can take the form of six distinct stages of activity:

1 Planning treated in 2.3–2.6.

2 Identifying resource requirements (in the context of the overall formulation of business goals and related activities; treated in 2.1 and 2.2).

3 Overviewing existing resources (either in terms of resources already acquired and possessed, or looking prospectively at how these can be located and acquired) (discussed in Chapters One and Two).

4 The financial management function, especially as an implementation of budgetary policy and planning, with the related activities of budgetary management and control, and the generation of cost data (Chapter Three in general, and in Chapters Five and Six in more detail).

5 Management information and decision making (Chapters Four and Seven).

6 Performance measurement and evaluation (Chapter Four and section 4.3 in particular)

Although these can be presented as a logical sequence of activities, the main point is that each should be an established function within the organization. Equally logically, the order might vary, and certainly many of the stages are taking place simultaneously, although not necessarily equally actively or intensively. For example, while the upcoming budget is being planned, other projects may be progressing to different stages.

Planning and budgeting are no doubt convenient terms to describe the whole sequence of processes. There is general agreement that they are essential processes, and furthermore they embody some essential managerial characteristics and dimensions.

1 The process draws managers' attention to the time factors involved in all managerial activities; it is true that there is often a time and a place for everything.

2 Emphasizing the sequential aspects of the process helps to clarify goals, aims and objectives, and the inter-relationships between each.

3 The best conditions for determining actual operational objectives are obtained.

4 Programme areas are established and are seen in overall and strategic terms; resource requirements as preconditions for the performance of activities can be ascertained.

5 In helping to draw the complete picture the singularity or overlapping of resource requirements can be established; resources can be used more intensively.

6 Improved knowledge of resource patterns can give managers the edge in being responsive to circumstances.

7 Managerial knowledge of resources can play a part in assessing reactive versus proactive behaviours, and in gaining a capacity for proactive response.

8 Since much managerial behaviour is about the global, strategic and overviewing approach to the organization, resource knowledge gives a stronger hold on interconnectivity and relationships within the organization.

Figure 2.3 is intended to provide a reductive statement about the resource requirements problem. Actual and potential demand for products and service are fundamental factors in making clear resource requirements.

The volume of resources required may well have been established by existing operational practices and needs; in this case the requirement/allocation problem is one of maintenance. However, forecasts and intelligence may indicate the emergence of new demands, or changed conditions in resource supply (price increases, changes in supplier). In this case the future needs element becomes stronger.

In some circumstances a completely new organization, service, product or programme is being considered. This will require a zero-based approach to resourcing, but it is likely that the resource requirements will be built up from a knowledge of the market, its requirements and forecasts of demand. Production volume anticipated will be a significant element in estimating resource quantities.

The interaction between resources (existing or planned) and future needs is a key element in which many factors require estimation, and in which uncertainty is reduced by forecasting.

Planning and budgeting are techniques and methods which support the whole process of allocation, with their respective emphases of planning (future needs) and budgeting (the quota of resources). Demand is the regulator of resource consumption but is only satisfied when services and products are output. The implication is contained

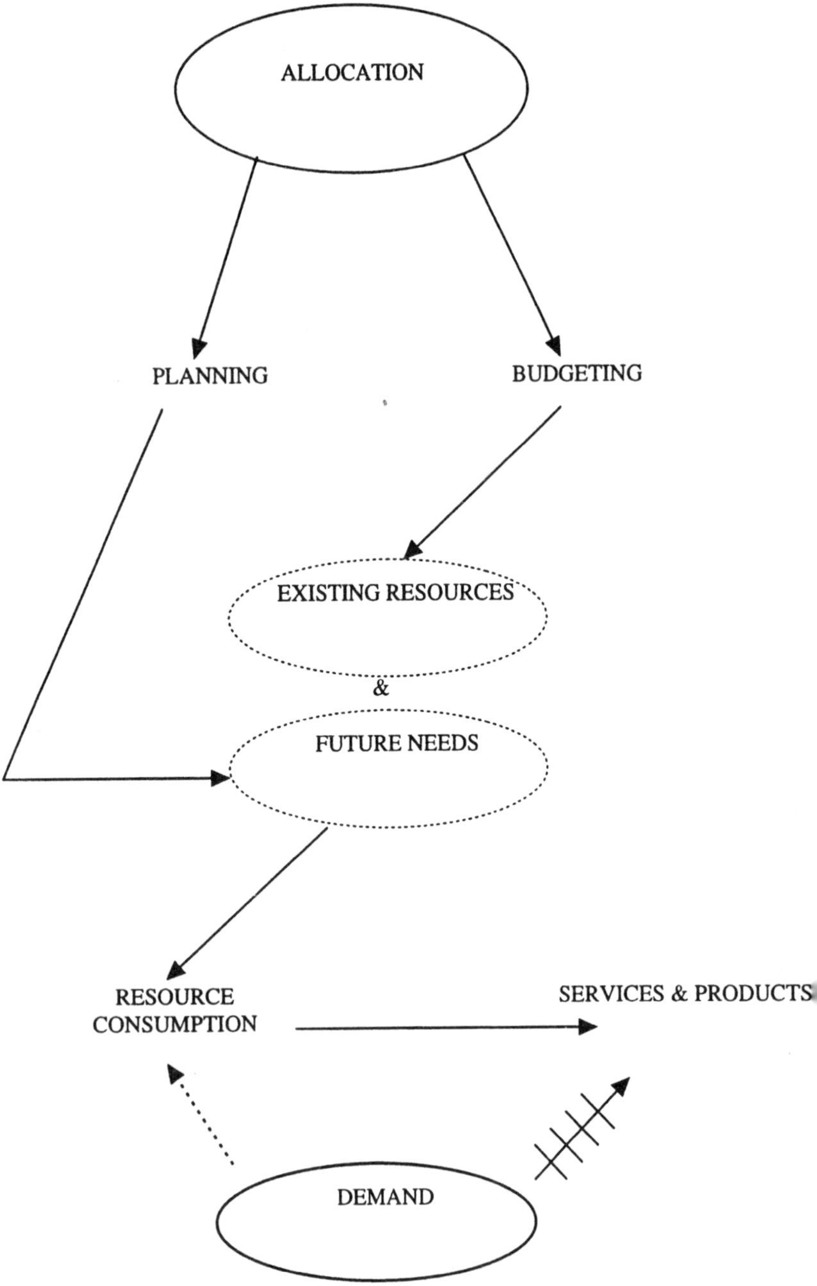

Figure 2.3. Resource requirements: a reductive statement

therein that too many resources may be consumed for insufficient product output. The feedback loop from this state to planning and budgeting is a strong iterative force in this model.

2.15 Resourcing levels for library and information services

There are three main aspects that affect financial planning and management:

1. The overall level of resources allocated to library and information activities in the economy and the distribution of these resources across the sectors of activity. The quantification of this has become more difficult as the information economy has developed. In the UK the Library and Information Statistics Unit (LISU) has started to monitor it (Sumsion *et al.*, 1993); similar work for the broader information sector has been undertaken by the PICT programme (Miles *et al.*, 1990).
2. The level of allocation to library and information activities by host organizations, and the financial investment required by free-standing information-providing organizations (e.g. online database producers, publishers, brokers, information centres etc.).
3. The distribution of resources internally within the library and information organization. Staffing levels and the proportion of staffing to total expenditure is a critical factor. Within materials budgets the distribution between serial publications and other formats is significant.

The organization manager needs to establish the normal level achieved and relate this to any standards of expenditure which have been determined. The management of these levels is part of the financial strategy and parallels the business planning dimension.

Standards for resource use

There has long been an appreciation of the importance of establishing work standards for libraries (for example, Gimbel, 1969), so as to establish levels for staff performance, job productivity etc. This same concern can be extended to develop normative standards for resource use. An understanding of such standards (assuming they can be developed and accepted) underpins vital contemporary concepts such as value for money and efficiency. In the context of work study and work measurement relationships between resource input and output have been explored as they effect cost measurement (see Chapter Five in particular). This understanding is essential for management and planning so that in each task area there is a move towards optimization.

Achieving programme balance: budgetary integrity

Financial management can be viewed as a process of striving to achieve an equilibrium in the conversion of resources to activities according to a proper formulation of goals. In reality the equilibrium is a temporary one rather than a steady state; real market and production conditions are dynamic, and the organization is continually responding to these forces. Managers aim to define the range within which the organization can operate, using variance analysis as a means of control; variation is permissible even outside the range, provided that the equilibrium can be restored (this means ultimately being able to control credit, having access to overdraft funds, stimulating additional consumption and generating more income or reducing spending). The methods and tools of financial management are available to provide managers with a capability. Some capacity is essential in every organization, but it becomes more and more a critical factor as complexity of production grows. Each organization can benefit from making an appraisal:

- what planning procedures are in place at the strategic level
- how formal and detailed are budgetary procedures
- how do these procedures operate, so that a report can be generated across the organizational year, by function and programme
- what information support is in place to underpin these activities
- what is the level of circulation of relevant information across the organization
- what and how effective is the co-ordination across organizational units.

These questions need to be put, and should have a proper home in each organization. Once the questions have been put, what are the answers?

2.15.1 Further reading

Resource management, planning and budgeting

Anderson, D. J. (1985) The high cost of planning. *Journal of Library Administration*, **6**(1), 9–16

Association of Research Libraries (1995) *Strategic planning in ARL Libraries*. Washington, DC: ARL/OHS. (Spec Kit 210)

Baker, D. (ed.) (1997) *Resource management in academic libraries*. London: Library Association

Biddle, J. F. (1992) *Planning in the university library*. Westport, Conn.: Greenwood Press

Blasingame, R. and Goldberg, R. L. (1985) Planning, another view. *Drexel Library Quarterly*, **21**(4), 1–131 (Special issue on the theme of planning)

Brophy, P. (1986) *Management information and decision support systems in libraries*. Aldershot: Gower

Budd, J. M. (1991) Allocation formulas in the literature: a review. *Library Acquisitions: Theory and Practice*, **15**(1), 95–107

Carrigan, D. P. (1991) The librarian/manager and resource allocation. *Library Management Quarterly*, **14**(2), 10–13

Castens, M. (1995) Financial management. In Cowley (1995) (ed.) *Management of polytechnic libraries*. Aldershot: Gower and COPOL

Corrall, S. (1994) *Strategic planning for library and information services*. London: Aslib

Coyers, A. (1985) The costs of a multi-site library service: a study of Brighton Polytechnic. *Aslib Proceedings*, **37**(10), 395–403

Donlon, P. (1991) Strategic planning in national libraries. *IFLA Journal*, **17**(4), 395–399

Ferriero, D. S. and Wilding, T. L. (1991) Mapping the future: strategic planning in a research library environment. *IATUL Quarterly*, **5**(1), 47–58

Financial management in government departments. (1983) London: HMSO (Cmnd 9058)

Galliers, R. D. (1991) Strategic information systems planning: myths, reality and guidelines for successful implementation. *European Journal of Information Systems*, **1**(1), 55–64

Gregory, V. L. (1992) Formula budgeting in academic libraries. *In Encyclopedia of Library and Information Science*, **49**, 259–267

Goldberg, R. L. (1985) A library planning model – some theory and how it works. *Drexel Library Quarterly*, **21**(4), 92–114

Gratch, B. and Wood, E. (1991) Strategic planning: implementation and first year appraisal. *Journal of Academic Librarianship*, **17**(1), 10–15

Hamburg, M. *et al.* (1974) *Library planning and decision making systems.* Cambridge, Mass: MIT Press

Hammell Carpenter, K. (1989) Forecasting expenditures for library materials: approaches and techniques. *Acquisitions Librarian*, **2**, 31–48

Hanson, R. K. (1991) Budgeting for monographs, serials and electronic databases – how should the tart be cut? *Journal of Library Administration*, **14**(3), 1–16

Hayes, S. and Brown, D. (1994) The library as a business: mapping the pervasiveness of financial relationships in today's library. *Library Trends*, **42**(3), 404–419

Heery, M. and Morgan, S. (1996) *Practical strategies for the modern academic library*: London: Aslib

Hunt, C. J. (1993) Academic library planning in the United Kingdom, 1993. *British Journal of Academic Librarianship*, **8**(1), 3–16

Jenkins, C. and Morley, M. (1991) (eds.) *Collection management in academic libraries.* Aldershot: Gower

Jenkins, C. and Morley, M. (1993) Collections. In M. B. Line (1993) (ed.) *Librarianship and Information Work Worldwide 1992.* London: Bowker-Saur, 71–104

Journal of Library Administration (1991) Budgets for acquisitions: strategies for serials, monographs and electronic formats. *Journal of Library Administration*, **14**(3) (special issue)

Katz, B. (1989) (ed.) The acquisitions budget. *Acquisitions Librarian*, 2 (whole issue devoted to the theme of acquisitions budget)

Kinnell, M. (1991) Environmental factors and strategies for managing change in UK public libraries. *International Journal of Information and Library Research*, **3**(1), 41–55

Kinnell, M. and MacDougall, J. (1991) Strategies for marketing public library and leisure services. *International Journal of Information and Library Research*, **3**(3), 167–185

Koenig, M. E. D. and Kerson, L. (1983) Strategic and long range planning in libraries and information centers. In *Advances in Library Administration and Organization* **2**, 199–258

Line, M. B. (1991) Strategic planning as an instrument of improving library quality. *Inspel*, **25**(1), 7–16

Lovecy, I. (1992) Budgeting in university libraries. *Serials*, **5**(1), 43–51

McKee, B. (1989) *Planning library service*. London: Bingley

Martin, M. S. (1994) (ed.) Library finance: new needs, new models. *Library Trends*, **42**(3), 369–584 (Special issue)

Molz, R. K. (1990) *Library planning and policy making*. Metuchen, NJ: Scarecrow Press

Orna, E. (1990) *Practical information policies: how to manage information flow in organizations*. Aldershot: Gower

Palmour, V. E. (1985) Some reflections on strategic planning in public libraries. *Drexel Library Quarterly*, **21**(4), 45–59

St Clair, G. and Williamson, J. (1986) *Managing the one person library*. London: Bowker-Saur

Senkevitch, J. J. (1985) Implementing a systematic planning process in two very small rural public libraries. *Drexel Library Quarterly*, **21**(4), 60–75

Van der Berg, S. (1993) *Research of unit costing of library operations in Bradford University Library*. Den Haag: Haagse Hogeschool (Sector economie en management) (report from a fieldwork placement at J. B. Priestley Library, University of Bradford)

Webbs, S. (1995) *Creating an information service* 3rd edn. London: Aslib

Wilson, A. (1979) *The planning approach to library management*. London: Library Association

Chapter 3

Financial management

3.1 Concepts

Some of the main elements of financial management have already been introduced in Chapter Two in the context of resource management. A recapitulation is given here bringing together the main elements which form the basic subject matter of this book (shown graphically in Figure 3.1(a–d)). To start the analysis some key concepts are identified and reviewed. A simple alphabetical order is used to introduce them giving no precedence to their importance, significance or systematic position in the field of financial management. Together they form part of the overall toolkit of financial management. Actual relative orders are more a function of circumstances, organizational experiences and scale of operations. In trying to plot the ideal form of financial management, all the concepts would be reflected in the make-up and functions of any given organization. More detailed definitions are listed in the Glossary.

Accounting

Accounting (making a reckoning by counting dealings in money) is a generic term which reflects two basic subsidiary activities. The first is a time constrained summarizing activity; historical financial accounting ensures probity in financial affairs by monitoring, tracing and recording financial and monetary flows and presenting them for inspection by auditors, managers and shareholders.

The second has a more technical dimension in the context of cost accounting; identifying and calculating quantities and flows within the cost data environment, so as to ensure that cost targets are met (e.g. through standard and unit costing, and through analyses of cost variances). This aspect feeds into budgetary control, and is related to the decision taking aspects as management accounting (considering the significance of cost values in decision making). The results of these recording and decision taking activities are then fed back to the picture viewed by the financial accountant.

Cost information provision has always been an essential part of accounting (as cost accounting), and is a necessary support to wider financial accounting activities. Financial accountability is both a legal and an operational requirement, reflecting a responsibility to stakeholders and shareholders. The ability to produce accounting statements and documents is vital. (See the alphabetical entry for a definition of cost.)

Proper budgeting is an important structural element of accounting, and this is followed through in cash accounting and

Finance	(Sources... Amount)
Income	(Sources... Amount... Regularity)
Expenditure	(Current... Capital)
Planning	(Strategic... Policy... Strategy... Implementation)
Resources	(Decision... Allocation)
Budget	(Plan... Control)
Costs	(Analysis... Patterns)
Accounting	(Money flows... Costs)
Management Accounting	(Costs for Decision)
MIS	(Data Systems/Sources)
Control	(Short term... Longer term)

Figure 3.1(a). Financial management: the key elements

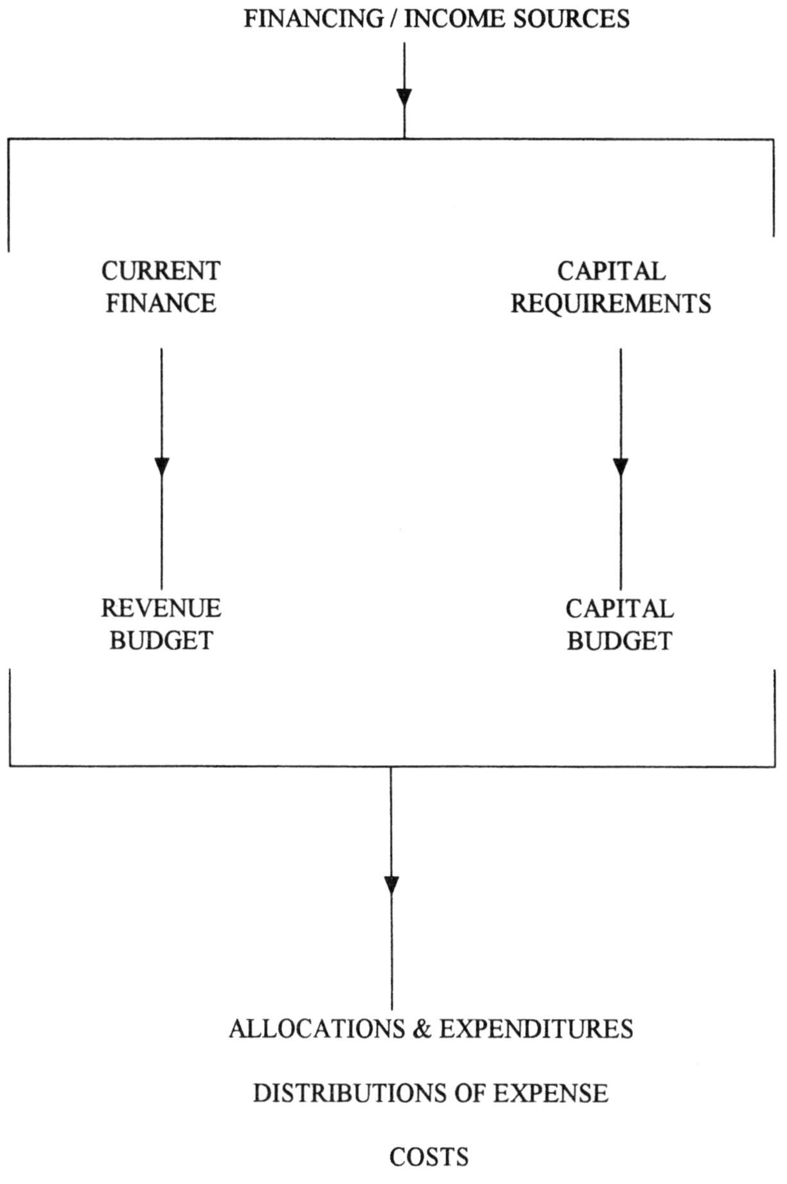

Figure 3.1(b). Financial management: a structure

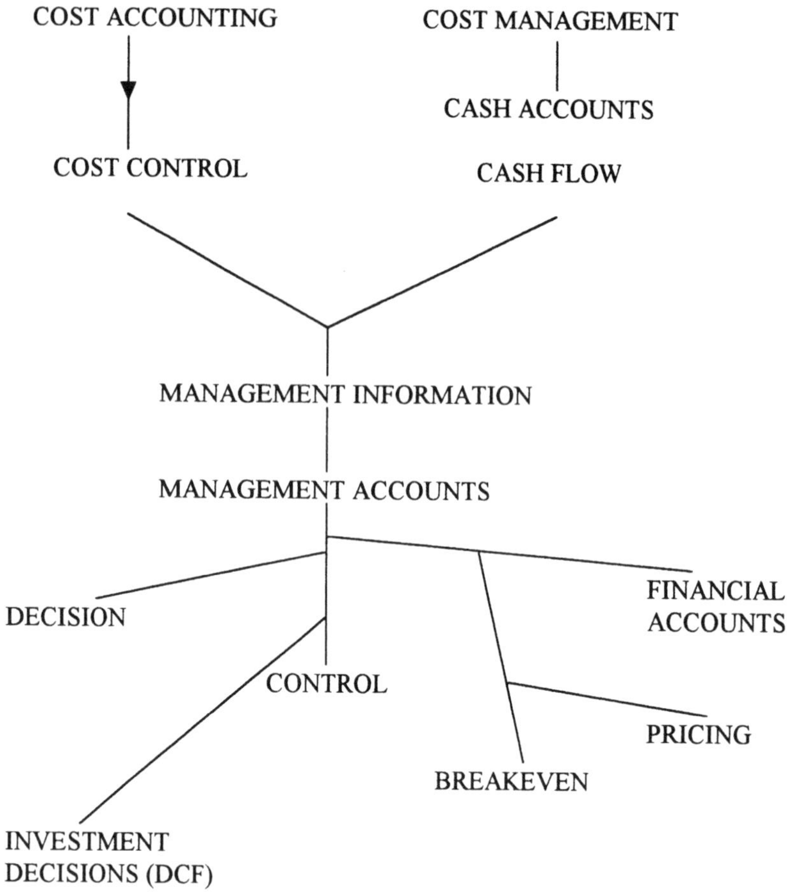

Figure 3.1(c). Financial management: the value of cost information

bookkeeping. Accounting has become heavily automated in commercial organizations, and this model of accounting can be replicated usefully to a degree, in library and information centres.

Management accounting

The use of cost data for decision making exploits the value of cost data in resource management. Management accounting in commercial organizations has tended to separate out from financial accounting into a discipline of its own, reliant on statistical analysis (quantitative business analysis).

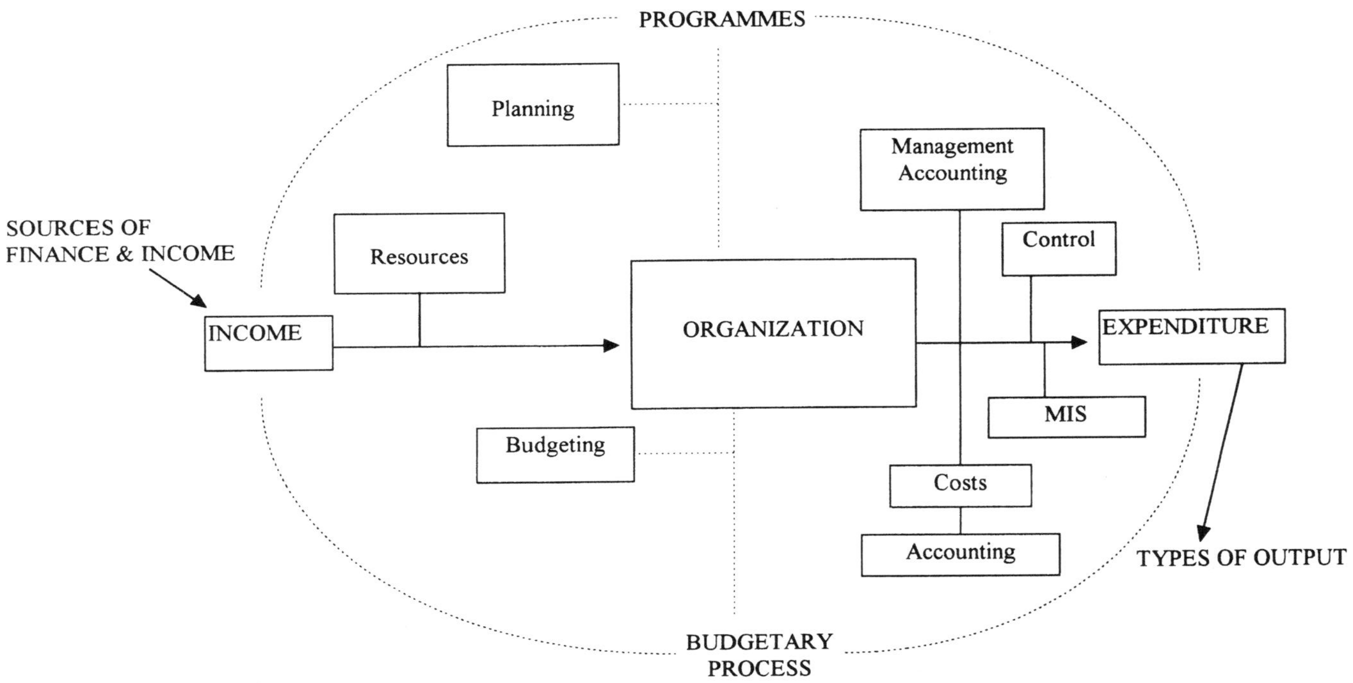

Figure 3.1(d). Financial management: a graphical presentation

Budget

A budget is the financial plan for the organization. Participation in and responsibility for budgeting activities may well be shared within the organization, but it is a key task of financial management and a focus of defined financial management responsibilities. These activities are covered further in this chapter.

Control

Control is a management function referring to the activities undertaken to maintain the state of the system within determined limits. In financial management sub-areas would include cost control, budgetary control and overall financial control. In complex organizations the degree of control that can be exercised is largely dependent on the substructure of information that can be generated about the system and the intelligence and other managerial qualities that can be applied to interpret it. Library and information centres have their own dimensions and characteristics requiring a professional and managerial capability of a distinct kind. There is great scope for control activities which can be brought together under the costing and budgetary planning methods advocated in this book.

Costs

Broadly speaking cost is the measure of what has to be given up in order to achieve something. A variety of cost terms is defined in the Glossary. Costing has always occupied a prominent place in financial management, but is still an underdeveloped activity in library and information centres (a point made earlier by Roberts (1984 and 1985), and still relatively true more than a decade later). But the move towards a business culture, greater attention to resource effectiveness and a recognition that economic and financial analysis is essential and beneficial continues to direct attention towards cost measures and measurement. Any technical difficulties in cost measurement in libraries will have to be overcome as a pragmatic necessity. The financial manager needs to know both costs and cost patterns.

Expenditure

Broadly defined as the financial outgoings of the organization, in a stricter sense the amount spent should be exactly defined by the agreed budgetary plan. The manager should see expenditure as not merely spending, as the simple outflow of monies to the point of exhaustion, but as outflow as the result of informed thinking and decision making, traceable back to agreed spending objectives and their physical consequences. All expenditures should be planned, regulated and controlled through a budget (see earlier entry). Capital expenditure must be separated from current expenditure.

Expenditures have to be authorised to permit budgetary control at the lowest level. The financial manager is responsible for ensuring that expenditures are covered by income in source accounts, or capable of coverage by expected income without penalty (e.g. an unexpected interest charge). The financial manager monitors revenue and expenditure budgets, using the full range of budgetary techniques, supported by technical and administrative assistance proportionate to the volume of income and expenditure.

Finance

This term (and its derivatives) is widely and often confusingly used. Its core meaning is money resources; financial management can be considered as the technique of managing money resources; financing can be understood as addressing the money/financial needs of an undertaking and the sources available to satisfy these needs. The term is often used co-terminously with income to denote the financial resources actually brought to bear on an undertaking. A useful distinction can be made between financial as relating to the broader aspects of money related affairs (especially the sourcing of money resources), and income as relating to the money actually obtained for the undertaking (see entry for a definition).

Income

Literally, income can be seen as the mirror image of expenditure. More specifically income is the money actually obtained for an undertaking. This said, however, much consideration is given to the financial aspects of income as defined earlier. The basic issue so addressed is the sourcing of income, either (1) as a grant (subsidy; allocation) from the host institution; (2) through income/revenue-generating activities; (3) through borrowing (with requirement to payback); or (4) as a sponsorship/gift. The total amount and the proportion from different sources are of course significant.

Other factors include the flow of income (regular or irregular), the control of credit and creditors, action on defaulters, and the costs of income generation and income raising. A division into *current* and *capital* income is also required, reflected in the revenue budget structure.

Management Information System (MIS)

An MIS is a tool to collect, handle, analyse and evaluate operational and financial data, so as to inform and improve the operational and financial management of the organization. The elaboration of a system reflects increased formality systematic capability, the application of technical means for data and information processing, and an end utility for improving management within the organization. Today MIS are a product of the application of information technology to business operations. Data are extracted from different stages and operations in the organizations, and through summaries, inter-relations of data and statistical analysis valuable information describing and indicating trends is produced. This information is then displayed in ways supportive of managerial decision problems.

Planning

Planning is a part of a systematic approach to management. It refers both to a process of selecting, revealing and formalizing arrangement, and to the creation of an agreed schedule of action. The philosophies and techniques of financial planning draw on all the resources and conditions related to planning as a major managerial function, ranging from the 'hard' technical systems such as project management methods to the 'soft' issues within human resource management (communication, consultation and political dynamics; see Raddon, 1997 for discussion). Planning is a form of project development and management dedicated to the purposeful achievement of goals and objectives. Planning introduces a rational element into management, although a realistic approach to planning recognizes the interaction of random and irrational events in the implementation and realization of the plan. Financial management can be said to begin and end with planning: and in the changing and dynamic organization the process does not end. The budgetary approach to developing financial planning is convenient, flexible and rewarding. This is the key to achieving financial management success.

Resources

Resources can be regarded as those things used by organizations that lead to the production of their characteristic outputs of goods, services and values. Such resources can be tangible and physical, as well as intangible (intellectual capital, human skill, business goodwill). Resources are generally acquired systematically by an initial outflow of income (showing as a resource raw material cost in the capital or the current account), and are then maintained by further income outflows (current expenditure).

Planning and management make certain rational assumptions about resource acquisition and use, but these can often be contradicted in practice. It is around these contradictions that debates about cost control, waste, efficiency, effectiveness, productivity and performance arise. The financial manager tries to be informed about the financial and accounting consequences of them, building on the review of resources (see Chapter Two) The greater proportion of expenditure will go to the acquisition of fixed resources (primary resources) and variable resources (resources for production) in line with the levels of production. Utilities and payments to organizations are consumed directly.

Expenditure on fixed capital may show irregular time patterns (significant in one year, but much less in another). Variable expenditures tend to have a more regular time pattern, often growing with the volume of business or declining with cutbacks in times of constraint. Awareness of such regularities helps budgeting, forecasting and planning.

A useful distinction is between those resources which accumulate for a significant period of time in the organization (e.g. collections of information materials), and those which are transitional, being converted through production into service, goods and products for consumption and/or sale.

A proportion of variable resources acquired become the equivalent of capital goods (e.g. the installed computer system with a life of say five years). The financial manager should try and assess the typical proportions of the status of resources in the organization (for example to forecast and plan replacement). Although other members of the organization play roles in resourcing, the financial manager should have a clear responsibility for decisions about choices (with proper professional advice), monitor allocation decisions, and be a party to performance and evaluation activities.

3.2 Sources of finance and income

Where a library and information centre is an independent trading organization it has to raise finance and generate income to resource the activities which support its goals as they are formulated in its business plan. Whatever the scale of activity the nature of the problem is the same. The most typical information organizations in these circumstances are publishing houses, online database producers and hosts, suppliers of networked bibliographical services, and information brokers and consultants. In short, these are the main commercial enterprises of the information industry. Matters relating to income generation and the revenue budget are further discussed in section 3.8.

However, the majority of library and information service centres are typically dependent on a host or parent organization. These conditions can occur in the public or the private sector; Section 1.5 provided an overview of the main categories of such types. The question of the requirement for a supply of finance in public organizations is the same as in the independent organizations just noted; but the nature of supply differs, and is influenced by a crucial question: how much should the host organization be spending on library and information support? It is not surprising that in the view of library and information professionals the amount is never enough; this is a recurring theme in the practitioner literature.

The truth or otherwise of the view of underfunding will always be debateable. And yet there is plenty of evidence that librarians do apply much pressure on their host bodies to maintain and increase funding, using factors such as materials price inflation, the need to invest in technologies, and evidence of user demand as levers. It is important that library managers are seen to press to the limit to try to improve funding, especially where no market orientated income generation is possible, or will yield worthwhile extra income.

Since the 1980s there has been a modification in practice to the two part model of direct external income or internal grant income. The creation of internal markets in organizations, through the creation of business and cost centres and the use of internal chargeback has introduced a third part to the model. Although it may bring little or no change in direct external income, it does create a psychological climate in which income and financial flows have a higher profile. With internal chargeback comes shadow pricing, and the internal customers/consumers become more sensitized to cost and value issues: if we are going to have to pay part of our budgeted expenditure to an internal provider (for information/library support) we will be aware of the opportunity cost (the money will not be available to spend on another resource factor).

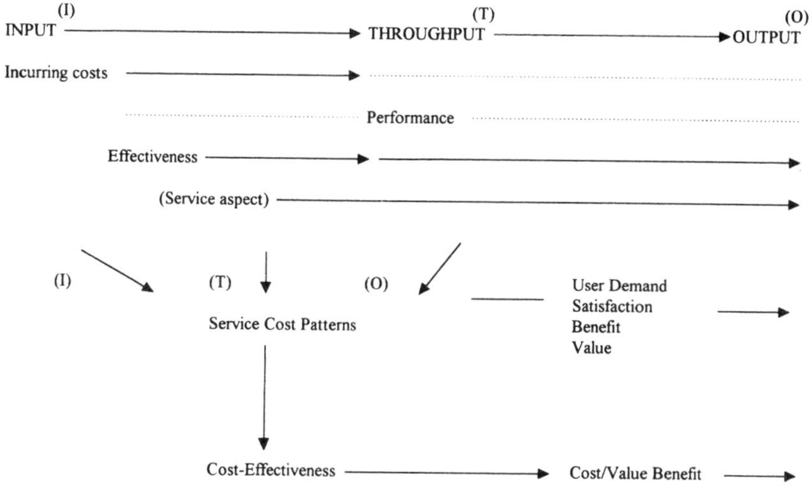

Figure 3.2. Resources and relationship to cost

Beyond these efforts lie the questions of the value of information and information services, and how it can be demonstrated in practical terms such as to influence policy decisions on funding. Performance measurement (discussed in Chapter Four) is a stratum for exploring such questions since it directs attention to questions of internal efficiency and effectiveness by focusing on the use of inputs and their treatment as service throughputs (see Figure 3.2). Performance measurement also evaluates output, which may be quite independent of value and benefit considerations. In theory there could be perfectly efficient libraries which delivered no value to users.

Evaluation requires both internal and external (user) judges, with the external view carrying the greater weight in claims for funding in host funded libraries. In commercial conditions it is the market which evaluates the consequences of decisions reflected in sales, consumption figures and market shares. This is not to confuse one approach (the external) with the other (the internal) and conclude that one is 'easier'; some library and information centres have no choice if they have a public service function. However, the market will deliver a clearer and usually less ambiguous signal about what action is necesary.

Ultimately one can see a resolution emerging where the requirement for funding is a function of the external evaluation of the library and information service either by host organization or market. This is realized and delivered in many different ways through professional practice. An important dynamic of the funding question is thus to do with the strength of value declared, and library and information managers are trying to increase the convergence on this point.

3.3 Planning and budgeting: the financial dimension

Planning and budgeting are at the core of financial management (see Chapter Two), although they have a wider influence and involvement in the organization. For example, service planning, marketing and sales planning are entities in their own right but have interfaces with financial planning which imply a strong level of co-ordination across the organization. Methodological issues which need to be addressed include the point at which planning involves formalities in communication, meetings, documentation and consultation (advantages are gained from an early stage). Also, a distinction is drawn figuratively between 'top down' and 'bottom up' methods; who, how, where and when issues may be less fundamental to success than giving clear goals and terms of reference to the process.

Exploratory planning will generate its own momentum in terms of questions posed and information requirements discovered; this is very creative but requires co-ordination. Another key aspect is the point at which financial constraint is introduced. Progress in planning may only be made when the financial parameters are drawn clearly; at this point some options will be eliminated.

The primary structural tool of financial management is the budget, already defined as the financial plan. In its simplest most useful form the budget could be presented as a tabulation with the rows represented by activities (the objects of expenditure) and the columns by the expenditures under different categories of expense); Table 8.1 in the EBIC case study is an example, and presents it as a line-item budget broken down by activities. This is more elaborate than the most extreme simple form of budget: a lump sum budget broken down only by categories of expense. However, even this simple form is normally given a useful elaboration by departments within the organization.

There is a perception that the scale of budgetary planning activity is proportionately related to the size and scope of the organization.

While this is broadly true, many larger organizations still have scope to employ more activity centred and programme-based budgeting, and many small organizations could still benefit from more explicit budgeting going beyond aggregate volumes of line-item expenditures. Although these comments put particular emphasis on the documented presentation of the budget, the remarks apply equally to the support and planning work leading to the preparation of these documents.

In the scale of organizations library and information centres have seemingly been able to operate hitherto on a very minimalist interpretation of planning and budgeting. As Allen (1989) has shown in her case study, this minimalist approach is capable of effective and beneficial reform, a point well made as early as 1974 by Hamburg. The case for planning library and information services is well and truly made; but the full implications have not been integrated into budgetary processes at all levels. Much can be learnt from the larger organizations which have successfully implemented *extended* planning and budgeting methods: many large North American academic and public library systems have done so, as has a large number of European national and large public library systems. But many others in the small to medium range have not progressed far beyond lump sum/line budgeting. Both generalizations need to be checked by inspection of individual systems, but these generalizations do serve as a warning and reminder. Further periods of macroeconomic and organizational change will speed up integration, but much may still rest on getting to grips effectively with cost measurement and cost accounting, to model choices and to monitor results during implementation.

As a permissible general conclusion about the library and information field certain larger public sector organizations such as national libraries, major state and public libraries, large and medium sized commercial information providers, and private sector organizational library and information centres have made the transformation to reform in both planning and budgeting systems. The norm for all library and information centre management should be standard business practice.

3.4 Cost centre development

The planning and budgeting stages should have provided a clear analysis of existing programme areas and helped to shape new ones. The programmes as the basic structural units of the ideal budget can then be used as the basis of structures for cost allocation, measurement and accountability. Programmes are complexes involving activities, operations, service, products – whatever units are meaningful and which best represent the way in which resources are grouped to facilitate productive processes. The active shaping and management of these units is at the heart of day-to-day and shorter term financial management. Cost centres form the basis of the financial control apparatus (see Figure 3.3). Jones and Nicholas (1993) provide a useful account of practical cost measurement under conditions of cost centre development.

Cost measurement (discussed in Chapter Five) focuses on these units, and their significance in unit costing. Cost centres provide a focus for cost-efficiency studies concerned with maximizing the effectiveness of spending (regardless of effectiveness in terms of objectives or performance criteria); elimination of waste, redundant operations and achieving productivity are goals. Cost-effectiveness extends the analysis by seeking the lowest cost/cheapest means of achieving defined objectives and/or obtaining the maximum value from a given spend.

3.5 Microfinancial management and procedures

All organizations irrespective of status, funding source or sector type need procedures to handle financial transactions of different kinds, including direct cash handling. These can be considered more properly as financial administration, but they are the overall strategic responsibility of the financial manager.

Typically these areas include (S. Pantry, 1994, personal communications):

- initiating orders for purchase, including the central area of acquisitions and ordering of information materials
- order authorization procedures
- order and invoice handling
- authorization of payments
- collection of cash and payments from clients (e.g. sales and till procedures)
- cash collection, accounting and cash management

COST CENTRE

Location, person or item of equipment (or group) for which costs may be ascertained for cost control.

SOURCES OF EXPENSE (Risk's Categories)	Type
COST CLASSIFICATION (Direct/Indirect)	Class
BUDGETARY EXPENDITURES (Amount of Spend £)	Quantity

Aggregated to a

COST UNIT

Product service or time period (or combination).. for copy control. May be a job, batch, contract or project group.

Sometimes COST UNITS referred to as COST CENTRES (colloquially)

As above

Aggregation can be referred to as:

BUSINESS CENTRE or BUSINESS UNIT

As above

In Budgetary terms referred to as:

BUDGETARY PROGRAMME/UNITS/CENTRE

THE BUDGET: BASIS FOR FINANCIAL MANAGEMENT

Figure 3.3. Cost centres: the basis of control

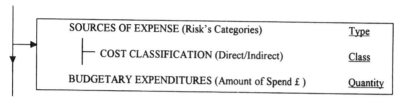

- cash account and bookkeeping
- preparation of cash and other financial summaries
- account preparation
- auditing procedures.

In addition there are tasks relating to budgetary monitoring and control:

- preparation of budgetary balances
- collation of budget reports
- analysis of budget reports and variance
- preparation of financial reports for management decision.

Some cost collection activities will also be involved:

- routine cost reports generated from budgetary data and current balances
- exploratory cost analysis and cost measurement (see Chapter Five)
- analysis of standard costs and cost variances.

3.6 Devolved budgeting and business units

The creation of systems of internal markets in organizations has been a characteristic reform of the last decade in the public sector of the economy in the major developed countries (and is a phenomenon spreading to developing countries). It is a major outcome of organizational reform consequent to the shift to free market activities in the developed and the developing economies. Library and information services are not immune to these changes. While the possibility of increased efficiency has been a justification, the notion that the market mechanism leads to the optimal allocation of resources has given the reform a stronger ideological colour when coupled with policies to reform public spending under the pressure of inflation, declining tax yields and other fiscal measures. When budgetary allocation is devolved to a unit the implication is that autonomy of decision is increased, together with greater responsibilty and accountability.

The providers of the funds can lay down the terms under which the funds are to be used, either by direction or negotiation; for example, by contracting to produce so much output. By the same token the unit to which the devolution is made can also begin to assert some autonomy and responsibility, especially when given powers to look for alternative income sources through trading activities.

The theory of internal markets in financial management may seem both rational and attractive, and to some extent it is. But its introduction has involved cultural and ideological change against long-standing traditions. It may have been introduced when the best conditions for success were not present. It is a complex problem with both social and economic connotations. What is involved is a redefinition of contractual obligations around another type of economic and organizational model. And often the parties involved have been neither willing nor equal to the change. The contemporary concern with organizational change and its management is derived partly from such circumstances as these.

What is clear is that the introduction of internal markets requires a planning and budgeting approach to financial strategy; the proper framework for the internal market is the key to its success, and this has to be consistent and evident across many levels (type of product, market conditions, consumer incomes). Internal markets may work if the right conditions can be created, and the play approximates to perfect competition. Consumers (of information services in this case) have to have incomes to purchase what is required, as much as producers have to have funding to organize production. Internal markets may be perfectable, but conditions for proper equilibrium operation have to be created. But once an internal market has been created the need for financial management is very clear (for example, as discussed by Jones and Nicholas (1993) concerning library services in the National Health Service in the UK).

.7 Market testing and contracting out/full cost recovery and commercialization

Market testing

The creation of an internal market of business units is often a precursor to further developments.

On the one hand market and trading opportunities may be revealed which point in the direction of the business unit being given full commercial autonomy, or near autonomy. The business unit has established itself, through good financial management and enterprise as a productive unit, able to control costs and produce competitively. With a market for its product there may be little reason to continue as a dependent unit within the host organization. It will thus achieve commercial status and its future success is measured by its profitability.

On the other hand the host organization may see a better opportunity to have its requirements met by other suppliers. Its own business units will then be market tested against outside competitors to see if they are able to stand the competition. The threat or the reality of market testing may have the result of improving the efficiency of the business unit within the organization. It will take appropriate action to maintain its position as the supplier of the service.

Market testing and competitive tendering are closely related approaches. Their introduction is always coupled with greater attention to questions of financial management; its advocates regard the process as stimulating and innovative. Its opponents see a neglect of public service obligation and a way of marginalizing activities which cannot fulfill financial and profitability criteria. Resolution of some of these issues has often looked to cost-effectiveness and cost-benefit analysis to produce some arbitration.

Publicly funded library and information services are potential candidates for contracting out/competitive tendering. Too little is known at present about the feasibility of these innovations for public information provision either in theory or in practice. It is certain, however, that any weakness in budgetary planning, costing or other financial managerial arrangements would soon be found out, to the ultimate detriment of market success.

The scope for commercialization of public service provision is one of the great economic and political issues of the closing years of the century. Public subsidization to organizations working to market discipline for the supply of public goods may be the best compromise. This could ensure supply of beneficial services and near optimal allocation of resources. Consumers have a role to play in making clear the benefits of the services received to decision makers. The jury is still out in this area, but the UK laboratory of the privatized utilities, healthcare provision and the railway service privatization point to lessons for the future management of the public domain (Hutton, 1995; Farnham and Horton, 1993).

Contracting out

Competitive tendering is a normal way of trying to obtain the best deal under market conditions, in the way of supplying goods and services inbound to the organization. A public organization uses competitive tendering (and has always historically done so) to obtain best value for money from external suppliers, as it is an accountable custodian of public funds, derived from taxation or borrowing against public assets.

Contracting out extends the notion of competitive tendering by literally giving a part of the organization's business to a third party under certain legal and contractual agreements. Generally speaking it refers to a contracting out of current operations and assets; the host organization still retains the rights over capital assets. Competitive tendering is always used when services are being contracted out. Contracting out is an arrangement for a defined period of time, often referred to as the franchise period. The contractor undertakes provision to an agreed service standard and is entitled to the surplus (or loss) over the period. The host organization, as the customer receives service, is spared current operating costs, and retains the capital assets.

The service agreement between customer and contractor is a key ingredient in the arrangement. The organizational customer can see it as service provision without financial risk, but the end user may not share this view in that the service or product is more clearly regulated and defined. Such arrangements do not allow for an unregulated margin in which optional activities or benefits may be gained seemingly without payment or charge at the point of use. Contracting out tends to provide more limited social goods benefits and to set the scene for later more strictly enforced pay-for-use arrangements.

Contracting out is a more radical whole organization approach which seeks to apply the logic of the market and competition to a major area of supply. A substantial segment of a public organization's activities is offered to contractors who will then offer the service, as if it were delivered by another organization.

Popularly, contracting out has come to be known as 'privatization'; a normal enough word, which has over the last ten years in the UK acquired other often pejorative connotations. Contracting out could be commissioned just as much by a private sector organization, but this case is more usually seen as selling off part of the organization completely.

Privatization (of a formerly public service) is the ultimate stage of the shift to market orientated activities. Whatever the public may choose to think is the full meaning of contracting out, it is but one stage short of privatization. A contract may end with the service brought back into the former host organization (in practice this does not seem to happen often, and privatization may sometimes appear to be the preferred option). But privatization does involve the disposal of public capital assets once and for all, the crucial difference being that the ownership of assets passes from the state to the new private owners. In this option competitive tenders are invited for the whole business, and rather than the lowest price being sought (as in contracting out) the objective is to achieve the highest price for the former public owner.

The consequences of these arrangements for publicly funded library and information service are clear and interesting. If a publicly funded library is fully privatized can it be considered as a distinctly 'public library' in the traditional sense of the word? The answer must surely be no. This said, the financial solutions available to such public information organizations must fall within a mixed mode (short of privatization). There may indeed be varying degrees of public subsidization and privately contracted management (with opportunities for supplementary income generation and profit taking), but falling short of full privatization with disposal of public assets into private ownership.

Contracting out is a phenomenon with a much wider range of application than in the UK alone. The reduction in direct state participation has, or is still having a major impact on the economies of the developed countries; those with a market economy as much as those with formerly centrally planned economies.

The library and information profession, especially the publicly funded sector, has seen the matter in a rather different light. Contracting out has been feasibility studied by several UK public library authorities, and in the mid-90s debate seemed poised between reaction against and some steps towards what is perceived as a rather threatening innovation. Just as the library professions are absorbing the message of better economic management internally, another challenging issue started to loom large. In 1997 the UK debate appeared to be moving away from contracting out. Whatever the end result it is clearly a sensitive subject.

The question as to whether or not the public library can be fully privatized still has to be resolved both ethically and practically. Many see the progression towards contracting out as being just a short step from privatization. Whether the concept would be more ethical or practical if it were less emotively described is to be seen. But there does seem to be a clear line between a publicly funded library service which uses the full range of business and market orientated methods, and one in which ownership is no longer in public hands.

Contracting out is an interesting technical and business approach to be sure. Some value might be achieved if it helps to focus the debates more clearly on the general public requirements, and on ways in which they might best be satisfied, given funding alternatives, subsidization, trustee arrangements and subscription methods. The matter could be seen in other ways as a social overhead even to the extent that public welfare need not be confused with direct state support.

These issues are fine exercises in political economy. Very well managed publicly funded library businesses could be seen as the sources for the delivery of value to whoever chose to consume their services. It may be pertinent to observe that higher education libraries enjoy some degree of immunity from the criticism levelled at public libraries (because they try to be all things to all people and rarely succeed), precisely because the benefits deliverable to end users are more clearly perceived. Clear public policy objectives with sound and rational financial management would be a good platform for necessary public libraries and information facilities (of all kinds) whichever shade of political opinion may prevail.

3.8 Income generation and the revenue budget

From financial dependence to financial independence

Income generation refers principally to the development of products and services for sale to provide revenue for the library and information centre budget. The term may also be used to cover revenue derived from grants, sponsorship or donation over and above the normal source of income as an internal subvention or institutional allocation, but the former sense of 'product for sale' seems to be the dominant contemporary usage.

This usage is very familiar to commercial, private sector and market orientated organizations which are habitually accustomed to survive and grow by their ability to sell product and gain revenue. But for public sector funded organizations there is still some novelty, unfamiliarity and even trepidation about the need to generate income. As the reader of this text is well aware the situation has been changing progressively (see Chapter One) over the last decade and provides the impulse for the attention devoted in this book to financial and resource management, and its extension into business planning and commercial culture.

Revenue budget under financial dependence

In the traditional public sector, units within the organization (such as library and information centres) received allocations of funding (authorizations to spend) usually on an historical basis. Decision making was concentrated at the centre, although some budgetary planning information (proposals and requests) originated at lower levels giving a sense of involvement. However, most approaches were convention- and procedure-driven, allowing subordinate units relatively limited opportunities to engage in any business context or financial managerial environment. Service units had, with few exceptions, no commercial context. This lack of economic motivation and limited financial responsibility was professionally acceptable and went largely unquestioned. The concept of revenue budget was usually nominal in this situation.

Private sector library and information centres tended to share this limited culture in professional practice, although their host organizations decidedly did not. There were of course exceptions, but more significant in this sector was the likelihood of more vigourous responses to change when general organizational and financial pressures changed. These changes were taking place during the 1970s, and in the UK clearly so after 1979. In the private sector the expenditure budget had always been more rigorously viewed, and so when changes on the revenue side came the shock was lessened. But the same cannot be said for the reforming public sector institutions in the 1980s where attention has had to be focused on both revenue and expenditure budgets. Special libraries in the private sector were better prepared for change.

Although internal adjustments have been required in both private and public sectors, the external pressures have been very significant. Thus it would be incorrect to suggest that the supply side of funding has been the exclusive problem, although much income generation activity has been a response to making up for financial shortfalls. The development of the information economy and the growth of the demand side has been a potent force for change and innovation.

Rather than seeing revenue problems as a source of restriction and inconvenience, the opposite view can be taken: growth in the information economy is associated with opportunity to develop new products and services and open up new markets. On the one hand this could be regarded as too idealistic a stance, rationalizing the bad into the good; on the other hand the environmental changes are largely irreversible, and pragmatism suggests an approach going along with the momentum and managing change to mimimize the disturbances which are inevitable. Norton (1988), Smith (1988), Brindley (1993) and Webber (1989, 1993) provide a range of contemporary viewpoints on the topic.

Revenue budgets under the business environment

Over the longer term the innovations experienced during the last two decades in organizational environments are likely to be seen in a more favourable perspective. What is most essential and realizable is the overall growth in the quantum of information economic activity; this is the only way in which uncertainties in the future of public service libraries will be resolved. The maxim must be that desired and essential growth is funded out of income, generated by revenue-earning activities, where direct public funding falls short. The changes are as much psychological as economic.

In this context, diversity of funding should be a longer term professional aim, but at the same time it is essential to remember that income generation requires:

- energy
- entrepreneurial spirit
- time to plan
- expertise
- resources to get the project moving initially.

This last requirement involves resources which are not often readily available in the publicly funded sector, so it has been advocated that involvement of the private sector can help to overcome this deficiency (Office of Arts and Libraries, 1987). There have been discussion fora and reports and commentaries in the UK (and elsewhere) which have reflected and confirmed this. The current library and information plans evolving in different regions in the UK are promising effective collaborative ventures between private and public sectors, against the background of wide ranging cultural change in national life (which is, of course, not without its critics, e.g. Hutton, 1995).

By twinning the public sector resources and capabilities to the private sector's ability to exploit and add value to the basic information commodities held in many libraries, there is an opportunity to present products which can be of great benefit to the user. Examples of this range from industrial sponsorship of events, encouraging commercial publishers to exploit public information assets (especially historical and artistic ones), to joint initiatives involving the application of new technologies (e.g. the proposed British Telecom sponsorship of Internet links in public libraries and schools).

Income generation: a political context

The OAL report (Office of Arts and Libraries, 1987) declares that joint ventures between private and public sectors do not necessarily lead to charges for information. What it does do is to provide value added services for those consumers (industrial, commercial and professional firms) who wish to pay for added value and customized information services. This in no way detracts from the provision of services to those customers who are unable to pay or who do not wish to pay for the information (e.g. students, people on low incomes) but it does require a clear policy statement and commitment to bring it about; this element may be the one absent in practice (Nicholson, 1992).

Brenda White (Oakeshott and White, 1991; White, 1992) further investigated changes and developments which had taken place since her earlier case studies reported in Oakeshott and White (1987). Attention was given to an examination of charging policies, and also of guidance to libraries considering joint ventures on external services.

The debate has continued on whether there should be charges for library and information services. The 1988 UK government Green Paper on 'Financing our public library services' (1988) and the Library Association's 'Guidelines on charging' discuss the options as does the Library and Information Services Council (1988). The LA guidelines accept that:

> It is not considered practicable for all conceivable library and information services to be provided by the public sector free of charge to all who demand them in all circumstances . . . the task is then to define (a) which services should be fully supported from the public purse; (b) which

services should be partially supported; (c) which services should not be supported at all (being charged at cost); (d) which services should be provided at a profit (either within or outside the public sector). Consequently there will be many variations of what might actually happen in local circumstances, with different types of customers and demands.

Gradually there has been a recognition that a purist concept of free libraries and information was never likely to be fully achieved as the scope of the information field has widened and increased expectations. Professional fundamentalism has been upheld in some quarters but it will lead to frustration and disappointment as the goal is not reached and as the goal point charges. Instead of seeing the problem as resistance by exclusion of charges, increasingly the perspective is of deciding what can and should remain 'free at the point of consumption', and making sure that it remains so. The blanket approach to policy does not provide the most fruitful solutions in the long run. Selectivity and considered choices are part of the cultural style of the 1990s.

Currently, direct charges are made by public library authorities for a number of services and these can be grouped in five main categories identified by John Beard in a paper presented to a seminar, 'The impact of charges in the public library service', organized by the Federation of Local Authority Chief Librarians and the Library Association in 1988 (Jones, 1988). These categories are:

- those services for which a profit can be seen on each operation (e.g. photocopying)
- those services considered to be of added value for which a charge is made to cover replacement costs (e.g. loan of video/audio cassettes)
- those services provided within the overall framework of the library and available from time to time on a charged-for basis (e.g. renting a meeting room)
- those services for which, by present law, only a nominal charge can be made (e.g. reservation charges)
- those services which are partially or wholly recharged to other departments of local government or sectors of government.

So it appears that any charges such as these do not appear contrary to the idea of a basic (public library) service free of charge at the point of consumption.

Winkworth (1992) looked at income generation in academic libraries and argued that they are public institutions and that any income raised is justified for reasons other than profit. There are many examples in various library and information services in the UK and other European countries and the USA of free and fee-based services co-existing. The Health and Safety Executive's Information Services in the UK offer both kinds of service, as indeed does the British Library both to recover costs in some and to compete aggressively in others. Many more examples have been reviewed in the OAL Report No. 16 (Office of Arts and Libraries, 1987). As opportunities widen with the expansion of markets such as the European Union the information provider will inevitably have to respond, and will find capability derived from the degree of financial management introduced into organizational practice.

Information is a raw material for many 'production lines'. If the information specialist can recognize the opportunities or be retrained to do so then the profession itself will be able to develop beyond today's thinking and action. Surveys of contemporary practice on charging is provided by Yates-Mercer and Pearson (1992), Pearson and Yates-Mercer (1992) and Brindley (1993).

Linking income generation to the cost centre concept

As the new economic thinking becomes absorbed into library and information centre management, the priority is for techniques and structures which will support the fullest developments. Cost centres have traditionally been identified for cost accounting and control purposes. When the concept is elaborated it becomes a structure for autonomy, responsibility and enterprise; it emerges as a focus for interpreting and responding to the market and demand. The market is the source of income, and the cost centre (and the business centre) is the means of focusing resources and structuring income and expenditure to optimize production.

The concept of cost centres has already been discussed, and it can now be related to income generation. As the information centre has traditionally been dependent on the parent organization, the decision to move away from such integration has to be considered carefully. As an independently operating unit it will have to invest to provide the service (expenditure), and make charges for use (income). Aggregation of cost centres leads to the definition of proper business centres, integrated to seek income, use resources and control expenditure.

Thus the information manager becomes a true financial manager, with all the attendant results that such autonomy and independence bring. Plans of work will then need to look at earning and income potential as well as expenditure consequences. There is a dramatic difference between orientating activity around 'what shall we spend' and 'what income are we likely to earn', or 'what will be the contribution to revenue of a given activity'.

The means of generating income

There are two levels at which to consider this problem:

- higher level service and product strategies
- lower level initiatives.

Most library and information services have been developing a familiarity and experience with lower level intiatives. Sometimes this results in an ad hoc approach, but often it is a stage on the road to greater formality. Integrating lower level intiatives at an appropriate time could encourage stable and progressive growth. A review of these initiatives follows, and an evaluation of the way in which they can be exploited for creating a higher level service and product strategy.

Fines, reservation charges, reprographic services, document supply
These can be conveniently grouped together as commonly used library income generators. They are characterized by being embedded in typical library activities (circulation activities, photocopying, inter-library lending) and as such their support is largely accounted by fixed costs or as marginal costs often absorbed by 'more efficient working'. While they need to be monitored managerially, they do not usually have a high start-up requirement or incur project maintenance costs. However, librarians have become more aware of the impact of these first step income generators, and there are capital and some current spending implications in buying reprographic equipment and taking out servicing and leasing contracts.

Reprographic services Most libraries view copying as a profitable activity. Leasing a copier to support this activity is likely to be the most cost-effective way, and pricing can reflect rentals. Service contracts cost money but ensure eliminating waste of staff time. The implications of copyright legislation are now taken more seriously than ever, and in the UK the Copyright Licensing Agency can ensure compliance; library malpractice is now costly and illegal. Although user self-service copying is the norm, services undertaken by staff for customers need to ensure recovery of costs for all work including billing and administration, as well as handling and delivery.

Advertising

Advertising and promotion can generate income, using public library space and space in library produced publications, including promotional material such as book marks, carrier bags, library produced events listing material and so on. Although income is likely to be small in volume it could be regular. Public libraries can capitalize on the high volume of passing traffic. The commercial advertising and media world has many examples of persistent, low intensity, but steadily profitable revenue opportunities (selling space on public transport for advertising is a case in point). Sometimes advertising is paid for in reciprocity of message carrying, and while beneficial the opportunity for revenue-generating promotion should not be neglected.

Selling library space

Public libraries may occupy prestigious locations with a reservoir of space which should be regarded as a revenue-generating asset. The leasing or franchising of space to commercial facilities has become increasingly attractive to public authorities to yield additional revenue. Such assets may not be in the exclusive control of the library, but the example is a powerful one. Sales and merchandizing operations may be an integral part of library, gallery and museum business, and if such opportunities exist they should be taken to use space effectively, recognizing that selling incurs cost and resources, and that profitability has to be assessed. Hence the attraction of leasing out, and the library adopting a rentier function where the lessor carries all the risks, and the library confines itself to providing leasable accommodation.

The introduction of a retail bookseller to a major library is advantageous to all parties, and what goes for libraries may also be so for higher education institutions, and museums, galleries and theatres. Ticket booking agencies and catering facilities are other kinds of distributive enterprise with an affinity for library positioning and clientele. The London Borough of Sutton, the British Library and British Museum are good instances of this approach to arts, libraries and retailing. In general the galleries and museums world has taken a lead in this activity, exploiting the affinity between culture, public/consumer aspirations and merchandizing. Libraries can no doubt do more in this field, but need to think through such projects clearly: all such revenue-generating opportunity incurs costs and risks, and an understanding of markets and market behaviour is essential. The enterprise becomes a natural cost/business centre.

The most significant factor promoting these activities, apart from economic necessity is culture change in the professional community. Public service is not inevitably the prerogative of the publicly funded enterprise, and over the years such enterprises have failed to sustain a high level of customer service. It has also to be said that the reputation of private enterprise for good customer service was not consistent. Both domains are being challenged and tested by the customer care culture, promoted through the total quality management (TQM) perspective.

Consultancy

Selling professional LIS skills is a very complex subject. In the current economic situation many small businesses are setting up in a wide variety of backgrounds. Not many will be able to afford an information specialist but all will need information. It is possible that the LIS may be able to fill a particular gap in the information services already available. It is a task for the LIS to identify such gaps and match to their expertise. This could be:

- links with specialists in a subject field
- document supply services based on collections
- sharing the training of staff
- online searching and other retrieval activities
- provision of language services and translation.

It has been noted that one of the greatest difficulties is the reluctance of LIS professionals to sell their services; circumstances are now working to change this. Gurnsey and White (1989) in their book on information consultancy recognized this problem and are among a growing number offering advice in the information-broking field.

Contracting out/in

There has been growing momentum in libraries to contract out housekeeping routines, such as the use of bibliographic co-operatives and bookbinding; reduction in expenditure and participation in economies of scale have been the main reasons. Traditional and electronic publishing activities also make extensive use of contracted out services. Contracting in needs to be addressed by libraries as potential for income generation; supply of services to business and science parks has been identified and in a few situations actually practised. In many ways the contracting out and in situations are complementary. Economical contracting out of routine support and housekeeping tasks frees services to deploy resources to income productive activities. The library and information centre needs to make a strategic audit of its competitive strengths and seek the best mix of activities. Library and information centres may yet discover potential in information facilities management; facilities management emerged as one of the new features of organizational life in the 1980s, and the model needs to be applied to the opportunities provided by the growing information services market.

Electronic services: databases and multimedia

With the increasing use of computers in libraries there is a growing potential to set up information services and products using these technologies and to market and sell them. The libraries' bibliographic databases, OPACs, electronic products in CD form, and the library function as a gateway and network node open up a feedstock of electronic data and information for commercial gain, as well as for public dissemination. The library is in an advantageous position if it can develop product from its own sources, because setting up its databases on external hosts requires additional stages of negotiation, forming agreement, testing and prototyping, and establishing a tariff for commercial use with arrangements for payment of revenues and royalty.

The marketing and sale of electronic services and products of this kind is a good illustration of the requirements of such commercial revenue activities. While product design and production inhouse is a task, the success of the activity is dependent on marketing, promotion and sales effort, which should be properly identified as to time and expenditure. Proper project budgeting is essential and this should be assimilated into overall budgetary planning. Traditional methods of marketing and promotion can be used (see Roberts (1989) in Kinnell, 1989), but electronic networks and videotext services can also be used to boost promotion.

Information searching

There is great scope in the library and information centre to expand the concept of 'added value services'. Most library and information centres offer parts of a 'menu' of standardized services (such as loans, photocopies, provision of reference tools etc.). But often what the customer wants is that extra service which will save his/her time. It may also be required because the customer does not have the necessary expertise to carry out the task, which could involve location of sources, retrievals, data analysis and report production. This is an added value service. Customized information searching is increasingly required by business and technical clients who can absorb realistic costs into their projects. The library and information centre has to have proper business sense to engage in this kind of revenue-generating activity, knowing the expenditure of effort required, and confidently pricing to recover costs plus. Include in these costs: staff time asking questions of the customer; staff time carrying out the search; online and CD charges; document supply and handling costs.

Publishing, reading lists and bibliographies

Over the last decade many library and information centres have realized their traditional role as publishers, and many more have begun to see the natural potential for this activity (e.g. Carson, 1988). The accessibility and convenience of desk top publishing (DTP) has driven enterprise in this activity. Low print runs and ease of design and production, as well as potential for rapid updating are attractive characteristics.

Compiling reading lists, bibliographies and subject catalogues naturally extends and uses professional skills, and realistic pricing can open up markets. But the potential is even greater, and areas such as local studies and history and directory publishing have shown revenue-generating promise. Sometimes lists and documents are really sales catalogues and promotional aids, so their production costs need to budgeted for.

There are degrees of involvement in publishing activity, and sometimes the library should work in conjunction with another organization to share editorial and marketing expenses. Libraries may be a fruitful point of initiation of a publishing project in terms of archives, records, illustrations or other collections, but still need to seek appropriate authors and editors.

Seminars and courses
Organizing seminars and courses can be lucrative. Once the formula for holding seminars and courses has been worked out the library and information centre may identify a whole range of possibilities. Partners within and outside the organization can be found. When special sources of expertise are required these should be bought in and costs recovered. Some working capital/petty funds are also usually necessary.

In terms of product the right speakers and programme are key assets in selling an event. There are standard checklists for arranging public events, which cover both the arrangement of the programme and the supporting activities such as promotion, registration and sales, catering, services to speakers and participants, and dissemination and publicity after the meeting. Expenditure implications of all these stages need to be noted and built into the budget. Collection of revenue needs firm organization, especially in dealing with credit and default for payments.

Retailing and merchandizing
Public, general and some scholarly libraries have begun to appreciate the potential of their location and context for selling publications, cultural items and often popular gift type merchandise; the British Museum/British Library, Bodleian Library Oxford, and National Library of Scotland provide examples, and major public libraries many more. The activity has progressed from marginal selling over the ticket or circulation desk to a dedicated and purpose-built location. The normal methods of retail practice must be applied to the sales point. Similar developments have taken place in museums and galleries. The bringing together of libraries, arts and performance facilities in cultural centres can maximize the potential of this kind of income generation. A library sales point or a franchise-selling operation within a library moves income generation to a higher level and strategic focus.

Training, consultancy and other services
Since the mid-1980s libraries have become less intimidated and more realistic about the potentialities and benefits of entrepreneurial activity of various kinds. The British Library has led the way (as it should) in building professional confidence in a time of market orientated and market led activities. It has become a major provider of value added commercial services in document supply, publishing, consultancy and training activities. Traditional professional feelings and values are

not necessarily compromised by commercial and business activities. What is essential is that such enterprise should be successful. Libraries and information centres are evolving into multiple goal/mission organizations; success in commercial activities can be used to complement success in public value activities, upon which traditional library and information centre expertise has been built.

High level and strategic level income generation

As libraries have explored the potential for income generation and seen the necessity of backing up such activities with sound financial management, these initiatives may come to occupy a more strategic role in the overall financial and resource management of the organization. Income has progressively become more multiple sourced; when non-grant/non-institutional income allocation reaches the 10–20 per cent level income generation is both high level activity and strategic. Loss of such revenue budgeted income becomes strategic when the result would be a weakening of organizational capacity, requiring layoff of staff, loss of markets and clients and closures of service points and reduction in service levels.

Library and information centres need a positive approach to these matters, starting with clear policy formation on commercial and enterprise strategies, organization of resources for commercial projects, information systems, money management procedures, and marketing and customer policies. Integration of elements is crucial for success.

Income can thus be variously classified as:

- institutional grant allocation
- revenue budgeted activities
- retail merchandizing
- library use charges (fines, reservations, document supply)
- value added library and information services
- consultancy income and research income
- training and other events
- income from use of space and accommodation (hire and rental)
- publishing activities (in general)
- grants, gifts and sponsorship.

This provides the basis for a revenue budget framework with a recognizable programme structure which can be related to expenditure and activity programmes.

The choice of income generation activities is very wide. Library and information businesses will have to address these choices at a strategic level in the light of market opportunities and production capabilities. When activities are selected the priorities are to operationalize them in organizational, managerial and production terms. Each activity has to be planned in business mode, and identified as a programme, e.g. having a business centre and cost centre; an expenditure and revenue budget has to be drawn up with a proper operational plan for implementation.

Pricing

Price represents an exchange value whether seen from the point of view of the producer/supplier or from that of the consumer/buyer. In a classical market situation price levels are established through the interaction of buyers and sellers; the theory implies perfect information about offers and intentions, a so-called state of perfect competiton. In the real world the situation is considerably less perfect and more complex since consumers have less interaction in practice.

However, competition between suppliers may produce similar results which to an extent will benefit consumers; if there are more suppliers in the market the competition between each will push towards a price equilibrium from which consumers will benefit. The overall theory of the market suggests that in this way resources are allocated most efficiently, and that this will result in optimum pricing.

Market interaction is not the only factor at work. The cost of production as a component of price formation is very significant. Producers therefore seek to control costs and thereby leave a greater margin for surplus return (profit). The pattern of production costs is thus critical in all business pricing decisions. Profitability is achieved through responses to competitiveness, and profit maximization is certainly a fundamental business motivator. Revenue is maximized by keeping overall production costs low and competing for market share to maximize turnover and revenue. Pricing levels are therefore important in relation to volume of demand, level of sales, financial turnover, income levels and profitability.

The other significant factor is consumers' propensity to consume; this is a function of needs and requirements for satisfactions provided through goods and services and a willingness to sacrifice resources (income) to obtain these satisfactions. The consumer reads the information signals contained in prices, relates these to needs and acts accordingly constrained by level of income and alternative requirements. Consumers tend to prioritize their expenditure decisons. Lower prices contribute to stimulating consumption. Consumers' interests may be best served by having a range of supply alternatives and adjusting prices in order to gain market share.

Between the supply and the demand side there are many other factors such as market and marketing strategies, product quality, distribution and delivery strategy, fashion, and consumer psychology which influence pricing.

Pricing is a substantial aspect of business stategy and planning, and as the information market moves into commercial mode and/or into a state of higher financial awareness the topic has a much higher profile. Information production may have a market price or a shadow price if the market is subsidized as it is in publicly funded information provision.

The relation between costs and prices is substantially determined by financial management strategies. This fact underlines the approach taken throughout this book. The professional debate is complex and complicated by views of the nature of information and information service, and by different intepretations of the commoditization of information. Whatever the status of information per se the delivery of it to the customer by information and library services has to acknowledge the resource sacrifices made and the inevitable cost and price components. The business of organized information supply has to take account of these factors irrespective of the professional and philosophical debates surrounding information as an economic good. Further reference to pricing and charging is made in Chapter Eight and Section 8.4; some additional readings are also listed as an introduction to this topic of growing importance.

3.9 Growth and contraction: financial implications

Libraries are not unfamiliar with the concept and implications of growth, but historically it has been focused on the physical aspect of collections, and their housing and storage. Such growth has not lacked financial implications: it has been a special concern of academic and research libraries and of national libraries. This aspect will continue to be a problem for libraries.

However, there is another meaning to growth which owes more to the business and commercial culture of the market. The search for profitability drives the business preoccupation with growth in terms of market share, exploitation of mass markets, increasing turnover and reducing costs, obtaining economies of scale and seeking an aggressive response in a competitive marketplace. Gains in profitability are not necessarily linked with expansion and growth, but where they are the manager must give attention to growth both in capital funding and in income.

Library and information services have moved and are continuing to move decisively into business and market mode. Growth is becoming related to prospects for survival, and information managers must therefore consider financial growth as a corollary of developing a business strategy while maintaining their traditional competence at managing collection growth and its physical and spatial consequences.

This new concern for growth should not be seen merely as a concern for the quantity of monies involved, but through its concomitant business and market awareness. The library and information centre is to be viewed increasingly through its sense of purpose. Growth is thus about purpose, optimism, relevance, adaptability, innovation and progressive change and shaping to the needs of customers. A growth in demand for finance alone is without purpose, but the growth culture is a measure of health as much of as expansion. Such positive growth is more likely to bring about a purposeful expansion of need for funding, and therefore the skill of managers is to prepare for this in the most effective way.

Contraction, whether of the organization or of its demand for finance and resources, needs to be given the equivalent attention as growth. Contraction and the removal of financial resources can clearly be negative. But contraction is also a component of a healthy organization's strategy if it is dictated by circumstances and needs and is not going inevitably to lead to the collapse of the organization. Some strategic contraction (or reduction) may be the most suitable course of action in the short term. Growth of the wrong kind could pose dangers and therefore indicates a prudent contraction. Information managers need therefore to use the repertoire of growth and contraction and its financial consequences according to circumstances and with intelligence and understanding.

3.10 Capital funding and strategies

The sourcing and management of capital funds is both an initial and continuing preoccupation in the commercial business. This is well reflected in methods of financial analysis and accounting procedures. Public sector library and information services have usually been dependent on their host and/or funding organizations, and remote from centres of investment and capital decision making. Such situations provide little incentive to address properly questions of capital funding. But the introduction of market disciplines into the information industry is changing this position. There are several levels of analysis.

1 The auditing and valuation of capital assets (fixed buildings, plant and equipment) is a basic requirement. This provides a basis for estimating depreciation rates (and allocating depreciation to fixed/overhead costs) and for developing a plan for renewal of assets (planning for future capital investment and spending).

2 Identification of capital requirements for maintenance and new projects. Larger organizations have a mechanism for managing capital spending. Bids from departments are called for on a regular basis (budgetary cycle) or when it is known that capital funds will become available.

3 Sourcing of capital funds. Increasing business autonomy and market discipline gives the organization a broader range of capital sources in the financial market. Banks and finance houses offer capital at market rates of interest. The viability of the project for which capital is sought is the key factor. The borrower can examine the payback period by discounted cash flow (DCF) analysis, and the provider of capital will want to look at business plans and future income projections. For many library and information services this is new territory. The Private Finance Initiative (PFI) in the UK is a typical development of this new financial culture, getting private investors to invest in public services; but the problem for library and information services is that there is no clear prospect of profitable returns.

In the public sector there has been some diversification of capital sourcing over the last decade. Public agencies have become providers of venture capital in the form of project grants (the

European Union is a good example). Leasing of equipment is a method that has also developed to satisfy capital requirements.

4 Matching proposals to available funds. Traditional inhouse capital projects analysis will require the prioritization of alternative projects. Taking the capital requirement to the market is less a case of matching to funds than of substantiating the viability of a project. The analysis of risk assumes a greater importance, and estimates of market demand and projection of revenue flows are critical.

5 In business organizations the capital flows can be divided into working capital (essentially shorter term) and investment capital (longer term) requirements. Working capital is required to pay for materials, to finance credit periods to customers, or to cover bad debts. A contingency fund or reserves also shares these functions.

Library and information businesses are gradually becoming accustomed to deal with capital fund management as a part of overall financial strategy and management.

3.11 Projection and forecasting

The growing awareness of the significance of capital-funding management highlights the importance of the ability to make projections and forecasts. Projected resource costs (especially staff costs) and demand projections are key elements in capital projects analysis. Routine library and information service statistics and evolving capacities in management information have a part to play in increasing financial management competence. The collection of statistics and trend analysis such as that carried out by the Library and Information Statistics Unit at Loughborough University (Sumsion *et al.*, 1993) becomes more significant.

As the library and information sector acknowledges market disciplines the quality of forecasts and the appropriate time horizons chosen for analysis affect the quality of decision making.

3.12 The changing budgetary environment

A substantial part of the discussion so far has been concerned with the internal financial environment of the organization. However, this is ultimately responsive to the external environmental conditions; to the business environment of the library and information services community. There are several ways in which to categorize these features.

Legal and corporate environment

Legislative features of a general or sectoral character define corporate requirements: these include the Companies Act, the Health and Safety at Work Act and the Data Protection Act. Sectoral requirements include the Public Libraries and Museums Act, the Copyright legislation, the British Library Act and various legislation relating to the provision of education.

The financial implications of such legislation refer to the presentation and publication of accounting data, the provision of an annual report, the registration of the enterprise, the need to appoint auditors and many applications concerning taxation (notably the implications of the value added tax). There are also wider implications sometimes depending on the public or private sector framework.

Library and information centres in the private sector have always had to ensure compliance with such legislation, but significant and evolving changes in the public sector are taking place. The creation of de facto businesses within public sector organizations as part of financial and economic reforms, and the hiving off of activities through contracting out is already affecting library and information services. These changes are bringing such traditional public sector activities into the mainstream of corporate and business life with all its legal consequences.

Obtaining capital project finance and increasing the supply of resources for enterprise schemes generally has been one area of difficulty in the traditional public sector. Public service managers have not had the option to go independently to the financial market to increase their access to capital funding. Public sector finance in the UK has always been dominated by the Treasury, and the mechanism for distributing public funds by a complex system of bidding and top down allocation, often determined by the pecking order of government departments.

Treasury regulations (and those of most public monetary authorities in all countries) have constrained expansionist and enterprise tendencies on the grounds of the need for overall control of public expenditure and co-ordination; if the rules were changed what was good for one would be good for all the others, and chaos might be the result in macroeconomic policy. Recent illustrations of this have been the access to and redistribution of receipts from the sale of public housing (in the UK) from 1979 onwards; another was the refusal until recently of restrictions on leasing of rolling stock by British Railways Board, but this has now been overtaken by UK rail privatization. For a long time it has simply not been possible for universities and county councils to go directly to the capital markets to obtain funds for new library buildings. The UGC report on capital provision for university libraries (the Atkinson report) was a good example of the distorting effects of Treasury policy on the library economy.

Legislation does not, however, prescribe the way in which corporate enterprises should set about organizing their internal financial affairs, but it does provide the driving force for the ultimate discipline required and underlines the practical necessity of sound budgeting, supportive costing and proper financial accountability to shareholders and stakeholders. Proper financial management is thus all about proving the means to achieve this corporate responsibility.

We cannot forecast the likely development of the library organization economy with any precision but the evolution of matters is clear enough. Financial management within the public sector is already becoming tighter and more rigorous than ever before. The opening up to enterprise type activities has begun (Bawden, 1988); the pressure of events will drive along related reforms; a stronger and more formal legal base for financial matter is just a matter of time, and the differences between the public and private sector will be reduced (Farnham and Horton, 1993).

The evolution of new practices and models

The last two decades have been characterized by developments in the corporate and business world which are the response to changing global conditions and to the impact of information technology. These changes cover business structure and organization, the deregulation of the financial markets in many countries, innovations in fiscal and financial policy, and the application of the results of academic study, research and policy discussions. This section can be no more than a guide to those which are already having an impact on the library and information community. As a conclusion the most significant elements in this debate are restated.

Cost centre management

For a commercial business organization cost centre management is no novelty; proper financial accounting could hardly take place without it and any failure to apply it or any deficiency in it is probably the result of neglect or incompetence.

In the public sector, and in libraries in particular, sound and appropriate financial management according to the prevailing paradigm has often been achieved without detailed and specific cost centre management. The preference and requirement was often seen in global and aggregate terms; numbers were not so crucial; professional judgement about the rights or wrongs of actions could take the place of cost and accounting data. Of course it was essential that the numbers added up and that overall accountability could be achieved. And there have always been exceptions to the level of general practice, as a study of the literature can demonstrate, but the test is one of wide innovation in practice and this has not been the norm in library and information service operations.

But matters have been changing since the 1970s and library and information service professional management practice is slowly converging with the business norms (Bailey, 1989, is a useful review of theory and practice). Many librarians still regard accountants with suspicion and even disdain, and would like to keep them out of their libraries, but this is Cnut before the waves.

The construction of the discussion in this book has, we hope, been convincing enough to show that the financial/business approach is no more than common sense and can in all circumstances contribute something.

But even more the trend of the environment in library and information service management is providing the justification. Pessimists may say that librarians have not had much choice and have had to go along with the grain of policy. But realists can see that changes in method may achieve more by helping to facilitate a development that in the long run will strengthen the management of libraries, and make them better equipped for survival and more competitive in establishing their place in the information market.

The cost centre approach is partly a by-product of the will to impose better financial and budgetary planning and control on the organization. It thus has to be shown as this, rather than merely as an arid imposition with little connexion to the real business of library and information professionalism.

Business units

Business units show the value of a cost centre approach, since they represent the strongest relationship between choices of inputs allocated to goals and functions and the likely achievement of outcomes. Furthermore, business units are likely to be profit centres as well as being clearly defined unitary or collections of budgetary programmes. A business unit will show a high degree of autonomy, making the fullest use of financial management methods mandatory.

Customer–contractor principle

The growth of commercial discipline has served to introduce higher levels of formality into the relationship between supplier and customer. This will take the form of more explicitness in the obligations between the two parties and introduces a higher level of demand for certainty in financial matters. At the very least a substantial degree of cost knowledge is assumed upon which to base projections of delivery, pricing and qualitative and quantitative standards.

Competitive tendering

Tendering is the process of exploiting competition in a market for the right to supply. This is a method by which to test and evaluate the potential to use private sector contractors to provide a service or a system which may previously have been carried out inhouse in the public sector. There are no limits to the nature of the activity; it could be used as a means to supply books and journals to a library and information service, eliminating the need for inhouse capability.

In the initial stages it could be establishing the commercial costs of the service required. It may be a way for the library and information service to offload an activity which is consuming inhouse resources beyond a justifiable level of benefit. The more competitive the supplier environment the lower the price of such services. A key question for the library community is the extent to which a market of alternatives exists for supplying such services and the level of competitiveness. Such markets can develop; witness the growth of a library systems automation supply market, and the growing market for computer hardware and software supply and bibliographical data.

3.13 Summary and progression

A number of key areas of financial management has been highlighted following the overall definition of elements: these are a source of income/funding; a method of planning and budgeting; a facility to identify cost centres (closely allied to programme structures); and a range of microfinancial management procedures. These are necessary whether the library and information centre is a unit in a host organization or a free standing commercial activity.

Cooper (1980) provides a good bibliographical review of the literature to c. 1980; Blagden (1982) and Prentice (1983) offer readable overviews for the non-specialist. Robinson and Robinson (1994) discuss planning and budgeting relations, and Campbell (1994) considers organizational change and budgeting. Smith (1983; 1991) gives a detailed if orthodox treatment of costing and accounting, while Braunstein (1989) reviews the wider economics perspective.

In the last decade and impacting on the library and information industry are other refinements and developments in financial management. These are affecting traditionally publicly funded non-commercial organizations and centres within a host organization, and take the form of cost recovery, pricing of services, internal chargeback, and a generally tighter and more aggressive approach to financial mangement.

3.13.1 Further reading

Financial management

Abbott, C. and Smith, N. (1992) Management. In M. B. Line (1992) (ed.) *Librarianship and Information Work Worldwide 1992.* London: Bowker-Saur. pp.165–200

Aren, L. J., Webreck, S. J. and Mark, P. (1987) Costing library operations – a bibliography. *Collection Building,* **8**(3), 23–28

Aslib Proceedings (1980) **32**(1)–**32**(4) *Proceedings of the 53rd Aslib Annual conference on Economics of Information* (Four issues of the volume devoted to financial and economic aspects in papers delivered to the conference)

Blagden, J. (1982) Financial management. In *Aslib handbook of special librarianship and information work* 5th edn. London: Aslib 53–73

Bosanquet, N. (1983) *After the new right*. Aldershot: Dartmouth Publishing

Braswell, R., Fortin, K. and Osteryoung, J. S. (1984) *Financial management for not-for-profit organizations*. New York: Wiley

Braunstein, Y. M. (1989) Library funding and economics: a framework for research. *IFLA Journal*, **15**(4), 289–298

Broadbent, M. and Cullen, J. (1993) *Managing financial resources*. London: Butterworth-Heinemann

Brown, E. F. (1979) *Cutting library costs: increasing productivity and raising revenues*. Metuchen, NJ: Scarecrow Press

Bryson, J. (1990) *Effective library and information centre management*. Aldershot: Gower

Buckland, M. K. (1988) *Library services in theory and practice* 2nd edn. Oxford: Pergamon

Campbell, J. D. (1994) Getting comfortable with change: a new budget model for libraries in transition. *Library Trends*, **42**(3), 448–459

Comedia. (1993) *Borrowed time? The future of public libraries in the UK*. Gloucester: Comedia

Cooper, A. (1980) *Financial aspects of library and information services: a bibliography*. Loughborough: Centre for Library and Information Management (CLAIM Report No. 5)

Cronin, B. (1994) (ed.) *Marketing of library and information services 2*. London: Aslib

Dahlgren, A. C. (1989) Costing library system services: a national survey. *The Bottom Line*, **3**(2), 20–26

Farnham, D. and Horton, S. (1993) (eds.) *Managing the new public services*. London: Macmillan

Feeney, M. and Grieves, M. (1994) (eds.) *The value and impact of information*. London: Bowker-Saur

Financing our public library services: four subjects for debate. (1988) London: HMSO (Cm 324)

Genaway, D. C. (1989) Administrating the allocated acquisitions budget: achieving a balanced matrix. *Acquisitions Librarian*, **2**, 145–167

Hayes, R. M. (1989) *A long view of a broad scene: means to prepare for strategic management of the modern large library*. London: British Library (BL R&D Report No. 6049)

HM Treasury (1989) *Government accounting: a guide on the accounting and financial procedures for the use of government departments*. London: HMSO

Jones, L. and Nicholas, D. (1993) Costing medical libraries: the feasibility of functional cost analysis. *Health Libraries Review*, **10**(4), 196–201

Kesmer, R. M. (1994) The library as information center: a utility model for information resource management and support. *Library Trends*, **42**(3), 373–394

Koenig, M. E. D. and Feeney, A. (1992) The context of library and information work: three timely issues. In M. B. Line (ed.) *Librarianship and Information Work Worldwide 1992*. London: Bowker-Saur. pp.1–24

Line, M. B. (1976) The principles of cost recovery for inter-library loans. *IFLA Journal*, **2**(2), 81–86

Line, M. B. (1986) The survival of academic libraries in hard times: reaction to pressures, rational and irrational. *British Journal of Academic Librarianship*, **1**(1), 1–12

Line, M. B. (1994) Libraries and their management. In B. C. Vickery (1984) (ed.) *Fifty Years of Information Progress: A Journal of Documentation Review*. London: Aslib. pp.189–223

Lowry, C. B. (1992) Reconciling pragmatism, equity and need in the formula allocation of book and serial funds. *College and Research Libraries*, **53**(2) 121–138

McKay, D. (1995) *Effective financial management in library and information services*. London: Aslib

McClean, N. (1987) A bigger slice: cost justification for library and information services. *Aslib Proceedings*, **39**(10), 293–297

Manley, K. (1994) *Financial management for charities and not for profit organizations*. Hemel Hempstead: ICSA Publishing

Martin, M. S. (1994) (ed.) Library finance: new needs, new models. *Library Trends*, **42**(3), 369–584 (Special issue on library finance)

Midwinter, A. and McVicar, M. (1992) *Public library finance: developments in Scotland.* London: British Library (LIR Report No. 85)

Orna, E. (1996) Valuing information: problems and opportunities. In Best, D. P. (ed.) The fourth resource: information audit management. Aldershot: Gower. pp.18–40

Prentice, A. (1983) *Financial planning for libraries.* Metuchen, NJ: Scarecrow Press

Revill, D. (1991) (ed.) *Working papers on management issues: finance.* Brighton: Council of Polytechnic Librarians

Richardson, P. R. (1988) Cost containment: the ultimate advantage. New York: Free Press

Roberts, S. A. (1984) (ed.) *Costing and the economics of library and information services.* London: Aslib (Aslib Reader series Volume 5)

Roberts, S. A. (1985) *Cost management for library and information services.* London: Butterworth

Robinson, B. M. and Robinson, S. (1994) Strategic planning and program budgeting for libraries. *Library Trends*, **42**(3), 420–447

Smith, G. S. (1991) *Managerial accounting for libraries and other not-for-profit organizations.* Chicago: American Library Association

Spyers-Duran, P. and Mann, T. (1985) (eds.) *Financing information services: problems, changing approaches, and new opportunities for academic and research libraries.* Westport, Conn.: Greenwood

Whitehall, T. (1980) User valuations and resource management for information services. *Aslib Proceedings*, **32**(2), 87–105

Winkworth, I. (1991) Management. In M. B. Line (1991) (ed.) *Librarianship and Information Work Worldwide 1991.* London: Bowker-Saur. pp.187–212

Budgetary planning

Baker, D. (1992) Resource allocation in university libraries. *Journal of Documentation*, **48**(1), 1–19

Chamberlain, C. E. (1986) Fiscal planning in academic libraries: the role of the automated acquisitions system. *Advances in Library Administration and Organization*, **6**, 141–152

Chen, C. C. (1980) *Zero-based budgeting in library management: a manual for librarians.* Phoenix: Oryx Press

Clements, D. W. G. (1975) The costing of library systems. *Aslib Proceedings*, **27**(3), 98–111

Ford, G. (1991) Finance and budgeting. In C. Jenkins and M. Morley (1991) (eds.) *Collection management in academic libraries.* Aldershot: Gower. pp.21–56

Hamburg, M. *et al.* (1974) *Library planning and decision making systems,* Cambridge, Mass: MIT Press

Humphreys, K. (1974) Costing in university libraries. *Liber Bulletin*, (5/6), 8–32

Kelly, L. (1985) Budgeting in non-profit organizations. *Drexel Library Quarterly*, **21**(3), 3–18

Koenig, M. E. D. (1977) Budgets and budgeting: part 1. *Special Libraries*, **68**(7/8), 228–233

Koenig, M. E. D. (1981) *Budgeting techniques for library and information centers*. New York: Special Libraries Association

Koenig, M. E. D. (1984) Budgeting and financial planning for scientific and technical libraries. *Science Technology Libraries*, **4**(1), 87–104

Koenig, M. E. D. and Alperin, V. (1985) ZBB and PPBS: what's left now that the trendiness has gone? *Drexel Library Quarterly*, **21**(3), 19–38

Koenig, M. E. D. and Stam, D. C. (1986) Budgeting and financial planning for libraries. In *Advances in Library Administration and Organization*, **4**, 77–110

Library Association (1974) *Professional and non-professional duties in libraries* 2nd edn. London: Library Association

Library Management (1991) Special issue on Budgeting. **12**(4) (entire issue)

Midwinter, A. and McVicar, M. (1991) The public librarian as budget manager. *Journal of Librarianship and Information Science*, **23**(1), 9–20

Planning, programming, budgeting systems in libraries: a symposium (1975). Library Association East Midlands Branch

Prentice, A. E. (1985a) Budgeting and accounting: a selected bibliography. *Drexel Library Quarterly*, **21**(3), 106–112

Prentice, A. E. (1985b) (ed.) Budgeting and accounting. *Drexel Library Quarterly*, **21**(3) (special issue)

Ramsey, I. L. and Ramsey, J. E. (1986) *Library planning and budgeting*. New York: Watts

Reilly, C. R. (1986) Productivity measurement for fiscal control. *The Bottom Line*, 'Charter issue' [**1**(1)], 21–28

Risk, J. M. S. (1956) *The classification and coding of accounts*. London: Institute of Cost and Works Accountants (Occasional Paper No. 2)

Roberts, S. A. (1985) *Cost management for library and information services*. London: Butterworth

Robinson, B. M. and Robinson, S. (1994) Strategic planning and program budgeting for libraries. *Library Trends*, **42**(3), 420–447

Shreeves, E. (1991) *Guide to budget allocation for information resources.* Chicago: ALA (Collection Management and Development Guides No. 4)

Sullivan, D. S. (1991) Budgeting for users: rethinking the materials budget. *Acquisitions Librarian*, **6**, 15–27

Trumpeter, M. C. and Rounds, R. S. (1985) *Basic budgeting practices for librarians*. Chicago: ALA

Weinstock, M. (1979) Managing special libraries under financial stress: the role of budgeting, cost analysis and evaluation. *Australian Special Libraries News*, **12**(3), 101–103

Budgetary management and monitoring

Alley, B. and Cargill, J. (1986) *Keeping track of what you spend: the librarian's guide to simple bookkeeping*. Phoenix, Ariz.: Oryx Press

Clark, P. M. (1985) Accounting as evaluation, as reporting: the uses of online accounting systems. *Drexel Library Quarterly*, **21**(3), 61–74

Khoo, G. *et al.* (1991) Serials fiscal control using a flat file database management system on a microcomputer. *Serials Librarian*, **20**(1), 91–105

Martin, M. S. (1978) *Budgetary control in academic libraries*. Greenwich, Conn.: JAI Press (Foundations in Library and Information Science Vol. 5)

Midwinter, A. and McVicar, M. (1991) The public librarian as budget manager. *Journal of Librarianship and Information Science*, **23**(1), 9–20

Prentice, A. E. (1985) Financial reporting. *Drexel Library Quarterly*, **21**(3), 99–105

Roberts, S. A. (1985) *Cost management for library and information services*. London: Butterworth

Chapter 4

Information needs and requirements

4.1 Defining management information by the resource management process

Library and information service managers need cost data for the ultimate purpose of determining system and service performance. The general purpose of library and information service cost data is then to contribute to performance measurement. A great part of the need for cost data can be subsumed under this primary need. Since the previous edition of this work appeared (Roberts, 1985) this cost/performance relationship has been extensively reviewed and synthesized in a project undertaken by King Research Limited. Their results have been published in the form of a practical manual entitled *Keys to success: performance indicators for public libraries* (Office of Arts and Libraries, 1990). A number of points from this study are referred to and/or tabulated in this chapter.

Keys to success has received considerable and well deserved acclaim by the UK library community, and by implication by the US professional community from which much of its thinking derives. In trying to define performance measures the study also defines a wide sweep of management information measures; Brophy (1986) offers a synthesis of the field of management information, which can be read profitably in the context of the later work by King Research. By incorporating the cost element into performance measures where necessary and feasible, *Keys to success* also highlights core areas of the present work in so far as they are based on cost concepts and measures. *Keys to success* takes forward this author's original thesis about the vital significance of cost management.

In addition cost data have other specific uses such as helping to inform resource allocation decisions, to distribute fund allocations across a budget (by identifying resources needed and the time/cost implications of work plans) and to provide feedback to the manager about the relative differences between operations at various levels within the system (for example through indicating absolute levels of costs, and changes in costs and unit costs over time). For the purpose of identifying the need for management information on costs and performance a general model is described here to show the basic structure of the relationships encountered in a system which recognized the need for structured scientific approaches to management, and which was prepared to develop the necessary support systems of management information and performance measurement

Figure 4.1 is a generalized attempt to outline the central characteristics of the resource management process. It tries to identify and synthesize the main elements of library management, library performance and management information. The discussions which have taken place in the professional literature of management suggest a consensus view of this type. These are all elements which have to be viewed as part of a whole. Management systems themselves, such as those for costing with which this book is concerned have to be rooted in this overall structure. There is very little point in developing library costing unless the cost data can be fed through to the support of other management processes.

4.1.1 Specifying goals

The specification of goals, aims and objectives is fundamental and pervasive in any resource management strategy. Resource allocation plans depend closely on the specification of goals.

Goals are also needed in order to specify effectiveness criteria and their associated performance measures. In many situations these goals, aims and objectives are implicit and unstated; this position will invariably need to be reversed if resource allocation is to be co-ordinated and effective.

4.1.2 Standards

Standards for operations and procedures may be used to determine the realistic range across which the manager can, may or should

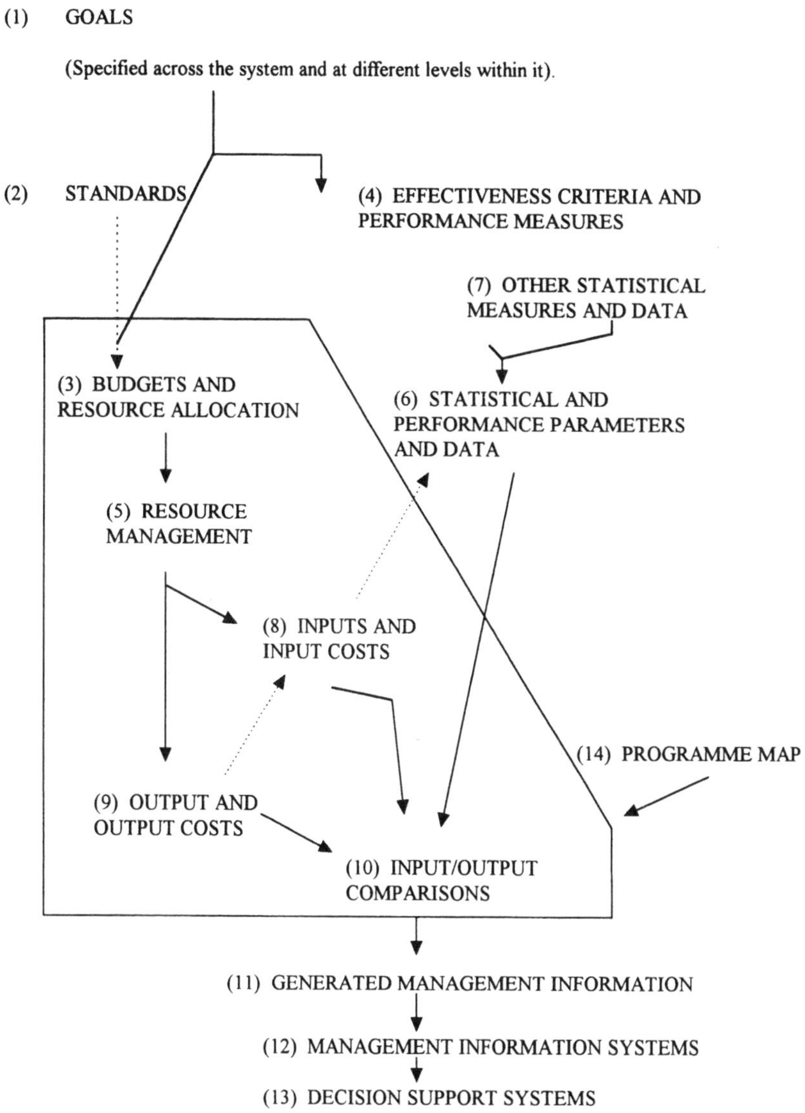

Figure 4.1. Resource management processes and management information

set goals. There is a crossover relationship (for simplicity this is not shown in Figure 4.1) between effectiveness criteria, standards and performance measures.

4.1.3 Budgets and resource allocation

Resource allocation is the primary economic task of the library manager, although it is not by any means the outstanding or dominant managerial task. The budget plan and other resource allocation tools and mechanisms will relate to the overall goals and subgoals, and will be fashioned and toned by reference to data on standards and norms. Goals and effectiveness criteria must have a mutual reference to one another, and hence with the budget. The programme structure for the service stands conceptually between the longer term goals and aims and the shorter term (usually) annual budget.

4.1.4 Effectiveness criteria and performance measures

Effectiveness criteria are a type of operational definition for the management and implementation of goals. A programme to achieve certain goals is set in motion and the manager judges the allocation of resources and results obtained in terms of effectiveness criteria (the King Research study would call these effectiveness indicators, and considers them one of four possible performance indicators, the others being operational performance indicators, cost-effectiveness indicators and impact indicators (p.25).

The effectiveness criteria themselves are realized in terms of performance measures. Many effectiveness criteria and performance measures will contain a strong cost and economic element. *Keys to success* properly defines effectiveness ultimately in terms of the user or client perspective. The definition in the present model is not inconsistent with this external view; it does, however, note that much managerial behaviour has to assume values in the first place for effectiveness criteria, which can then be confirmed by performance measurement studies.

4.1.5 Resource management

If the budget is a means of stating and translating goals into financial terms and is the basic plan for economic achievement, resource management is the process of achievement itself. Resource management has already been defined and discussed in Chapter Two and a considerable variety of issues noted. At the moment a sufficient definition could be the managerial combination of productive factors and elements to achieve goals. Many factors – physical, human, behavioural, social – affect resource management. For the purposes of management and cost information, data on input and output for each of the budgetary programmes are clearly a central consideration. There is a number of crossovers between resource management (input, throughput and output) and the other stages, but only one is shown in the figure. Output and input are given a connection to statistical and performance parameters and data.

4.1.6 Statistical and performance parameters and data

Performance measures are in a general sense parametric: that is they are a range with given limiting values which have instrinsic importance. Effectiveness criteria define parameters of performance which are needed for managerial control. The performance measures associated with the effectiveness criteria have a data content, and thus may be, but are not exclusively, statistical. Cost measures are important economic quantifiers which can be used in a number of areas of the model. For example, materials costs become transformed in acquisition budget statements. In a cost control system these costs have management accounting significance.

4.1.7 Other statistical measures and data

This sector or category of the model is a reminder that there are many varieties of statistical data and intelligence which are not directly related to the Goal – Effectiveness criteria – Performance structure already elucidated, with its related stream of allocation and resource management decisions. Many of these measures and data come under the general heading of internal or external descriptive statistics about the library and its environment.

4.1.8 Inputs and input costs

The definition of library programmes (see later in this chapter) within the goal structure and budget is the basis of the management of inputs in the system. For the current discussion in this book, the related matter of input costs is central. Input costs may be stated in time units or monetary units.

4.1.9 Outputs and output costs

Input and throughput on a programme-by-programme basis leads to outputs which are goal related and statements of output costs. Both input and output statements have to be consistent with the Goal – Effectiveness criteria – Performance measures structure already mentioned. In terms of cost and financial data alone, this consistency is achieved through management accounting systems which relate financial sacrifices to resources consumed and work done. The structure of these systems is such that goals and programmes and budgets and resource management can be related to effectiveness and performance. Thus a management accounting system will contain control information (for instance about acceptable ranges of unit costs for technical processing), and a means of reporting the current status of the system with respect to the relevant programme (technical processing).

4.1.10 Input/output comparisons

The input/output comparison is the main checking tool for the resource manager and allocator, in determining whether desired outcomes on Goal – Effectiveness criteria – Performance measurement have been achieved. Discordance between input and output will suggest an examination of throughput activities, and perhaps later reference to original goals, which may be overambitious or unrealistic. In practice this is not done in a simplistic way, since judgments and qualitative factors inevitably intervene.

But our capacity to measure the interactions which have taken place will probably appear simplistic in comparison. This is the dilemma of performance measurement; quantifying for the most part many factors which are unquantifiable. So far as cost factors are concerned there is some chance to obtain relatively good data, provided an effective management accounting procedure is set up and this will include a costing system. In the current state of performance measurement technique it may well be that relatively good economic data can be gathered, provided a coherent set of procedures is applied in management practice. The specification for cost measurement given in the King Associates study is one practical acknowledgement of the desirability of this (Office of Arts and Libraries, 1990, pp.88–92 for measuring costs, and pp.138–144 for a discussion of cost concepts).

4.1.11 Generated management information

Each of the areas considered so far will generate much information of potential use to management. This is the present situation in many libraries today, although the practices could not be said to be clear or dignified with the title of management information system. There are certainly many available library statistics, some performance measures, and some cost data.

4.1.12 Management information system (MIS)

The idea of a management information system for library management implies and suggests the formalization of all sources and types of information and intelligence from the point of view of collection, storage, analysis and dissemination. A management accounting system is one part of a total management information system. Reference can be made to Brophy (1986) for further discussion on these aspects.

4.1.13 Decision support systems (DSS)

Decision support systems can be thought of as higher level developments of management information systems. It is increasingly realized that a management information system in itself is not a sufficient tool for full decision making by managers (Bommer and Chorba, 1981). A DSS would contain a number of operational models which could provide specific answers to managers (for example, using computer simulation or gaming techniques). More recently, research into DSS in the context of performance measurement and management information systems has been carried out by Adams, Collier and Meldrum (1991), Bloor (1991) and synthesized in Adams *et al.* (1993).

4.1.14 Programme map

An area of the model of resource allocation has been defined as the programme map. This covers all the functional and operational areas with which the library and information service is concerned. In terms of cost and management accounting this embraces the functional and task descriptions which form the basis of cost centres and cost unit classification.

As a first stage in developing management information and management accounting systems the library and information manager should write a description of the service and its systems in these terms. This process will make use of systems analysis, but the final result should be one of system synthesis. Such a description would form the specification for designing a management information and management accounting system. It is important to be clear about what happens in the system, and to make sure that gaps in specification and structure can be identified (for example, what is the current level and practice of cost collection).

4.2 Defining categories of management information

Some of the very obvious information dependencies of library managers have been outlined in Chapter One, both generally and with regard to cost information. Lynch and Eckard (1981) went on to specify the types of information that should be collected about libraries.

1 Information on the institutional identity of the library.
2 Information on the target group to be served.
3 Information on collection resources.
4 Information on financial resources.
5 Information about library personnel.
6 Information about facilities and equipment.
7 Information on the various programmes and functions of the service.

Information on library programmes (7) can logically be broken down by any one or more of the categories (1) to (6). Furthermore, cost information could be considered a part of each of these seven categories.

Lynch and Eckard's typology is a useful one to consider generally since it has been put forward to contribute to a discussion on standards. This may be an optimistic hope, since the field of library management information is one that has resisted standardization. As yet this may not have been too harmful, since standardization is often necessary when technological innovations become important.

Many librarians would argue that they already have what might be called 'proto-management information systems'; in practice these are locally developed 'paper' systems (collections of documents, statistical summaries, working printouts etc.), sometimes effective, but lacking much coherence (for example, for inter-library comparison). But the time for standardization may not be far off. From the earliest days of library computer applications the possibilities for generating data which could be used for management information have been seen, experimented with, but never fully realized. But soon the available technology will be exploited properly for management information. The increasing computerization of library activities makes this inevitable.

This suggests that the time has come to be very much more explicit about the general lines and detailed content and operation of library management information systems; to see whether there are one or several general types and to start on prototype development. The need for agreement if not for standardization has again come into the foreground. Brophy (1986) provides a good review of the position and Harris (1987) provides typical illustrations.

The purpose of this section is not to spell out in detail, measure by measure, index by index, file by file what the content of one prescriptive management information system could or should be. Even though this is very tempting, the exercise would be presumptuous and meaningless without the participation of libraries and without extensive experiment.

But it is important to take on the alerting and stimulating function here, and quite proper to do so in the context of a book on library costing and management accounting. This is because the development of costing and accounting systems replicate many of the stages required in developing a management information system. It is an earnest hope that library managers will be stimulated to consider their needs in costing and accounting, so that they may also turn to questions of management information, and be led to a profitable integration of the functions of gathering, analysing and evaluating information. Nevertheless, the practitioner may start to consider this process by reference to the King Research study (Office of Arts and Libraries, 1990).

Some other examples of measures, indices and files are worth presenting for their stimulus value. In Appendix 1 tables are reproduced from Hamburg (1974) and Clements (1975), who have both made serious proposals for management information structures, all yet to be tested operationally.

The field of library statistics cannot be ignored either; this book is not the place to debate it, but there is already an extensive literature: the American Library Association (1966); Moore (1977a;

1977b); Brockman (1982). Brockman and Klobas (1979) carried out pioneering work. Library statistics themselves range over all the Lynch and Eckard categories. But disagreements about the nature and purpose of library statistics have to some extent distracted attention from the debate about welding all these parts together into some useful systematized structure, which is really capable of informing library manager decision making. Figure 4.2 tries to sketch out the main relationships and components which need to be considered in the development of these informing systems. By the early 1990s library statistics collection seems to have moved into a higher phase in the UK and USA; sector wide statistics were being collected more systematically, with a firmer analysis being carried out directed to more explicit policy goals.

There will be many views of what a library management information system might or should look like. As a result of some preliminary studies at CLAIM in the 1980s on management information and decision making, a function/process/information typology was developed to explore questions of the relationship between decision making and information handling by library managers. This typology is reproduced in Table 4.1. A rationale for development has since been elaborated by Brophy (1986). Major library systems in higher education in the UK, USA and Australia have put much effort into refining practical management information bases, stimulated by the changes in organization and funding in higher education and the ever present drive for efficiency and value for money.

A consideration of this structure shows that the Lynch and Eckard scheme can be mapped onto this typology, which itself goes further (but logically) into performance measurement; a view consistent with the theme of the inter-relationship between costing and performance which is discussed at some length in this book.

However, there should be at least some agreement, even now, on the basic tasks of library management information design, and if this can be reduced to some precepts they might be that:

1 It has to provide the means of describing, assessing and weighting alternative courses of action in the short, medium and long term.

2 It has to distinguish between recurrent and capital expenditure and projects, and between past, present and future states.

3 On the basis of identified objectives, it has to accommodate priorities and allocate time between programmes (taking time

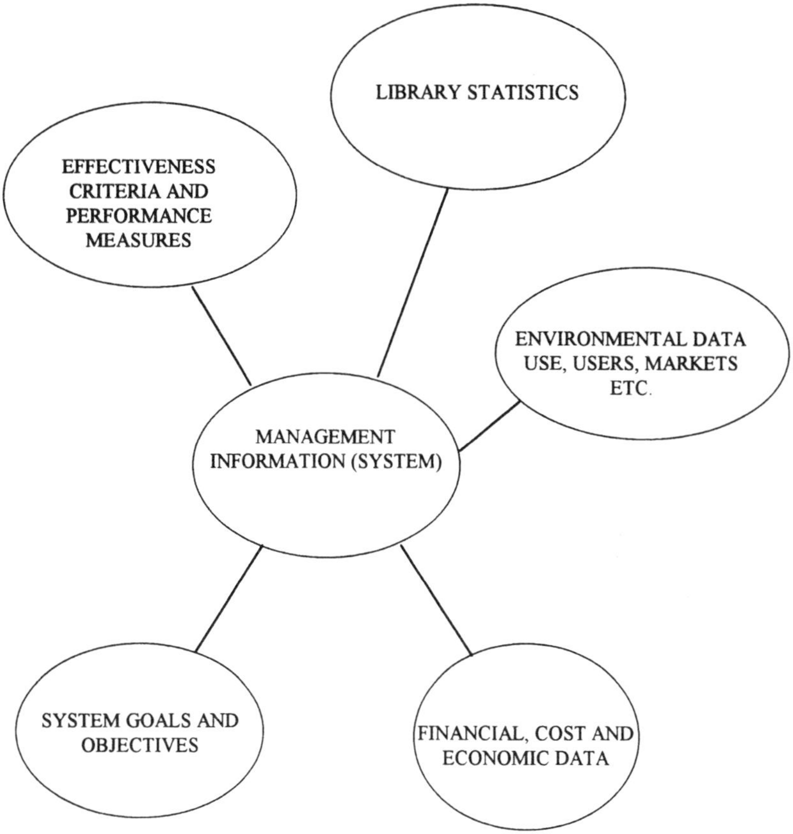

Figure 4.2. The components of management information

to mean more generally the proportions of effort and activity distributed across functions).

4 It has to indicate the ways of allocating resources at input, monitor performance during throughput, and assess performance at output.

These tasks also cover some of the foundations of managerial economics for libraries, and operationally many of the functions of the more advanced techniques such as decision support systems (see 4.1.13).

The principles and practices described in this book are directed toward the long-term development of management techniques for

TABLE 4.1 A schema for management information

Function	*Process*	*Information*	
Primary functions and processes	*Managerial activity*	*Typical current statistical data*	*Prescriptive management information requirements*
Resources for library provision	Investment decisions. Knowledge of system	e.g. Budget and expenditure; types of stock; staff; equipment	May resemble statistical data closely, but often more detail and specificity required
Distribution of resources provision	Allocation decisions	e.g. By function, by form, by type, etc.	Information required on programme by programme basis
Provision (supply) of services	Management of functions and services. Control decisions	e.g. Crude output measures by function, form, type etc.	Refined input and output measures required. Staff, output and process data
Consumption (demand/use) of services	Demand management. Control decisions	e.g. Data on users and use, but often crude and general	Greater refinement. More regular monitoring required
Assessment of effectiveness	Measuring efficiency and productivity	e.g. Input/output and performance measures. Usually very few	Greater integration with supply, demand and control information
Benefit/value measurement	Justification. Political roles	Not always considered or collected	Regular monitoring required. Mixture of 'hard' and 'soft' information
Impact measurement	Comparison, evaluation feedback, planning and development	Perception of change over time. Some simple measures but usually of output rather than impact	Accumulation of time series. Long term reporting systems required. Integration of all management information

management accounting and managerial economics, aimed at assisting the optimal allocation of resources to library and information services.

At some stage in management development within the organization the manager will need to review existing procedures and practices in this area. In the light of this review decisions may be taken to introduce new methods of collection of management information for resource planning and performance measurement.

The conceptual framework for resource allocation offered here is a systems orientated one. The areas of conceptual development and practical application are derived from a systems typology of input, throughput, output and performance. An information system is developed in parallel with this typology to form part of a resources management system. This system can be based on the traditional sources of management documentation, for instance, the estimates, budgets and internal manuals of practice, plus any long-term documentation and practices employed in the organization. In addition many novel procedures to collect additional kinds of cost and performance data are likely to be needed.

The extent to which this complex is developed and the speed of development in any given library will vary widely; there is no stock formula for development applicable to any one library management. The manager has to judge the pace of change, and a gradual acclimatization to the ideas and concepts, combined with practical experience gained, will determine the extent of the innovation. Setting up the system requires the willingness to change and a good deal of flexibility and effort on the part of staff at most levels. The motivation to adopt these styles of management – basically a scientific style – will be a key drive in the operation.

4.3 Performance measures

Despite the prominence in this discussion on the centrality of cost studies and cost measures for library management, there is no intention to diminish the emphasis which the library manager wishes to give in the longer run to performance measures. Put into perspective, it is suggested that many performance measures are incomplete if a cost and/or economic dimension cannot be included. Therefore in many ways cost measurement is a necessary condition for the development of performance measures, either primarily, because the performance measures contain a cost element derived from resource use, or because the performance measure then raises further questions which can only be answered from a cost and/or economic point of view.

Because the development of general economic theories and general performance theories about libraries is still an intractable topic, there has been a tendency to consider cost and performance measures more as separate concerns rather than as closely inter-related factors. This intractability has to be overcome, so that the ideal relationship between all the indices of library and information service performance can be developed into practical techniques and measures which can be properly applied in management, and which make a tangible contribution to improving the performance of libraries.

One way to ameliorate these difficulties is to ensure that a proper structure for library and information service cost measurement, and management accounting is developed. The ability to generate cost data and cost measures on a routine basis will make it so much easier in practice to motivate the development and application of cost measures. Access to a management accounting system, and the data it can provide all have one crucial benefit at least: it will remove the tedium and intrusion which have traditionally been associated with the implementation of library and information cost studies. More than anything else this will help the library manager to be managerially efficient in handling all types of management information and managerial intelligence.

Performance measures embrace a number of types of data with which library managers are already familiar. Some are no more than descriptive data about inputs to the library; others are of a more refined and complex nature, although there is no inherent reason why a performance measure should be complex and obscure.

The library and information service manager should therefore consider:

- library statistics, collected for internal use or for outside bodies
- data relating to the inputs of resources
- throughput data; measures of activity and process of conversion of input to output
- performance measures; output, impact, effectiveness and benefit measures
- management information (consisting of data generated from the first four points)
- decision support and intelligence.

Cost and economic data are a thread which runs through all six areas of systems and management data handling. Purpose-designed systems and procedures ensure that consistency and transferability of economic indices can be achieved, and is one of the purposes and functions of a library management accounting system.

The study of library and information service performance has developed actively particularly since the 1970s. A tradition of study has grown up, notably in the USA and the UK, but also in Germany and Scandinavia. Much pioneering work was done in the late 1970s. Monographs by Lancaster (1977; 1993), Blagden (1980) and Morgan (1995) provide different approaches to overview the field. There are also treatises taking a mixed theoretical and empirical approach exemplified by Buckland (1975; 1988); Hamburg (1974); Morse (1968) and Raffel and Shishko (1969). Surveys of the literature and various topical themes have been produced by Allred (1979), Du Mont (1979) and in bibliographic form by the Public Libraries Research Group and CLAIM (Ward, 1982). Reviewing serials such as the *Annual Review of Information Science and Technology*, *Advances in Librarianship* and *Libraries and Information World Wide* also carry overviews of the literature on performance and evaluation studies.

The bibliography compiled by Ward (1982) could be used as a benchmark, because the study of performance and evaluation entered a second generation in the 1980s under the influence of financial constraints, changing information economic environments and the growing and widening impact of the information and communication technologies. The recent study by King Research Limited (Office of Arts and Libraries, 1990) could be viewed as a contemporary synthesis of the debate, with a strong feeling for the urgency of greater dissemination of ideas and the absorption into practice of the relevant principles (see Tables 4.2 and 4.3).

The approaches have been many and varied with little consensus on what types of performance indicators need to be kept. One hope is that the King Research proposal may become a popular statement of methods for measuring input, output, effectiveness and domain values, as well as for calculating measures and derived indicators. Tables 4.2 and 4.3 provide a summary of the King Research perspective.

Many of the studies carried out and reviewed include an economic element in them, albeit not always strong. But for all the interest in the questions of library and information service performance the impression left is one lacking coherence and consensus.

TABLE 4.2 Performance measures used to calculate indicators (after Office of Arts and Libraries 1990/King Research Ltd., 1990 pp.11–12)

Service input cost measures

(1) Amount of resources applied to services
(2) Amount of money/funds applied to services
(3) Relevant attributes of resources applied to services

Service output measures

(4) Quantity of output
(5) Quality of output
(6) Timeliness of output
(7) Availability of service
(8) Accessibility of service

Service effectiveness measures

(9) Amount of use
(10) User perception of attributes
(11) User expressed satisfaction
(12) User indicated importance
(13) Purpose of use
(14) Consequences of use

Service domain measures

(15) Total population size
(16) Total population attributes
(17) User population size
(18) User population attributes
(19) Size of geographic area
(20) Geographic area attributes
(21) Information needs

For example there hardly appears to be agreement about the basic terminology, so that we are left without generally evaluated and accepted definitions of such concepts as performance measure, effectiveness criterion, value, satisfaction, benefit and impact. Some examples of varying approaches even at the simplest level of statements about performance measures can be given in the three listings reproduced from Lancaster, Hamburg and Daniel respectively (see Tables 4.4 and 4.5), which are exemplified in a multitude of other examples from the literature.

It is very clear that more empirical studies by practising managers are needed before these ideas can be consolidated into a useful corpus, which can then be used to evaluate the economic perfor-

TABLE 4.3 Performance indicators (after Office of Arts and Libraries, 1990/King Research Ltd., 1990 p.26)

Operational performance indicators
(1) Productivity
(2) Cost per output
(3) Cost by attribute levels
(4) Productivity by attribute levels
Effectiveness indicators
(5) Turnover rate
(6) Amount of use by attribute levels
(7) User satisfaction
(8) User satisfaction by attribute levels
(9) Amount of use by satisfaction levels
Cost-effectiveness indicators
(10) Cost per use
(11) Cost per user
(12) Cost per capita
(13) Cost by satisfaction levels
Impact indicators
(14) Users as a proportion of population
(15) Use per capita
(16) Needs fill rate

mance of libraries, and to associate performance measures of the various kinds with resource allocation and cost data. All that can be said at present is that the development of management accounting and management information practices is likely to prove beneficial to progress in this area, not least by extending the range of measurement and data collection.

4.4 Evaluation

Evaluation can be used as a term to describe the many different kinds of process connected with performance measurement and effectiveness analysis. There has been a tendency for writers on these themes to make this distinction, and this consistency will be helpful in making a similar rationalization in the terminology of library costing and management accountancy in this book. Evaluation is an aspect of the managerial mind and style as a well as a process of deriving

TABLE 4.4 Examples of possible performance criteria applied to various services of a library (from Lancaster, 1977)

	Technical services	*Public services*
Quality	(1) Selection and acquisition. Size, appropriateness, and balance of collection (2) Cataloguing and indexing. Accuracy, consistency and completeness	(1) Range of services offered (2) Helpfulness of shelf order and guidance (3) Catalogue. Completeness, accuracy, and ease of use (4) Reference and retrieval. Completeness, accuracy and percentage success (5) Document delivery. Percentage success
Time	(1) Delays in acquisition (2) Delays in cataloguing and other processing (3) Productivity of staff	(1) Hours of service (2) Response time (3) Loan periods
Cost	(1) Unit cost to purchase (2) Unit cost to process Accession Classify Catalogue	(1) Effort to use. Location of library. Physical accessibility of collection. Assistance from staff. (2) Charges levied

measures related to activities, which are informative to management. A system which possesses a facility for cost measurement and economic accounting may find it easier to cultivate analytical and systematic approaches to the assessment of performance, output measurement, or whatever aspect of evaluation is chosen.

Evaluation refers to the process by which the value of something is determined or established. In the field of library and information studies the concept can be usefully understood as a generic and comprehensive idea which encompasses the many and various ways in which the worth of library and information services can be estimated or measured. What is essential is to realize the intimate bond between performance measurement specifically and evaluation studies in general.

The evaluation could be personal and individual or collective and corporate; the evaluation could be expressed verbally as a qualitative judgment, it could be expressed in terms of relative quantitative values, or in some combination. The process of evaluation could be informal or formal. If it is going to be more formal and have

TABLE 4.5 General structure of performance and cost measures

Performance measures (from Hamburg, 1974)

X	Per unit of work	
X	By task, task area or programme	Activities/operations
X	Staff category (producer)	
X	Programme, function	
X	Staff category	outputs/products
X	Unit of output, product	
X	Document set	
X	Population set	Use (consumption)
X	Time period	

Performance measures (from Daniel, 1976)

(1) Inventories (e.g. of competencies; ALA behavioural requirements analysis checklist)
(2) Checklists of criterion statements (e.g. Fulton for school library media programmes)
(3) Measures with library/user orientation (conditions for 1 or 2)
(4) Operational research techniques
(5) MRAP (a type of inventory/checklist method)
(6) Cost-effectiveness and cost-benefit
(7) Combined measures/unitary measures 'e.g. Hamburg (1974) – document exposure'
(8) Proxy measures (e.g. unobtrusive measures of change after program implementation; pre- and post-use studies)
(9) Circulation measures
(10) Technical processing measures
(11) Measures of reference
(12) Collection evaluation measures
(12a) Document delivery, failure tests, coverage tests
(13) Comprehensive studies e.g. DeProspo *et al.* (1973)
Availability of materials
Use of facilities
Nature of staff and user interaction

particular consequences for future decision and action it might also have to be demonstrative and to show evidence which is more objective than subjective in order to be convincing. If the formality of the evaluative process is to be increased then the evaluative activity might best be carried out with some degree of independence, for example by a third party who lacks bias or interest in the subject of the evaluation. The external judgmental element in evaluation is usually the most highly valued, at least because it introduces independence and freedom from internal bias (although that is not to say that external views are unbiased).

However the problem of evaluation method is solved, the process of evaluation and the results obtained within the evaluation will draw the evaluator to look at the performance of the system being evaluated. This is particularly the case when the evaluation is motivated by system management needs, rather than exclusively by end user requirements. The selection of appropriate performance measures and the measurement of actual performance achieved is therefore a central issue. Indeed, this is the basis for the present discussion. This perspective establishes the tie between performance measurement (aiming to be objective and quantitative) and final evaluation (involving a subjective judgement of value, benefit or similar qualitative expression).

The system undergoing evaluation (in a library and information service context) gains a significant part of its integrity and capability from the resources deployed to it. These resources are limited and in an economic environment were allocated more or less rationally to the system by decisions which weighed different options and choices. In the financial environment these resources were paid for and they carry costs. The budgetary systems which form the financial tools for the manager help to make these choices and costs evident, and provide the manager with a level of control over the system.

It is clear that the budget manager is deeply interested in the performance of the resources allocated to a given system. In this way the measures of performance chosen and the actual measurement of performance are integral to the budgetary process. This is the argument we continue to explore in this chapter.

Performance measurement and evaluation are clearly two distinct concepts. Performance measurement does not necessarily provide the evaluative measure or evaluation sought. Although a performance measure may be used as a substitute evaluative tool, this tends to give a provider orientated evaluation; such usage is often carried out because it is managerially or administratively convenient, or when an end user evaluation is not possible, feasible or convenient. This substitution of concepts and measures is inevitable in practice, although it is as well to keep the theoretical or pure distinction in mind when thinking through a problem which might require the use of one or other or both of the concepts and techniques. Where performance measures can be easily derived there is a tendency to extend their usage even if this is theoretically problematical.

Evaluative procedure (particularly end user-based) can be conducted without reference to performance standards and measures; for example, when an individual user evaluation is sought. The user can and will, perhaps even should express a truthful opinion about the quality and worth of library and information service received.

But the real challenge comes when the consequences of the relationship between performance (provider centred) and evaluation (user focused) are addressed.

In terms of the total management of a system (increasingly the total quality management of a service) the manager is bound to have to elicit and address the implications of these two primary concepts. When this is done in a coherent way with a very concrete operational purpose in mind the value could be very significant.

The absence of expressed user satisfaction from an end user-based service evaluation could be clearly correlated with the performance rates and factors observed in the system. When the manager then goes on to relate these observations in a planning, budgetary and resource framework, and clearly elicits the cost and financial significance the conclusion could be clear. This could range from increasing output levels, and therefore reducing unit costs; by noting the paucity of demand and drawing the conclusion that if service is required the user will have to be charged; or it could be that the service is no longer viable on account of poor levels of performance, and should cease to be offered. Whatever action might emerge, it is clear that the boundaries between different values of the condition are critical to managerial decision making. In a fully fledged commercial environment the weight of these indicators should be clear.

The formalization of enquiries into the performance and evaluation of library and information services has become a focus for investigation and research in the field and provides a primary point of contact between theory and research on the one hand and practice and management on the other. Data and measurement methods hold a common interest for the manager and the researcher alike, and this illuminates the crucial area of contact between resources, activities, financial aspects and the ways in which different outcomes might be achieved in practice which depend upon appropriate applications of management and professional skills. Put very simply, for emphasis, the end product often depends not only on the quantity of resources used, but as much on the managerial knowledge applied by the practitioner. Our contention is that skill in financial management really does count in the achievement of successful library and information performance.

4.5 Cost measurement, output measurement and evaluation

In many library and information services the amount of cost data collection is inadequate to maintain managerial influence in economic decisions at the highest level. There are a few libraries where a much greater level of cost information is available either regularly or on an ad hoc basis. But even in these it would be rare to find a system where budgeting, accounting and performance measurement systems are related and integrated. Still less is one likely to find a total managerial structure which relates library goals in a programmatic sense, through the various apparatus of economic management, to the type of management information systems and information handling which many commercial enterprises regard as essential.

It has been suggested by numerous commentators on library economics that these lacunae stem from the lack of influence of the profit motive at work in library operations, and from the fact that a majority of libraries do not operate in a commercial market. There is considerable truth in these views, but there are now many library services or parts of them which are orientated to profit making in an increasingly conventional sense (or at least cost recovery) and which operate in commercial conditions or markets. These conditions, becoming more and more common in the last decade, do not seem to have brought the full realization that library and information services managers need a full repertoire of managerial economic and accounting tools at their disposal and an ability to use them fully. It sometimes appears as if budgeting and performance studies take place in a cost vacuum.

Yet the interest in the performance of library and information systems and services is a strong and growing one. Library and information economics is a developing field, although the focus is on the economics of information as a commodity, rather than on the economics of library and information services as organizations. Service performance has an essential economic element, but this element will never be fully understood if it proves impossible to provide full cost data about aspects of library and information operations. It is here that the relationship between costing, accounting and performance is closest, first of all conceptually, but then essentially in practice. The relationship can be realized through cost data collection by taking account of the physical activities of the library, and structuring them for economic management in terms of resource allocation (budgeting methods of all kinds, and budgetary decision making), resource management procedures and through regulation and control mechanisms.

Output measurement is one of the technical aspects of performance measurement, and cost measurement should be a major part of that process of measurement required in any evaluation programme. Cost measurement gives an essential perspective to the assessment of performance but it does not provide a substitute when other measures, for example, related to behavioural aspects of service delivery and consumption are called for. Cost measures may be essential, but they are very often of greater value and significance for management if complementary to other measures.

As far as the present discussion is concerned cost-effectiveness, both as performance measure and criterion of effectiveness, provides the focus and legitimate concern. Cost analysis, as a contributor to cost-effectiveness analysis, has to be seen boldly in context of performance measurement and library and information evaluation. Activities and actions in library and information operations consume resources, and the manager needs to know through measurement the rate and nature of consumption – cost provides the ideal measure and economic analysis the ideal vehicle. This point is rarely made explicit by the majority of writers on evaluation and performance measurement, but it is clearly discernible in the professional writings of Hamburg and Lancaster. It is perhaps implicit in the writings of the majority of writers on library and information operation evaluation, although their explicit concern may be with usage, demand, value, satisfaction, impact or similar intangibles concerned with the final output of service activity.

It has already been suggested that terminological confusion may have been an impediment to the coherence and consolidation of library and information evaluation studies. Cost and economic study may yet serve only to confuse the picture a little further, if claims are made for it as a panacea for the manager–evaluator. Table 4.6 tries to make a small contribution by suggesting in sketch form some of the directions which might lead to a clearer conceptual understanding.

Evaluation (1) is chosen as the general term, with at least three useful subordinate concepts (2a, 2b and 3). Against these concepts are what might best be called aspects: such as the distinction between micro- and macroevaluation made by King and Bryant (1971); between output and evaluation measures made by Mohr (1979), although the use of 'evaluation' may cause confusion

TABLE 4.6 Concepts of evaluation

Concept	*Scope*	*Aspects*
(1) Evaluation	Collective name for the general process (see Blagden, Lancaster)	Sub-concepts (aspects) include internal/external (e.g. output/impact) and macro/micro
(2a) Performance measures and measurement	Characterized by orientation to *activities*. A range of different types of studies of activity associated with library and information service	Complemented by other types of measurement and assessment, not exclusively related to *activities* themselves (e.g. social, educational, cognitive etc.)
(2b) Effectiveness analysis	Different types of studies of activities focusing on the specific degree to which objectives are achieved by different levels of performance	Often concerned with the aspects of *demand, use, satisfaction, value, benefit, quality*, etc.
(3) Criteria and parameters for evaluation	The methodological bases for 1, 2a and 2b	Especially measures designed to illuminate the more general aspects of effectiveness (see above) e.g. speed, depth, penetration, coverage, accessibility, cost; measures of retrieval effectiveness

(perhaps 'valuation' would be better); and between internal and external, corresponding to output and evaluation (internal evaluation is concerned with service outputs; and external evaluation is concerned with the impacts and effects such as benefit, value, satisfaction etc. on the user or client).

What certainly cannot be escaped by the clear headed cost examiner and accountant is that evaluation and performance studies are a multidimensional field of discourse. There are many problems of a theoretical nature which will only be resolved through testing based on useful operational definitions; there is a 'chicken and egg' problem here. Yet there is useful agreement that the evaluation and performance study begins with the identification and specification of goals and objectives. The UK Public Library Research Group (PLRG) and American Library Association work on public library evaluation has established this without doubt, and it may be possible now to combine evaluation and managerial economics by starting

TABLE 4.7 A spectrum of measures and information

Increasing usefulness for management decision ↓			Decreasing structure, order, certainty ↓
	* National library surveys and accounts (Statistics originating with British Library, Department of Education or Office of Arts and Libraries in the United Kingdom; Brockman-AARL Statistics on higher education libraries in Australia)		
	* Library (descriptive) statistics HEFCE and SCONUL series on university libraries in UK; LISU series LIBGIS (USA)		
	* Activity measures	= Input statistics = Throughput statistics = Efficiency measures	
	* Performance measures	= Output measures = Impact measures = Effectiveness measures = Benefit incomes (value, satisfaction etc.)	
	* Management information	= Principally statistical	
	* Decision support and intelligence	= Statistical (quantitative), but increasingly qualitative	

with an obviously goal centred emphasis to management programmes. The similarity between goals and objectives setting, programme development, and functional analysis to derive cost centres should be perceived as a way to develop an economic style of management; one that is economic in managerial time, and stylistically relevant to managerial economics.

In the long run it should be possible to look towards an evaluation and performance context for library management which is not seen as a separate battery of tools but as an integrated part of a continuous process of management. Table 4.7 tries to show very simply how this might develop by positing a spectrum of data and measures.

This is consistent with the general flow of argument from cost data to management information discussed in this text. This spectrum moves generally from a greater to lesser degree of structure, order and certainty. Descriptive library statistics should be highly specific and structured, although they are not necessarily meaningful to operational management (the so-called 'problem' of library statistics) in crude form.

At the other end of the spectrum, decision support and intelligence is both more complex and less structured. The paradox of less structure at the higher levels of the spectrum is resolved by the fact that the deeper knowledge of the system obtained provides what is needed to compensate for the lack of structure. The more dynamic environment can be handled more adequately with knowledge than by data alone. This argument holds true if the progression from data to information to knowledge is maintained; it seems to be maintained at the level of metatheory in information science and information management, so therefore, why not in this case. More sophisticated management information and information processing methods are required, which at least in theory are more specific and meaningful to operational management; that is, they are decision supportive. Performance measures (and more generally middle range evaluation) are located in the middle of this spectrum, and activity measures include the majority of sources of cost data in a system.

4.6 Financial data and cost data

The *Penguin Dictionary of Economics* (Bannock, Baxter and Rees, 1972) defines finance very simply as 'the provision of money when and where required'. In all kinds of commercial enterprise finance and financial management has two main foci: first, the securing of long-term funds and capital; second, the provision of money (i.e. finance) to procure resources for the current economic operations of the firm.

Financial management is a very significant managerial responsibility, and the finance director of any concern a key figure in management, with extensive internal and external responsibilities. A large segment of the management information system will consist of the financial information system; the feeding of cost data to this system, and hence the relationship between management accounting and financial management will be explicit.

Because most libraries exist as units within host institutions and are financed in the long term by some form of fixed grant, supplemented with earned income from market operations, the external function of financial management is more limited. Of course, the library manager is concerned with external finance and provision of monetary resources for the system, but rarely is the need met by going out to the financial market (usually the banking system).

However, budget preparation and budget justification are central tasks for the library manager which cannot be neglected and approximate to the financial realities of the commercial enterprise manager. Internal financial management for the library manager is just as important, if not more so. Within the total financial resource obtained the 'when and where' of money within the system is, in direct monetary terms or in resources, a prime concern for the manager. Budgetary control, the maintenance of management accounting, and all kinds of cost and performance study contribute to the overall roster of financial management tasks.

Some further clarification of the relative meanings of the terms costing and accounting is helpful. Costing is one of the techniques of study concerned with the economic measurement of (library) processes, and relates to the monetary (and time) sacrifices made in the disposition and allocation of resources to activities and productive uses. Accounting is used to denote the manner in which costs, as defined earlier, are categorized and presented for the purposes of record and for the use of management. This entire process can be described as management accounting. A management information system should encompass the management accounting apparatus. Costs are described as complete quantities (total costs), or else are broken down by categories of expense, which are necessary to facilitate the construction and comprehension of accounts.

There may be points where it is difficult to distinguish in practice between costing and accounting, since the accounting system is rich in cost data, which can be secondarily analysed to produce further elements of cost information. In this case it might be safer to define or confine the concept of costing to the initial or primary measurement of cost, when the degree of monetary or time sacrifice is first recognized and calculated. The secondary and subsequent handling of cost data can then usefully be described as management accounting.

To summarize, there are three levels of monetary and resources activity; financial management broken down into external (obtaining sources of funding) and internal (monitoring and controlling both funding and resources); management accounting (the internal subdivision of financial management, undertaken on an active controlling basis); and finally costing (with important subdivisions such as work study, and performance studies). In effect, and arising from this analysis cost data are the common thread across the whole scale of financial activity and its related manifestations as different kinds of financial data.

4.7 Cost data: needs, requirements and strategies

In the preceding sections the range, scope and pervasiveness of cost data has been discussed in terms of a general managerial economic model of a library and information operation, encompassing goal setting, resource allocation and management, performance measurement, and management information systems. The needs and requirements for cost data are set in the context of this conceptual model of library management. The purpose of this section is to indicate more precisely the specific aspects of cost data required, and the strategies for cost collection which can be developed to produce relevant usable data.

For the purposes of management and accounting, library operations have to be broken down to reflect the managerial responsibilities in the library, or the functional aspects of library work, or a combination of both.

The traditional manner of library cost accounting and financial accounting has been to use a structure which reflects the functional categorization of library work (e.g. by task) and or the managerial organization of the library (e.g. line management responsibilities). Most commonly this has employed a pattern based on departmental structure, with further apportionments according to functional category. Reader services, technical services, administration and educational work are examples of the categories used in both approaches. This is an input orientated approach, which emphasizes the block allocation of inputs of staff and materials to departments and broad functions. This schema is reflected in the budget with line-items for the main inputs broken down by departmental responsibility, adminstrative unit or by function. Such a schema can be adapted to generate output/product costs although these can be of a very general, often imprecise nature.

Another method, of more recent development, and certainly of more recent innovation, is to develop a closer specification for management and financial accounting which pays more attention to the exact types of output, general services or specific products in various areas of library and information service. In its most developed form the management and financial accounting would not be structured at all in terms of departmental, broad function or administrative categories, but in terms of different outputs and products. Budget and accounting categories would be identified in terms of programmes related to the different outputs. Such a scheme emphasizes the unit nature of output and the unit nature of costs. The main use of this kind of approach has so far been in programme budgeting, such as programming, planning and budgeting system (PPBS) and zero-based budgeting (ZBB). See Chapter Two (and Sections 2.9–2.11) for a wider discussion and Chapter Eight for a general example.

In practice the intelligent application of both structures and approaches is useful, helpful, and sensible. The ideal management accounting system would be able to produce different reports for management, based on a whole variety of different centres and structures, outputs and products. If an organizational approach to budgeting and accounting is useful to management then it should be used. However, one would like management to realize that to use only this approach to budgeting and accounting is limiting and impedes the development of a full grasp of the total economic aspects of the library system.

The essentials of needs, requirements, and strategy might be summed up as follows: the needs are for basic financial accounting (a statement of the income and expenditure flows in the library), a budgeting system, a management accounting system (which is designed to give the manager, cost and other cost related reports on a frequent basis), some means of applying tests based on effectiveness criteria and associated performance measures, and information support (statistics, management information and intelligence, decision support).

The requirements are the specification of a structure which can ensure a relationship between budgeting (resource allocation), management accounting (control and resource management), and performance measurement. The most likely way to achieve this relationship is through the definition of a programme structure with elements of organizational, managerial and functional categories, and outputs and products in it, which allows for the full development of a structure of cost centres for accounting purposes.

The specific strategy which the library manager adopts to achieve all this will depend on the type of library and information system in question. But the needs and requirements and the basic strategy for meeting them are common to all library service situations, as they are indeed to enterprise management in general. A small library may not need such an elaborate system, although it should contain all the conceptual essentials. A medium sized library organization with several departments, several levels of staff, and more than perhaps half a dozen staff or upwards will need a more elaborate system. Host institution requirements can determine the point at which more complex systems and procedures are elaborated. In some situations the library system may have to develop with, or conform to, other accounting systems. In other situations the library service may develop different methods. Large libraries and large systems will need well elaborated systems. Increasing organizational complexity, more numerous stages of production and numerous outputs will as a general rule indicate greater elaboration of accounting and the related systems.

In all its different dimensions cost study is both analytical and synthetic. The final needs for management are usually for total and summarizing measures. The requirements of a costing system to satisfy these needs necessitate different degrees of analysis and dissection. There is no hard and fast rule as to how far the analysis and dissection should go. Judgements about these matters depend on the kind of information sought and the ease with which it can be obtained. The manager's judgement is determined by wider needs, and above all by an understanding of the concepts of cost study and accounting; it is with these two latter factors that this discussion is especially concerned. A working knowledge of the concepts enables the manager to construct whatever structure is appropriate to the system in question.

4.8 Managerial and economic structure

It is not the purpose of this text to explore prescriptively questions of managerial style and technique: numerous works on library management and management generally offer copious discussions and suggestions. However, there is good ground for believing that some success in management derives from the fulfilment of certain structural conditions and needs. The manager tends to be more successful at fulfilling managerial functions and objectives when there is a high level of insight and perception about the system in question.

There has already been considerable professional debate about the organizational and communication structures of libraries, and both aspects are important for the behavioural and resource aspects of management. The 'thinking manager' will come to categorize usefully the system managed, and develop conceptual models and perceptual skills for operational management. Resources are allocated to functions, staff are allocated to jobs, staff and objectives are matched to achievement, and effectiveness and performance monitored; these are but a few of the modes in which the manager operates either consciously or subconsciously; information flows are developed and decisions considered within such contexts.

Managerial thinking about the system managed as an economic system rooted in different types of economic structure is much less developed or prevalent, although there are exceptions. But the generally low level of library costing undertaken and the underdevelopment of management accounting techniques by library managers, alone point to grave deficiencies in economic management. Indeed, it is a thesis of this text that library management lacks a developed body of managerial economic thought and tools to enable it to fulfil adequately the economic functions within management.

The development and implementation of costing methods on a wide basis in libraries can, it is argued, represent a first vital step towards attaining a perception of the economic structure of the library system, and to achieving a library managerial economics. The application of operations research to library problems, the widespread interest in library evaluation, effectiveness and performance study, and the development of effective information bases about library operations suggests that the right directions are being signalled, if not generally followed.

In commercial firms a neglect of cost study would be absurd, illogical and a folly. And it is not 'commercial pressure' alone that makes this so, but more the appreciation that the task of the enterprise itself concerns the effective management of resources. Resources are limited and finite, so that the commercial choice is solely between survival or failure. For library and information service operations of whatever kind the message is just the same; there can be no confident neglect of cost study in resource management and economic structures have to be made explicit in libraries and their management, just as management structures have already become.

4.9 Further reading

Goals and performance and the study of performance and evaluation

Performance and evaluation topics are widely discussed in the professional literature at a theoretical and practical level. Orr (1973) has attempted an overall theoretical integration on the basis of a logical examination of principles and Lancaster (1977, 1993) has offered syntheses of the literature and critique of method. Ford (1989), Abbott (1990) and Winkworth (1991, 1993) provide a finer focus on theory and method. Moore (1989) and Office of Arts and Libraries (1990) address the need to synthesize and package the concepts and methods for operational use. The short list of readings which follows will help to guide the reader into the mainstream of this key topic.

Totterdell and Bird (1976) and DeProspo and Altman (1973) are classic studies in the public library context. Morgan (1995) considers applications in academic libraries with a strong practical emphasis.

Abbott, C. (1990) What does good look like? The adoption of performance indicators at Aston University Library and Information Services. *British Journal of Academic Librarianship*, **5**(2), 79–94

Abbott, C. (1994) *Performance measurement in library and information services*. London: Aslib

Blagden, J. (1980) *Do we really need libraries?* London: Bingley/Saur

Blagden, J. and Harrington, J. (1990) *How good is your library: a review of approaches to the evaluation of library and information services*. London: Aslib

Blagden, J. (1983) *Do we really need libraries? Proceedings of the First Joint Library Association Cranfield Institute of Technology Conference on Performance Assessment*. Cranfield: Cranfield Press

Brockman, J. R. (1980) *Academic library management research: an evaluative review*. Loughborough: Centre for Library and Information Management

Chacha, R. N. and Irving, A. (1991) An experiment in academic library performance measurement. *British Journal of Academic Librarianship*, **6**(1), 13–26

Circle of State Librarians (1992) *Developing quality in libraries*. London: HMSO

Circle of State Librarians (1993) *Performance and potential of librarians*. London: HMSO

Curran, C. C. and Summers, F. W. (1990) *Library performance, accountability and responsiveness: essays in honour of Ernest R. De Prospo*. New Jersey: Ablex Publishing Corporation

Ford, G. (1989) A perspective on performance measurement. *International Journal of Information and Library Research*, **1**(1), 12–23

Goodall, D. L. (1988) Performance measurement: a historical perspective. *Journal of Librarianship*, **20**(2), 128–144

Hannabuss, S. (1987) The importance of performance measures. *Library Review*, Winter, 248–253

Hoeglund, A. and Moore, N. (1991) Measure the performance of your public libraries and your planning will be easier, more rewarding – and more successful. *International Library Review*, **23**(1), 31–47

Kantor, P. B. (1984) Objective performance measures for academic and research libraries. Washington, DC: ARL

Kelley, P. M. (1991) Performance measures: a tool for planning resource allocation. *Journal of Library Administration*, **14**(2), 21–36

Lancaster, F. W. (1977) *The measurement and evaluation of library services*. Washington, DC: Information Resources Press

Lancaster, F. W. (1993) *If you want to evaluate your library* . . . 2nd edn. London: Library Association Publishing

McClure, C. R. (1986) A view from the trenches: costing and performance measures for academic library public services. *College and Research Libraries*, **47**(4), 323–336

Midwinter, A. and McVicar, M. (1990) Public libraries and performance indicators: origins, developments and issues. *Library Review*, **39**(5), 10–22

Moore, N. (1989) *Measuring the performance of public libraries: a draft manual prepared for the General Information Programme of Unesco*. Paris: Unesco (PGI89/WS/3)

Morgan, S. (1995) *Performance assessment in academic libraries*. London: Mansell

Office of Arts and Libraries (1990) *Keys to success: performance indicators for public libraries*. London: Office of Arts and Libraries (Library and Information Series No. 18)

Orr, R. H. (1973) Measuring the goodness of library services: a general framework for considering quantitative measures. *Journal of Documentation*, **29**(3), 315–332

Pantry, S. (1988) Performance activity indicators. *State Librarian*, March, 2–4

Revill, D. H. (1985) The measurement of performance. In J. Cowley (1985) (ed.) *The management of polytechnic libraries*. Aldershot: Gower and COPOL. pp.104–134

Revill, D. H. (1990) Performance measures for academic libraries. In *Encyclopedia of Library and Information Science*, **45**, 294–333

Van House, N. A. *et al.* (1987) *Output measures for public libraries.* 2nd edition. Chicago: ALA

Vickery, B. C. and Vickery, A. (1987) The evaluation of systems. In B. C. Vickery and A. Vickery *Information science in theory and practice.* London: Butterworth. pp.261–269

Ward, P. L. (1982) (ed.) *Performance measures: a bibliography.* Loughborough: Centre for Library and Information Management and Public Libraries Research Group (CLAIM Report No. 15)

Webb, S. (1991) *Best practice? Continuing professional development for library/information staff in UK professional firms.* London: British Library (BLR&D Report No. 6039)

Wills, G. and Oldman, C. (1977) The beneficial library. In C. M. Oldman (1977) (ed.) *The value of academic libraries: a methodological investigation.* Cranfield: Cranfield Institute of Technology

Winkworth, I. (1990) Performance indicators for polytechnic libraries. *Library Review*, **39**(5), 23–41

Winkworth, I. (1991) Performance measurement and performance indicators. In C. Jenkins and M. Morley (1991) (eds.) *Collection management in academic libraries.* Aldershot: Gower. pp.59–93

Winkworth, I. (1993) Into the house of mirrors: performance measurement in academic libraries. *British Journal of Academic Librarianship*, **8**(1), 17–33

Chapter 5

Methods of cost measurement

5.1 Service cost structure: input, throughput, output, and budgets and costs

The typology of input, throughput and output provides the focus for the development of methods and techniques designed to elicit the cost structure of a library and information service. The way in which input, throughput, and output can be further defined and categorized has already been suggested: according to categories (contexts) of function, department, organization, personnel, material, and programme and/or product (see Table 5.1 and Section 4.7).

The organizing systems for providing cost information and cost structure are the budget (planned expenditure (and revenue)), the financial accounts (actual expenditure (and revenue)), and the managerial accounts (costs related to decision making). The means of establishing, assessing, and controlling costs are provided with this framework.

A cost analysis must first of all identify the categories and components of input, throughput and output. This has to be done irrespective of the scale of the costing exercise. There will inevitably be some boundary problems to face.

5.1.1 Input

It is recommended that input and input cost are used to describe the resources available to the system (or that part of it being analysed) prior to their activation in functional work. These inputs

TABLE 5.1 Categorization of input, throughput and output activities by context

These contexts can be used at input, throughput and output levels:

Function

A function is defined as a subsystem of a library and information operation. There is no absolute restriction on the scale of a function, although most will be substantial, since they will be composed of subfunctions and elements which are treated as subordinate cost centres and cost units. Functions can be identified at input, throughput or output levels.

Department

A department is an organizational unit within a system which can be defined in terms of function and staffing and location within a management structure. A department can embrace several classes of staff and multiple functions. A department can be concerned with input, throughput and/or output activities.

Organization

An organization or organizational unit within a system can embrace several functions and departments or be considered to represent one specific function or organization. The concept of organization is useful in that it frees management thinking from overrigid departmental and functional thinking. The concept of organization can be helpful in defining multifunction programmes and programme areas. For example technical services departments are organizational rather than departmental by these definitions, since in a large library they may cover the accessions and order departments, cataloguing and classification, physical processing and distribution departments.

Personnel

Staffing is the major expense category, in most service enterprises and libraries are no exception. It may thus be important, necessary and useful to categorize input, throughput and output activities in terms of dominant personnel involved. In a small library where each member of staff has many functions this could be a sensible and practical way of developing accounting and control (this is the traditional method of line responsibility).

Material

An obvious way to collect library management information on costs and/or performance is according to material handled – according to monographs, serials, reports, non-book media etc. in the contexts of technical services, use, storage etc. This is an example of the development of major programme categories, specific to the needs of the enterprise concerned and its management.

Programme and product

Any one of the preceding five categories can form the basis of defining and/or constituting a programme or product in a library. A programme will have input, throughput and output stages, while a product will usually concern throughput and output, with input activities listed as categories of expense.

include the traditionally accepted categories of expense – labour, materials, services, and overheads etc. At this level the concepts of 'resource', 'cost' and 'expense' are almost synonymous. The costing of these will often be historic, for example based on actual expenditures as shown on invoices, debits, financial report statements etc. However, it may be possible to predict likely budgeted expenditures, for instance using regression analysis. Part of the task of cost analysis is indeed to attempt to predict likely future patterns of cost, as much as to establish current costs, or failing that, historic costs.

5.1.2 Throughput

Throughput costs should cover all stages of the functions involving work done with activated library resources, up to the stage of the emergence of final outputs. Some intermediate outputs will inevitably be identified at the throughput stage, and these must be defined and distinguished from final output. Throughput costs can be specified using the variety of categories already suggested – functional, organizational, departmental etc.

Input cost data feed across to studies of throughput costs; thus staff and material expenses have to be identified before throughput cost studies can be made. Throughput cost studies are essentially about how resources are divided up, distributed and spent across a whole range of library activities. These activities have to be carefully defined first, and there may be several appropriate ways of then making a cost study, depending on the level of detail, accuracy and frequency of information required.

It is during costing of throughput that differences of scale of cost study and cost structure are most evident. Different methods of studying cost produce different qualities and quantities of cost data. One method is to study tasks and jobs and their content using work measurement and time study; this is of great importance when detailed information is required. However, the same library operation or function or product can be cost studied in other ways. A crude cost study without recourse to detailed work measurement, and only the crude description of tasks and jobs and estimation of staff times spent is another variety of approach. On another occasion a crude allocation of gross expenses to different contexts or programmes may be made (a cost allocation study). The costing of intermediate and final output may require work measurement, time study and crude cost study in combination, together with output measurement to produce unit times and unit costs. Cost studies can be done at regular or infrequent intervals, and regular ad hoc studies can be carried out as well as regular systematic studies (continuous monitoring of a function or process, which is the basis for regular management accounting).

5.1.3 Output

Some managers may choose to treat intermediate outputs as final outputs for some purposes. This is legitimate and appropriate. The cost of producing bibliographic records is in many ways a final stage of output, although in terms of the cost of service to users, the cost of bibliographic tools can be regarded as an overhead charge or intermediate output. It is at this stage that attempts to overrigidly define costing rules and protocols can be irksome and inflexible. Much of the costing of final output in practice comes down to calculating unit times and unit costs. Overall resource allocations and expenditures are reduced to a convenient unitary form of output. Whatever procedure is chosen, the outputs have to be clearly defined, and then related back through to the stages of input and throughput. Each manager and each library has to write its own set of protocols.

However, there is often a wish for inter-library and inter-function comparison, so that common bases have to be found. Suggested common structures for cost study were a preoccupation of the investigative programme at the Centre for Library and Information Management (which was the stimulus for the predecessor of the current work (Roberts, 1985)) and have been addressed elsewhere (the work of the Centre for Interfirm Comparison is relevant (Harrington, Carruthers and Moffat, 1981), as is that by Jones, (1981), by the administration of the British Library, and later by King Research (Office of Arts and Libraries, 1990) and in the USA by the Association of Research Libraries over a period of years. Most schemes have so far failed to win general acceptance.

Improving structures for cost study through refining schemes of description and measurement is critical for the success of output measurement. The ramifications of this extend back to the beginning of the budgeting process. Analytical budgeting techniques such as PPBS and ZBB usually require thorough and ambitious statements of expected outputs and outcomes, which have not only to be specifically identified and defined, but also have to be measurable to facilitate the control and evaluation of performance. Thus in the long run costed output measures are necessary and are of greater value to management than cost data alone. The cost analyst has the task of relating the contribution of units of input and resources consumed to the outputs of the system. Unit times and unit costs can relate to individual outputs achieved in different parts of the system, and such data should be produced where possible.

But it may also be necessary to deal with aggregates of output in terms of a complete section of a library, a group of staff, or a range of services. Along with aggregation of outputs goes the aggregation of cost data, and this requires a clear vision and established procedures if it is to be achieved. Not all cost data will be related, either to final or to intermediate output, although most costs can be finally, allocated (or distributed) to an area of output, and in the long run all should be accounted for financially.

Cost data with different degrees of relationship to output are all managerially useful, but costs related to final output have a special relevance – these latter cost data may be taken to form a small but highly significant set of managerially useful costs (MUCs), which can form the basis for specific resource allocation decisions. Nevertheless, management cost accounting spans all levels of activity, thus being more or less valuable for decision making.

In planning to meet the costing information requirements of output measurement a degree of selectivity has to be exercised and can be illustrated. The number of task elements and activities related to library and information service is very large. A preliminary list prepared in conjunction with the predecessor of the current book listed over 1500 (unpublished). It would be convenient if task and activity descriptions corresponded exactly or closely to final forms of output (or throughput) and other associated measures. There is a tendency for this to happen, especially at aggregate levels of activity (e.g. total technical processing, total reader service activity). But many outputs and output measures can only be established when defined in terms of their (smaller) constituent tasks and activities and this is a laborious but necessary exercise.

The result is that the processes of work measurement and cost data collection do not fully converge naturally and consistently with the expectation of gathering the most significant (output related) information for the management information system, management decision and resource allocation. This suggests that the manager and cost accountant has to find some means of reconciling these differences.

In terms of management information systems discussed in Chapter Seven, there has to be scope for transforming the content of different sets of data and information to form the most useful files of fully processed information. The practical implications of these theoretical points are that cost measurement and output measurement are not always interchangeable even though they lie on the same spectrum of studies of enterprise performance. However, the management information system could provide the vehicle for the convergence of cost and output measures.

5.1.4 Budgets and costs

The library budget can be both a plan for resource allocation and expenditure and a tool for predicting the target levels of cost to be achieved (refer to Chapter Three for a wider discussion of budgeting). Historic costs and standard costs can be used to prepare the budget, and the variances analysed as spending proceeds. Expected levels of output would also have to be identified. During each budgetary and financial cycle the manager has to update, revise and supplement the cost data picture of the service. Cost studies using the input, throughput, output structure provide means of intermediate scale for achieving this. Finally at the highest level of scale a management accounting system requires a regular and systematic coverage of activities and generation of costs, covering historic, present and expected levels of activity. Every major function has to be supported by a system which records the expenditure of resources and time in productive and unproductive activities. It is management's task to ensure this support as part of the general process of management in the service.

5.2 Types of cost study for library and information services

Five different types of cost study are reviewed here. A knowledge of their potential, and an ability to employ them gives the library manager the basis upon which to build an information system for managerial accounting, decision making and economic analyses. The five types form a hierarchy of increasing complexity and diversity of application.

Cost analysis is the basic mode of study which provides information for the other descriptive and analytical methods. Cost analysis can be carried out and its data presented in a variety of ways (see notably Sections 5.4, 5.6 and Chapter Six). Cost analysis requires the measurement of resources input to the system, an understanding of the nature and type of work carried out and especially an appreciation of the use of time by labour (through measurement or a substitute for it). Data from cost analyses can be fed into accounting, estimating, budgeting and performance measurement procedures.

Cost distribution and/or cost allocation studies (the terms are often used interchangeably) look at resource allocations, flows of resources and activities, especially in the throughput or transfer stage. These are useful descriptive procedures, providing a general view of the costs carried in different parts of the library system. These analyses help to understand the outcome of previous resource allocation and financial decisions, and corrections can be applied through budgeting process.

Unit costing and timing uses cost analysis data with measures of output to give cost/unit indices; these are often used as performance measures. As a summarizing measurement technique unit costing and timing is attractive to managers, but it must be used with discretion because of the sensitivity of unit costs to volume, the problems of variable to fixed costs, and the difficulties of the treatment of overheads.

Cost-effectiveness studies are used for performance appraisal, planning and decision. Costs of existing processes and model cost data for the alternative options under consideration are required and obtained through cost analyses or cost estimation. Cost-effectiveness studies are systems orientated: which of several methods performs best according to the effectiveness criteria specified, and does so at a given level of costs.

Cost-benefit studies, in the proper sense, are rarely carried out for library and information service provision. Yet, the appropriateness of cost-benefit analysis for the appraisal of major investments is obvious, especially when public goods and services are concerned and welfare considerations of social cost and social benefit uppermost. Cost-benefit studies draw on cost data from the other four types of cost study.

The collection of raw cost data (cost analysis) is the key to all the other types of derivative cost study. Library and information service managers can implement cost studies of a basic as well as an increasingly sophisticated kind. A library which sets out to design, implement and operate a cost study programme will gain managerial strength through greater economic insight and more effective decision making – choosing the right alternative and realizing it through effective resource allocation.

At this point it is worth introducing both a note of clarification and one of caution. During the process of revision of this text the need to make fundamental changes of principle in the discussion was addressed. After hopefully adequate and informed consideration, the bulk of this chapter still stands as written in the predecessor work (Roberts 1985). However, the question of making generalizations about practice is not nearly so simple. What is clear and true is that the managerial and economic environment has changed at a pace and has been discussed in Chapter One at some length.

The revision has tried to acknowledge that by a more extensive review of the financial and environmental context, and by updating the literature reviewed. It is reasonable to assume that the major bibliographic databases of the field would give a sound impression of the coverage of professional writing; examination of these sources fails to show a significant increase in writing and investigation about costing topics which might be proportionate to the scale of the environmental changes. Given the economic and business changes what conclusions, if any, can be drawn from this?

First, nothing may have changed since the mid-1980s: cost analysis and its related practices are still underdeveloped in spite of everything. Second, cost analysis practices have changed; much more measurement is being done, and service management and practice is rich in cost data; but no one has the time to report this in the literature. This may be hard to believe, since professionals usually make it their business to tell their peers about what they are doing. Third, there may be unfortunate problems in bibliographical control and dissemination of this topic and its literature; having searched and found little (and little new), the author would tend to infer that this was a true reflection. From reasons two and three a combination of unreported successes and problems in bibliographical control does seem rather unlikely.

However, the answer (or truth) may be found in a fourth position, which states that managers/information professionals must determine their own circumstances, and provide their own (truthful) answer. The way to do this is to follow the programme of this book, and then report and discuss what you find. Ten years hence we could be thus better informed. But for the moment, and as far as UK (European), North American and Anglo-American tradition goes, professional opinion would tend to find some answers (and many good methods) in the review made by King Research (Office of Arts and Libraries, 1990).

5.2.1 Cost analysis

Cost analysis is the basic tool of cost study – it is principally the measurement of the monetary (and time) sacrifice made to achieve certain ends. Cost analysis deals with the question of 'how much does it cost to do Y' or 'what is the cost of X'. In practice cost analysis can be applied to a great range of phenomena, events, stages and processes of operations. The analyst isolates those areas of task which are considered relevant to the given end, and on which information is required for descriptive or decision making purposes. At the most detailed level monetary expense incurred is identified on a task-by-task or operation-by-operation basis. Cost analysis is a very flexible tool, in that almost any part of a system can be selected for scrutiny. A range of standard techniques and procedures can be applied over a wide span of circumstances.

To make an effective analysis of cost requires the ability to define the unit 'X' or 'Y' which is being costed. This unit is referred to as the cost centre or cost unit. The object of the monetary sacrifice may be a recognizable organizational or service unit (e.g. the maintenance of a cataloguing department or inter-library loan office etc.) or an end product (e.g. all the technical processes applied to an item of literature, an inter-library loan transaction etc.). The object of cost analysis may also be a necessary but subsidiary part of an operation, one or two stages removed from the final end product.

Sometimes the methods and techniques of cost investigation are impeded by the nature of the phenomena studied, and this interaction has to be understood for practical reasons. For example, specific managerial or intellectual tasks or elements may be difficult to describe and isolate in practice, so judgements have to be made to account for their influence on cost patterns.

There are two basic kinds of cost analysis methods:

- work measurement methods
- estimation methods (really a subclass of the former).

Work measurement

This carries with it the connotation of precision, or at least attempted precision. Work measurement techniques are the best tools available for practical library cost analysis (see Section 5.6 for a summary). Besides categorizing the system unit under study, the methods of operation employed, and determining the factor inputs, work measurement attempts to measure the precise quantities of factors consumed (principally labour) and time apportioned to constituent functions and tasks. It encourages work study and time study, and uses different devices to collect the data required (work diaries, activity or work sampling etc.).

Work measurement approaches to library cost analysis are often used to determine standard times and job norms, and to explore ways of making procedural and system changes. These approaches are not solely concerned with cost analysis but help to inform other areas of library operations, practice and management related to resource allocation (see Smith and Schofield, 1971; Thomas, 1971) and Gilder and Schofield (1976).

Estimation methods

Estimation methods are frequently used in libraries to cost analyse where exact work measurement poses problems of introduction or practical difficulties of implementation. The quantities of factor inputs allocated per time period are estimated on a basis of observation and discussion with staff, or regrettably by even more subjective methods. Monetary costs are calculated from, or scaled down from gross annual expenditures for the total system or for major expenditure headings. These methods often give relatively accurate estimates, and may supplement work measurement based studies which of necessity are undertaken less frequently (Roberts, 1981). The danger is that over a period library managers will neglect to carry out more accurate measurement studies.

There are operational reasons for the popularity of cost estimation. The annual budgetary cycle is a relatively short period, and the demands of precise cost analysis compete with other managerial tasks for attention. Budgeting usually has a higher priority, is concerned with total expenditures, and is partly a political process, so that latitude in the formulation of proposals and estimates is often required and sometimes legitimate. It may, therefore, be politically convenient to make a less detailed appraisal of some functions and subunits, in order to emphasize the entirety of the budget. The urge to cost processes in detail will be less. Of course, funders, accountants and auditors may take a different view, but in practice management information and judgement are weighted against each other by the different parties concerned.

Accounting is another matter. Expenditures must be accounted for, and taken on a functional basis this can provide a rough and ready historic cost analysis. This intermediate stage in costing may often be the limit to the process. But accounting categories are not always those of most use for financial and resource management – determining the future allocation of resources. So a gap remains to be filled by specific cost analysis; at some point work measurement may have to replace cost estimation and historic costing as the basis for costing.

In the long term the estimation methods have to be complemented not only by the application of work measurement methods, but by an integrated approach to library budgeting, accounting, management information and performance evaluation – by a move in the direction of costing and accounting systems which are the standard practice for business enterprises. In a well accounted system, where the regular work load can be frequently monitored for output and performance, managerial interest in costs at the operational rather than at the strategic level becomes more concerned with variances from standard costs than with the detailed cost performance of all centres and units.

For management purposes historic costs of operations performed, without reported times, are of little use for comparative purposes. Comparisons are needed either from one institution at different periods, or between different institutions. Comparative cost analysis requires the use of similar investigative procedures, methods and treatments. Without these considerations cost comparisons are contentious. The lack of comparability within or between systems and institutions is perhaps the most unsatisfactory aspect of present day library cost study; witness the contentiousness of estimates of inter-library loans costs, or the cost-effectiveness of new technology applications in different types of library.

5.2.2 Cost distribution and/or cost allocation

Whereas a cost analysis should be a thorough attempt to assess the actual or real costs in a system unit (preferably by work measurement, but by estimation if necessary), cost distribution is a means of extracting similar information, usually over a wider range of units or the total system, with less effort. Cost distribution study selects the units to be reviewed and attempts by estimation to allocate the actual monetary amounts and flows to the units (departments, functions or programmes) in accordance with some generally agreed scheme. A common source for allocatable cost data will be projected or actual expenditures in the budget or financial statement (balance sheet).

Of course, cost analysis data can be used in a cost distribution study, but at the risk of mixing more accurate data with less. In a cost distribution study gross costs of labour, materials, overheads etc. are divided between the cost centres and cost units using a variety of criteria: for example, number of full-time staff per centre could be used as a basis to allocate staff costs and other costs on a per capita basis. Some analysts would then try and relate cost distribution data to output data to generate unit costs; at this point some argue the tendentious nature of the exercise, because extensive use can lead to errors and inaccuracies which may become cumulative.

If a library employed a general cost collection routine, it would, through continuous cost analysis, have all the information necessary to construct accurately an overall cost distribution for its system. Certain problems of definition, double counting, apportionment and aggregation would have to be solved, but conceptually, and probably in practice, it could be done. At the moment few libraries are in a position to do this. Its achievement could normally be undertaken only with a fully fledged computer-based accounting and management information system. To do so manually would take an excessive amount of clerical effort, disproportionate to benefit in terms of management information yielded.

A cost distribution study can be appreciated conveniently by contrasting it with budgeting. The budget is an expenditure plan, showing monetary flows consonant with the goals and objectives prescribed for the system. The budget shows projected total expenditures, which may or may not be achieved in practice. Cost accounting systems monitor the progress of actual expenditure within the budgetary framework, and these rely on appropriate techniques of recording and analysis. In a cost distribution a period of account is taken and the actual total expenditures are allocated, usually by estimation, to the centres and units being assessed.

In other words cost distribution study maps the burden of costs actually incurred at a level of generality comparable to the budget. The cost distribution can be checked against the periodic accounts (they should tally or the difference satisfactorily explained), and against the budgeted expenditure for the period (again these should tally or have explicable differences). Cost distribution studies can be seen as a means of supplementing normal budgetary control, e.g. dealing with programme/product items as against line-items.

Cost distribution could be described as 'soft' cost analysis. It is a useful synthetic technique, but it is usually done retrospectively. Its use, therefore, is in evaluating financial performance, and in looking at strengths and weaknesses in the system as indicated by the relative distribution of actual expenditures. A cost distribution study could be used as a preliminary to a major redrafting of the library budget. In some ways cost analysis and cost distribution are complementary, and do not strictly replace each other. Each is appropriate to particular situations and management information functions.

The synthetic and synoptic property of cost distribution study is its main value. As an indicator of the system wide distribution of monetary resource flows, and as a device for relating actual expenditure to projected expenditure, it is of great importance. What is more the distribution can be studied in a variety of ways: by department, by function, by product, by staff grade, by process. This flexibility makes cost distribution study a useful managerial probe and evaluation device.

The trade off between cost analysis and cost distribution emphasizes the rather elusive nature of cost study. The objects of cost study and the costs incurred are rarely static; change and fluctuation is the norm. To know the 'costs' of, or to, an organization is in many ways something of an abstraction; a managerial and informational goal which is rarely fully achieved. Cost analysis and cost distribution really need to be seen as different levels and intensities of cost and financial information provision. A cruder estimation and distribution of costs may be quite sufficient for informing budget preparation, where political factors often precede economic ones. Managers who can display the financial workings of their system by a judicious use of cost distribution studies will find themselves in a relatively strong position when it comes to stating the system performance level to a funding body, and for justifying past resource consumption and future proposals.

The most usual form of cost distribution study arises out of the need to look at the overall financial and cost distribution of the library system. A general picture of monetary flows and distributions is usually required for:

- strategic planning
- budget construction
- management review
- demonstrating to governing and funding bodies the effectiveness of the present system or making a political case for adjustments in resource allocation

- providing general measures of financial performance for inter programme and time series comparison.

Cost distribution studies have an important role to play as diagnostic and prognostic tools. For example, different loadings for staff, materials, overheads and service costs can be identified between functions, departments, sectors and products. The 'programme' element in cost distribution relates it very closely to overall budgeting systems such as PPBS, and it certainly enables recognition of the sectoral contribution to output which may be lost in a straight cost analysis (usually only carried out over a short duration) and not explicit enough in straight unit cost data.

5.2.3 Unit costing and timing

Performance measurements depend to a large degree on the ability to specify the nature and quantity of output. Units of output have to be defined, and final costs related to levels of input and any necessary intermediate outputs. Unit costing and unit timing are essential tools for the managerial economist and for financial accounting, as they are two of the basic output measures available to managers. Once units of output have been satisfactorily defined in a system, output can be related to the original inputs, throughputs and intermediate outputs.

In a library there are many potential outputs which can be defined, and related to time and cost data. Whatever the unit of output, it must be 'unitary' in nature; in practice this means that it should be operationally evident and capable of unambiguous definition.

If units of output (final or intermediate) can be defined in this 'unitary' fashion, the manager will have a convenient measure of cost/performance, and/or cost-effectiveness at his disposal. A management information system should be designed so as to provide unit time and unit cost data. Unit times will tend to be fairly stable if standard operational procedures can be defined and set. Unit costs, however, may vary because of sensitivity to volume and over time because of changes in input, total costs, technical procedures and inflation.

Unit concepts in costing are important to the following areas:

- establishing unit times for job, task and process elements for further analysis or synthesis

- the development of 'standard' and 'norm' values for jobs, tasks and processes, either in time or cost terms
- relating factor inputs consumed to output produced, in time or cost terms; this is the commonest form of unit cost – the cost per specific unit of output, in monetary or time terms
- calculating actual performance rates in time or cost terms for a given subunit of the system, and not solely for specific units of output.

Libraries are familiar with the scope and uses of data of the first and third type and many make use of reported times, or collect them for their own systems, and incorporate them for costing purposes at the current factor prices. The fourth type of data are a more general case of the third, although not necessarily related to specific units of output. The second type of data are often considered desirable, for planning and control purposes, but there is little agreement about standards, or their empirical verification.

5.2.4 Cost-effectiveness measures

The term cost-effectiveness is notoriously susceptible to misunderstanding and misuse. Its correct use assumes an understanding of a number of related terms: in particular those of cost-efficiency, cost-benefit and value.

Cost-effectiveness is a measure of the efficacy with which various means will achieve a given goal or level of performance judged to be satisfactory. In a cost-effectiveness analysis the focus is on the level of output achieved or of goals satisfied. The cost-effective solution or option is the one which maximizes output and performance while keeping costs to a minimum; it is not necessarily the minimum cost solution (which might fail to deliver the level of output specified by project objectives or performance criteria).

Cost-efficiency has to be distinguished from cost-effectiveness. Cost-efficiency refers to the maximizing of the effectiveness of spending, regardless of the effectiveness in terms of stated project objectives or performance criteria. Cost-efficient spending implies the elimination of wasteful operations to achieve a given level of output at minimum cost. It does not necessarily maximize performance.

Cost-effectiveness (output orientated)	*Maximize output at a given level of cost* (not necessarily the least cost solution)
Cost-efficiency (input orientated)	*Minimize cost at a given level of output* (not necessarily the most effective solution in terms of goals or performance)

Cost-effectiveness, performance measurement and evaluation have come to occupy part of the central ground in library management debate. The cost-effective library is seen as the desirable state, providing the greatest level of performance consistent with given levels of expenditure and resource consumption. Cost-efficiency does not necessarily relate to the maximum level of performance desired. Cost-effectiveness is, however, usually consistent with a high level of cost-efficiency. In cost-effectiveness analysis there has to be a relationship between service goals and objectives and the users' (or consumers') needs, requirements, values and perceptions. Services set their goals, and therefore their performance levels, in terms of their likely response to user expectations.

Cost-effectiveness, cost-efficiency and performance analyses have always been hindered by the difficulties of measurement. Defining the performance level, and measuring performance (as output), needs, requirements, values, satisfactions and perceptions are all notoriously difficult The professional literature seems unanimous on this point.

Cost measurement does not give the whole picture, but is essential to the development of performance measures. In some ways cost becomes and serves as a measure of performance – sometimes a crude one, but never the ultimate one. Cost-effectiveness analysis is only as good as the cost data on which it is based. Hence accurate cost analysis is an essential part of cost-effectiveness and performance studies.

5.2.5 Cost-benefit measures

In the same way that the terms cost-efficiency and cost-effectiveness are sometimes confused or misapplied, so with cost-benefit. 'Cost-benefit' should not be used as a substitute for cost-effectiveness. The terms refer to two specific and different techniques. In some cases a cost-benefit analysis is in reality more akin to a 'value of benefit' analysis (in which values (levels of benefit) are assigned subjectively either by suppliers or consumers) than to an analysis in which benefits are assessed in cost terms. However, a full cost-benefit approach will consider the relative values (benefits) from options available, and try to estimate their associated costs. Different options may have different qualities of cost-efficiency and cost-effectiveness.

Cost-benefit analysis is a technique which tries to determine and evaluate the social costs and benefits of investment to help decide whether or not a project should be undertaken. The emphasis on social costs and benefits distinguishes it from other techniques of investment appraisal. The technique tries to measure the losses and gains in economic welfare to society as a whole of a particular project and different options for carrying it out; hence the focus on value concepts as much as cost concepts.

Cost-benefit analysis is an important tool of the welfare economist. It encourages consideration of impacts beyond the confines of the immediate production of a good or service. The option which provides the greatest cost-benefit level is not necessarily the most cost-efficient or cost-effective, since the criteria of judgement are based on a broader assessment than the productive cycle or stages of a project itself.

Cost-benefit measurement looks at resource allocation and economic performance 'in the round' or 'in the broad context' and actually tries to incorporate the measures and measurements derived from the choice–decision model. It is essentially a capital appraisal tool, and while cost-effectiveness analysis can be used for this purpose it is more suited to ongoing appraisal of production systems, and to shorter term operational decision making.

Cost-benefit analysis is potentially very appropriate to decisions about resource allocation in public welfare projects such as library and information services, where outputs are not always direct and tangible. Such elements as value to users (consumers), time and energy savings and externalities can be measured or assessed and incorporated in the decision model.

The contrast between cost-benefit analysis and cost-effectiveness analysis is that between a long-term view and a short to medium view.

When the choice between options can be determined in cost-benefit terms, the manager can then look at the production side to determine the most cost-effective (and cost-efficient) means of delivery of goods and services.

Cost-value analysis is less specific and less precise or formal than cost-benefit analysis. Measurement of value tends to be more subjective and qualitative than objective. Clearly, value is related to performance, and benefits are assumed to have value. Cost may provide a means of helping to measure some aspects of value, performance and benefit.

As in cost-effectiveness analysis, the ability to provide cost measurement for benefit assessment depends on the ability of the library system to provide cost data regularly. Without a general cost accounting system to provide data about internal operations, and a knowledge of wider environmental cost factors and implications, the library manager will not be in a position to implement cost benefit analysis as part of investment appraisal routine.

5.3 The categorization of costs

5.3.1 The nature of cost

Broadly speaking cost is the measure of what has to be given up or sacrificed in order to achieve an objective. Costs can be measured in different ways, but monetary values are usually the commonest sort. This section is concerned with monetary costs, which may nevertheless be derived from time 'cost' data.

This discussion on the nature of costs is derived in accordance with the conventional terminology of cost and management accounting; see for example Batty (1968), Baggott (1977), Knott (1983), Risk (1956) and numerous standard textbooks. However, it is important to develop a framework and set of conventions relevant to library and information applications. This practice is acceptable provided the conventional terminology is introduced where possible and related to what is already familiar and accepted in library and information management.

5.3.2 Classification of costs

The classification of costs is the basis of all cost accounting systems. It is the identification of each item of cost, and the systematic placement of like items of cost together according to their common characteristics. The process is an essential step in the summarization of detailed costs. Costs are classified by major functions or contexts (see Section 5.1) and within these costs are collected by cost centres and cost units.

A *cost centre* is a location, person or item of equipment (or group of these) for which costs may be ascertained for the purposes of cost control. A cost centre consists of an aggregate of lower order functions known individually as cost units.

A *cost unit* is a product, service or item (or combination of these) in relation to which costs may be ascertained for the purpose of cost control. The cost unit may be a job, batch, contract or product group depending upon the nature of the production in which the enterprise is engaged. Ultimately all cost centre costs are allocated to, or apportioned to, or absorbed by cost units.

Within cost centres and cost units, costs are further classified into *cost elements* or *categories of expense* (basically material costs, labour costs, other expenses). Cost elements are treated as direct costs (allocated) or indirect costs (apportioned).

Direct costs are referred to as prime expenses (directly traceable to the production of a cost unit or activity of a cost centre). *Indirect costs* are called overheads, and ultimately have to be absorbed by all cost units.

5.3.3 Library and information services models and accounting categories

A good starting point is to relate the familiar library and information services descriptions to the conventional cost and management accounts basis. Library systems analysis for computer applications has provided the sort of scheme which can help reconcile library and accounting usage. The Birmingham Libraries Co-operative Mechanization Programme (BLCMP) is a good example (see Appendix 2), and efforts have been made to have this conceptual model accepted as a standard (Ford, 1973; Humphreys, 1974). The classificatory basis consists of the five levels:

- subsystem
- procedure
- function
- element
- step.

The following equivalence is offered for discussion and use.

Accounting model	Library service model
Functions (may also be defined by/as dept., organization, programme or product)	Subsystem (subsuming procedures)
Cost centres	certain aspects of and types of subsystem Function (related to procedures) Some groups of elements
Cost units	Certain functions Elements Steps

In the library service model procedures are subsumed within subsystems and are related to functions at a subordinate level of analysis.

There is a rather uneasy equivalence between the terms of the library model and the accounting model. The terms in the library model overlap the categories of the accounting model. The incompatibility is a natural consequence of two valid views of reality. The idea of equivalence is only necessary and useful in so far as it helps to create the awareness that is needed in handling a cost study problem.

Management has to work with two models in the real world – one descriptive and functional (library model), the other analytical and abstract (accounting model). The bridge between the two models comes from understanding the processes of the enterprise, and being able to isolate and relate the components (system and task descriptions) to the management information being sought (cost analysis).

In the library model 'costing' takes place within functions, by identifying elements and steps (a work measurement process). Humphreys (see Appendix 2) gives a clear example of this for cataloguing (processing subsystem/catalogue function). A list of 'jobs' is given for the cataloguing section. Each job (task) can be treated as a cost centre, but there is considerable flexibility depending on what information is required, from what level and in what depth. Within the cost centre, cost units can be identified. Cataloguing (element (b)) is a cost centre; cost units could be defined in terms of material handled (new titles, new editions, standing orders, theses). Or a functional approach could be taken, cutting across the types of material – in this case cost units could be identified as location of items and movement to cataloguing work station; preparation of catalogue copy; checks made on bibliographical data in library etc.

5.3.4 The framework of cost accounting

Table 5.2 outlines a conceptual framework for costing studies presented in such a way to suggest requirements of a cost accounting and financial information system. The costing and accounting procedure can be viewed in terms of a two dimensional matrix. One dimension consists of activities and structures; the other consists of categories of primary expense.

Activities, structures and categories of expense can be, and in fact have to be, coded for the purposes of recording, manipulation and analysis. This is conventional accounting practice. The basic matrix is shown in a transformation in Figure 5.1; it is essentially the same structure. The area of cost analysis is represented by the rectangle outlined in heavy lining in Table 5.2. Other types of cost study are also included in this area, and their relationship to basic cost analysis has already been described (Section 5.2).

5.3.5 The identification of tasks, activities and structures, and the coding of cost centres and account categories

The various ways in which library and information activities and structures can be described and coded for the purposes of costing has been considered in the work on costing carried out at CLAIM. Many other cost studies such as those by Gimbel (1969), Leonard *et al.* (1969) and Humphreys (1974) have also tackled this problem. No workable consensus has emerged from all these experiences of cost study. More than two decades later the situation is still broadly the same. Practically, this means that these earlier studies can be used as a basis for contemporary investigations, bearing in mind the need to incorporate new divisions and elements derived for instance from more general information management applications. The structural principles are still broadly valid.

TABLE 5.2 The main concepts of costing

Basic concepts	*Activities and structures (objective classification)*	*Categories of primary expenses (subjective classification)*
		Expenses can be categorized in various ways
Concepts for method and technique	Tasks. (Task descriptions and account codes) Cost units. (Defined and coded) Cost centres (and responsibility centres). (Defined and coded) Programme (as cost centres). (Defined and coded) Other means of division of activities and structures	By categories of primary expenses. e.g. Risk's nine categories. e.g. Cost elements (materials, labour, expenses, etc.) (Coded appropriately – see *Figure 5.3*) As *direct* expenses and *indirect* expenses. (Coded appropriately – see *Figure 5.3*).
Information needed	Costs sought	Summation of expenses to produce final cost

Whatever tasks, activities or structures have to be costed for operational purposes, it is necessary to have a means to identify and distinguish between the various component elements for descriptive purposes. For recording, aggregating and retrieving cost data it is almost always essential and practically very useful to employ a task coding for the construction of cost accounts.

The relationship and degree of integration between individual library operations and tasks, the functional classification of library work, and the identification of cost units and cost centres has been stressed. An understanding of this relationship is necessary in order to design cost studies, and to operate accounting procedures and financial management information systems.

Given some consensus on the description of library and information tasks, an appropriate structure of cost units and cost centres can be established. The cost centres (representing functions) can be responsibility (line) orientated or programme orientated. There

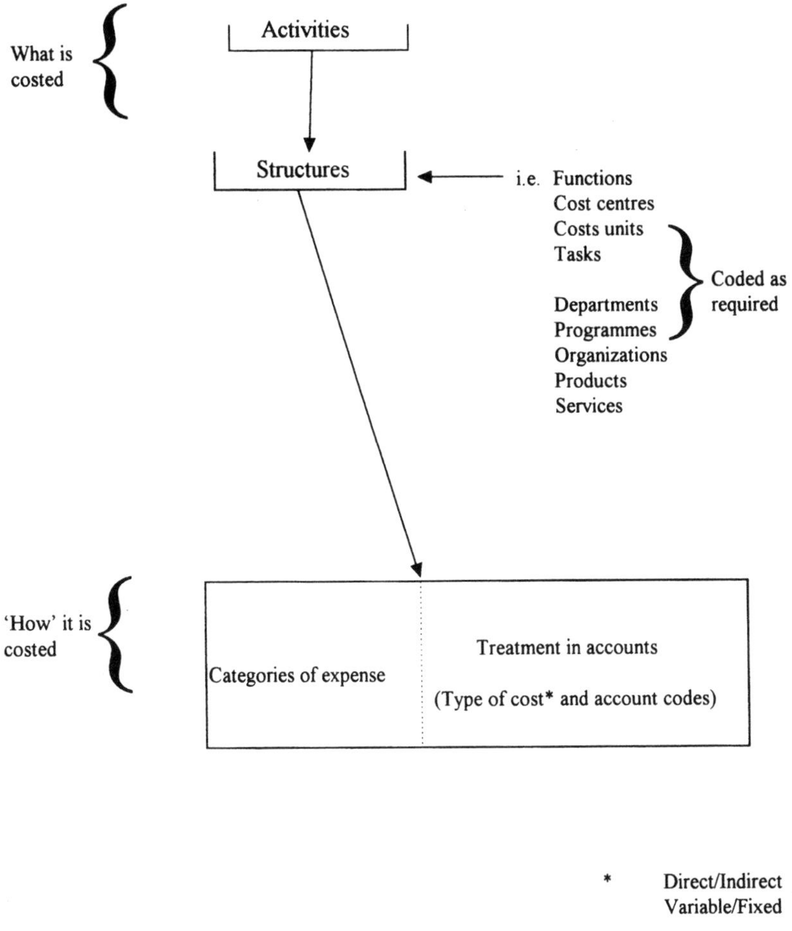

Figure 5.1. Summary of costing concepts and categories of expense

is often a need and value in presenting costs and accounts from both perspectives. In general, responsibility (line) accounting is insufficient for management information purposes, although it still tends to be the dominant form used.

A possible Task Description Listing was prepared by CLAIM with suggested codings, which could be adapted as a working model to the needs of different libraries. The simple codes can be used for reference data collection, data processing and cost account presentation (a summary is given in Appendix 4).

TABLE 5.3 Categories of primary expense (after Risk)

Categories	*Treatment in accounts*	
	Type of cost	Accounts code (after Risk) (see Appendix 3 for indicative example)
(1) Payment to and for employees	Direct and indirect	100–199 direct labour 200–299 indirect labour*
(2) Charges for materials	Direct and indirect	000–099 direct materials 300–399 indirect materials*
(3) Outside services (not elsewhere classified)	Mainly indirect	
(4) Payments for information and knowledge	Mainly indirect	
(5) External payments for protection, continuity and development	Mainly indirect	General charges Group I (400–499)*
(6) Charges, for the use of facilities	Mainly indirect	
(7) Ex-gratia payments	Mainly indirect	General charges Group II (500–599)*
(8) Payments for the use of purchasing power	Mainly indirect	
(9) Payment of taxes	Mainly indirect	

Expenses (or cost elements) have to be similarly described and coded. The nine categories outlined by Risk (1956) form a useful guide to the totality of information and the level of detail (see Table 5.3 and also Appendix 3). This scheme can be adapted for library use, and it enables the manager to distinguish between different costs to some considerable level of detail. The distinction between direct and indirect expenses is fundamental. Indirect expenses are basically the overhead expenses which have to be apportioned to cost units and cost centres. A practical example of revenue and expense codes is shown in Figure 5.2.

The general relationship between the task, activity and structure coding (for cost unit and cost centre identification) and the coding and classification of cost and expenses is shown in Figure 5.1.

The main concepts are embodied in the form of the data collection and recording instruments which are used in a cost study. Staff

PROGRAMMES & COST CENTRES		PROCEDURES							
System / programme Phrase	Sub-system / sub-programme Letter	Functions Number	Element / Step Number	Payment 100 - 199 (1)	200 - 299	Charges 00 - 99 (2)	300 - 399	General charges 400 - 499 (3)	Do. 500 - 599 (9)
(A) (GEN)	(A/Z)	001/009	001/999						
¦	¦	¦	¦						
(G) (PRO)	(A/Z)	Example: Internal editing of an EBIC Bulletin (see chapter 8.0) Code for salary costs: G.0.140 (extendible).600 (e.g. Proofreading) (from Table A4.1 G = Production 0 = In-house production 140 = Information Analyst							
¦									
K (ATT)	(A/Z)	900/999	001/999						

Source: Appendix 4 (Summary task description listing)

Source: Table 5.3 (after Risk, 1956) and Appendix 3

Figure 5.2. A sample generalized coding scheme (EBIC example)

timesheets will indicate task units, ideally identified by codes, and these are transferred and aggregated when cost data are processed. Costs sought are produced as final costs by the summation of expense items. For each task unit or cost centre, expenses can be analysed at different levels of detail as required; for example, by using all of Risk's categories.

5.3.6 The nature of primary expenses

The nature of primary expense categories is well summarized by an extract from Risk's discussion of cost accounting principles (Risk, 1956):

> A primary expense is defined as one which cannot be divided into two or more distinct types of expenditure; that is, a primary expense account holds one type of expenditure only. A cost centre has been defined as the smallest accounting unit for which costs will be collected; it may be physical location or an activity, or merely a convenient resting place for certain primary expenses, not falling readily into any other cost centre.
>
> An accounting statement may be said to be in *subjective form* when the expenditure is listed according to the totals of each kind of primary expense, that is, according to what has been the subject or nature of the expenditure, such as wages, salaries, insurance, materials, etc.
>
> On the other hand a statement is in *objective form* when the expenditure is grouped according to the purpose or object for which the expenditure has been made.
>
> Thus there is a two-dimensional classification of expenditure, first according to primary expenses, and secondly according to the object function.

This is illustrated in Figure 5.3.

5.3.7 The expenses incurred in library and information operations

This section takes a more detailed look at the types of current expenses incurred in library and information services. The practical treatment of these categories in cost studies of library and information services is indicated. Not every library would find it necessary, worthwhile, or advantageous to obtain, analyse, and present cost data in quite the detail envisaged in a standard industrial enterprise scheme such as the one provided by Risk (Appendix 3). Some of the industrial and commercial categories are inappropriate or occur rarely.

(1) Type of expense: A, B, C, D, ...
(2) Type of activity: I, II, III, IV, ...

Subjective

Type of expense	Objective / Department						Total
	I	II	III	IV	V	etc.	
A							a
B							b
C							c
D							d
etc.							
Total	1	2	3				Grand Total

Figure 5.3. Analysis of expenditure

But the principle of approach is the same. Subjective and objective accounts can be identified; objective accounts can take a responsibility (line) approach and/or a programme approach. Expenses have to be broken down into useful categories and cost accounts constructed so as to provide a variety of views, cuts or perspectives from whatever data can be obtained about the activities under review. This is one of the essences of cost and management accounting – the use of some very basic and elemental cost data to construct other indices which reflect the special needs of a problem (e.g. marginal costing, or breakeven analysis on a product run) and the needs and views of managements as resource allocators (e.g. the current level of unit costs, the anticipated costs of a new project or product, or when to make an investment decision etc.).

Payments to and for employees (category 1)

Invariably payments to and for staff represent the largest item of expenditure in a library and information service. Typically, between

50 and 80 per cent of expenditure is consumed under this heading. Direct expenditure will take the form of wages and salary payments, but most organizations will have to carry indirect or staff overhead costs. The most common indirect staff costs are for social and health insurance payments: these may or may not be charged directly to the library budget, and so may or or may not be recorded as expenditure, but the payments still have to be accounted for when total costs of a programme or function are calculated. Indirect staff costs range up to as much as 50 per cent of direct costs for staff in any given department.

Thus staff costs must be identified in terms of direct and indirect expenditure (supported by the direct budget of another department or programme). Costing practices have to take account of wage and salary rises and increments, as well as bonus and other special payments.

A library will often have to rely on the host institution accounting for details of staff expenditure. Many wage and salary payments are the subject of national or standard rates and scales. The librarian must ensure that internal records are kept up to date with this information. The timing of payments and awards has to be known. All these factors have a bearing on the calculation of staff costs and are especially important in preparing the staff items in expenditure estimates and budget proposals.

Charges for materials (category 2)

Documents and other information materials form the primary category within materials expenditure. After staff expenditure has been determined the bookfund or library materials budget usually represents the main part of library resources over which real decision power can be exercised: for example, through the book selection practices followed. The usual need to deal with a range of suppliers, and the fact that regular payments take place and contracts are entered into means that materials expenditures have be very well recorded and accounted.

Once the bookfund has been determined and allocated, usually over one financial year, the accessions and book order section must take steps to see that the orders, and their current position, are accurately documented, and that a running balance of each fund is kept when orders are placed, committed and paid for. The book order department usually provides the nearest analogy to those departments of a business enterprise where current cash accounts are kept in a regular and systematic fashion. There is often a link to the central accounts and payments system, if the library information unit operates within a host organization, and management and financial data are provided by this system.

The total materials expenditure, the average cost per item and the amount spent per fund or department are the most common cost measures kept both for current management accounting and control, and for estimate and budget preparation.

Various library materials price indices are produced. In the UK the *Bookseller*, the *Library Association Record*, and the Library and Information Statistics Unit (LISU) at Loughborough University with its Academic Book Prices Index, produce indices for books and periodicals. In the USA several indices are regularly summarized in the *Bowker Annual* and the *Library Journal*. Other European countries (notably Germany) and Australia also produce library material price and cost indices.

Other materials charges will be for office and business equipment and supplies. Annual charges for equipment may often be considered as part of materials expenditure. Recurrent maintenance and cleaning charges may also be entered under this heading. In practice for sundry small items expenditure the allocation to one or another heading may well depend on local circumstances, and be a very flexible process.

Outside services (category 3)

Expenditure on services supplied by outside contractors is becoming increasingly common in library and information services, especially since the development of computer-based bibliographical services. Most outside services of this type quote prices, rates, and tariffs, which mean that anticipated expenditures can be budgeted for in advance. Outside service suppliers often permit the negotiation of special rates and terms for their services, and current costs and volume of consumption have to be reappraised from time to time to see whether or not more advantageous terms can be obtained.

Traditional items of expenditure under this category have included the purchase of catalogue cards from centralized services such as the British National Bibliography and the Library of Congress. The contemporary equivalent is the acquisition of downloaded bibliographic records from cataloguing services like Blaise and OCLC. Often professional fees for auditors and accountants have to be paid, and more frequently libraries are calling upon the services of external consultants to perform a variety of special technical and managerial tasks. Nowadays the purchase of special information services is the major category under this heading, and this stems from the developing role of the library as an intermediary and broker within a range of information networks. Again, the actual charging practice for costing may vary; annual fees may be charged under the outside service category, and connect time charges as a material expense. With CD Rom and multimedia products, which are part material and part service in nature, the best approach is one of consistent allocation to a category; undoubtedly, large sums may be spent on such media, which gives them a capital or fixed cost orientation.

Payments for information and knowledge (category 4)
This category of primary expense is of greater significance to the business enterprise, since it covers payments for professional services necessary to meet the legal obligations placed upon companies, for example to retain the services of lawyers, accountants, business consultants and medical and social services. These are payments from one business usually to another professional business. The library and information unit will from time to time have to make payment to professional bodies and library co-operatives and networks. Payments for the education and training of staff should also be included under this heading.

External payments for protection, continuity and development (category 5)
More and more frequently library and information units are considering the desirability of ensuring adequate insurance cover for their materials and equipment. In a period of inflation it is likely that library stocks may be both undervalued and underinsured. Similarly there is a renewed interest in a whole range of security systems. Capital and recurrent charges can be incurred under this heading of expense which may be quite significant in the budget of a large research, educational or public library.

Charges for the use of facilities (category 6)
A library and information unit will often have to make direct payments of rent, mortgage, lease payments, rates on property and local taxes for the building premises it occupies. Sometimes these payments will be indirect, being absorbed within the budget of the host institution. Indirect payments should not be neglected when costing library operations. Accommodation charges may include an element of maintenance and upkeep costs. Whether direct or

indirect these payments may represent a substantial charge, and therefore a significant element in costs.

It may be preferable to charge equipment costs under this heading, rather than under materials, especially if the items concerned can be classed as capital goods. Office and computer equipment are principal items in this area, and purchase costs, debt charges and depreciation have to be identified.

Other expenses (categories 7–9)
These expenses are less frequently encountered in library and information services, but are noted here for completeness. A library might wish to add its own special account headings in this area to complete its classification of costs.

Ex-gratia payments From time to time the library may have to make ex-gratia payments to its staff or clients, or to those from whom it has received goods and services. Hospitality payments could be included under this heading.

Payments for the use of purchasing power The interest charges on a loan used to buy capital equipment are a payment for the use of purchasing power. With the increasing use of new technology and equipment in libraries, such charges may become a more significant element of expense.

Payment of taxes In most cases the library and information unit is part a host institution, which will usually arrange through its central financial machinery to be responsible for tax liabilities. For costing purposes the manager should try to become aware of the real tax liability incurred by the unit. The business enterprise is in a much more difficult, involved and complex position with respect to tax liability – one reason why management accounting for this sector is and needs to be so much more sophisticated than in welfare organizations such as library and information services.

.3.8 Revenues

For costing purposes almost the entire focus of attention is on expenditure categories. However, a management accounting system will also make provision to record sources of revenue and income. Information on income and revenue is especially important in budgeting since past, present and future allocations have to be monitored and compared. The majority of library revenue for publi and academic libraries, and many special libraries comes in th form of a grant from the parent body. The revenue distribution i shown in the allocation of the budget. The revenue contributio of different sections of the library is an important consideration too especially income earned from the sale of services.

Cost studies and management accounting in effect show th diminishment of revenue through spending. Programme orientate accounts showing revenue allocations and cost flows (expenditures unit costs etc.) can provide a detailed and powerful source c management control over resources. Cost distribution studies ca supplement the general picture; and detailed cost analysis an unit costing will give more depth. Cost-effectiveness, cost-benefi and cost-value studies can give even greater depth, qualitatively an quantitatively, to management knowledge. The effectiveness c expenditure from revenue can become fully known through progression of cost study and management accounting methods The manager's interest in the revenue section of accounts refers t the disbursement of revenue (spending) as much as to the source of that revenue.

A wider discussion of income generation and revenue budget can be found in Section 3.8 above.

5.4 Calculation of costs

Specific costs relating to any stage in the sequence of library processe are obtained by converting labour (or sometimes machine or othe process) times to monetary values using salary and wage rates (c machine hour rates, for example) and by adding other expens elements as appropriate (e.g. staff overheads, direct materials etc.).

Many specific costs can and will be aggregated by programme section or management responsibility to provide more gener higher level cost measures. For example, specific costs from th main stages of technical processing (book order, through cata loguing to physical processing) can be aggregated to give a tot cost for book processing. Costs can be reconstructed to highligh different aspects of the performance and economics of the system Budget projections and actual expenditures can be manipulate as in a cost allocation study to provide specific measures b programme, section, responsibility or period of time, and comple mentary cost measures produced and evaluated.

Once basic time data and categories of expense have been identified for a given function or task the process of costing is one of addition, combination and transfer of cost flows according to the accounting structure of the system. The principal pitfalls concern the problem of double counting of costs or the failure to allocate full costs to a particular activity or programme; this is simply the equivalent of overcharging and undercharging.

For costing activities it is usually most convenient to reduce staff (or machine) costs to a consolidated hourly rate, although for budgeting and aggregated analysis annual rates can be used. The manager should have a clear idea of the staff cost structure currently in force. It may be useful at some point for the manager to synthesize (determine an appropriate consolidated rate from direct and indirect elements) the appropriate staff costs for internal use, but it is also common for staff costs to be 'supplied' by the host organization's finance department, and in practice there may be some haziness about full staff costs (especially over and above social benefit overheads).

In government departments and large firms or public authorities the librarian may use consolidated staff costs by different grades of staff, which may include realistic full overhead costing. The manager needs to have the latest salary and wage scales to hand. Where long salary scales exist with many employees at different points on them the practice of using median salary is common. It hardly needs to be emphasized that there is often sensitivity about discussion of handling of salary data for costing purposes.

By comparison materials costs should present fewer problems. The regular filing of all invoices and records of invoices passed for payment will cover most categories of materials costs. Published materials price indices should be used and a collection maintained for reference and use in budget preparation. Other categories of expenses should be treated in a similar fashion, with a helpful filing system used for maintaining documentation. Data should be kept and regularly updated on the prices of various services consumed by the library, noting discounts and direct debits. Services obtained on subscription should be carefully monitored to note that payments have been made and to scrutinize any changes and increases in price. Certain expense cost items may be difficult to procure, particularly for shared utilities and centrally provided services: lighting water, gas, cleaning, rate payments and local taxes. The manager should develop some liaison with appropriate finance officers so that these figures which compose elements of the general library overhead are up to date and accurate.

The whole question of overheads and indirect cost computation is usually complex and prone to difficulty; this is the experience of industry and commercial concerns, and is no less so in the public and welfare sector when an effort is made to obtain realistic figures. Once the overhead elements are known it is essential to oversee this area of costing by up-to-date information and by liaison with finance officers in host institutions. A thorough knowledge of indirect costs is essential if 'full costs' are to be known. When pricing decisions have to be made it may be essential to allow for full cost recovery.

In looking at the total cost structure of the library service decisions will have to be made about the allocation and apportionment of overheads/indirect costs. This is important at the estimate and budgeting stage, and when cost allocation studies are undertaken. Overheads for buildings can be conveniently reduced to a rate per square metre per annum. So far as a library is concerned it may be useful and necessary to distinguish between internal overheads and external overheads (the proportion of total institutional costs carried by the library or information unit).

5.5 Capital charges, current costs and overheads

Business enterprise accounts have to distinguish between current and capital flows. At the same time the manager has to be aware of relationships between the two kinds of monetary flows. Systems of taxation and tax liability recognize the relationships between capital and current accounts, and the financial strategies of enterprises try to order their affairs to gain the maximum advantage in minimizing their tax liabilities. Government fiscal policies can ease the burden of investment by offering tax allowances against capital commitments.

Capital financing in library and information units is by and large a different process from that of the business enterprise. The host institution (and there usually is one especially in the public sector) is responsible for the management of capital spending and for any financial aspects of capital account transactions. The library and information unit therefore usually receives its capital in the form of an allocation or grant, which is earmarked for spending on certain previously agreed projects. Such organizations do not have a direct relationship with the capital market, nor they carry the financial obligations of this. In theory this makes the job of the library manager a lot simpler than that of his counterpart in industry and commerce when it comes to financing investment and capital budgeting.

In many cases the library manager has to take little account of capital flows in management accounting, because the library itself does not have to finance the capital. However, for management accounting and costing, capital costs have to be identified as fixed costs, and are often best dealt with by a reduction to some kind of annual overhead charge. This annual overhead should take account of the cost of capital and depreciation charges. In comparison with commercial enterprises, libraries rarely have to enter the complex business of asset valuation.

Accounting for overhead costs (as fixed or indirect costs) is a major issue in an organization, so that actual total operating costs can be calculated with all possible precision, and so that the direct element in cost is clearly identified. Failure to account for all sources of overhead and to allocate them fairly is a common source of financial and cost inefficiency. What is invisible is often forgotten, with serious consequences which may be discovered too late.

There are two sets of overhead to bear in mind. First, as argued earlier, capital charges must be distributed as an annual overhead charge, which will include depreciation allowances. Second, a portion of annual variable costs needs to be treated as overhead (semi-fixed costs), mainly to account for common costs and charges that cannot be allocated directly to a given unit of output or cost centre. Terminology can be confusing here, so the organization needs to make its definitions and usage clear. The total annual variable costs can be regarded as the sum of the current expenditure budget (and made up of the direct variable costs plus the indirect (or semi-fixed) costs.

Another characteristic to bear in mind derives from the relative nature of capital and current spending. For example, the construction of a library building represents a capital amount for the library, but for the building contractor it represents current expenditure on labour and materials. Likewise, many smaller capital expenditures in a library have a strong current cost element in them too. For instance, the establishment of a computer-based information unit, would over a year include direct capital expenditure on equipment, plus a whole range of current operational expenditures.

Clearly, all the input costs of service establishment have to be identified and divided between fixed and variable expenses (indirect and direct costs to use an alternative but equally acceptable terminology). When in the case of a library the capital is really a grant sum the relative flexibility of current and capital accounting conventions is apparent. At the level of output costs, the fixed and variable distinction is important when pricing decisions have to be taken and especially when marginal costs are required to appraise volume/price relationships.

Reducing capital charges and other fixed costs to a standard overhead charge is a useful technique when trying to synthesize a whole range of operational and programme costs. The library manager may find this the best compromise to overcome many difficult technical problems of costing programmes over a long period.

Full lifecycle costing is likely to become more important to library managers as they are faced with the prospects of technological change and initiatives such as long-term depository storage programmes; consolidating many individual cost elements to an overhead rate provides an attractive means of introducing cost control to long-term planning. Stephens (1988) provides a library application and Smith (1991) reviews the matter in Chapter Five of his study; the topic is treated in most standard works on industrial cost accounting and cost management.

The concept has proven attractive to acquisitions and collection management librarians trying to gain an appreciation of the total costs of holding an item in stock, and for appreciating the lifecycle of a book from purchase to disposal. The next step is thus to move from a lifecycle process to a lifecycle cost. These questions arose from the debates in the 1970s about research library buildings and storage and relegation alternatives. The results of these explorations tended to have some shock value when it was realized that a lifecycle cost of a book could be several factors greater than the purchase cost. One major question is how far to draw the cost boundary, both upstream and downstream of the item itself.

Life cycle costing is also gaining credence as an environmental or 'green' accounting tool. The total environmental cost of a course of action has to include pollution costs and environmental control costs. So if information in all its forms and guises becomes the resource, its lifecycle costing needs to be known. The information society is creating significant information environments; so the costs of user actions and user behaviour in information and communication can be better understood if subjected to a lifecycle approach. Whatever the application decision making should be improved through lifecycle costing. However, the foundation for such studies must lie in greater facility to produce and manage cost data as part of the normal run of events. All the more reason then for giving cost measurement its due attention.

5.6 Measurement of labour time input

5.6.1 Method study and work measurement

Work measurement, as a method of studying labour time spent on a task, is complementary to method study. Together, these two techniques make-up the field of work study, which forms an essential first stage in the analytical costing of work operations, particularly where tasks are well defined, structured and observable. The purpose of this section is to give a concise introduction to the main principles of work measurement. The cost analyst will need to consult more specialized texts for further guidance: for example, Gilder and Schofield, (1976); Gimbel, (1969); Leonard, (1969); or standard textbooks e.g. Barnes, (1963); Currie, (1972); Knott (1983). A summary of method study and work measurement practices are shown in Figures 5.4 and 5.5. This introduction is heavily indebted to the excellent outline on work study prepared by the International Labour Office (1958).

Method study is the principal technique for reducing work content, which is primarily a matter of eliminating unnecessary movement on the part of material or operatives and of substituting good methods for poor.

Work measurement is concerned with investigating, reducing and subsequently eliminating ineffective time (time during which no effective work is being performed, whatever its cause). It is also an important technique in establishing work standards/time standards. For costing purposes it may be sufficient to investigate the use of time. By using work measurement techniques, methods can be standardized and reliable valid time data obtained. Adverse cost patterns might suggest the need for further action on eliminating less effective procedures.

Work measurement provides the basic information necessary for investigating, organizing and controlling library activities in which the sacrifice of time plays a significant part. However, it is by nature better suited to the investigation and assessment of repetitive tasks with a high physical work content. Since much library work consists of non-repetitive tasks with a high mental activity content which is not physically observable, the more formal industrial applications

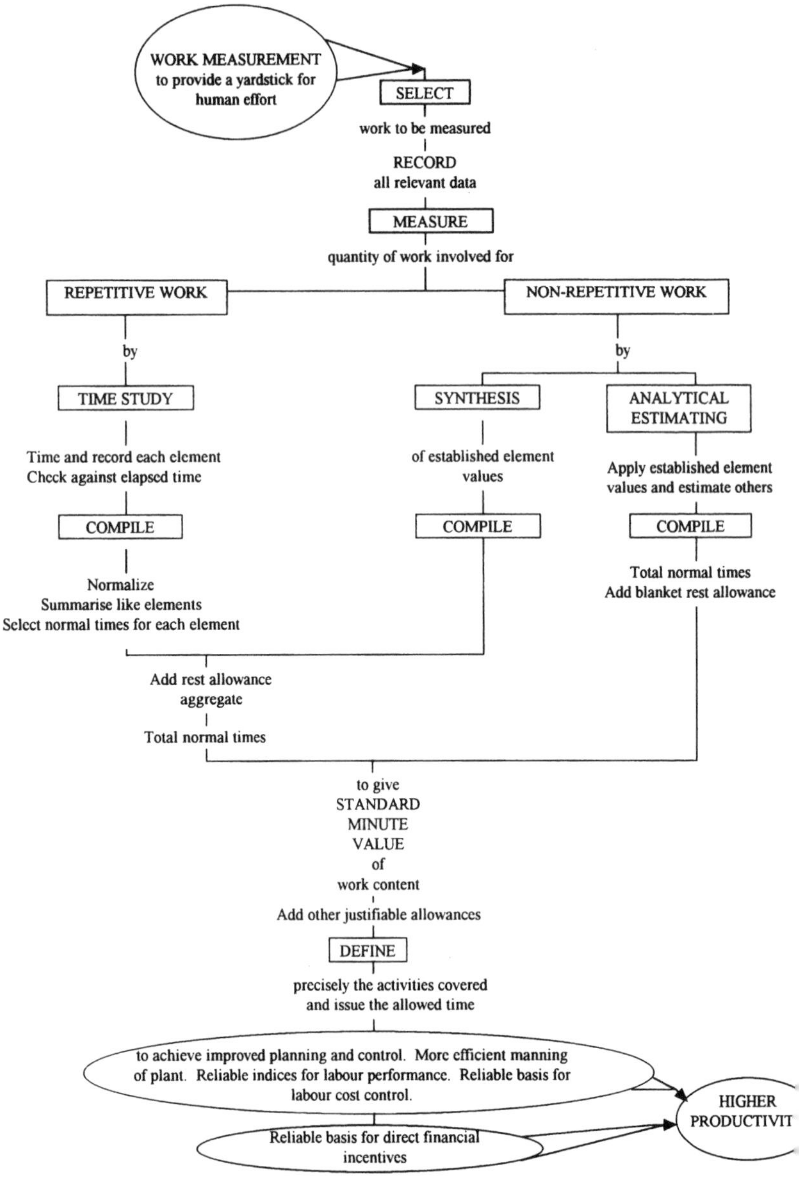

Figure 5.4. Method study (after Imperial Chemical Industries Limited)

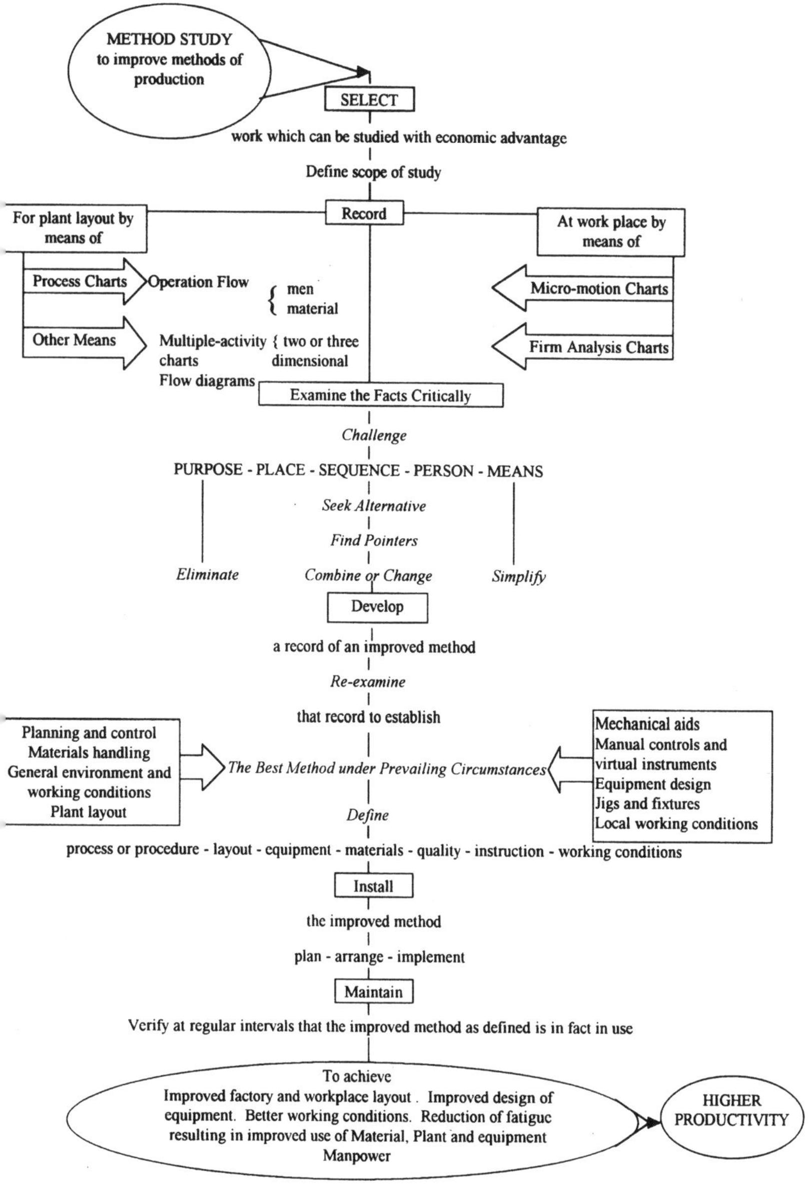

Figure 5.5. Work measurement (after Imperial Chemical Industries Limited)

of work measurement for time study will be limited. Nevertheless, work measurement principles provide the basis for developing methods of time measurement appropriate to library work and cost calculation.

More generally, in the process of assessing work and setting standards, work measurement may be used:

- to compare the efficiency of alternative methods. Other factors being equal, the method which takes the least time will be the best time
- to balance the work of members of teams and between sections, departments or functions
- to determine the optimum mix of man–machine–material interaction and activity.

Once time standards are available they may be used:

- to provide information on which planning and scheduling of production can be based, including equipment and labour requirements for carrying out the programme of work and the utilization of available capacity
- to provide information on which estimates for budget, charging and service delivery can be based
- to set standards for equipment utilization and labour performance, which can be used for the above purposes and for incentive and motivational purposes
- to provide information for labour cost control and to enable standard costs to be fixed and maintained.

The basic steps of work measurement

SELECT	the work to be studied
RECORD	all the relevant data relating to the circumstances in which the work is being done, the methods and the elements of activity in them
MEASURE	each element in terms of time over a sufficient number of cycles of activity to ensure that a

	representative picture has been obtained (time study)
EXAMINE	(i) the recorded data and time elements critically to ensure unproductive or random elements are separated from productive elements
	(ii) the recorded times of each element and determine a representative time for each
COMPILE	a time for the operation which will provide a realistic standard of performance and will include time allowances to cover suitable rest, personal needs and contingencies
DEFINE	precisely the series of activities and method of operation for which the time has been allowed and issue the time as a standard for the activities and methods specified

It will only be necessary to take the full range of steps if a time is being established as a performance standard. Where work measurement is being used solely as a tool of investigation of ineffective time before or during a method study, or to compare the effectiveness of alternative methods or to collect time data for costing, only the first four steps are likely to be needed.

5.6.2 Time study

Time study is a technique for determining as accurately as possible from a limited number of observations the time necessary to carry out activity at a defined standard of performance.

There is a number of well established methods, techniques and protocols for collecting time data. The relevant sections in the ILO manual provide an excellent introduction, and many textbooks cover the ground thoroughly.

There are seven basic steps in making a time study.

1 Obtaining and recording all the information available about the job, the operator and the surrounding conditions likely to affect the carrying out of the work.

2 Recording a complete description of the method and breakin down the operation into elements.

3 Measuring with a timing device (usually a stopwatch) an recording the time taken by the operator to perform eac element of the operation.

4 At the same time assessing the effective speed of the workin of the operator relative to the predetermined 'normal' speed.

5 Converting the observed times to 'normal times'.

6 Determining the allowances to be made over and above th normal time for the operation.

7 Determining the 'allowed time' for the operation.

In a time study the job, process or operation is broken down int elements. An element is a distinct constituent part of a specifie activity or task composed of one or more fundamental motion and/or machine or process activities selected for convenience o observation or timing.

A work cycle is the complete sequence of elements necessary t perform a specified task or activity or to yield a unit of production It may include elements which do not occur in every cycle.

A detailed breakdown into elements is necessary:

- to ensure that productive work (or effective time) is separate from unproductive activity (or ineffective time)
- to permit the rate of performance to be assessed more accu rately than would be the case if the assessment were made ove a complete cycle
- to enable elements involving a high fatigue component to b isolated and to make the allocation of rest allowances mor accurate
- to enable time standards to be checked so that the later omissio or insertion of elements can be quickly detected
- to enable a detailed job specification to be produced
- to enable standard time values for frequent recurring element to be established.

Elements may be repetitive, constant, variable, occasional o foreign:

- repetitive elements recur in every cycle of a given activity or task
- constant elements identical in specification and time occur in two or more operations
- variable elements are those in which time of performance varies with some characteristic of the product, equipment or process
- occasional elements do not occur in every cycle of the task, but occur at regular or irregular intervals
- foreign elements are not a necessary part of the operation or activity.

There are certain general principles which govern the selection of elements.

1 Elements should be easily identifiable with definite beginnings and endings, so that once established they can be repeatedly recognized.

2 Elements should be as short as can be conveniently timed by a trained observer. A range of 2 seconds to 20 seconds is considered optimal.

3 Elements should be as unified as possible.

4 Manual activities and times should be separated from machine activities and times.

5 Constant elements should be separated from variable elements.

6 Elements which do not occur in every cycle should be kept separate from those that do.

The importance of proper selection, definition and description of elements must be emphasized. The amount of detail in the description will depend on a number of factors.

Small batch jobs which occur infrequently require less detailed element descriptions than those in which output is greater.

Movement from place to place generally requires less description than hand and arm movement.

Elements should be checked through a number of cycles and written down before timing begins.

The foregoing remarks apply specifically to detailed work measurement time studies, but they apply equally to other methods of time and work measurement calculation, particularly analytical estimating.

For the library and information manager the most problematic area is deciding on the elements to be measured. For example how far should cataloguing or reader service tasks be broken down to differentiate meaningful segments of work, which can and should be separately measured. Aggregates of elements will ultimately become co-equivalent with cost units and cost centres and other functional categories having management information significance.

5.6.3 Time accounting conventions

For practical purposes time and cost studies require the use of certain conventions for providing a common basis for cost analysis and time rate calculations. It is very important that these conventions are recognized, understood and used properly. The following provides general guidance.

Total working time It is necessary to know the total working time for which labour is available for organizational purposes; in many circumstances this will be defined contractually. The most helpful convention is to take beginning to end working times e.g. 0900 to 1230 hrs and 1330 to 1700 hrs for five days per week (with the main meal break not counted for remuneration purposes).

For costing purposes the time needed for statutory leave and agreed absence on medical or social grounds are included.

The total working time is required to calculate the hourly salary rate and logically this has to be derived from the total number of hours which the employer has to pay staff in order to retain their services (e.g. total annual work hours). The non-productive element of total working time is a retention cost for labour (e.g. rest breaks and relaxation time allowances).

Available working time This is the actual time available for productive work and is important when estimation methods and exceptional task reporting is used to assess times spent on different tasks. For example, in an inter-library loan section the time spent on non-inter-library loan work would be assessed and then subtracted from the available working time; the balance of time (for which detailed task investigation and measurement may not be carried out) is then assumed to be spent directly on inter-library loan tasks.

The value chosen for available working time for cost study purposes should exclude minor refreshment and comfort breaks (for which it is useful to agree a standard value), vacations and leave of absence and agreed relaxation time (a standard percentage allowance-based performance rating, and conventionally appearing to vary between 10 and 20 per cent). These exclusions are deducted from the total working time, and the net remainder is the available working time.

Relaxation time allowance The determination of an adequate relaxation allowance is often a source of controversy. The International Labour Organisation (ILO) favours 18 per cent total working time, but many library studies have used 16 per cent.

Unit times It is quite feasible for a unit time to be made up of actual output time (available working time), or from total time (total working time) which includes nominally non-productive time. Every time study should make quite clear which convention is being used.

5.7 Generalized cost measurement models

5.7.1 The concept of a generalized cost measurement model

The desirability of a common focus and common concepts for library service cost studies is implicit throughout this discussion. This goal is worth pursuing to gain greater clarity of understanding in the costing of library operations and to achieve more comparability between cost studies. It will not be easy to achieve any of this in practice, so the best that can be done is to aim for a compromise solution. As yet no generalized cost measurement model which can describe the cost position of a library and provide the manager with information for decision has been developed and tested. Thus, in the discussion of task categorization (Section 5.3.5) mention has been made of a number of schemes. At the present time the final choice on use has to be left with each manager, and field testing and adaptation are still essential before acceptable standards can be promulgated.

There are some cost studies reported in the literature which may have more general applicability and may thus be the basis for future development. These may serve as preliminary models for a more general model of methods and practices, which in the long term should be the desirable goal. However, the working experience and approval of library managers in general would be required. Particular cost studies can be rated against these desirable criteria.

A generalized cost measurement model would need to have the following basic characteristics.

1 It would have to be applicable to many different types of library and information service, and therefore would need a highly developed task categorization and description of library and information work.

2 A set of definitions of inputs and associated expenses would be a primary feature.

3 Methods of time and cost recording and data collection would have to be harmonized and standardized, recognizing that exceptional cases requiring specific treatment would exist.

4 Methods and techniques of processing, analysis and interpretation would have to be explicit.

5 Ideally, performance measures related to output cost would have to be defined, so that costs are being generated for a clear and explicit purpose (compare with the concept of managerially useful costs and measurements, already discussed). In the long run, costing for the sake of establishing cost alone is not enough; costs have to relate directly to performance structures, and decisions taken on options using a cost performance discriminator.

6 Operational definitions for manual and computer application would also be needed.

No set of standards for library cost studies has yet been written, although the desirability and benefits of such a scheme have been long recognized. It has been difficult, if not impossible, to identify one or two cost studies in the literature that meet all the desirable requirements identified in this discussion.

5.7.2 Measurement or estimation?

One of the major technical problems in practical cost analysis is work measurement – assessing the labour time spent on tasks. It has to be accepted that special work measurement studies, and any prolonged monitoring by or of specific individuals of the time budget and work output are irksome. Attempts to simplify measurement and recording procedures introduce greater generality, and often less reliability and validity into results.

To circumvent some of these problems the practice of estimating time budgets instead seems to be widely prevalent – this is done by employee self-appraisal or by supervisors. Staff availability data and cost data can be extracted from line budgets. Some reviewing with staff has to be done, but a qualitative (rather than a quantitative) approach is taken. 'Reasonable' estimates are produced and these can at least be checked and revised periodically. Where work is organized clearly by section and subsection, job title and work content often correspond, and the estimates can be used with some confidence. Some questioning on 'exceptional' tasks is often necessary, but estimation of time budgets for costing has to be done with discretion. It is less suitable where staff are involved in multiple tasks which legitimately might have to be cross-allocated to different cost centres. Estimating techniques are often appropriate for the small library and information unit, where the pressures of time and work prohibit a work measurement exercise (e.g. staff spend short spells on very many tasks).

It has to be acknowledged that estimation of time budgets is a convenient solution to data collection. The possibility of gross errors (and even important minor ones) can be reduced by nominating a costing co-ordinator in the library. Regular monitoring could bring an element of quality control to the library processes themselves, regardless of the value of the exercise for costing. Alternatively, more formal work measurement studies could be carried out periodically, perhaps on a rotating basis between departments.

Estimating output, and allocating output to time budgets and work areas or functions can be an equally difficult task. There should be some balance or control between the nature and level of data collection about inputs and the same for output data in terms of quality and consistency, validity and reliability. The development of more embracing cost accounting systems by library management and more refined and worker acceptable methods of collecting such data could ease the difficulties. All this points to the need for everyone to know the uses to which cost data are to be put. Where staff motivation towards achieving a target level of performance in the library is high, and where management style is participative rather than directive there is likely to be greater acceptance of work measurement and costing procedures. Removing the element of fear, which in turn creates employee hostility, is crucial.

Estimation is useful for preliminary studies and for 'hunch' and 'hypothesis' testing in a system. On the basis of these preliminary studies it might be necessary to proceed to more formal work measurement in certain areas. What is required is an intelligent and flexible strategy for combining estimation and work measurement. Ideally, over a period of time the levels of resource flows and time allocations should be accurately estimated to a high degree of confidence for the main programme areas. Work measurement can then be used to fill in the details of specific operations, and cross-programme activities. This accounting strategy could be described as analysis downwards rather than synthesis upwards.

Work measurement has been adapted and used in libraries although it hardly rates as a popular standard technique. Gimbel (1969) and Leonard *et al.* (1969) have carried out detailed and wide ranging studies to obtain unit times and costs; these are both classic library studies. From time to time studies are reported in the literature. To date there has been virtually no consistency of method and surprisingly little borrowing and adaptation from other studies. One attempt to develop a preferred practice is to be found in the administrative effectiveness procedure developed by the Library Management Research Unit (Centre for Library and Information Management, 1980). This package contains all the main information and guidance required for a simple but effective library work measurement study. The outline of work measurement given in Section 5.6.1 provides managers with the groundwork for basic appreciation.

5.7.3 Cost analysis and cost studies: methods and practices summarized

In categorizing cost studies the process of cost analysis has been identified as the basic element (Section 5.2.1), and as a series of steps for implementation (see Chapter Six). The defining features of cost analysis are that a sequence of measurements and observations are actually carried out around the course of a given process. If actual sequential observation and measurement is not possible the cost analysis should strictly be called cost estimation.

Inputs are identified in terms of productive factors (labour, materials etc.), the quantities allocated to the process are established, and their costs identified, either as input prices or as costs likely to be incurred (principally through labour time expended at the appropriate labour cost rate), but also from calculations dependent on aggregate measures such as overhead and depreciation rates.

Throughput (or the stages of the process when work is performed) is identified using systems analysis and description and relevant cost indices constructed using input data, which can be used to monitor and assess performance. Work study and work measurement (time measurement) can be carried out as part of standard cost analysis technique. The managers' interest in throughput will be principally focused on efficiency, effectiveness and productivity. The optimization or maximization of performance is sought at the throughput stage. Efficient throughput should ensure effective output. A cost analysis at the throughput stage is concerned with performance during the actual work process. A cost analysis at this stage can be performed at various levels (the staff member, the equipment used, the organizational section) and for various stages or elements in the process.

Output may be registered in intermediate or final terms. Most output cost analysis is concerned with assigning a cost (or time) to a unit of production (however defined in terms of the process studied). An output cost analysis is the summation of the calculated input costs and their conversion as throughput. Input cost provides the basic cost platform of minimum expenditure, and in theory could be equated with fixed or non-variable costs. Throughput cost (with its usually high labour element in libraries and service industries) determines the actual incurred costs for the process and can be substantially associated with the concept of variable costs. The throughput costs can vary widely – often wildly – depending on the efficiency of management in controlling work processes. The management role is crucial in terms of cost reduction and cost minimization, and the productivity rate of any process is substantially determined at this stage.

Output cost is also concerned with volume of production, and the final productivity of capital (materials, labour etc.) applied to a process. Output cost analysis is the basis for developing cost performance measures, or cost as a performance measure, and for using cost as one method of price setting.

The other types of cost study (cost distribution (and the related studies of expenditure distribution, allocation and budget), unit costing, the determination of various indices of economic costs and management costs, cost-effectiveness and cost-benefit) all depend on cost analysis in full or in part but may have to be supplemented with cost estimation as a substitute for full cost analysis.

The distinguishing feature of cost analysis is that it is concerned with actual (i.e. concurrent) measurement of the productive process. Cost analysis can be a one-off or a continuous process. Above all it should be confused neither with cost measurement derived from budgeted or actual (i.e. historic) expenditures (both of which are often (but misleadingly) called cost analysis), nor with a retrospective (non-concurrent) analysis, which should also be called cost estimation. A 'cost distribution' based on aggregate expenditures (applied retrospectively) is not a cost analysis (in the strict sense of the word). 'Cost distribution' based on a budget proposal is more correctly referred to as a budget distribution or allocation.

A cost distribution is a legitimate cost study tool, but it does not conform to the criterion for cost analysis – the concurrent, ongoing, actual sequential collection of cost data from a productive process.

The 'active' emphasis in cost analysis is the reason why time study (work measurement) is given its primacy as a tool of analysis. Work measurement is labour orientated – it is the study of people carrying out work. The increased role of machinery in library work requires other distinctive techniques of costs measurement and cost analysis (fixed costs forming a greater feature, reflected in any unit costs which are derived).

Figure 5.6 attempts to show the relationship between time studies and cost studies. Methods (1) to (5) are different methods of assessing times spent on tasks, and the time data derived from them form an essential element in cost analysis and cost estimation.

Direct time studies (1) use work study and work measurement techniques; these methods are only really suitable for analysing certain types of operation and task times. Some library technical processes with an industrial or repetitive element can be treated in this way, but the method is unsatisfactory with irregular, varied or intellectual tasks (for instance where the work input necessary to complete a job is not solely performed at one defined work station).

Work diaries (2) can be used when a variety of tasks is being performed. This permits an independent staff orientated approach to measurement which may be acceptable, especially for relatively short periods of time; using exceptional task reporting the range of the technique and its acceptability can sometimes be extended.

Activity sampling (method 3) can sometimes provide an economic solution to field data collection, and applications to library work have been quite successful, yielding useful and reliable time data. The library operations which have to be costed often consist of many component tasks and it may be possible to derive useful

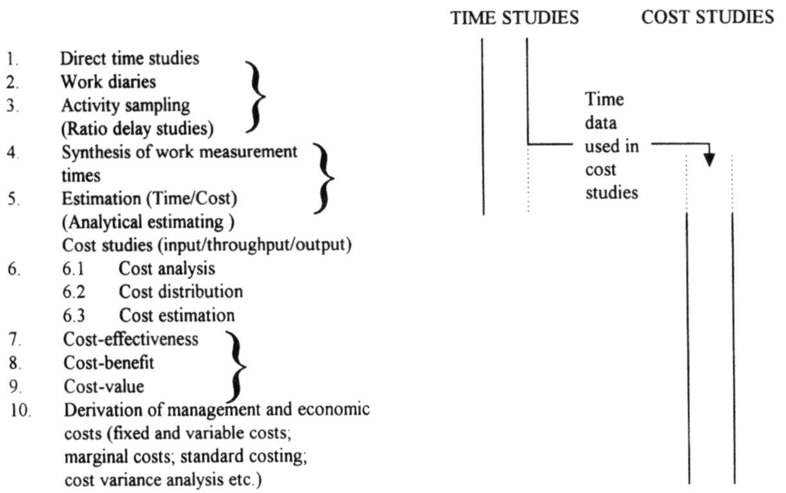

Figure 5.6. Relationship between time and cost studies

overall times by synthesizing appropriate unit times (method 4). The drawbacks of cost estimation have to be balanced against the convenience of collecting and usefulness of having even crude data, and the same can be said for estimation of times (method 5).

The threefold division of cost studies, and the separation (for analytical purposes) of input, throughput and output have already been discussed (method 6). Methods (7) to (9) use a variety of cost studies to provide cost data to construct cost-performance measures. Only when a full cost analysis of a service is possible (or of its component operations) can proper management and economic costs be constructed with any reliability (method 10).

Figure 5.7 is a slightly modified restatement of Figure 5.6 to suggest the ways in which cost study methods might be used, or tend to be used in practice by library managers. This interpretation of present methods is not inconsistent with the practices advocated in this report. Many library managers estimate costs and times by broad function. This is done by taking a comprehensive view of all functions and areas, or by partial coverage, possibly using exception reporting. Crude estimation of times and/or measuring time over restricted periods has to be used even at this broad level, but will often lead to adoption of more comprehensive work measurement and time measurement using diary methods and variations.

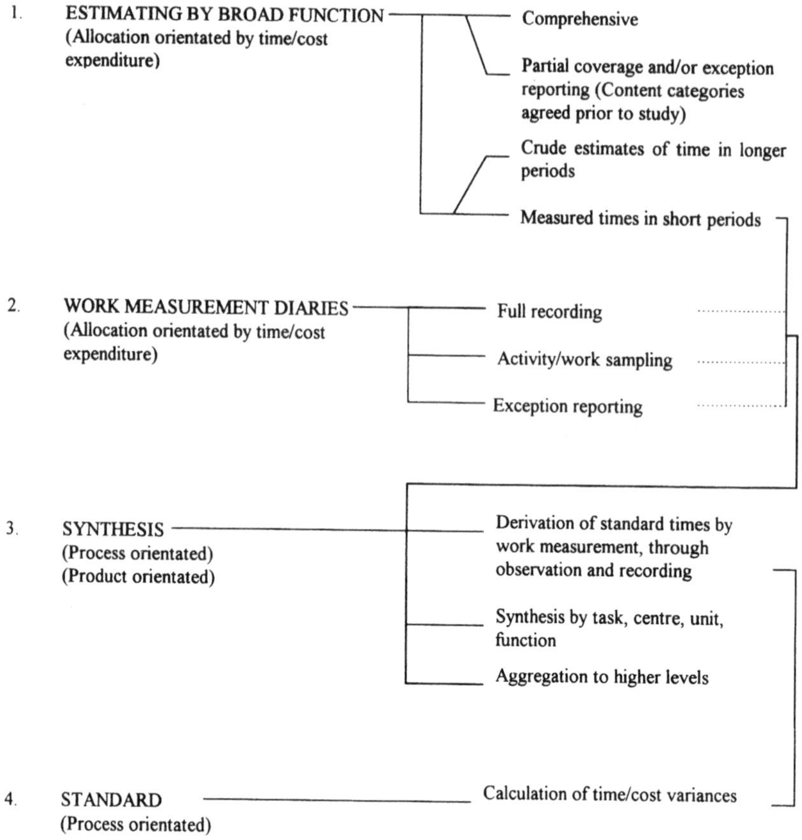

Each of the four methods has an input/output balance or emphasis.

Figure 5.7. A practice orientated categorization of cost and time measurement

Groups (1) and (2) are essentially analytical; group (3) underlines the role and relevance of synthesis once adequate analytical data have been obtained. The derivation of standard times for a whole variety of library operations is a key tactic in management accounting, since it permits the introduction of standard costing systems and cost variance analysis (group 4). A plentiful supply of analytical cost data provides a platform for thorough explorations of library and information service costs and economics. For example, the ability to model costs of different methods of resource allocation depends on synthesizing standard costs from analytical cost data.

Figure 5.8 looks at the various methods of cost study as representing a system of input/output analysis. The purpose of the diagram is to map the relationship between the different methods discussed, trying to be consistent with the stricter definitions advocated; for example, drawing a more specific distinction between cost analysis and cost estimation. The output range gives some idea of the different types and derivations of cost data available to the library manager. The sequential relationship to a management information system and the ultimate extension to a decision support system is the obvious conclusion.

Figure 5.9 suggests that costing and accounting tools form a general hierarchy of methods, with work measurement being a fundamental starting point and source of data. The implication of this statement is that in the larger type of library and information system or enterprise, these functions become increasingly well differentiated, and form definite areas of managerial responsibility. In effect, such a listing becomes a checklist for organizational structure.

5.7.4 The wider dimensions of cost analysis: a commentary

While it is often simple to collect a one-off cost for a library operation by identifying the desired activity and/or context, isolating the labour, material and overhead costs and sampling all these inputs for an appropriate period of time, a more wide ranging and systematic approach to the whole spectrum of library cost factors requires the use of different procedural tools. It is then important to realize that in very many cases the one-off cost which has been isolated stands in relation to many others; this immediately raises the question of boundaries and definitions which have to be accommodated in categorization of tasks and costs. This is especially true when comparative costs are sought, because the necessary control of boundaries and definitions is a fundamental part of the comparative technique. Most libraries therefore require a means to collect cost data about many items and situations over many programmes and sectors. Anything more than a simple one-off cost collection for an activity has to be considered in general terms in an overall management framework.

Library services are very often complex organizationally and technically, and recognition of their cost structures and cost patterns has to take this into consideration. While simple and inclusive cost indices are sought for their desirability and applicability as management information, the information and support systems

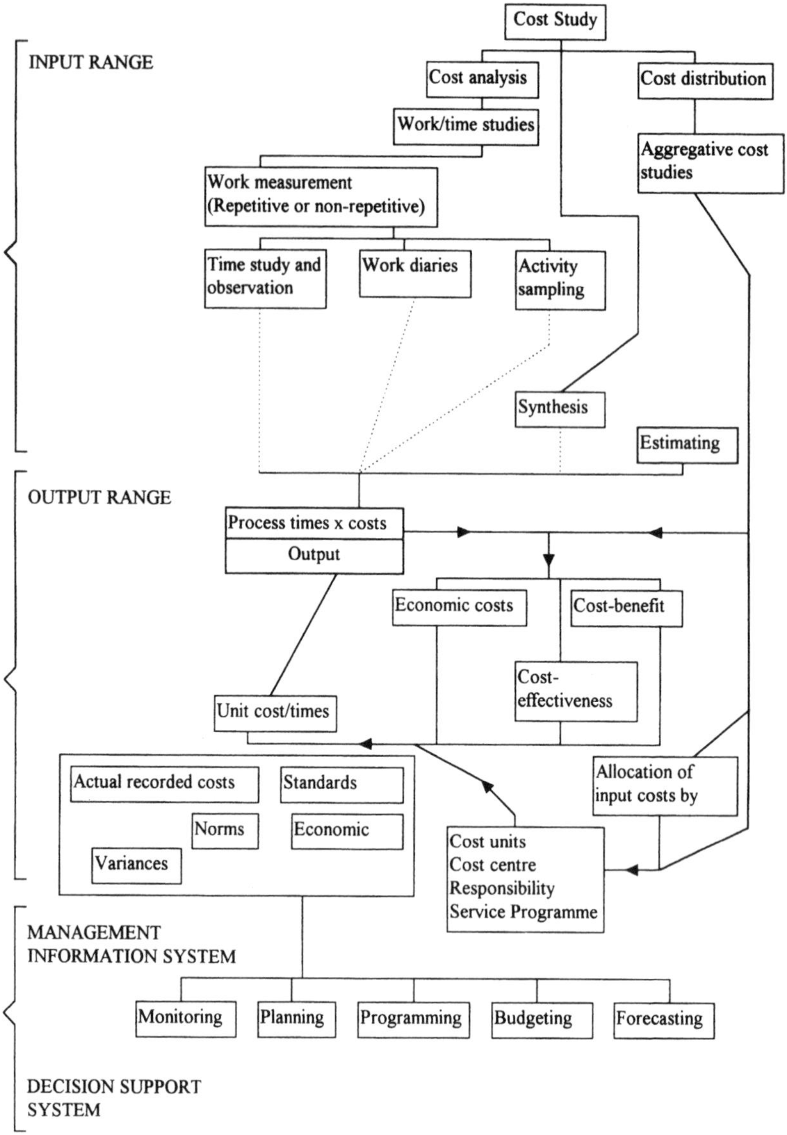

Figure 5.8. Costing and input/output analysis

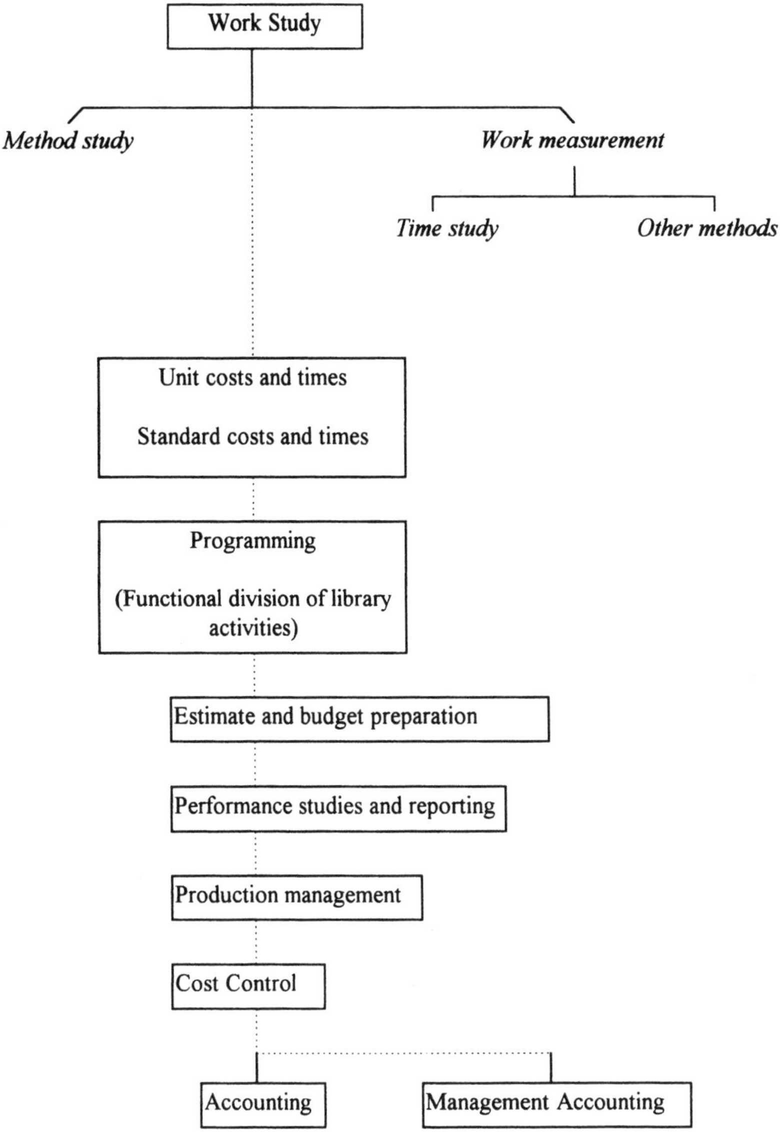

Figure 5.9. Work measurement methods in the hierarchy of costing and accounting tools

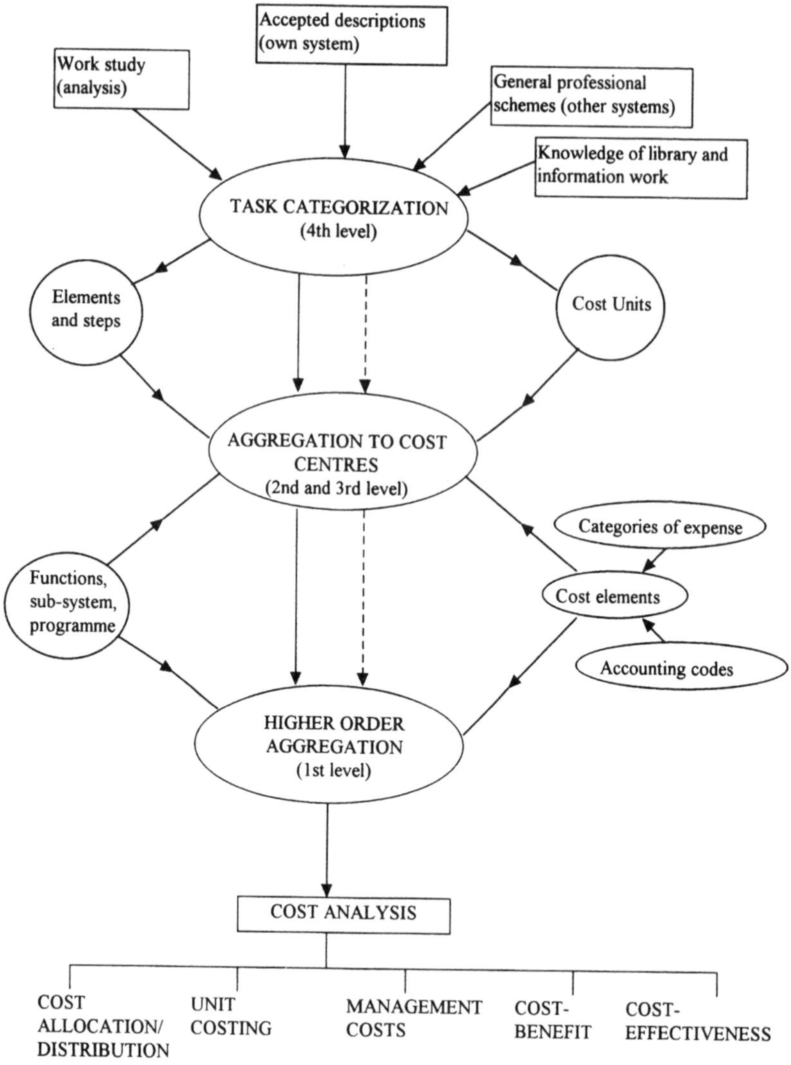

Figure 5.10. The dimensions of cost study: summary

required to produce these data may be far from simple in structure and operation.

Figure 5.10 attempts to summarize the various dimensions of cost studies covered so far in this discussion. All the stages down to cost analysis are concerned with the identification of processes and elements for costing, and with the structural framework for cost study. Crudely, the framework provides the inputs for basic cost study. The five further applications of cost analysis are different forms of throughput and output cost. All these elements have already been discussed in detail. The cumulative effect of these stages is to provide the library manager with a structure for management cost accounting.

It is perhaps only in the larger library or system that more than several cost methods will be necessary, although there is some value for all library managers to speculate upon the variety and structure of cost studies as a means to a better economic understanding of their systems.

5.7.5 Further reading

Managerial and economic terminology

Bannock, G., Baxter, R. E. and Rees, R. (1972) *The Penguin dictionary of economics*. Harmondsworth: Penguin Books

Batty, J. (1968) Terminology of cost accountancy. In J. Batty (1968) (ed.) *Cost and management accountancy for students*. London: Heinemann

Keenan, S. (1996) *Concise dictionary of library and information science*. London: Bowker-Saur

Kempner, T. (1976) (ed.) *A handbook of management*. Harmondsworth: Penguin Books

Prentice, A. E. (1977) The lingo of library finance. *American Libraries*, **8**(10), 550–552

Basic approaches to cost study

Association of Research Libraries (1977) *Determining indirect cost rates in research libraries*. Washington, DC: ARL/OMS (Spec Kit 34)

Association of Research Libraries (1979) *Cost studies and fiscal planning in research libraries*. Washington, DC: ARL

Association of Research Libraries (1980) *Indirect cost rates in research libraries*. Washington, DC: ARL/OMS (Spec Kit 84)

Association of Research Libraries (1986) *Technical services cost studies in ARL libraries*. Washington, DC: ARL

Association of Research Libraries (1987) *Technical services cost studies in ARL libraries*. Washington, DC: ARL/OMS (Spec Kit 125)

Clements, D. W. G. (1975) The costing of library systems. *Aslib Proceedings*, **27**(3), 98–111

Coffey, J. R. (ed.) (1980) Operational costs in acquisitions. *Acquisitions Librarian*, **4** (Whole issue devoted to this topic).

Cummings, M. M. (1989) Cost analysis: methods and realities. *Library Administration and Management*, **3**(4), 181–183

Durrance, J. C. (1986) Costing library services: PLA's first cost finding manual. *Public Libraries*, **25**(1), 36–37

Funk, R. (1981) Kostenvergleich in Hochschulbibliotheken. *Liber Newssheet*, (5), 5–20

Humphreys, K. W. (1974) Costing in university libraries. *Liber Bulletin*, **5**(6), 8–32

Kantor, P. B. (1989) Library cost analysis. *Library Trends*, 38(2), 171–188

Kountz, J. (1972) Library cost analysis: a recipe. *Library Journal*, **97**(3), 459–464

Landau, H. B. (1969) Cost analysis of document surrogation: a literature review. *American Documentation*, **20**(4), 302–310

Leimkuhler, F. F. and Cooper, M. D. (1971) Cost accounting and analysis for university libraries. *College and Research Libraries*, **32**(6), 449–464

Lutz, R. P. (1971) Costing information services. *Bulletin of the Medical Library Association*, **50**(2), 254–261

Marron, H. (1969) On costing information services. *Proceedings of ASIS*, **6**, 516–520

Miller, R. A. (1936) Cost accounting for libraries: a technique for determining the labour costs of acquisition and cataloguing work. *Library Journal*, 7, 511–536

Murfin, M. E. (1993) Cost analysis of library reference services. In *Advances in Library Administration and Organization.* **11**, 1–36

O'Donovan, K. (1991) Costing library services towards a model for the NHS. Proceedings of a seminar and workshops held at the University of Newcastle upon Tyne 13 December 1990. *Health Libraries Review.* **8**(2), 120–141

Office of Arts and Libraries (1987) A costing system for public libraries: a model system development by Cipfa Services Ltd. London: HMSO (Library Information Series No. 17)

O'Donovan, K. (1991) Costing library services towards a model for the NHS. Proceedings of a seminar and workshops held at the University of Newcastle upon Tyne 13 December 1990. *Health Libraries Review*. **8**(2), 120–141

Pierce, A. R. and Taylor, J. K. (1978) Model for cost comparison of automated cataloguing systems. *Journal of Library Automation*, **11**(1), 6–23

Price, D. S. (1971) *Collecting and reporting real costs of information systems*. Washington: ASIS (ED 055 092)

Price, D. S. (1974) Rational cost information: necessary and obtainable. *Special Libraries*, **65**, 49–57

Richmond, E. (1987) Cost finding: method and management. *The Bottom Line*, **1**(4), 16–20

Risk, J. M. S. (1956) Information services: measuring the cost. *Aslib Proceedings*, **8**(4), 26

Rosenberg, P. (1985) Cost finding for public libraries: a manager's handbook. Chicago: ALA

Rowe, D. (1974) Application of the theory of the firm to library costing. *Australian Library Journal*, **23**(3), 108–111

Sessions, V. S. (1970) The cost and costing of information storage and retrieval. *Information Storage and Retrieval*, **6**(2), 155–170

Shoffner, R. M. (1975) Comparative cost analysis. In *Information Roundup, Proceedings 4th mid-year meeting*. Washington: ASIS. pp.1–32

Smith, G. C. K. and Schofield, J. L. (1971) Administrative effectiveness: times and costs of library operations. *Journal of Librarianship*, **3**(4), 245–266

Topping, J. R. (1974) *Cost analysis manual: field review edition*. Boulder, Colo.: National Center for Higher Education Management Systems at Western Interstate Commission for Higher Education (Technical Report No. 45)

Vinson, M. (1988) Cost finding: a step by step guide. *The Bottom Line*, **2**(3), 15–19

Waldhart, T. J. (1992) The process of cost justification. In *Advances in Library Administration and Organization* **10**, 113–127

Wilson, J. R. (1973) Costing for libraries: a summary review of the recent literature. In F. Slater *Cost reduction for special libraries and information centers*. Washington, DC. pp.2–21

Wooster, H. (1965) Post mortems can be fun: the cost analysis of information systems. *Library Journal*, **90**(30), 2968–2973

Cost accounting tools

Alley, B. and Cargill, J. (1982) *Keeping track of what you spend: the librarian's guide to simple bookkeeping*. Phoenix, Ariz.: Oryx Press

Armstrong, A. (1972) Analysing industrial information service costs: a simple checklist. *Aslib Proceedings*, **24**(11), 635–639

Axford, H. W. (1975) The validity of book price indexes for budgeting projections. *Library Resources and Technical Services*, **19**(1), 5–12

Brutcher, C. *et al.* (1964) Cost accounting for the library. *Library Resources and Technical Services*, **8**(4), 413–431

Duchesne, R. M. (1973) Analysis of costs and performance. *Library Trends*, **21**(4), 587–603

Ford, G. (1973) *Library automation: guidelines to costing*. Lancaster: Library Research Unit

Franklin, B. R. and Egan, G. J. (1989) Harnessing accounting theory: scrupulous costing can re-vitalize university library systems. *The Bottom Line*, **3**(3), 21–24

Hall, A. C. (1973) Identifying operational costs. *PLA Bulletin*, **28**(5), 183–189

Helmkamp, J. G. (1969) Managerial cost accounting for a technical information center. *American Documentation*, **20**(2), 111–118

Hewgill, J. C. R. (1977) Management accounting and library activities. *Aslib Proceedings*, **29**(9), 304–309

Ludwig, R. (1969) The objects, tasks and methods of the calculation of costs with models for the application of costs in research libraries in East Germany. *Zentralblatt für Bibliothekswesen*, **83**(10), 571–591 (in German)

McKinley, M. (1970) (comp.) *Computer assisted job cost accounting: report for the acquisition department*. Davis: University of California (Report AC-Q 7)

Mitchell, B. I. (1978) *Cost analysis of library functions: a total system approach*. Greenwood, Conn.: JAI Press

Moisse, E. (1976) Costing information in an independent research organization. *Information Scientist*, **10**(2), 57–68

Pateman, J. (1989) Cost centre management, a new concept in branch librarianship. *Service Point*, (45), 8–11

Revill, D. H. (1989) Cost centres and academic libraries. *British Journal of Academic Librarianship*, **4**(1), 27–28

Rider, F. (1936) Library cost accounting. *Library Quarterly*, **6**(4), 331–381

Sayre, E. and Thielen, L. (1975) *Cost accounting procedures for public libraries: a model.* Denver: Colorado State Library (ED 136 739)

Cost measures and related measures

Armstrong, A. (1972) A cost determining formula for library staff. *Library Association Record*, **74**(5), 85–86

Armstrong, A. (1972) Analysing industrial information service costs: a sample checklist. *Aslib Proceedings*, **24**(11), 635–639

Axford, H. W. (1972) (ed.) *Proceedings of the LARC Computer-based Unit Cost Studies Institute, September 16–17, 1971*. Tempe, Ariz.: LARC

Brockman, J. R. and Klobas, J. E. (1979) Contemporary issues in the economics of Australian academic libraries. *Australian Academic and Research Libraries*, **10**(4), 230–236

Drake, M. A. (1977) Attribution of library costs. *College and Research Libraries*, **38**(6), 514–519

Gilchrist, A. (1971) Cost-effectiveness. *Aslib Proceedings*, **23**(9), 455–464

Hawgood, I. and Morley, R. (1969) *Project for evaluating the benefits from university libraries: final report.* Durham: Durham University (OSTI Report 5056) ED 051 824

Jacob, M. E. L. (1970) Standardized costs for automated library systems. *Journal of Library Automation*, **3**(3), 207–217

Kissel, G. (1972) Problems of measurement and evaluation of costs and value in documentation and library systems. *Nachrichten für Dokumentation*, **23**(6), 257–269 (in German)

Lancaster, F. W. (1971) Cost-effectiveness analysis of information retrieval and dissemination systems. *Journal of the American Society for Information Science*, **22**(1), 12–27

Lyders, R., Eckels, D. and Leatherbury, M. L. (1979) Cost allocation and cost generation. In R. D. Stueart and R. D. Johnson (1979) (eds.) *New horizons for academic libraries; papers presented at the First National Conference of the Association of College and Research Libraries*. New York/London: Saur/Bingley. pp.116–122

Magson, M. S. (1973) Techniques for the measurement of cost-benefit in information centres. *Aslib Proceedings*, **25**(5), 164–185

Mason, D. (1973) Programmed budgeting and cost-effectiveness. *Aslib Proceedings*, **25**(4), 100–110

Morris, D. E. (1992) Staff time and costs for cataloging. *Library Resourc* *and Technical Services*, **36**(1), 79–95

Nachlas, J. A. and Pierce, A. R. (1979) Determination of unit costs fo library services. *College and Research Libraries*, **40**(3), 240–247

Nightingale, R. A. (1973) A cost-benefit study of a manually produce current awareness bulletin. *Aslib Proceedings*, **25**(4), 153–157

Pitkin, G. M. (1989) (ed.) *Cost-effective technical services: how to track an justify internal operations.* New York: Neal-Schumann

Revill, D. H. (1973) Unit times in studies of academic library operation *Aslib Proceedings*, **29**(10), 363–380

Robertson, S. E. *et al.* (1970) Standard costing for information system *Aslib Proceedings*, **22**(9), 425–427

Standera, O. R. (1974) Costs and effectiveness. *Journal of the America* *Society for Information Science*, **25**(3), 203–207

Vickers, P. (1976) Ground rules for cost-effectiveness. *Aslib Proceeding* **28**(6–7), 224–229

White, H. S. (1979) Cost-effectiveness and cost-benefit determinations i special libraries. *Special Libraries*, **70**(4), 163–169

White, H. S. (1985) Cost-benefit analysis & other fun and games. *Librar* *Journal*, **110**(3), 118–21

White, H. S. (1990) Hiding the cost of information. *The Bottom Line*, **4**(4 14–19

Wilkins, A. P., Reynolds, R. and Robertson, S. E. (1972) Standard time for information systems. *Journal Documentation*, **28**(2), 131–150

Wilkinson, J. B. (1980) Economics of information: criteria for countin the costs and benefits. *Aslib Proceedings*, **32**(1), 1–9

Chapter 6

Implementation of cost measurement

6.1 Defining needs and requirements

This chapter is concerned with some of the specific issues and problems which arise in implementing a programme of cost collection in a library or information unit. The comments apply principally to cost analysis, but are broadly relevant to all types of cost related study. In practice there is a spectrum of cost study through and across which the library and information manager may wish to operate. On the one hand there is crude cost estimation, ad hoc cost analysis, and various kinds of budget and expenditure distribution study. Then there is more rigorous and systematic cost analysis, using work measurement to study library functions, and various in-programme costs. These precise data can be used in cost-effectiveness, cost-benefit and cost-value studies, although often less precise data are regrettably used in these kinds of study. Then there is the implementation of full management accounting, which requires cost study and cost coverage over all areas of service operations, with regular reporting and means of cost control. At this stage such management accounting data may be used as part of a wider management information system.

Before making cost studies and collecting cost data the manager needs a clear idea of the specific reasons for doing so, and to be able to answer the kinds of questions covered on the needs checklist (Section 6.2). At this stage a general need for cost study has been assumed, as a means of servicing budgeting, control, planning and performance measurement procedures. When the general and specific points on the list have been checked, the manager will know whether or not these preliminary assumptions are valid, and can then proceed to design cost studies, collect fresh data or continue any existing data collection.

6.2 Cost study needs: a checklist

General

- What cost information is currently collected?
- Is there a regular cost reporting system?
- If there is an irregular cost reporting system, when are data produced?
- Has a library and information service activity or problem suggested a need for cost data?
- Can the problem need be met by current cost data?
- What kind of cost information is needed?
- What decisions depend upon the cost data collected?
- Is this a one-off or a recurring need for cost data?

Specific

- Who will use the cost information?
- What will the cost data be used for?
- What will be done with or to the information after its initial collection use?
- When are the cost data required?
- From what date should collection begin?
- For how long should collection be undertaken?
- What level(s) in the system is (are) going to be subject to cost study?
- How does the cost information relate to other levels of the system and its constituent parts?
- Where is the cost information to be collected?

- Who is to collect/process/analyse the cost data?
- Is existing cost/management information being updated?
- Is the information needed/defined by the problem available elsewhere?
- Is there 'substitutability' of cost data?
- How durable are the cost data once they have been collected?
- How do current data relate to earlier data (if they exist)?
- How reliable/accurate do the cost data need to be?
- What sorts of error levels are likely and how tolerable are these?
- What sort of cost study will meet the need for cost data, following examination of the situation by this checklist?
- What implications are there for the future by collecting these data now?
- What resources can be devoted to a study in the light of depth, urgency and priority of need?
- How much original fieldwork investigation is required and can be undertaken within the system?
- What balance (if any) is required between measured, estimated or applied (standard) values of cost data?

6.3 Study design

When the library manager carries out a cost study it is useful to have a checklist of the main stages against which progress can be noted. The main areas of a cost analysis study (and to some degree all types of cost study involving field data collection) can be broken down into four kinds of approach: procedural; methodological; technical; post-study.

6.3.1 Procedural approach

In this approach points on the checklist should:

- identify the general and specific needs for cost study
- establish involvement of library personnel and responsibility for cost centres

- develop operational definitions and descriptions of systems and functions
- define the topics for measurement (people and/or systems)
- identify a systems study and a methods study
- involve a time study and/or cost study
- consider staff participation and project management
- develop project design with respect to all the other aspects.

6.3.2 Methodological approach

An approach of this sort implies:

- appreciation and understanding of costing methods
- modifying ideal conditions and theories to suit practice
- sampling (time period, people, length of study, scale of study)
- appreciation of likely errors and sources of error
- reliability of methods and procedures
- task categorization and development of cost units, cost elements and cost centres.

6.3.3 Technical approach

A technical approach involves:

- writing instructions and procedures for study and collection of data
- briefing participants
- documentation (data collection forms, instructions etc.)
- analysis procedures.

6.3.4 Post-study

Elements of importance in post-study are:

- feedback to participants
- implementation of results

- follow-up and updating
- improvement of methods and procedures.

6.4 System description

The purpose of system description in a particular cost study is to ensure that all the contributory tasks and elements of a process or function are identified and accounted for. The system description then provides a reference guide or map of the functions costed. The description also serves as a source of information for method study. In the light of cost patterns identified it may be necessary to recast a given process, and the system description can help re-organize work flows, identify critical points, and form the basis for a monitoring mechanism to assess future performance: it is thus a basic tool in the practical allocation and reallocation of resources.

Diagrammatic aids (such as structure charts, flow diagrams and listings) are the best means to build up a system description although some supporting narrative may be necessary, especially when descriptions are to be archived in staff and procedural manuals. The description need not be elaborate provided that the essential elements of the situation are revealed and conveyed. In practice this stage of cost study may be rough and ready, and it will serve its purpose if it helps library staff to discuss critically those library operations for which they are responsible that may become the topic of a cost investigation.

6.5 Data collection and field measurement

The time period of the study must be carefully defined and all parties notified and briefed adequately. Documentation must have its message reinforced by the direct and accessible presence of the cost co-ordinator. Simple and clear explanatory instructions should accompany any forms and data collection instruments. Preliminary briefing sessions should be held, and extra care given to details of implementation at the beginning of the study period.

When direct time studies of staff are to be carried out a good relationship must be cultivated between the investigator and the staff concerned and frank preliminary briefings are crucially important, so that when the field studies are carried out there is the minimum of intrusion and the maximum of confidence entrusted in each party. Even when self-recorded diaries and/or activity sampling is used these principles should not be neglected. The subjects of the study should know to whom they can turn for advice. No participant should feel the burden of an unresolved problem, since this can lead to misunderstandings and errors in recording.

It is both practical and convenient to collect field data records regularly, say once a week in a monthly study, and the investigator should check completed records as soon as possible thereafter. Ideally, of course, a study should be designed with clarity and forethought such as to minimize any difficulty in field implementation.

One drawback to note in library cost studies presented in the literature is that they rarely report operational details of method and implementation in a helpful fashion; the treatment is usually cursory. This makes it difficult to compare actual practice library by library. Informal contact between libraries which have carried out or are carrying out cost studies should be encouraged.

6.6 Work measurement practice

There are numerous accounts of industrial applications of work measurement, and some very clear textbook expositions. Time studies need no more than simple, readily available equipment – clipboards, stop watches (and some practice in their use), and data recording sheets. Work measurement diaries can be based on purpose-designed forms. Activity sampling requires the use of a random alarm device or no more than reference to a list of randomly selected times. It is usually best to write instructions to subjects for each study and to be as specific as possible.

Some examples of data recording forms are given in Appendix 5; the essential elements of any form are reference details on the subject for future identification, and entry columns for times spent, task codes and units of output (if available). A column or space for investigators' notes is useful, especially as many studies can still be conveniently analysed manually. The investigator will need summary sheets and there is usually an amount of transcription to be done. Checking for errors in transcription is very important. Summary sheets should show expense categories so that costs can be computed from one array of data. Time reporting sheets which can be used for regular data collection are not likely to differ much in detail from those used in ad hoc or special studies.

6.7 Processing and analysis of results

Processing and analysis can be treated as one operation usually performed by the investigator, although in a large or complex study these stages will nowadays be machine assisted. Processing will already have begun with transcription of data to summary and analysis sheets. The use of task and account/expense codings greatly simplifies the operation and reduces confusion and error. In a system where cost studies are a regular feature all these conventions will be ready to hand and previously tested.

Presentation of results can either be in full, based on the format of model expense accounts (see Table 5.3 and Table 6.1), or in some brief summary for management use: for example, just a list of unit costs of operations. The analysis and reporting will depend to a large degree on management style, preference and end use of cost and account data.

The Centre for Library and Information Management has produced a model work measurement and costing package in its ATLAS (Aids to Library Administration Series). It gives step-by-step instruction on how to set up a work measurement procedure to generate times for production of unit times and unit costs.

Reference to the model forms and instructions provided may be found useful by those making a beginning at timing and costing library procedures (Centre for Library and Information Management, 1980).

Unit times provide the basis for standard costing procedures. Any survey of unit times reported in the library literature shows the range of reference values which can be obtained for tasks and processes in a variety of libraries. An approximation of a mean value (for example taken from several studies) is possibly the best that can be obtained. Any claims for absolute standard values (except those for small and clearly defined task units) need to be treated with some caution, because local conditions are likely to have a strong influence on values. Some pragmatism is acceptable since a complete correspondence of tasks and unit times is neither necessary nor a practical proposition, although in theory a complete coverage would allow wide scope for synthesis from basic operations up to major functions. Given this, rather than relying on a synthetic approach to building up unit costs, it is better to collect unit costs directly 'at the source' as and when their relevance is recognized by management. The necessity to collect unit times and costs presupposes the ability to define an appropriate unit of output; self-evident but not always easy to apply in practice.

TABLE 6.1 Standard expense headings adapted for library and information units

Category		*Typical expenses/sources of revenue*	*Data source*
Expenditure			
(1)	Payments to and for employees	Wages and salary payments (direct costs). Social and health insurance payments etc. (indirect costs)	Parent body. Accounts Department
(2)	Charges for materials	Documents and information materials	Bookfund accounting. Materials price index
(3)	Outside services	Outside contractors and suppliers. Computer based services. Some subscription services. Certain maintenance services for premises	Standard tariffs. Negotiated terms
(4)	Payments for information and knowledge	Professional services. Membership subscriptions	Invoiced costs
(5)	External payments for protection, continuity and development	Insurance	Invoiced costs, often paid by Parent body
(6)	Charges for use of facilities	Accommodation, maintenance, equipment	Costs apportioned by Parent body. Overhead charges (often standardized)
(7–9)	Other expenses	Ex-gratia payments (e.g. payment to temporary staff) Contingency fund. Tax payments	Direct payments made to payments by Parent body
Revenue		Grants, fines, donations. Earned income from services	Parent body. Budgetary allocations. Working accounts.

6.8 Factors affecting implementation of cost studies and use and interpretation of data

No cost collection system or exercise can ever be totally comprehensive or completely reliable. Even in the best designed studies some assumptions and compromises have to be made, for instance in the categorization of tasks and functions or in the degree to which work measurement and field work can be implemented upon staff. Provided that the assumptions and compromises are well known, the validity and reliability of cost data can be maintained and will not seriously impair the implementation of cost studies and the use and interpretation of cost data in policy and decision making.

The library manager is faced with taking decisions on the depth and frequency of cost study; these factors can affect interpretation and use of cost data. To reach the stage of having continuous monitoring which is both economical to maintain and relatively unobtrusive, means developing a proper system of management accounting as a recognized arena of managerial responsibility. Economy is achieved by sampling operations to collect time, work and cost data, or by developing reporting systems which have low impact on staff but a high yield of information (for instance weekly reports, noting exceptional or non-standard tasks). It is rarely necessary or practicable to have more or less continuous field collection and monitoring of costs. This may be necessary in process industries, but is less so in service operations. In the former, regular accounting and documentation procedures have been developed (cost and works accounting); these are described in any standard textbook on the subject, and it can be readily appreciated that they are inappropriate to whole areas of library work.

Library organizations generally resemble industrial organizations only superficially; for example, storage, distribution and pricing functions are very different in libraries compared to industrial manufacturing enterprises. However, a library management accounting system will attempt to be regular and permanent in its ability to provide and control costs, as is consistent with the methods available to collect costs.

Ad hoc and one-off cost studies and cost analysis can be very useful if properly conducted, but if conducted at the wrong moment may provide a false picture. This is a strong argument for some regular management accounting in all libraries, especially where activities may be subject to cyclical trends. For instance the ad hoc costing of inter-library loans in an academic library is affected by the time at which the study is made in the academic year, since the level of traffic may vary, and the response (and productivity) of staff is sensitive to this. This is to say that cost studies have to be supported by the manager's knowledge of the system, and its sensible application to the types of costs studies implemented.

Managerial use of cost data requires above all a confidence in the quality of those data. This requires the recognition of management accounting as a significant task, and the intelligent use of the variety of methods available consistent with the effort needed to collect costs and the objectives of cost use.

6.9 Developing a cost and management accounting system

There are still many libraries that have never collected cost data on their operations, although hopefully this is a declining number. Important questions for many library managers will then be the 'why' and 'when' should a cost and management accounting system be developed, as distinct from the occasional collection of cost data or no collection at all.

In Chapters One and Four an attempt was made to answer the question 'why' satisfactorily and convincingly. Chapter Five discussed methods and techniques, and in this chapter some specific problems of implementation have been covered. The questions of 'when' and exactly 'what' remain to be dealt with. The simplest response to the question of 'when' is best answered by saying that action is necessary whenever doubts enter the manager's mind about what is going on in the service from the perspective of most effective resource allocation, productivity, efficiency and performance. When the manager is faced with economic decisions the question of cost data is never far away. When that economic dimension has become a central part of management discussion the librarian should already have reached the point where cost study tools are being used in the system.

The manager's response to the problem of 'what' to do will clearly be a graded one. The very smallest library will not need an elaborate system of data collection, processing of accounting information and presentation of results, but in outline its needs will be met by the same principles underlying full and elaborate systems. First of all the functional structure of library activities has to be recognized and productive objectives identified, especially as they relate to activities, products and services achieved through the conversion of resources by labour.

The functional structure of the library operation is mapped by systems description and analysis. A programme structure which recognizes objectives and functions has to be drawn up, and this is translated into budgetary terms which relate to inputs and their costs, in terms of planned expenditure. At this stage the budget itself will contain much latent and implicit cost information (largely historical). It is the purpose of cost analysis to test out in the real world the cost assumptions upon which the library operation rests, using the many cost study methods at the manager's disposal.

The statements about library functions and programmes represent the kinds of throughput (or conversion) activities in the library. Programme outputs should be capable of direct relation to original objectives. For the purposes of costing and accounting, functions, programmes and activities have to be categorized in terms of tasks and operations with a coding system which can permit the description and manipulation of data in accounts. The coding system has to include the types of expense incurred as well as the objects of those expenses. The categorization and coding of tasks and expenditures occupies a central place in any costing and accounting system, and is the link between the structure of programmes and functions, the extraction and isolation of costs and the ultimate relation of output and performance to all that has gone before to achieve it.

During the course of the budgetary cycle, and of the progress of managerial activity, costs have to be determined, compared and controlled, internally and externally. As the scale of library operation increases coupled with the wishes of the manager to know and understand the system in greater detail, it is likely that ad hoc, and one-off cost study will develop into something more permanent and sophisticated. When regular cost information can be produced, the library manager has de facto implemented the basis of a cost and management accounting system.

6.10 An action programme and checklist

In the majority of libraries cost studies need to be approached on two essentially complementary levels. In practice the first is probably more common than the second.

The first approach stems from the need to obtain the costs for specific operations, and is rooted in the fact that library management is in practice dominantly object and/or problem centred rather than systems orientated, conceptual and holistic. An action programme for costing is thus likely to focus on the need to continue, expand or initiate discrete cost measurement of various segments or aspects of operations. Although it would be desirable to repeat such studies, in practice this is not often done, and may stem from a lack of attention to the second level of costing.

The second level of cost study is the implementation of a regular cost accounting system operating across all main systems and programmes of the library. Such an accounting system should be capable of generating management accounting data in any required form (e.g. by cost centre, category of expense etc.). In the ideal world (or library) the order of approach should logically be the reverse. A regular programme wide cost accounting system clearly can do both jobs: provide the broad and comprehensive view, as well as the object or problem centred locus required for operational management. Such a cost accounting system dispenses with the difficulty engendered by the one-off approach typical of the discrete study: the ability to repeat analysis using a standardized base for study is a consequence of the system itself. Of course, even with a regular cost accounting system there may be occasions when a special project or circumstance necessitates a discrete study, but then it will be possible to use the regular cost accounts as a source of information for the special project by deriving standard costs, unit costs, overhead rates or whatever else is needed from the main system.

In the majority of libraries a regular management accounting system (which would be real time and online) is still a dream, and one of which some librarians still have to be convinced of the value, appropriateness or necessity.

Installing a management accounting system in any organization is a major task. Whether or not a particular library has arrived at this position the points checklisted in this section can serve to direct thought about both levels of cost studies. A gentle initiation and familiarity with problem and object centred discrete cost studies may help to clear the way for installing more ambitious and comprehensive costing and accounting procedures.

An action programme checklist for cost studies

Objectives

Check the reasons why cost measures are needed (see 'Needs checklist' in Section 6.2). Develop general and specific objectives for the cost measurement studies.

Performance evaluation

Will the cost measures when collected contribute to an increased knowledge of the performance of the service?

Are the cost measures being collected to supplement other kinds of performance measure and performance evaluation?

Have the costs already been collected or can they be obtained from some other source?

System knowledge

Can you implement the necessary actions and procedures to obtain sufficient system knowledge to design and implement the cost study? Categorize by programme, function, department or other administrative breakdown and/or by unit or type of input, throughput or output to obtain meaningful and useful cost categories.

Budgets and programmes

A programme structure for the service provides a basic and useful analytical framework for study. The programme structure can be used as the basis for the estimates and budgets, and for the management accounting apparatus. Develop a programme structure for the service (for example, using sources of the type reproduced in Appendix 4). Try to supplement or recast budget presentations in terms of the programme structure. Think of costing, accounting and performance measurement in terms of programme structure. Remember that standardization is often necessary for effective measurement.

Input/output and throughput

Develop an analysis of service activity using these aspects and combine this with the ideas on programme structure, functions and tasks.

Cost reports

The results of cost studies (general/specific; regular/irregular) must be presented in the framework of a cost report structure. The more general and regular the studies the more formalized and more useful cost data and reports are likely to be.

Begin to see cost data in the perspective of more embracing management information and decision support systems.

Staff roles

Develop a chain of responsibility for collecting and evaluating cost data. Allocate responsibilities for specific cost studies. Ensure time and resources for successful endeavour and results.

Discussion and evaluation
The discussion and evaluation of results is of utmost importance at many levels of staff and management. Analysis, policymaking, control and feedback are important and widely distributable functions.

6.11 Management measures and checklists

Three checklists have been compiled listing the main component measures useful to library managers for assessing financial performance, management accounting and general economic management of their services:

- input measures include the primary expense categories
- throughput measures include measures of intermediate output as well as the main elements of library and information service programmes
- output measures relate as far as possible to the final goals and objectives of the service (and include measures of impact and benefit).

The measures listed on the three checklists cover most of the major categories of managerially useful measurements and their associated managerially useful costs.

There are two other categories of measure which are much more difficult to establish, but which need to be borne in mind. Impact measures are related to marketing and value concepts, and although not always considered by managers in cost and accounting exercises they have implications for output management and for evaluating service objectives. Benefit measures have to be assessed subjectively, although costs can be applied to them semi-objectively. When considering either impact or benefit it is very useful to back up assessments of both measures with the cost implications of achieving these output results.

6.11.1 Input measures

(1) Input measures include primary expense categories, which after Risk (1956), using standard account headings involve:

- payment to and for employees (labour, staff)
- charges for materials

- outside services
- payments for information and knowledge
- external payments
- charges for use of facilities
- ex-gratia payments
- payments for the use of purchasing power
- payments of taxes.

(2) Other categories used in estimate and budget preparation (according to specific local usage) include:

- staff
- materials (by source, type of material, vote etc.)
- services
- sundries
- overheads (e.g. for common services consumed).

(3) Allocations of estimates, budgets, sources of expense etc. divided/distributed according to departments of the service, categories of staff and user constituencies are also considered.
(4) Discrete isolation of input costs is carried out according to type of programme and/or function in the service, broken down by subcategories if required, e.g.:

- special cost studies of services and operations at the input level;
- one-off cost studies, e.g.:

  input cost measures defined according to various schemes (see Appendix 1; Hamburg, 1974; Clements, 1975).

(5) Unit costs of inputs.
(6) Standard costs of inputs, including variances, have to be established as the final element in the input measures checklist.

6.11.2 Throughput measures

(1) Throughput measures imply the allocation of costs across the service according to programme and/or function or by other criteria of categorization, e.g.:

- total cost of reader services division
- total cost of technical services division etc.

(2) Unit costs at throughput level are also involved, e.g.:

- obtaining an inter-library loan
- lending a document to a requesting library
- as intermediate outputs, e.g.:

  unit cost per title catalogued within the bibliographical records section.

(3) Throughput measures should also take into account standard costs at throughput level, including calculation of variances.
(4) Differences between budgeted expenditures and costs and actual expenditures and costs according to programme and/or function or object of expenditure should be noted most particularly.
(5) Management or economic costs of throughput activities are also included, e.g.:

- total costs
- average costs
- fixed and variable costs
- marginal costs.

6.11.3 Output measures

(1) These relate as far as possible to the final goals and refer to total costs across the service according to programme and/or function or by other criteria of categorization, e.g.:

- total cost of document delivery to user
- total cost per hour of document exposure (cf. Hamburg)
- cost of adding an item to stock
- annual cost of storage per shelf metre
- total annual cost of inter-library lending, technical services etc.

(2) The checklist should include unit costs of final outputs (these may subsume some measures identified under the previous category, or some throughput measures), e.g.:

- unit cost of adding an item to stock
- average costs of borrowing an item on inter-library loan
- average costs of lending an item on inter-library loan
- average cost per issue from different collections in stock (e.g. student loan, long loan)
- average cost per reader of reference or information enquiry
- average cost per computer search of external databases.

(3) Standard costs at output level can be usefully established, and calculation of variances may be made.
(4) Comparisons of total actual expenditure against budgeted expenditure should be made at a more general or gross level of activity than in the first category on this checklist.
(5) Management or economic costs of final outputs should be calculated e.g.:

- total costs
- average costs
- fixed and variable costs
- marginal costs.

There may be difficulties in calculating these costs at both general and specific levels of activity, and of distinguishing between intermediate and final outputs.

These checklists were first presented in the predecessor work by Roberts (1985), and can be read and usefully compared with material in the King Research study (Office of Arts and Libraries, 1990), especially Section 4 'Examples of performance indicators for library services and operational functions', which includes a range of cost measures, and reinforces the message about the value of cost studies to management practice.

6.11.4 Further reading

Investigating and describing systems

American Library Association (1943) *ALA glossary of library terms*. Chicago: ALA

Aslib Research Department (1970) The analysis of library processes. *Journal of Documentation*, **26**(1), 30–45

Atherton, P. (1977) *Handbook for information systems and services*. Paris: Unesco

Buckland, M. K. *et al.* (1970) *Systems analysis of a university library: final report on research project*. Lancaster: University of Lancaster Library (Occasional Paper No. 4)

Burkhalter, B. (1968) (ed.) *Case studies in systems analysis in a university library*. Metuchen, NJ: Scarecrow Press

Burns, R. W. (1971) A generalised methodology for library systems analysis. *College and Research Libraries*, **32**(4), 295–303

Chapman, E. A., St Pierre, P. L. and Lubans, J. (1970) *Library system analysis guide*. New York: Wiley-Interscience

Grosch, A. N. (1980) Application of systems analysis to the special library. In E. B. Jackson (1980) *Special librarianship: a new reader*. London: Scarecrow

Leimkuhler, F. F. (1966) Systems analysis in university libraries. *College and Research Libraries*, **27**(1), 13–18

Leimkuhler, F. F. and Cooper, M. D. (1971) Cost accounting and analysis for university libraries. *College and Research Libraries*, **32**(6), 449–464

Lubans, J. and Chapman, E. A. (1975) *Reader in library systems analysis*. Englewood, Colo.: Microcard Edition Books

Mahapatra, M. (1980) Systems analysis as a tool for research in scientific management of libraries: a state of the art review. *Libri*, **30**(2), 141–149

Martin, G. P. and West, M. W. (1975) Basis for resource allocation: analysis of operations in a large library system. *Library Trends*, **23**(4), 573–586

Smith, D. (1980) *Systems thinking in library and information management*. London: Bingley

Swedish Work Simplification Committee (1960) *Organisation och arbetsmetoder vid kommunala bibliotek*. Stockholm. In H. Gimbel (1969) *Work simplification in Danish public libraries: the report of the Work Simplification Committee of the Danish Library Association.* Chicago: American Library Association

Thomas, P. A. (1970) Tasks and the analysis of library systems. *Aslib Proceedings*, **22**(7), 336–343

Thomas, P. A. (1971) *Task analysis of library operations.* London: Aslib (Aslib Occasional Paper No. 8)

Wright, C. and Tate, D. (1973) *Economics and systems analysis: introduction for public managers.* London: Addison Wesley

Work measurement

Divilbiss, J. L. and Self, P. C. (1978) Work analysis by random sampling. *Bulletin of the Medical Library Association*, **66**(1), 19–23

Drott, C. M. (1969) Random sampling: a tool for library research. *College and Research Libraries*, **30**(2), 119–125

Ferguson, A. W. and Taylor, R. (1980) What are you doing: an analysis of activities of public service librarians at a medium-sized research library. *Journal of Academic Librarianship*, **6**(1), 24–29

Flowers, J. L. (1978) Time logs for researchers: how useful? *Library Acquisitions. Practice and Theory*, **2**(2), 77–84

Gilder, L. and Schofield, J. L. (1976) *Work measurement techniques and library management: methods of data collection.* Cambridge: University of Cambridge, Library Management Research Unit (LMRU Report No. 2)

Gimbel, H. (1969) *Work simplification in Danish public libraries: the report of the Work Simplification Committee of the Danish Library Association.* Chicago: American Library Association

Goodell, J. S. (1971) *A case study of catalogers in three university libraries using work sampling.* PhD Thesis, Tallahassee, Florida State University

Goodell, J. S. (1975) *Libraries and work sampling.* Littleton, Colo.: Libraries Unlimited

Haarala, A. R. (1978) Results of work study of inter-library loan and information services at Helsinki University Library. In N. Fjallbrant and K. McCarthy (1978) *Developing effectiveness for the next decade: Proceedings of the Seventh Meeting of IATUL May 16–21, 1977.* Goteborg: IATUL. pp.173–179

Heinisch, I. (1975) Work study fundamentals in determining staffing needs. In R. Funk (1975) (ed.) *Personalwirtschaftliche Probleme in öffentlichen und wissenschaftlichen Bibliotheken* [Personnel Management Problems in Public and Academic Libraries]. Berlin: Deutscher Bibliotheksverband. pp.101–130 (Materialen der Arbeitstelle für das Bibliothekswesen, 9)

Hersey, F. H. (1989) Workload measurement systems for librarians. *Bibliotheca Medica Canadiana*, **10**(3), 111–116

Heydrich, I. and Boeck, A. (1974) Investigations into the expenditure of work in leading libraries. *Mitteilungsblatt*, **24**(3), 240–244 (in German)

Kozumplik, W. G. (1967) A time and motion study in library operations. *Special Libraries*, **58**, 585–588

Leonard, L. E. *et al.* (1969) The Colorado Academic Libraries Book Processing Project time methodology. *Library Resources and Technical Services*, **13**(1), 115–141

Local Authorities Management Services and Computer Committee (1976) *Staffing of public libraries.* 3 volumes. London: HMSO

Logsdon, R. H. (1954) Time and motion studies in libraries. *Library Trends*, **2**(3), 401–409

Marsterson, W. A. J. (1976) Work study in a polytechnic library. *Aslib Proceedings*, **28**(9) 288–304

Sacher, H. I. and Schulze, A. (1975) Application of a work time analysis for cost calculation in libraries. *Zentralblatt für Bibliothekswesen*, **89**(3), 116–126 (in German)

Schultz, J. S. (1970) Program budgeting and work measurement for law libraries. *Law Library Journal*, **63**(3), 353–362

Smith, G. C. K. and Schofield, J. L. (1971) Administrative effectiveness: times and costs of library operations. *Journal of Librarianship*, **3**(4), 245–266

Spencer, C. C. (1971) Random time sampling with self-observation for library cost studies: unit costs of inter-library loans and photocopies at a regional reference library. *Journal of the American Society for Information Science*, **22**(3), 153–160

Spencer, C. C. (1980) Random time sampling with self-observation for library cost studies of reference questions. *Bulletin of the Medical Library Association*, **68**(1), 53–57

Tam, P. W. K. (1978) *Work study in the library cataloguing department.* Hong Kong: University of Hong Kong, Department of Industrial Engineering

Voos, H. (1966) Standard times for certain clerical activities in technical processing. *Resources and Technical Services*, **10**(2), 223–227

Woodruff, E. L. (1957) Work measurements applied to libraries. *Special Libraries*, **48**(4), 139–144

Practical Considerations

Aslib Engineering Group (1972) Conference on costing library and information services. *Aslib Proceedings*, **24**(6), 325–362 (various papers)

Havard-Williams, P. (1980) Can financial management be taught to librarians? In *Proceedings UK Serials Group Conference, 1979*. Oxford: Blackwell. pp.89–96

Sturt, R. (1972) Teaching costing techniques to librarians and information scientists of the future. *Aslib Proceedings*, **24**(6), 350–355

Tuttle, H. W. (1970) Standards for technical service cost studies. *Advances in Librarianship*, **1**, 95–111

Western Interstate Commission for Higher Education (1976) *Librarians handbook for costing network services*. Boulder: WICHE

Cost studies: some guideline sources

Association of Research Libraries, Office of Management Studies (1977) *Determining indirect cost rates in research libraries*. Washington: ARL (SPEC Kit No. 34)

Association of Research Libraries, Office of Management Studies (1979) *Cost studies and financial planning*. Washington: ARL (SPEC Kit No. 52)

Aubry, J. (1972) A timing study of the manual searching of catalogs. *Library Quarterly*, **42**(4), 399–415

Baldwin, E. V. and Marcus, W. E. (1941) *Library costs and budgets: a study of cost accounting in public libraries*. New York: Bowker

Beyersdorff, G. (1974) *Cost-performance analysis in public libraries of the Federal Area*. Berlin: Deutscher Bibliotheksverband

Beyersdorff, G. (1978) Kosten-Leistungsrechnung in Öffentlichen Bibliotheken. *Bibliothek: Forschung und Praxis*, **2**(3), 198–206

Birmingham Libraries Co-operative Mechanization Project (1972) *Costing catalogue systems in three libraries*. Birmingham: BLCMP

Bryant, P. and Needham, A. (1975) *Costing different forms of library catalogues*. Bath: University Library (BUCCS Final Report: Paper No. 7)

Cayless, C. F. and Merritt, C. G. (1977) The keeping cost of periodicals. *Australian Academic and Research Libraries*, **81**(4), 178–185

Cooper, M. D. (1972) A cost model for evaluating information retrieval systems. *Journal of the American Society for Information Science*, **23**(5), 306–312

Druschel, J. (1981) Cost analysis of an automated and manual cataloguing and book processing system. *Journal of Library Automation*, **14**(1), 24–49

Dubois, D. (1972) *Library labor cost accounting system*. Los Angeles: California State University and Colleges

Ellsworth, R. E. (1969) *The economics of book storage in college and university libraries*. Metuchen, NJ: Scarecrow Press

Hargrove, L. and Stirling, K. H. (1970) *California State Library: processing center designs and specifications: Volume V: Cost analysis*. Berkeley: Institute of Library Research

Hayes, R. M. (1996) Cost of electronic reference sources and LCM (Library Costing Model). *Journal of the American Society for Information Science*, **47**(3), 228–234

Jestes, E. C. and Laird, W. D. (1968) A time study of general reference work in a university library. *Research in Librarianship*, **2**(7), 9–16

King, M. (1980) On costing alternative patterns for Com-fiche catalogues. *Program*, **14**(4), 147–160

Klintoe, K. (1971) Cost analysis of a technical information unit. *Aslib Proceedings*, **23**(7), 362–371

Koenig, M. E. D. (1971) SCOPE: a cost analysis of an automated serials record system. *Journal of Library Automation*, **26**(3), 129–140

Lantz, B. E. (1978) Manual versus computerised retrospective reference retrieval in an academic library. *Journal of Librarianship*, **10**(2), 119–130

Leonard, L. E. *et al.* (1969) *Centralised book processing: a feasibility study based on Colorado academic libraries*. Metuchen, NJ: Scarecrow Press

Leung, S. W. (1987) Study of the cataloging costs at the University of California Riverside. *Technical Services Quarterly*, **5**(1), 57–66

MacQuarrie, C. (1962) Cost study: cost of ordering, cataloguing and preparation in Southern California Libraries. *Library Resources and Technical Services*, **6**(4), 337–350

Maier, J. M. (1969) Analyzing acquisitions and cataloguing costs. *Library Resources and Technical Services*, **13**(1), 127–135

Mosley, I. J. (1977) Cost effectiveness analysis of the automation of a circulation system. *Journal of Library Automation*, **10**(3), 240–254

Pierce, W. (1949) *Work measurement in public libraries: a report to the Director of the Public Library Inquiry*. New York: Social Sciences Research Council

Reichmann, F. (1953) The costs of cataloguing. *Library Trends*, **2**(2), 290–317

Ross, I. and Brooks, J. (1972) Costing manual and computerised library circulation systems. *Program*, **6**(3), 217–227

Ross, R. M. (1977) Cost analysis of automation in technical services. In J. L. Divilbiss (1977) *The economics of library automation: papers presented at the 1976 Clinic on Library Applications of Data Processing*. Urbana-Champaign: University of Illinois, Graduate School of Library Science. pp.10–27

Sayre, E. and Thielen, L. (1990) Cost accounting: a model for a small public library. *The Bottom Line*, **3**(4), 15–19

Shercliff, W. H. Tipper, D. M. and Needham, C. A. (1973) *College of Education Libraries Research Project: final report*. Manchester: Didsbury College of Education

Snyder, H. and Davenport, E. (1997) Costing and pricing in the digital age: a practical guide for information services. London: Library Association

Swank, R. C. (1956) Cataloguing cost factors. *Library Quarterly*, **26**, 303–317

Tesovnik, M. E. and De Hart, F. E. (1970) Unpublished studies of technical services time and cost studies: a selected bibliography. *Library Resources and Technical Services*, **14**(1), 56–67

Tucker, C. J. (1974) A comparison of the production costs of different physical forms of catalogue output. *Program*, **8**(2), 59–74

Van den Berg, S. (1993) Research of unit costing of library operations in Bradford University Library. Den Haag, Haagse Hogeschool-Sector Economie & Management (Report from a fieldwork placement at J. B. Priestley Library, University of Bradford)

Vickers, P. H. (1976) *Information management: final report on project 2: extension and revision of the COST1 Accounting Scheme to interactive systems of the network*. Luxembourg: DG/STIIM/CEC (EUR 5627e)

Vickers, P. H. and Rowat, M. (1977) *Information management: development and use of models for the prediction of costs for alternative information systems: final report on project 3, phase 1*. Luxembourg: CEC (EUR 5693c)

West, M. W. and Baxter, B. A. (1976) Unpublished studies of technical services time and costs: a supplement. *Library Resources and Technical Services*, **20**(4), 326–333

Woods, R. G. (1972) *The cost of cataloguing: three systems compared.* Southampton: University Library

Wynar, B. S. *et al.* (1963) Cost analysis in a technical services division. *Library Resources and Technical Services*, 7(4), 312–326

Chapter 7

Developments in managerial economics

7.1 An integrated approach to budgeting, accounting, costing and performance measurement

The inter-relation and integration between the four major management processes of budgeting, accounting, costing and performance measurement is a recurring theme and philosophical standpoint in this discussion. Budgeting, accounting and performance measurement have received a variety of treatments in the professional literature, with the first two areas being very well covered in the literature of general and financial management; more recent developments in performance measurement have already been considered in Section 4.3. The following discussion is intended to reinforce professional attitudes towards costing and accounting for library and information services within the general framework of financial management and budgeting.

To implement a strategy of active development information and library service managers need to identify positively the scope and limits of these four processes in their own organizations. Budgeting and accounting may very often involve practices and processes shared with a host organization; therefore, questions of internal and external significance are raised. For example, how dependent or independent is the library budgeting process in terms of the host organization; have steps been taken to exploit fully the accounting procedures provided by the host? Cost measurement and performance studies might be thought of as more exclusively library service concerns, but this is not necessarily so; for example, in a public library system the local authority corporate management services will have more than a passing interest in this area, although their activities are sometimes viewed with suspicion by library and information managers (and departmental managers generally).

Other (external) agencies are clearly interested in the performance aspect of library and information services, and in this area above all it may be very beneficial for the library to be seen to take the initiative in measurement, information gathering and monitoring. Performance measurement in libraries should be treated as a necessary professional task, although it can draw profitably on the experiences and findings of agencies outside the library itself. Long-term management development in libraries necessitates a clear and definite position on each of these managerial responsibilities. This means that the manager should write a specification for each area of responsibility, in terms of existing practices, and in terms of the potential application of the kinds of models discussed in this volume and in the professional literature.

In recognizing the need for an integrated approach between these areas of managerial responsibility each information and library manager should:

1 Make a statement of current organizational practices (in the library service, and in the host institution if applicable).

2 Identify specific personnel responsibilities for initiation, monitoring and control in these areas of managerial economics.

3 Clarify and describe the existing procedures followed and identify the possibilities for implementing new procedures, especially those which are likely to produce a closer integration of these four functions.

4 Design and activate a timetable for the activities concerned noting particularly the cyclical nature of many of them, the critical pathing aspects, and dependencies on other sources of data.

5 Design appropriate methods of reporting the stages of the various procedures, and institute proper methods of review and evaluation.

6 Develop means of relating and applying the information generated by these activities and their associated information systems to policy-making activities in the library and information service.

Technical change and the newer applications of computer technology are going to have some dramatic effects on each of these managerial activities. First of all there is likely to be a general impact on management practices and managers, with fundamental implications for the structures of information and library management. These impacts were revealing themselves in the early 1980s, when the predecessor to this work was being written; see for example Centre for Library and Information Management (1982); Botten (1982); Finer (1982); Roberts (1982a).

Subsequently these developments and impacts have become recognized as a field of activity and study in their own right generally referred to as strategic IT and strategic management of IT. This field has a massive literature within management typified by works such as Earl (1989) and Ward, Griffiths and Whitmore (1990). The wider perspective of the impacts of technology on information and library service were addressed in the British Library commissioned study *Information UK 2000* (Martyn, Vickers and Feeney, 1991) and by Bawden and Blakeman (1990). The mainstream professional journals cover the topic regularly from the technical and practical level of hardware and software requirements, implementation, performance and evaluation to studies of impacts on organizations and the management of change.

Already the implementation of computer-based systems in libraries has elicited demands for a better understanding of their effects, costs and benefits. Decision making in resource allocation is gradually becoming a more sophisticated process. There is a greater awareness of the risks of faulty decision making, and a search for a better means of technical support derived from improved budgeting, costing, accounting and performance measurement methods.

New technology brings with it the means of significantly better control over many library activities. Computer-based cataloguing and circulation systems, for instance, have information-handling capabilities which can be exploited to provide management information. Such systems have to be closely integrated with other types of management information handling and systems, of the kind discussed in Section 7.3. The technical problems and significance of such developments are now much better understood than a decade or more ago. But the effective development of such systems will certainly be aided if component procedures in the areas of budgeting, accounting, costing and performance measurement are refined and systematized.

De facto software standardization appears to have been achieved to a degree through Windows applications as a dominant market leader, and the edge has now moved onto Web publishing and Intranets. Converged office systems open up a realm of potential for operations and financial management. But these developments have again only served to underline the importance of knowing what you want to do in an organization; the technology is less and less the problem. However, defining your objectives is all, so that in the end the technology is only the means of providing what you require. The question remains both to be asked and answered: what kind of financial, resource, budgetary and information management/management information structures and systems does the organization need.

Turnkey library automation systems generally accommodate management information processing in their system modules, but explicit financial management software and modules are relatively less developed and prominent than their bibliographical and information retrieval counterparts. Systems such as Geac, BLCMP, Dynix and Cairs need to be assessed for their potential contribution to greater integration in financial and resource management. The library automation literature is to be consulted here through periodicals *Program* and *Vine* (in the UK) and the *Journal of Library Automation* (in the USA), and increasingly as technologies converge attention and the forum shifts to the literature of intranets, hypertext/hypermedia and advanced office systems. Any turnkey system with modules for library fines, charging and billing, cash handling, and serials subscription and general acquisitions management provides a good interface to more general organizational procedures of financial and budgetary management. An invoice-creating and handling system can be regarded almost as a mirror image of a budgetary control system.

General database and statistical packages such as Excel can clearly be used to handle the required financial functions, but many users find themselves on their own when it comes to exploiting the software in a specific situation. The UK CTI LIS *Resources Guide* offers surprisingly little in financial management applications software for training purposes (Computers in Teaching Initiative, 1997).

On the other hand multipurpose spreadsheet software (like Excel) is now user friendly enough to make a customized application for an information and library unit. So for example the EBIC budget matrix in Table 8.1 can simply be transferred to a spreadsheet. The critical task though is to know enough about the process of budgeting and costing to design the protocols for your customized application; for example, defining suitable budgetary programmes, and defining these as fields in the database. With the basic matrix and data established variable modelling can be undertaken.

Matrices for income and expenditure can be created, and subunits aggregated and disaggregated as desired. Unit cost and times can be treated as constants (or as variables) and related to different levels of output or demand and run through a model to produce budgetary estimates. It is hoped in some way that the approach taken in this work can help to bridge this gap in developing protocols for customized applications. Cost analysis methods can be applied to develop unit times and costs, sound functional programme units can be described, and the resources required estimated (metaphorically analogous to the builders' quantity surveying). These steps in themselves would be a realization of the type of integration argued for in this present discussion.

It will thus be necessary to examine the financial needs and environment of the organization, and move to creating a clear capability to address the budgeting, costing, accounting and performance needs of the system. The results will provide the clarity to design the financial management system, and identify the data flows and data which can be handled by the software chosen for the management information system. This is no trivial task because it is in effect imposing the burden of creating an information strategy and a strategic information system on the information service and library organization. The measure of the problem is to be found in the reality that many small and medium scale commercial enterprises have failed to succeed in this endeavour.

7.2 Sources of statistics, performance measures and management data

While the development of new and different sources of management information could be seen as a panacea for some of the present ills of library and information service management, there must be no illusion that operational library management information systems are already available fully formed and ready for use. They have frequently been a topic for speculation and discussion, but have more rarely become an object of experimental testing or practical realization. However the climate of opinion has been changing progressively. The real reduction in levels of funding for library and information services experienced in the industrialized countries since the late 1970s (and which has continued without interruption into the 1990s) has shown managers that to produce the same or more with less resources means a greater self-knowledge of systems and activities. This has been coupled with a more critical and sharp edged use of management techniques and methods, not least in the areas of resource allocation and budgeting. Consequently, higher standards of costing, accounting and performance measurement have been called for and are still required.

In the absence of off-the-peg solutions to library management information (at least for the time being), it is sensible to maintain, and reappraise if need be, the existing sources and types of statistics, performance measures and data. For this reason a short discussion is interposed between discussing the primary objective of integrating budgeting, accounting, costing and performance aspects of management and the means by which this integration could be achieved – the development of purpose designed library management information systems.

Table 7.1 shows briefly the current state and relations between three areas of data which are or can be made readily accessible to library managers. The first group of descriptive statistics (of information and library activities) in one form or another is kept almost universally by library and information service managers.

There is still a good deal of professional debate about library statistics and often dissatisfaction with the records kept, the means of collection and the use to which they might be put. There is still an implicit tendency to confuse descriptive library statistics with management information or decision support information; this confusion will continue until the desired shape of specific library management information systems becomes clear.

Some illustration may help to make the point. Raw statistics of library stocks, however 'interesting' or revealing, on their own have little value as management information as a preface to decision and action. If they tell you your library is full, you still have to deal with the problem. The stock statistics are of more value if broken down by subject, and even more so if a use element is noted; adding a time dimension to that use gives more value. The addition of information on storage costs and an element for collection maintenance (covering a staffing element) further increases the value of the data. At this point the data are getting much closer to useful management information, but have acquired four more dimensions. The final level of addition in this illustration can be made only if

TABLE 7.1 Sources of statistics, performance measures and management data

	Primary sources	*Secondary sources*
ibrary tatistics	*Internally derived* Departmental and sectional records. Annual report statistics and compilations *External/published sources* Material, data etc. supplied by/to/for external professional and governmental organizations	*Standards* e.g. Lynch and Eckard (1981). Inventory of library statistics practices (1972) Information and advice provided by professional and other agencies *Reviews of the literature* e.g. Moore (1976); Moore (1977)
'erformance easures	*Internally derived* Internal studies carried out as required, with 'outside' methods. Data and measures generated from Management Data Systems, and from formal systems such as PPBS and ZBB budgeting. *Externally derived* e.g. Use of inter-firm/library comparison techniques	*Professional literature* There is an extensive, widely scattered literature of original papers, reports and reviews. For initial orientation see *Further Readings* sections in this volume. Professional groups and conferences provide ideas and discussion for practitioners
lanagement ata	*Internally derived* From descriptive statistics and performance measures sources. From formal budget systems, automated services (catalogue, circulation etc.), and inhouse research/surveys *Externally derived* e.g. National statistics, user survey data	*Published data sources* e.g. National social, economic and cultural statistics, e.g. census data e.g. Policy-making studies and material generated by external agencies e.g. General and professional knowledge e.g. External data on markets, market research etc.

ne organization has cost measurement capacity (supported no oubt by good budgetary systems), and then has the technical infor- nation management capacity to produce, handle, report and analyse ne data.

Descriptive library statistics can be, and often are improved and iscussed critically. In this manner they can certainly provide some ind of interim solution to the library manager's management information problem. Standardization of library statistics is urgently needed, but the implementation of proposals for standardization is mostly slow and sporadic. Costs (especially unit costs) are often considered as a library statistic, but it is preferable to treat such output indicators as performance measures (consequent on operating a proper budgetary system). But the illustration should serve to make the point about the sense of purpose and relative complexity required to furnish useful management information.

A greater interest in the methods and scope of budgeting, costing and accounting procedures should help to improve considerably the general environment in which library statistics are generated and handled. There are convincing arguments to be made for the fact that standards for description of activities and terminology for costing can be equally useful for library statistical description. A programme description and definitions of cost centres can be helpful in statistical description and for regular costing and accounting. Performance measurement is thereby later benefitted from the trouble taken to standardize the concepts and units of measurement at a much more elemental and basic stage in library management practice.

Performance measures are the second important group of existing data. There are many models for library and information service performance measures and very few accepted standards. The studies by King Research (Office of Arts and Libraries, 1990) and papers such as those by te Boekhorst (1995) and Carbone (1995) may be part of a move towards defining some de facto standard, but the truth is that only time and practice will tell. The professional debate in this area is still at a raw stage although gratifyingly lively. Performance measures and evaluation criteria are inseparable. Sometimes it is possible to draw up the evaluation criteria, but to be less successful at measuring the performance itself. The professional awareness of evaluation and performance among library managers is high; sometimes negatively (to be avoided if possible) but also positively (as a process which begins with establishing operational aims and objectives, and is pursued by genuine attempts to establish the performance parameters of a service).

The third group of existing data has to be loosely identified as management data; this is perhaps everything that cannot be specifically considered as a descriptive library statistic or as a performance measure. Such management data may be internally generated (in which case may have many of the characteristics of a library statistic) or external in which case they are environmental data. It is not eas to categorize this group of data since they range from hard quantitative data to qualitative impressions, and also encompass political and other kinds of intelligence, which undoubtedly are very influential in determining library managers' styles and approaches to resource allocation and decision making.

These three rough types and categorizations of management data are very important for developing an integrated approach. It is these by and large which constitute the manager's base for decision making. At the moment they are manifestly imperfect tools for managers to use, largely because there is no coherent framework which they naturally generate or encompass to permit ease of handling – input, processing and analysis. This situation defines the need and scope for purpose designed library management information systems which collate, integrate and elaborate upon these relatively plentiful raw data.

7.3 Management information systems and related developments

7.3.1 Resources management systems and management information

The previous paragraphs have sketched out a background to management accounting, resources management and management information and show how cost and performance data feed through these operations as a constant theme. The practical realization of these operations within particular library and information service managements remains another question.

Figure 7.1 sketches out the principal features of the main structures of a resources management system and a management information system. The central part of an applicable operational system is a number of information files: input, throughput, output and performance files each with subsections (e.g. section, programme, operation, product etc.).

The subsections in the input files would relate to the inputs of resources (categorized, for example, as quantities and costs as primary expenses), budgetary headings (for example, by library processes, or more explicitly by goal-orientated programmes), and by section or department (by line responsibility and by cost centres). Similar sub-sectional files for throughout, output and performance can be defined.

The information files themselves relate, as can be seen, to the functions within the resources management system (planning and

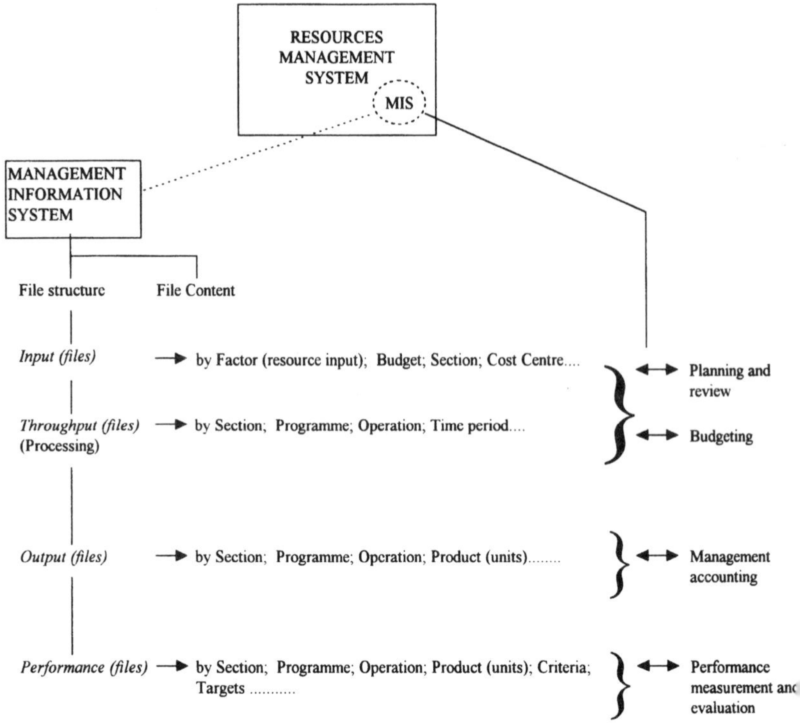

Figure 7.1. Resources management systems and management information systems

review, budgeting, managerial accounting, and performance measurement and evaluation). The information files in practice serve both the resource management system and the management information system; in fact, two indissoluble parts of a whole. Both systems could be subsequently developed as a higher order decision support system.

So to summarize:

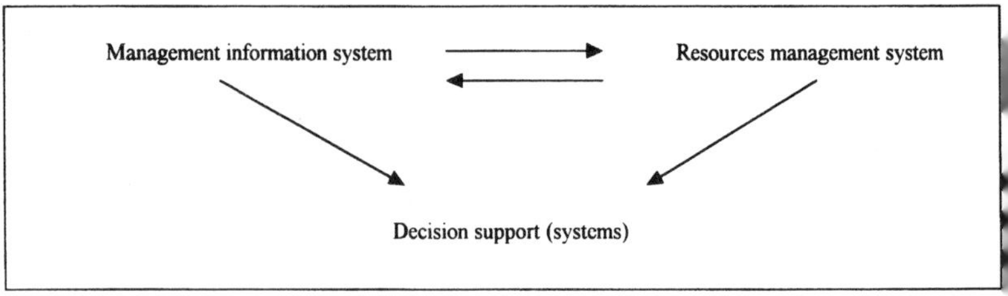

7.3.2 Planning and review

Policy making (including goal and objective setting) and planning, and the regular situation reviews which are necessary, form the basis of resource management (see Chapter Two for a more extensive discussion). There are various traditions and variations in practice depending on the style of management adopted and the type of library and information organization in question. In many 'one man bands' and other small library and information services the functions are concentrated in one person and distinctions between operations blurred. In larger hierarchical organizations, the functions may be concentrated and more sharply defined. More complex organizational patterns require more explicit procedures and information flows. Resource and information management systems are needed and can be adapted to these different managerial environments and circumstances.

7.3.3 Programming

The concept of programmes and programming has recurred throughout this discussion of library and information service costing and accounting. A programme is generally defined as an area of resource allocation and management structure, which can be individually identified and sustained. Any element which can be operationally defined can be regarded actually or potentially as a programme. In practice programmes are most frequently product and/or service oriented. Programming is concerned with the definition, management and administration of programmes. Service goals and objectives should be used to describe activities and define programmes, and these can then be translated into budgetary and accounting formats, elements and terms.

During the general promotion of service plans and developments the manager should give some thought as to how to make programme elements explicit: that is in terms of budget definitions and headings, data and statistical collections, job descriptions, reporting procedures, and evaluation and performance analysis. Over a period of time the basis for programmes may well change, and the implications of such changes have to be assessed across the whole system.

7.3.4 Budgeting

Drawing up estimates and drafting a budget is still often likely to be the main financial and accounting task of many library and information service managers. This is no more than a minimum, which less and less should be seen as an exclusive exercise, but more as supplementing other measures of accounting, control, monitoring and performance measurement. Besides being a tool of justification and something which has itself to be justified, the budget should be seen as a good method of visibly stating and describing the programme structure of service activities. Once developed the budget should be vigorously related to means of budgetary control.

7.3.5 Accounting and management accounting

For library and information service management usage the distinction between financial accounting and management accounting can still be drawn as it is in business enterprises. Very few library and information services have to present full stewardship accounts on the lines of business financial statements and profit and loss accounts, but they have as great a need for management accounting as commercial business. Cost data collection is at the heart of management accounting: this must be repeatedly emphasized. But full management accounting requires a system for handling and presenting cost data, as well as a style of management which shows a positive attitude to the role of cost data as a tool for detailed and exacting resource management.

7.4 Management information systems

Morse (1968) writing on management information systems states:

> neither the computer expert nor the librarian (for different reasons) really know what data could be useful for the librarian to have collected, analysed and displayed, so he can make decisions with some knowledge of what the decision implies. What is needed before the computer designs are frozen is for models of the sort developed in this book to be played with to see which of them could be useful, and to see what data are needed and in what form, in order that both models and computer... can be used effectively by librarians. (pp.141–142)

There has already been discussion of the elements of management information systems (especially 1.4, 4.1 and 4.2) and strong suggestions as to the central place that they could occupy in management accounting and library and information service managerial economics. The management information system plays a role in a wider resources management system. This is of central importance to the service manager although discussion of form and operation of such systems cannot be attempted within the scope of this book. However, it is important that this final section sketches out the practical form which a library and information service-based management information system might take, and to suggest how service managers might begin to experiment with the concepts of management information in their own systems.

7.4.1 Basic characteristics of library and information service management information systems

There are several basic aspects of a management information system to consider. At one level there is a view which regards management information as an all pervasive phenomenon of management, with information providing the focus for decisions about allocation of resources and economic activity (see Table 4.1). At this level the attitude of the manager to management is an important factor determining the stance chosen.

At the other level there is a focus on management information (and the management of that information) with more moderate objectives, which regards it as a potentially useful artefact of the management process and the productive activities of the system. At this level the management information system is in some ways more solely confined to being an information or data-carrying system. The management information system is thus mainly, if not entirely, a technical system – an information system with the distinguishing features of a set of collection and input procedures, a set of files, a means of manipulating those files, and ways of obtaining analyses and processed outputs from those files.

So far as library and information services stand at present there appears to be a willingness to consider both levels of management information and systems and their implications. Service managements have already gone a long way towards identifying the problems of delivery of service and the roles of management in providing those services. The domain of management information however, still rests at best in many organizations on a foundation of descriptive library statistics; these tend to be of little prescriptive value although they may be useful for between-system comparisons; see Moore (1976); Moore (1977b); Lynch and Eckard

(1981) for some historic viewpoints, and contrast this with the late developed views of MacDougall (1985), Brophy (1986), Harri (1987) and King Research (Office of Arts and Libraries, 1990). The growing body of comparative and contemporary statistic garnered systematically by bodies like the LISU (and its contribu tors) in the UK, and those of the ARL and RLG in the USA sho at least an enrichment of the empirical base for macro and micro statistical intelligence (management information at the higher level)

Given this pluralistic state of affairs it is uncertain what majo innovations in library and information service management infor mation systems will take place from these organizational statistica systems alone, partly since the potential to develop managemen information systems from most present library statistical reportin systems is very limited by a lack of standardization (seen most whe inter-organizational comparisons are made). And it must be note that once the internal data and measures are made, they ar inevitably used for comparison (one usually reports, in som fashion, favourable internal measures) to put one's organization i a better light or to justify some action or claim.

The deficiency resulting from the above mentioned aspects lie in the lack of means provided by these statistical reporting system to integrate the managerial activities of resource allocation an resource management through all stages of the system. Hence th emphasis in this discussion on alternative approaches using a input, throughput, output typology related to the fundamental area of goals and objectives, programming, budgeting, accounting an performance measurement.

The development and implementation of a library and informa tion service management information system therefore mean radical changes in management style, and a much tighter drawin together of management, systems and process activities. The firs stage will entail the creation of a system of management informa tion files as the specific means of sustaining the wider and mor pervasive approach to management and management informatio needed for the long-term economic management of library an information services.

A sketch of the system of management information files require has already been given in Figure 7.1. The structure and substruc ture of the files is provided by representations of functions programmes, organizational divisions or staff responsibilities. In generalized management information system there will be four basi sets of files: the first three essential files are for input (which wi be related to estimate and budget files and initial resource allocations), processing (concerned with the conversion of input to output, i.e. throughput, and with the appropriate means of analysing and transforming input and throughput data to give the final measures), and output (which displays the transformed input and throughput data in terms of final measures, according to the different file structures chosen according to management purpose). The fourth set of files will consist of performance and evaluation data from all sources (including cost data), which through manipulation of the other three files can be related to all stages of resource allocation and processing from input.

Practical experience to date with library management information systems fully categorized in this way is fairly limited (see discussion earlier in Section 7.1). The historic exemplar is by Hamburg (1974) who makes extensive use of the model system specified by Hayes and Becker (1970). Extracts from the Hamburg and Hayes and Becker documents are reproduced in Appendix 6. It is clear that these proposals differ in specific outline from the generalized MIS discussed in the preceding paragraphs, mainly because many more subfiles not directly related to management cost accounting data are included. Nevertheless, the general concepts behind these different interpretations are similar, except that our present discussion chooses a model using cost data needs as a starting point.

Both models converge in the sense that they are flexibly structured. The four file model can be expanded in its structure (for instance to cover all the detail required of the serials subsystem). The different functional aspects of the Hayes and Becker model could each be expanded and extended to focus on the cost aspect, by progressively detailing the resources allocated to each subsequent resource-consuming process. However, the fact that some items, such as personnel service reports, would not be suitable for such treatment does not invalidate the basic contention. The data content possibilities for a library management information system can be gauged by considering proposals from Hamburg (1974) and Clements (1975); in practice these proposals could be fine tuned to represent contemporary conditions.

The managerial tasks of planning, controlling, measuring and monitoring add up to a formidable complex of operations requiring many skills for successful accomplishment. Figure 7.2 is a very crude attempt to summarize some of the main relationships; these are highlighted in the following explanation.

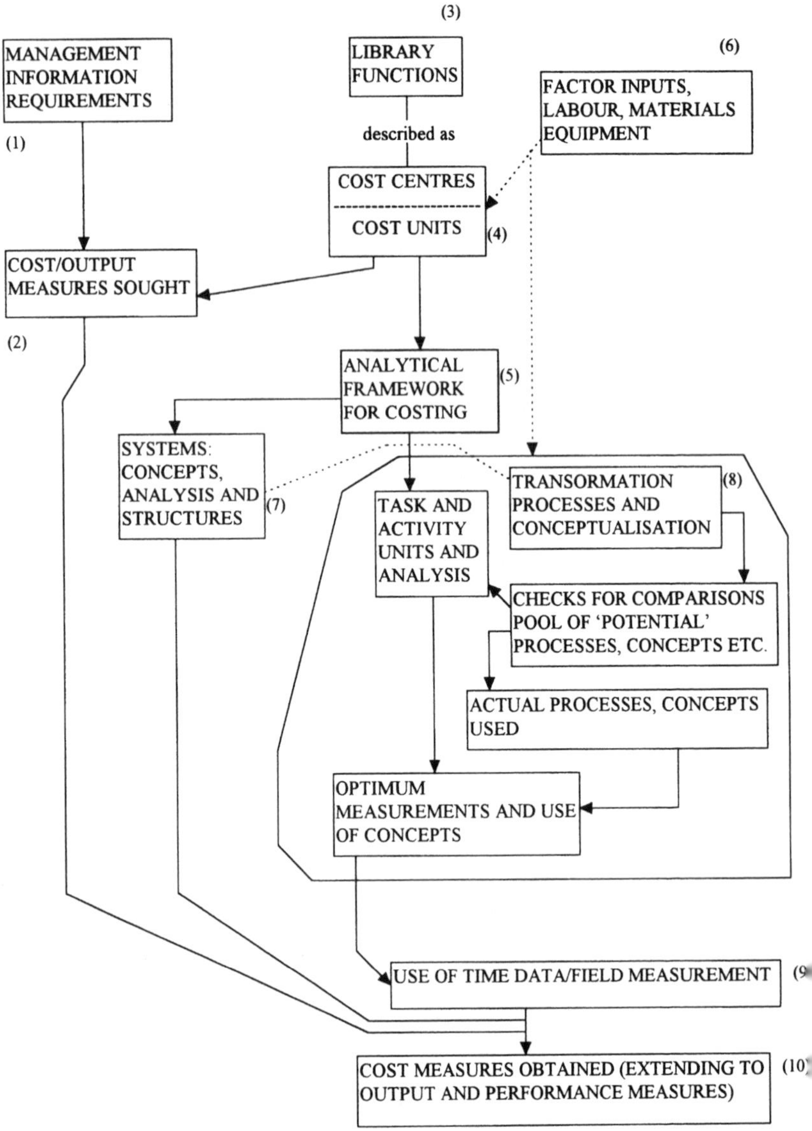

Figure 7.2. Management information, costing and optimum measurement

- The management information requirement (1) is for cost measures related to output.
- These cost measures (2) relate to service (library/information) functions (3).
- The service functions (3) which are described for costing purposes in terms of cost centres and cost units (4), are derived from an analytical framework for costing (5).
- Resources are allocated to functions in terms of productive inputs (6).
- The analytical and systems frameworks (5) and (7) are used to make conceptual and informational transformations (8) similar to a black box interpretation. At this stage the model is difficult to sustain in a simple form because it attempts to represent the mental process of the manager trying to balance out goals and objectives with the resources available and the processes by which the productive objectives can be attained.
- The cost and output measures sought (2) are also likely to be used as one of the criteria for integrating and differentiating at stage (8) between the tasks and activities performed, the objectives sought, and known norms and targets.

  If it can be simply described this process is a comparative procedure using conceptual and practical tools from costing, accounting and systems analysis combined with managerial skills and judgement.
- Cost, time and other operational data (9) are generated from a management information system during this comparative process, so that the requirement specified at stage (2) is met at stage (10).
- Stage (10) is the descriptive and analytical measures of output, cost and performance obtained.

Another way of looking at the purpose and objectives of a management information system for decision purposes is to relate the expected and/or actual output to the amount of input required. It will thus require a configuration (for example, files and protocols) capable of handling data on:

- programme input measures

- programme consumption measures
- programme output measures
- programme performance measures.

These requirements bring the information system into close proximity with the management accounting system, which is concerned with output measures and their input costs, and with variations in input cost (per unit of output). General management information handling and handling of accounting information are thus closely related or mapped upon one another. This is the essential point to be grasped.

7.4.2 Manual systems

It is feasible to develop a manually operated management information system with the appropriate files, procedures and analysis capabilities. A small library or information unit might find this an attractive proposition and an alternative to something more elaborate. In the past when computers were not available this would have been the only possibility, although some mechanization by use of a tabulator system would have been available. Nowadays, the choice is not between manual or computer, but a progression from simple to more complex. The simple stage is the recognition of the need to collect data and the action of doing something about it (a manual task at first). The more complex stages are the consequences of reacting to this need.

However, with the acute competition for managerial time it is most unlikely that even the smallest library would want now to set up a manual system, except as a pilot exercise. With PCs as virtually standard equipment there can nowadays be little justification for not starting to develop some kind of management information system: by keeping lists and data files (manually at first, and then converting data to machine form) the first step has already been taken; relating files one to the other is a natural second step, requiring mastery of relational database software (a training task which will soon bring results). When this stage is reached the manager will have experienced and understood the need, and will usually want more. The turnkey library automation system is one solution; other solutions use versatile general purpose software, which is relatively easy to use and customize.

Whether the final system chosen is manual or computer based there is still a great deal of manual and intellectual preparatory effort involved initially, which in some guise or other will continue when the system is set up. Staff have to be familiarized with recording and logging procedures. The implementation of such a management information system would have been preceded by extensive discussion and examination of the existing library system and its components and activities, as well as any future development plans. Whether computer or manual procedures are involved files and records have to be maintained once the system is set up and some of this work will be done off-computer. The system has to be programmed to perform the required analyses, and purchased software may require adaptation. Finally, the manager and staff must have sufficient time to interpret and consider the implications of the results; this process should ideally have more time assigned to it than system development and running.

There is a role for a small manual system as a pilot project for a more ambitious and permanent computer-based system. As to the design of such a system, there is at present still rather little library and information service experience to build on. The principles sketched out here and some of the reports mentioned in the reading lists will hopefully prove inspirational. The techniques of costing discussed in this book will, however, assist in determining the size of the costs segment in the management information system, and the measures most likely to prove useful.

7.4.3 Computer-based systems

The advent of the computer age has revolutionized the development of management information techniques in industry and commerce. The modern management information system is the product of massive computer applications. Taking the library and information service as an example of a complex enterprise organization, the contrasts in the area of management information could not be stronger. Some preliminary remarks on this have already been made in Section 7.1, and the discussion in the previous section shows how fluid is the boundary between 'old' manual and 'new' computer concepts. Still relatively few of even the largest libraries have yet developed an integrated manually based management information system, and even fewer have taken advantage of the possibilities of computer-based applications to the maximum extent.

Some historic examples of the trend can be noted. At California State University, Northridge, (Mitchell 1978) and in some pilot studies for LARC by Axford (1972) there is evidence of computer applications to costing at a fairly detailed level. But even these very promising initiatives have not matured into the development of more comprehensive library-specific management information systems. The area of computer-based library management information systems awaits major innovators on the back of what has already been achieved in library automation turnkey applications (see Section 7.1 above for some remarks). When this innovation takes place it will be gratifying to see the system designs include a strong element of cost data handling. The need for such systems and the advantage they can confer on managements has hopefully been demonstrated in this book. The wide dissemination of mini and microcomputer equipment and electronic office systems provide ample opportunity for experiment and innovation by library managers.

There should be scope for adaptation of small commercial management information packages for library use (Dewey, 1992). These opportunities should be seized together with a long awaited reform of library statistics-gathering programmes; work by Lynch and Eckard for the American Library Association (1981) was a noteworthy and helpful example of what could be done.

7.4.4 Accounting and cost control in management information systems

While management information system functions can be wide ranging and could be seemingly ever expanding, it is worth emphasizing that two major functions of such systems must be accounting and cost control. These two functions will amount to a sizeable capacity for budgetary control. The management accounting aspect can be achieved by a suitably differentiated structure of files to give sectional, responsibility, and programme account statements with cost data presented down to cost centre and cost element levels. Output cost measures can be derived from these, and variation in index values provides one of the main means of cost control. The accounting and cost reports provide no more than the first data-oriented stage in facilitating management economic decision.

7.4.5 Reporting cost data in a management information system

A computer-based management information system will be an interactive one, so that instant reports and displays of cost and other data can be provided. Over a typical one-year period a pattern of reporting could be developed. For instance, reports could be presented in a cumulative form at weekly, monthly and quarterly intervals with the possibility to draw on a backfile of records for annual trend analysis, and point by point comparisons. Visual display and printout would be the media used. All these reports would derive from the files and structures built into the system (section, responsibility, programme, etc.), and could be enhanced by aggregation (for instance, building up sectional data to compute annual storage costs per volume). This would provide a capability to generate data for various resource-modelling exercises. The computer and software technology is available now for all these simple, unsophisticated but highly useful operations.

7.4.6 Practical development of a library and information service management information system

A consideration of the simple practical issues of establishing the costs of library and information operations has been guided by the assumption that this aspect of service management has a wider context. The discussion has led to an appraisal of cost data within the wider sphere of management information systems, which in the long term should help contribute to the process of management decision in resource allocation and the development of a body of knowledge on library managerial economics.

The state of the art in library and information service costing is far from perfect and the development of service management information systems still peri-embryonic. However, the art can and will be improved by library and information service managers if some progress can be made toward standardization of concepts and techniques.

Innovations in systems may have to come from the computer rather than the library field, but the willingness of library and information service managers to experiment will be crucial to the process, and could show the commercial systems innovators that a worthwhile market for providing hardware and software exists. The key themes of the literature on library and information service costing appear always to have been ones of hope, expectation and despair. In reality there are not one but two problems – the second is of management information. The way ahead must be to solve both cost and information problems using the same methods and techniques, and for this reason the argument in this book is that costing and management information are the two sides of the same coin.

7.5 Development of managerial and economic models

7.5.1 Role of formal models in resource management

In the day-to-day running of libraries and information units the manager will make very little if any use of formal models of resource management. On the contrary, the management of resources tends by and large to be conducted on an empirical and pragmatic basis, relying on only a minimal level of formal procedures and their associated documentation. This is certainly the general picture; there are exceptions, but often only for restricted or small areas of allocation. There will be very few library and information service managers who do not prepare some kind of estimates, draft a budget, and have some means of monitoring expenditure, but it is a minority who build upon this basis – hardly avoidable – an apparatus to relate inputs to throughput, output and performance appraisal; and in so doing relate budgeting, accounting, costing and performance.

Pressure on resources and the need to justify resources committed to library and information activities is gradually modifying practices and attitudes, and could lead to the wider development and application of more formalized models and procedures for the management of resource allocation, the measurement of output and performance and of justification for levels of support. The management information system with its subsystem for measuring cost and cost performance will itself be an element in the resources management system (RMS), which each library will find it useful to develop.

The occasional collection of cost and other performance data should gradually be made to assume a larger place in the scheme of management, until it is organized as a permanent feature of management routine. Given a more plentiful supply of performance data there will be opportunities to test out some of the existing formal economic models of resource allocation, and to develop new ones which need hitherto unavailable data. For example, acquisition/inter-lending models, library storage models and stock use/relegation models could all be used in an operational and more realistic fashion given a reliable source of cost and performance data. Possibilities exist to build these models into computer-based cost and management information systems and associated programmes, which need to be widely developed and applied in library and information services during the coming decade.

7.5.2 A structure for economic decision making

There are two essential aspects to economic decision making in a library: one is the technical support provided by an information system, to provide cost, performance and related data; the other is the organizational and social base provided by the library and its staff. Management information systems or resources management systems are little use on their own if not supported by the organizational and social base of the library; some aspects of the social base have already been mentioned in the preceding sections on decision making and objectives. Management information is about the things and the people within the management process and the system managed; there is an indissolubility about both and a symbiotic relationship exists between them.

The degree of formality and explicitness of these relationships and processes varies with the type of library and information unit, and especially with the factors of staff size and number of levels or zones in the structure. Where there are perhaps more than three or four professional staff (with differentiated responsibilities) and more than two grade levels or zones, plus a possible geographical spread of resources, the need for formal and explicit procedures is evident.

In other words, the need for economic decision structures and management information systems is related partly to the general level of organizational complexity. In the smaller unit (falling below and about the threshold levels just mentioned) it is important to take note of the possibilities of formal systems, procedures and models. In larger systems, whether serving industrial, special, educational or public communities there can be little justification for ignoring the need to embrace a formal system, procedures and models. Cost measurement is close to the heart of these systems and models, and an early appreciation and acquaintance with the possibilities of costing and management accounting will both ease and stimulate the use of formal structures and tools for economic decision making. Some of the social aspects of economic decision making are suggested in the schematic chart in Figure 7.3.

7.5.3 The relationship between cost measurement and studies of effectiveness, performance, impact and benefit

At the risk of repetition it is important to emphasize the development of a clear relationship between cost measures and the different kinds of output and performance measures applicable to library and

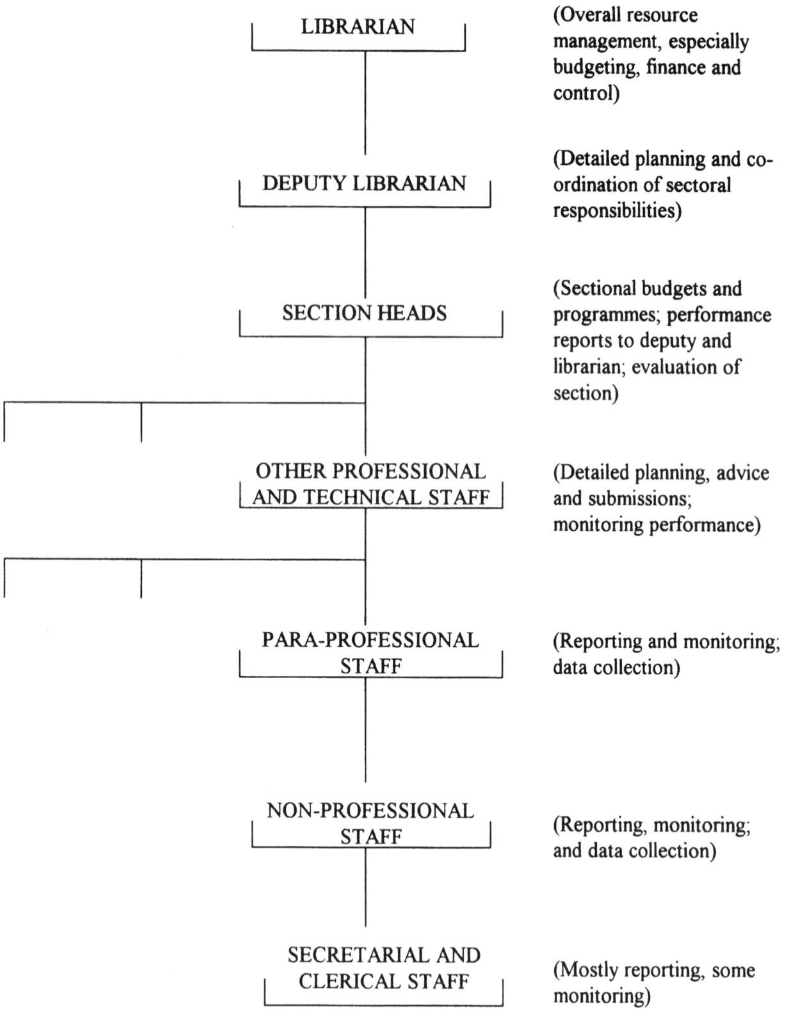

Figure 7.3. A schematic library management structure with economic decision making and information gathering responsibilities

information services. Mohr (1979) in a review of the costing programme at the California State University, Northridge distinguishes between use-oriented and system-oriented evaluation. Both these types of evaluation are directed towards final output and the latter is characterized by attention to the external or 'surface' aspects of the system.

It seems reasonable and useful to enlarge this categorization and consider a third type of evaluation related to the system-oriented type, which should be called internal evaluation. Internal evaluation looks at the progression of relationships between input and throughput in relation to output. Mohr's view is that output, impact, effectiveness and benefit should always be treated as a perspective of internal studies. This is an agreeable approach, even if one which may prove difficult to put into practice. In terms of management information, and resource and economic management, it could be solved partly by focusing attention on well structured goals and objectives, which are given practical form in the programme statements of the library, and reflected therefore in the budgetary and accounting procedures. Statements of operational objectives may thus form the basis of an explicit relationship between these evaluation concepts which are at the heart of resource management technique.

7.5.4 A forward view

The matters discussed in this book more often reflect what libraries should do (and what many library managers obviously intend to do or hope to do) rather than what is actually done in practice. While it is quite commonplace among library managers to bemoan the state of library management, the real grounds for doing so are not always as strong as emotional preference might suggest. However, in the realm of library economic management the bemoaning does have a strong correspondence to the facts and practices in the majority of services. There are notable exceptions.

The very largest library systems do have formal procedures (often quite elaborate budgets and management controls) for economic management, but these may be both antiquated and arcane; they will have probably grown up with the organization, rather than have been considered as entities in themselves for their own development, appraisal and management. In the mid-1980s the British Library had *ab initio* implemented a major scheme of internal costing and management accounting, which could hopefully be discussed as a model for adaptation to other library systems. Other major national libraries (in the USA, Canada and Germany, for example) were then following this trend. But the great majority of library and information services are medium or small units, which may need different and sympathetic forms of methods and implementation.

The suggestions and proposals made in this book will, it is to be hoped, also stimulate rather than stifle debate. The way ahead is through the efforts of librarians and managers taking the basic concepts and ideas and applying them to the circumstances of their libraries and information services. At the outset there is no prospect of a common solution, but with an honest internal appraisal many are likely to come near to certain points of view espoused in this book. For instance, the relationship between costing, accounting, budgeting and performance measurement; the need for standardization in costing and accounting procedures; and the desirability of comparable methods and measures (the value of which was demonstrated early on by the work of the Centre for Interfirm Comparison (Harrington, Carruthers and Moffatt, 1981) and by Jones (1981) and Roberts (1982c)).

While the general source for the ideas expounded in this discussion is the application of conventional management science to libraries, a more specific source derives from a quiet but persistent movement in librarianship begun in the 1960s directed towards a quantitative and analytical approach to management problem solving in libraries. In the USA this approach came under the general heading of operational research with Morse (1968), Raffel and Shishko (1969), Leimkuhler (1972) and Hamburg (1974), as its best known exponents historically.

The ideas of conceptual abstraction and modelling as well as systems analysis have been at the heart of this trend. As such, these ideas should continue to inspire and enrich the study of library performance and the practical development of better economic management techniques. In Britain a number of research projects (especially at Durham and Lancaster Universities) were begun in the late 1960s, and have become influential as guideposts for work in this area: Hawgood and Morley (1969); Buckland *et al.* (1970). It is regrettable that this vein of library management research seems to have rather died down in the last decade; this may be a reflection of a lack of funding for such work, although it may have been compensated by more inhouse investigation, the results of which are not widely published.

The momentum of work on these topics may have lapsed but it has not disappeared from the scene altogether; it may now be labelled as policy research or organizational planning. Library resource management and economic management are concerns as pressing as ever before. Given a chance to reconsider and implement improved methods of costing and accounting, the prospects for developing and implementing techniques already explored are greatly enhanced.

One should not be unaware, however, that there is a backlash (or perhaps some scepticism) against quantitative management methods in libraries. The reluctance to adopt such techniques hopefully reflects genuine pressures on where to focus priority of attention: that is, the behavioural aspects may have been relatively neglected, and there has been catching up to be done here rather than downright antipathy to scientific, quantitative and positivist approaches to management. Library management education may be of some help here, especially through continuing and in-service training programmes.

The purpose of this book may then be regarded partly as a trigger for a revivification of interest in a still neglected, yet essential area of library and information service management technique, which has considerable ramifications for progress in other areas of management. The ideas discussed, and the proposals made implicitly are offered as guides and signposts to assist library and information service managers to clarify issues in their own minds, and to help them take the crucial steps to initiate and implement schemes and methods in their own systems which have a maximum degree of useful similarity to those of their neighbours and colleagues.

7.5.5 Further reading

Programming and budgeting, costing and accounting

Chen, C. C. (1980) *Zero-base budgeting in library management.* London: Mansell

Citron, H. R. and Dodd, J. B. (1984) Cost allocation and cost recovery considerations in a special academic library: Georgia Institute of Technology. *Science and Technology Libraries*, **5**(2), 1–14

Cochran, M. L., Smith, A. C. and Bender, A. D. (1970) An application of managerial cost accounting to a science information center. *Journal of the American Society for Information Science*, **21**(2), 163–164

Eckels, D. C. and Lyders, R. A. (1978) The allocation of operating costs to users of a medical library. *Proceedings ASIS*, **15**, 123–125

Hamburg, M. *et al.* (1974) *Library planning and decision making systems.* Cambridge, Mass.: M.I.T. Press

Jennings, L. (1980) Zero-base budgeting and the management of library change. *Australian Library Journal*, **29**(4), 181–187

Jennings, L. (1981) Budgeting and decision making. *Australian Special Libraries News*, **14**(4), 96–107

Keller, J. E. (1969) Program budgeting and cost-benefit analysis in libraries. *College and Research Libraries*, **30**(2), 156–160

Koch, H.-A. (1985) Research on budgeting and standards for academic libraries in the Federal Republic of Germany. *Journal of Librarianship*, **17**(4), 268–292

Koenig, M. E. D. (1980) *Budgeting techniques for libraries and information centers*. New York: Special Libraries Association

Lee, C.-T. (1981) Acquisitions budget control in a CAE library. *Australian Academic and Research Libraries*, **12**(3), 174–184

Lee, S. H. (1977) (ed.) *Library budgeting: critical challenges for the future*. Ann Arbor: Pierian Press

MacNally, A. M. (1963) Budgets by formula. *Library Quarterly*, **33**(2), 159–171

Mason, D. (1972) PPBS (the Planning-Programming-Budgeting system): application to an industrial information and library service. *Journal of Librarianship*, **4**(2), 91–97

Niland, P. (1967) Developing standards for library expenditures. *Management Science–Series B*, **13**(12), B797–B808

Peterson, H. N. (1953) Performance budgeting, work measurement and the public library. *Wilson Library Bulletin*, **27**, 620–623

Shields, G. (1974) *Budgeting for accountability in libraries: a book of readings*. Metuchen: Scarecrow Press

Sizer, J. (1979) *Insight into management accounting* 2nd edn. Harmondsworth: Penguin Books

Waldhart, T. J. (1992) The process of cost justification. In *Advances in Library Administration and Organization*, **10**, 113–127

Weinstock, M. (1979) Managing special libraries under financial stress: the role of budgeting, cost analysis and evaluation. *Australian Special Libraries News*, **12**(3), 101–113

Management information systems

Adams, R. J. *et al.* (1993) *Decision support systems and performance assessment in academic libraries*. London: Bowker-Saur

Allen, G. G. (1985) The management use of library statistics. *IFLA Journal*, **11**(3), 211–222

Association of Research Libraries (1987) *Planning for management statistics in ARL libraries*. Washington, DC: ARL OMS (Spec Kit 134)

Auld, L. W. S. (1986) *Electronic spreadsheets for libraries*. Phoenix, Ariz.: Oryx Press.

Balmforth, C. K. (1981) Management information in university libraries: a case study of Sheffield University Library. In J. F. Stirling (1981) (ed.) *University librarianship*. pp.123–157. London: Library Association (Handbooks on library practice)

Barnes, M. E. (1994) 'Quick and Clean': a fast path to library spread sheet systems. *The Bottom Line*, **8**(1), 38–50

Breeze, H. (1987) Totaling and categorizing expenditures using dBase. *Library Software Review*, **6**(2), 68–73

Baumol, W. I. and Marcus, M. (1973) *Economics of academic libraries*. Washington: American Council on Education

Brophy, P. (1986) *Management information and decision support systems in libraries*. Aldershot: Gower

Burns, R. W. and Gladden, J. T. (1973) Suggested patterns for the accumulation of statistical cost information by a university circulation department. *Proceedings ASIS*, **10**, 31–32

Carter, M. D. (1984) Costing management information – a more formal approach. *Journal of Information Science*, **9**(3), 117–122

Childers, T. (1975) Statistics that describe libraries. *Advances in Librarianship*, **5**, 107–122

Clark, P. M. (1985) Accounting as evaluation as reporting: the use of online accounting systems. *Drexel Library Quarterly*, **21**(3), 61–74

Clark, P. M. (1985) Developing a decision support system: the software and hardware tools. *Library Administration and Management*, **3**(4), 184–191

Daniels, G. (1988) dBase III plus at the resources centre Plymouth Polytechnic Library. *Micromation News*, **22**(4), 4–6

Davis, B. B. (1991) Management concerns for the database for an integrated library system. In A. Kent (1991) *Encyclopedia of Library and Information Science*, **49**, 270–280

Dewey. P. R. (1992) *202+ software packages to use in your library*. Chicago: ALA

Evans, A. J. (1978) Management information from automated library systems. In N. Fjallbrant and K. McCarthy (1977) *Developing library effectiveness*. Proceedings of the 7th Meeting of IATUL, Leuven May 16–21. Goteborg: IATUL

Hamburg M. *et al.* (1974) *Library planning and decision-making systems.* Cambridge, Mass.: M.I.T. Press

Harris, C. (1987) (ed.) *Management information systems in libraries and information services: proceedings of a conference held at the University of Salford, July 1986*. London: Taylor Graham. [Well worth consulting as it presents views from various sectors at a time when MIS were invoking strong interest in the library community; can be read in conjunction with Brophy (1986) above]

Hayes, R. M. and Becker, J. (1974) *Handbook of data processing for libraries* 2nd edn. New York: Wiley-Becker-Hayes

Kantor, P. B. (1978) QUBMIS: Quantitatively based management information system for libraries. *Proceedings ASIS*, **15**, 174–176

Leonard, B. G. (1989) Using dBase III+ in administration: the San Jose University Library Experience. *The Bottom Line*, **3**(3), 17–20

McClure, C. R. *et al.* (1989) Design of a public library management information system. *Library Administration and Management*, **3**(4), 192–198

Mitchell, B. J. (1983) *ALMS: a budget based library management system.* Greenwich, Conn.: JAI Press

Runyon, R. S. (1981) Towards the development of a library management information system. *College and Research Libraries*, **42**(6), 539–548

Thomas, H. A. and Waghorn, C. A. (1986) *Management information systems for public libraries: costs, principles and outline research programme.* London: Inbucom Management Consultants (BLRD: Report No. 5893)

Library and information services resource management

Braunstein, Y. M. (1979) Costs and benefits of library information: the user point of view. *Library Trends*, **28**(1), 79–88

Brookes, B. C. (1970) Photocopies vs. periodicals: cost-effectiveness in the special library. *Journal of Documentation*, **26**(1), 22–29

Burges, T. K. (1973) A cost-effectiveness model for comparing various circulation systems. *Journal of Library Automation*, **6**(2), 75–86

Cooper, M. D. (1979) The economics of library size: a preliminary enquiry. *Library Trends*, **28**(1), 63–78

Dammers, H. F. (1975) The economics of computer based information systems: a review. *Journal of Documentation*, **31**(1), 38–45

Foggo, T. and Bartlett, G. (1993) *Financial management for librarians*. Newcastle upon Tyne: NTG/SCET (Open Learning package)

Lawrence, G. S. (1981) A cost model for storage and weeding programs. *College and Research Libraries*, **42**(2), 139–147

Lester, R. (1980) Inter-library loan: costs and benefits. In *London University Library Resources Coordinating Committee, Inter-library Loan*. pp.1–16 London: The University

Martyn, J. and Vickery, B. C. (1970) The complexity of the modelling of information systems. *Journal of Documentation*, **26**(3), 204–220

Mount, E. and Fasana, P. (1972) An approach to the measurement of use and cost at a large academic research library system: a report of a study done at Columbia University libraries. *College and Research Libraries*, **33**(3), 199–211

Overton, C. M. and Seal, A. (1979) *Cataloguing costs in the UK: an analysis of the market for automated cataloguing systems*. Bath: University Library

Pitt, W. B. and Kraft, D. H. (1974) Buy or copy? A library operations research model. *Information Storage and Retrieval*, **10**(9/10), 331–341

Price, D. S. (1977) Cost analysis and reporting as a basis for decisions. In *Proceedings of the 1976 Clinic on Library Applications of Data Processing*. pp.83–106 Urbana-Champaign: University of Illinois

Ruecking, F. (1964) Selecting a circulation control system: a mathematical approach. *College and Research Libraries*, **25**(5), 385–390

Welch, H. M. (1967) Technical service costs, statistics and standards. *Library Resources and Technical Services*, **11**(4), 436–442

Whitehall, T. A. (1980) User valuations and resource management for information services. *Aslib Proceedings*, **32**(2), 87–105

Williams, G. *et al.* (1968) *Library cost models: owning vs. borrowing serial publications*. Chicago: Center for Research Libraries

Towards managerial economics

Bommer, M. R. *et al.* (1979) Performance assessment model for academic libraries. *Journal of the American Society for Information Science*, **30**(2), 93–99

Bookstein, A. (1981) An economic model of library service. *Library Quarterly*, **51**(4), 410–428

Bookstein, A. and Kocher, K. (1979) Operations research in libraries. *Advances in Librarianship*, **9**, 143–184

Casper, C. A. (1981) Economic pricing models and their application to library service. In R. M. Mason and J. E. Creps (eds.) *Information services: economics, management and technology*. pp.129–145. Boulder, Col.: Westview Press

Cohen, J. (1977) Book cost and book use: the economics of a university library. In A. Kent and T. J. Galvin (eds.) *Library Resource Sharing: Proceedings of the 1976 Conference*. pp.197–224. New York: Dekker

Cohen, J. (1984) The economics of libraries. In *Encyclopedia of Library and Information Science*, **37**, 83–106

Cole, D. D. (1976) *Mathematical models in library management: planning, analysis and cost assessment*. Austin: University of Texas (PhD thesis)

Cummings, M. M. (1986) *The economics of research libraries*. Washington, D. C.: Council of Research Libraries

Dougherty, R. M. and Heinritz, F. J. (1966) *Scientific management of library operations*. New York: Scarecrow Press

Dudley, E. *et al.* (1991) *The economics of library and information services: an Anglo-German perspective*. London: Anglo-German Foundation for the Study of Industrial Society

Dunn, J. A. and Martin, M. S. (1994) The whole cost of libraries. *Library Trends*, **42**(3), 564–578

Feeney, M. and Grieves, M. (1994) (eds.) *The value and impact of information*. London: Bowker-Saur (British Library Research, Information Policy Issues)

Fletcher, J. (1977) *The library project: cost-effectiveness model for the comparison of alternative library systems*. Bangor: Institute of Economic Research, University College of North Wales (BLRDD Report No. 5345)

Hicks, D. A. (1980) Diversifying fiscal support by pricing public library services: a policy impact analysis. *Library Quarterly*, **50**(4), 453–454

Hindle, A. (1969) Models and measures for non-profit making services. In A. G. MacKenzie and I. M. Stuart (eds.) *Planning library services*. Lancaster: University of Lancaster Library (ULL Occasional Papers No. 3)

Kantor, P. B. (1979) A review of library operations research. *Library Research*, **1**(4), 295–345

Kantor, P. B. (1981) Levels of output related to cost of operations of scientific libraries. *Library Research*, **3**(1), 1–28 and **3**(2), 141–154

Kantor, P. B. (1986) Three studies of the economics of academic libraries. In *Advances in Library Administration and Organization*, **5**, 221–286

Kingma, P. B. (1996) *The economics of information: a guide to economic and cost benefit analysis for information professionals*. Littleton, Colo.: Libraries Unlimited

Line, M. B. (1979) The psychopathology of uneconomics. *Library Trends*, **28**(1), 107–119

Mackenzie, R. B. (1979) The economist's paradigm. *Library Trends*, **28**(1), 7–24

Marchant, M. P. (1975) University libraries as economic systems. *College and Research Libraries*, **36**(6), 449–457

Martin, M. S. (1978) *Budgetary control in academic libraries*. Greenwich: JAI Press

McPherson, P. K. (1994) Accounting for the value of information. *Aslib Proceedings*, **44**(9), 203–215

Moore, N. (1977) Economics in library management. In Gileon Holroyd (ed.) *Studies in Library Management Volume 4*. pp. 120–137. London: Bingley

Morse, P. M. (1968) *Library effectiveness*. Cambridge, Mass.: M.I.T. Press

Murphy, M. and Johns, C. J. (1974) Financial data for future planning at US Air Force Academy Library. *Special Libraries*, **65**(1), 4–11

Newhouse, P. and Alexander, A. J. (1972) *An economic analysis of public library services*. Santa Monica: Rand Corporation

Orna, E. (1996) Valuing information: problems and opportunities. In D. P. Best (ed.) *The fourth resource: information and its management*. pp.18–40 Aldershot: Gower

Pittsburgh University studies of collection usage: a symposium (1979) *Journal of Academic Librarianship*, **5**(2), 60–70

Raffel, J. A. (1974) From economic to political analysis of library decision making. *College and Research Libraries*, **35**(6), 412–423

Raffel, J. A. and Shishko, R. (1969) *Systematic analysis of university libraries: an application of cost-benefit analysis to the MIT libraries*. Cambridge, Mass: M.I.T. Press

Schauer, B. P. (1986) *The economics of managing library service*. Chicago: American Library Association

Slater, F. (1973) (ed.) *Cost reduction for special libraries and information centers*. Washington, D. C.: ASIS

Smith, G. S. (1989) Managerial accounting and changing models of administrative behavior: new methods for new models. *Library Trends*, **38**(3), 189–203

Van House, N. A. (1984) Research on the economics of libraries. *Library Trends*, **32**(4), 407–423

Wood, M. (1985) (ed.) *Cost analysis, cost recovery, marketing and fee-based services: a guide for the health sciences librarian.* New York: Haworth Press

Zais, H. W. (1977) Economic modeling: an aid to the pricing of information services. *Journal of the American Society for Information Science*, **28**(2), 89–95

Reviews of the literature and bibliographies

Aren, L. J., Webreck, S. J. and Mark, P. (1986) Costing library operations: a bibliography. *Collection Building*, **8**(3), 23–28

Bourne, C. P. *et al.* (1970) *Abstracting and indexing rates and costs: a literature review.* Minneapolis: University of Minnesota Library School and ERIC/CLIS

Bourne, C. P. (1977) *Summary cost data from 300 reports of library technical processing activities.* Berkeley: Institute of Library Research

Cooper, A. (1980) *Financial aspects of library and information services: a bibliography.* Loughborough: Centre for Library and Information Management (CLAIM Report No. 5)

Cooper, M. D. (1973) The economics of information. *Annual Review of Information Science and Technology*, **8**, 5–40

Dougherty, R. M. and Leonard, L. E. (1970) *Management and costs of technical processes: a bibliographical review, 1876–1969.* Metuchen, N. J.: Scarecrow Press

Griffiths, J.-M. (1982) The value of information and related systems, services and products. *Annual Review of Information Science and Technology*, **17**, 269–283

Hayes, S. (1988) Costs, costs, costs. . . give me a break: a brief bibliography. *The Bottom Line*, **2**(3), 30–33

Haynes, T. T. (1990) Costing acquisitions: an annotated bibliography. *Acquisitions Librarian*, **4**, 109–117

Hindle, A. and Raper, D. (1976) The economics of information. *Annual Review of Information Science and Technology*, **11**, 27–54

King, D. W., Roderer, N. K. and Olsen, H. A. (1983) (eds.) *Key papers in the economics of information.* White Plains: Knowledge Industry Publications

Koenig, M. E. D. (1990) Information services and downstream productivity. *Annual Review of Information Science and Technology*, **25**, 55–86

Mick, C. K. (1979) Cost analysis of information systems and services. *Annual Review of Information Science and Technology*, **14**, 37–64

Lamberton, D. M. (1984) The economics of information and organization. *Annual Review of Information Science and Technology*, **19**, 3–30

Olsen, H. A. (1972) The economics of information: bibliography and commentary on the literature. *Information, Part II: Reports, Bibliographies*, **1**(2)

Penner, R. J. (1970) The practice of charging users for information services: a state of the art report. *Journal of the American Society for Information Science*, **21**(1), 67–74

Prentice, A. E. (1985) Budgeting and accounting: a selected bibliography. *Drexel Library Quarterly*, **21**(3), 106–112

Repo, A. J. (1987) Economics of information. *Annual Review of Information Science and Technology*, **22**, 3–35

Repo, A. J. (1989) The value of information: approaches in economics, accounting and management science. *Journal of the American Society for Information Science*, **40**(2), 68–85

Reynolds, R. (1970) (comp.) *A selective bibliography on measurement in library and information services.* London: Aslib

Roberts, S. A. (1984) (ed.) *Costing and the economics of library and information services.* London: Aslib (Aslib Reader Series Vol. 5)

Roberts, S. A. (1993) Economics of information and the provision of information in the European economy. *Perspectives in Information Management*, **3**(1), 19–41

Spence, A. M. (1974) The economics of information. *Annual Review of Information Science and Technology*, **9**, 57–78

Stroetmann, K. A. (1991) Management and economic issues of library and information services: a review of German literature. *Journal of Information Science*, **17**, 161–173

Waldron, H. J. (1971) *Book catalogs: survey of the literature on costs.* Santa Monica: Rand Corporation (ED 053 775)

Wilson, J. H. (1972) Costs, budgeting and economics of information processing. *Annual Review of Information Science and Technology*, **7**, 39–67

Chapter 8

Applying principles to practice

8.1 A simulated cost and financial management study: introduction

Any attempt to illustrate the principles discussed in the body of this book by reference to practical examples is by nature a compromise. There are many different kinds of library and information service, and even within the broadly defined sectors of public, academic and special library services there is considerable organizational and institutional diversity (see Chapter One). Thus, what might seem to be an appropriate model description of a municipal public library might have to be substantially modified for a predominantly rural or regional public library system. To compromise by defining and describing a general organizational model for a public library, which could then be used to exemplify the needs and procedures of costing, accounting, budgeting and management information would be unsatisfactory to all intents and purposes.

The same arguments are equally true for academic libraries and for special libraries and information services. There are superficial similarities, for example in organizational structure and services offered, but to illustrate the application of principles to practice in detail requires taking actual examples of services themselves and exemplifying and analyzing accordingly. In effect, the learner has to examine one particular service and then produce what amounts to a case study based on that service; by analysing each segment and process in turn and applying the general principles enunciated, it is then possible to reconstruct the service or to overlay it with a costing, accounting, budgeting and management information framework, which can then be tested in practice and modified if necessary.

In the light of these comments the obvious question is how are the principles to be understood in the context of application if the determining standard is the real world of a specific library and information service rather than the abstract model? In management education much reliance is placed on the case study method of experiential learning.

Case studies are derived in various ways. Some are predominantly imaginative constructs based on the analyst/trainer's ideas and perspectives of a real world situation, permeated by the principal aim of meeting certain learning objectives. The learning objectives are given priority, and the case study is really a facilitating structure. The case material needs to be realistic enough to be credible, but does not need to (or even cannot) possess complete verisimilitude.

Other case studies are carefully reconstructed and often thinly disguised accounts of real circumstances of the business management situation, containing much supporting information and documentation. These case studies will also be used with specific learning objectives in mind, but greater priority will be given to confronting the learner with aspects of the real environment. Very often the questions posed have no specific or definite answer. The experiential learning is concerned with helping to come to terms with reality (and the effect this has on managers and others in the real world) rather than applying a given technique to solve a problem.

The main discussion of costing methods has already implied a high degree of generality for the principles and 'theories' themselves and their application. The tenor of discussion has often been highly normative and prescriptive. This approach is acceptable and useful provided there is no attempt to mislead about the context of application. Thus, the illustrative model presented here can be best appreciated if certain facts and limitations about the methods in general are borne in mind.

The illustrative model takes an imaginary specialized information service (with traditional library support) called European Business Information Consultants (EBIC) and on the basis of some essential data about it gives a narrative account of how the principles of costing, accounting, budgeting and management information can be applied to 'imaginary' practice.* The object is not to develop a ully worked out quantitative case study example, which in the end vould have no grounding in the real world, but to provide a strucure for making comments about principles and application in a nanner less constrained by the formal structure of the main text. This allows the author to contribute views on application which an be both provocative to and challenged by those who then go on to consider the needs of a library and information service over vhich they can exert real managerial influence.

The illustrative model is an imaginary and abstract case, used vith the specific learning goal of drawing the reader's attention to he theoretical principles and practical methods discussed in the ext, and encouraging the reader/learner to make his or her own nterpretation in the 'real' case of their own experience. The reader s left with a model to assist in applying principles; it is the eader/learner who must write the case study based on their own ife experience of a library and information service. The ideas xpounded in this book can only hope to provide inspiration and guidance.

It has been felt necessary to make this introduction to the illusrative example in order that both writer and reader understand its purpose and its limitations. To simply call the example a case study n applications of principles to practice would be misleading. It is an extension of the textual narrative providing more scope for interpretation and a means for eliciting useful questions.

The treatment is in five sections corresponding to the main text. To help re-integrate the case study into the main text and to show now text content can be used in actual practice a cross referencing nas been made to sections and chapters, giving an extended and deeper reference. This can be followed up in the last section 8.5

The EBIC study was originally developed by the author in an attempt to exemplify the principles of budgeting to students at Ealing College of Higher Education, School of Library and Information Studies (now Thames Valley University, London). It was used as a sequential exercise to introduce concepts of budgetary planning (especially the specification of programmes and their aims and objectives), budgetary development (focusing on programme resource requirements and relating these to categories of expenditure) and budgetary control (in the context of a number of problems caused by cost increases, changes in market conditions and he needs of longer term development plans). In the early 1980s there was still a certain novelty in the idea of commercial 'information businesses'; in the late 1990s he concept is common. With some revision for the present work EBIC is still fresh and relevant as a small business. However, the large commercial information and media businesses are now firmly in the corporate mainstream. Change in the last decade has indeed been rapid!

which offers guidance on the use of the book for practical purposes, summarily gathering together the themes of planning, budgeting, costing and accounting, control and management information, and finally performance and evaluation study.

Treatment of illustration

Context (see Section 8.1.1)
This section provides a brief description of European Business Information Consultants (EBIC), its environment, the problems it faces and the needs of its managers, together with some basic statistical data in the form of a simplified programme budget statement.
The reader should return to:

- Section 1.1 for a discussion of the service environment;
- Section 1.2 for a review of the financial management environment;
- Section 1.3 for discussion of the economic and financial pressures faced by libraries and information units (giving a justification for suitable financial discipline);
- Section 1.4 for a treatment of the need for management information;
- Section 3.1 for definitions of financial management concepts;
- Section 4.3 for a discussion of measurement of performance.

Needs and requirements (see Section 8.1.2)
A discussion is given of the needs and requirements of EBIC management for cost and related information, setting it in the overall context of the management of the service.
The reader should return to:

- Chapter Two for a general review of resource management strategies and techniques, and in particular Section 2.3 (business strategy), and Section 2.4 (business planning), and Sections 2.5 (the strategy of library and information service businesses), 2.6 (planning the productive process: constructing the business plan) and 2.7 (programme basis and definition).
- Section 4.6 for a discussion of financial data and cost data;

- Section 4.7 for a review of cost data: needs, requirements and strategies;
- Section 6.1 on defining needs and requirements for cost measurement;
- Section 6.2 for a checklist of cost study needs;
- Section 6.3 for a review and guidance on cost study design;
- Section 6.4 for a discussion of system description (as an important stage in defining programmes for budgetary planning and management).

Methods (see Section 8.1.3)
The different types of cost study and methods are examined and related to the needs of EBIC.

The reader should return to

Section 5.1 for a discussion of service cost structure: input, throughout, output and budgets

Section 5.2 for guidance on types of cost study for library and information service, with reference to Section 5.3 (categorization of costs) and Section 5.4 (calculation of costs).

Topics relating to current accounts and expenditure generally are covered in Chapter Three:

- Section 3.3 (planning and budgeting: the financial dimension);
- Section 3.4 (cost centre development);
- Section 3.5 (microfinancial management and procedures);
- Section 3.6 (devolved budgeting and business units).

Capital accounts are also treated in Section 3.10.

Topics relating to income and revenue budgets are covered in:

- Section 3.2 (sources of finance and income);
- Section 3.8 (income generation and the revenue budget).

Further reference can be made to

- Section 6.5 (data collection and field measurement),
- Section 6.6 (work measurement practice)
- Section 6.7 (processing and analysis of results).

Implementation (see Section 8.1.4)
Particular attention is given to the ways in which a small service can implement a cost management programme.

The reader should refer to Chapter Six (implementation of cost measurement) in general and to Section 6.2.1 (cost study needs: a checklist) in particular.

Managerial economics (see Section 8.1.5)
The broader view of cost and economic data is considered in terms of resource management models.

The reader should refer to:

- Chapter Seven (developments in managerial economics) for an overview; and to the following for finer detail:
- Section 7.1 (an integrated approach to budgeting, accounting, costing and performance measurement) for a discussion of theory;
- Sections 7.2 (sources of statistics, performance measures and management data), 7.3 (management information systems and related developments) and 7.4 (management information systems) for finer detail;
- Section 7.5 for a review of developments of managerial and economic models.

A final section (8.1.6) poses some questions which can be used with the material to widen the scope for further study of costing and related methods.

During the discussion comments are made about applications to other types of library and/or service where these highlight the illustration of certain points. The reader should be encouraged to do the same as often as possible.

8.1.1 European Business Information Consultants (EBIC) – the context

EBIC is a small limited liability company of information brokers and consultants with an office in the City of London, specializing in European business and marketing information. Its main clients are various of firms in the London region although it produces documentation services (intelligence bulletins) which have a wider national market (perhaps more potentially rather than actually). Its main clients and users are all concerned with production and distribution in the broad European market for manufactured goods and specialist services.

Since its establishment EBIC has maintained both traditional print-based documentation services and carried out specific information analysis projects for clients using its inhouse information resources and a variety of external library and information services in the London region, in addition to using wide ranging informal contacts in business circles. The firm was a little slow in grasping the potential of database services in the mid-1980s, but has caught up in its usage of online databases in commercial information and the social sciences as well as in technology. Having learned the lesson of a slow start the company has espoused Internet and WWW-based services with some alacrity to make sure they do not lose out again.

Currently its management is considering scope for physical as well as electronic expansion in the European information market area, to the extent of opening an office in a continental European city. Discussion of these proposals with its accountants and bankers led to some rather sharp criticism of internal management accounting and business strategy planning. These sources suggested an appraisal of budgeting and planning methods, greater attempts at cost analysis and control, and a more substantial effort to relate these to existing activities in the information market, and towards any planned expansion.

The first stage of this review was to analyze all the systems and operations of the firm, and from this emerged a budget plan on programme lines (Table 8.1 and Figure 8.1). Previously budgetary planning had been primitive, in fact little more than was contained in a line-item statement of projected expenditure by main categories of expense, and a set of financial accounts submitted at the end of each year. With a number of product lines (query services, consultancies, special reports, intelligence bulletins) it was difficult to distinguish precisely between different activities and resources used, to relate these accurately to each other, and to develop evaluation methods and performance measurement.

The present situation is as follows. In the current financial year budgeted expenditure (Table 8.1) is £802,000, which is allocated across 14 programme areas. There are 12 staff at four different levels with average annual salaries as indicated, to which a budgeted overhead of 20 per cent has been added.

TABLE 8.1 Current year expenditure budget—European Business Information Consultants (EBIC) (all figures quoted in £ Sterling)

Programme	*Staff*	*Staff cost*	*Material*	*Equipment and Consumables*	*Servicer*	*Total programme cost*
(1) Accommodation	0.1 Dep.	3,000		10,000	50,000	63,000
(2) Acquisition	0.5 IA 0.3 Cler	17,400	60,000	2,000		79,400
(3) Technical processing	0.5 IA 0.4 Cler	19,200		2,000		21,200
(4) Documentation collection	0.3 Cler	5,400		1,000		6,400
(5) Storage	0.1 Cler	1,800		1,000		2,800
(6) Information analysis	0.4 Dep 3.0 IA	84,000		6,000	150,000	240,000
(7) Information service	0.5 Dep 0.5 IA	27,000		3,000	135,000	165,000
(8) Publication	0.4 Dep 0.5 IA	33,000		6,000		39,000
	0.5 Cler					
(9) Marketing	0.3 Dep	9,000		2,000		11,000
(10) Staff services	0.2 Dep 0.2 Man	14,400		4,000		18,400
(11) Staff development	0.1 Dep	3,000		3,000		6,000
(12) Reprography	0.4 Cler	7,200		20,000		27,200
(13) General administration	0.8 Man 1.7 Cler	64,200		30,000	15,000	109,200
(14) Miscellaneous, travel	0.3 Cler	5,400		8,000		13,400
		294,000	60,000	98,000	350,000	802,000

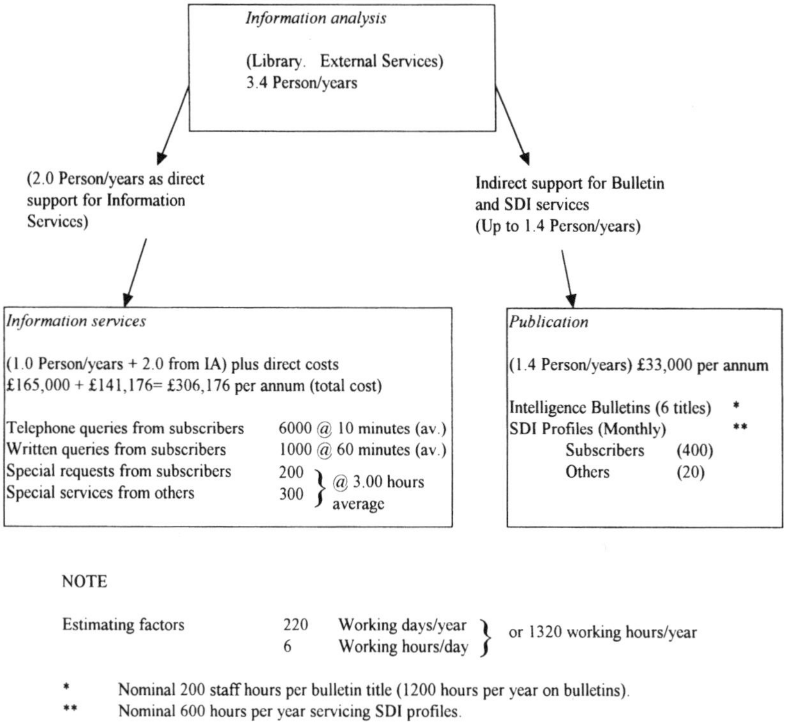

Figure 8.1. Basic activity data: information analysis, service and publication

Manager	(1)	basic salary	£35,000
Deputy Manager	(2)	basic salary	£25,000
Information analysts	(5)	basic salary	£20,000 (mean)
Clerical assistants	(4)	basic salary	£15,000 (mean)

The main material expense comes in the document acquisition programme estimated currently at 3,000 items at an average purchase cost of £20.00 per item. Other materials as such have been listed as equipment and consumables, e.g. reprographic materials in the case of the publication programme.

Computer time is rated at 150 hours connect time per week over the year at £40.00 per hour; this includes telecommunications costs for online searching and Internet access, and represents the bulk of the direct running expenses of accessing external databases and electronic networks; it also includes telephone costs associated with these information activities. Telecommunication costs are charged to programmes 6, 7 and 13. Accommodation rental and cleaning costs are charged as services to programme 1.

In this limited example the account cannot be expanded to take note of all the variety and nuances involved in running this information business. However, there are enough basic facts to construct an illuminative account of how the principles and methods discussed in the text can be applied. The object is to draw together some of the main ideas in such a way as to stimulate and interest others to do the same in the sterner school of the real world.

There are four main areas of context which have to be considered first: managerial environment, economic and financial pressure, need for management information and measurement of performance.

Managerial environment

The firm typifies many library and information organizations, which, at the current time, are experiencing a period of market and technological change. They are being driven to re-examine methods and procedures, especially in the area of systems, finance and resource management. Extension of activities into new areas cannot be undertaken without a positive appraisal of needs and consequences, especially in economic terms.

Typical questions would be as follows. What is the cost of producing the final product? What are the throughput and intermediate costs carried at different stages of production, and can these be reduced by more efficient and streamlined methods? Are staff resources adequate for the job; have staff received adequate training; do job descriptions need revision in the light of organizational change? All libraries in whatever environment must ask and answer these questions, before attempting to improve their economic management. Clarification of organizational aims and objectives is an all important preliminary.

Economic and financial pressure

Increases in resource costs for all the main categories of expense is the main pressure. There is the need both to maintain current and raise fresh revenue. This affects both the private sector (to reduce debt burden and increase the rate of payback on investment under prevailing market conditions) and the public sector (to compensate for loss of traditional sources of finance; to expand and innovate in certain areas not formerly considered viable).

Need for management information
Using line-item budgets EBIC did not possess enough basic system-wide information about its activities. The adoption of one of several methods of programme budgeting (which can be further adapted to a performance budget) is a basic step in providing more specific information. Programme definition provides the key to expanding the information base, by presenting a systematized structure, which can later be developed to furnish and sustain other types and methods of information support; decision support and expert systems may be a logical end product.

Measurement of performance
Until recently EBIC seemed to be content to occupy a traditional niche as a company. It has developed in a boom economy, offering services and products for which there was a steady market; its clients may still not yet have questioned whether EBIC is really supplying what they fully need (but that may be another question). EBIC has managed to retain its subscribers, keeping increases in charges in line with inflation. However, it has not really been able to tell whether its position in that market as a producer or supplier was optimal, and it could not easily respond to changes in market conditions. There is in short a certain amount of comfortable inertia. Nevertheless increased competition from later entrants to this part of the information market is creating an uncomfortable feeling, especially in the private thoughts of the deputy managers.

Clearly, cost-based performance measures can play some new part in the scheme of things to evaluate existing operations, and to appraise new operations proposed in response to changed conditions. For example, what contribution to costs and profitability is being made by the documentation services and the query services respectively? How could improved office automation and networked computing assist in present operations? Could staff reductions or redeployments be made or would circumstances force this? Has there been any clear market development policy, and have the financial implications for revenue and costs been appreciated? All these general management questions are also questions about performance.

Besides the expenditure budget two additional sets of data are needed at this stage in the narrative: (1) a listing of services and products, with information on production and sales volume (Figure 8.1), and (2) a statement of sources of revenue to cover current expenses of £802,000, supplemented by a note on the capital budget (involving long-term borrowing and debt service charges) (Tables 8.2 and 8.3).

8.1.2 Needs and requirements

The needs of EBIC management can be grasped initially by drawing a programme map showing interrelationships between various activities (Figure 8.2). A number of salient observations can be made about EBIC by taking together the data on manpower, budgeted expenditure, services provided and level of demand. Although the main technical relationship between the programme areas is in document and information handling (acquisition and storage, information analysis and information services areas) the marketing section seems to emerge with a key role which may be underresourced.

Using the programme map, the expenditure data (input and throughput) can be related to the output data, and from this unit costs/times can be generated (Figure 8.1). At this point the programme map should be compared with the procedural schema illustrated in Figure 5.2. The programme mapping corresponds to elements 1 and 6; it indicates lines of development for elements 2 (cost/output measures sought), 4 (description of cost centres and cost units) and 5 (analytical framework for costing).

TABLE 8.2 Revenue budget statement

Service	*Subscribers*	*Income source* *Others**	
Phone queries	1000 (± 50) annually @ £800/yr (all services)	n.a	Covered by Subscriptions
Written queries		n.a	Covered by Subscriptions
Special services		300 @ 3.00 hour/unit @ £75 hour	£67,500
Bulletins (6 titles per subscriber)		1000 @ £80 title/year (sold by title)	£80,000
SDI Profiles		40 @ 32 hours/year @ £75 hour	£96,000
	£800,000		£243,500

* *Also unspecified interest on reserves*

Table 8.3 Capital budget statement

Carried forward from revenue budget		£243,500	
Liabilities:	Interest on bank loans (£200,000 with two years to run)	–	£30,000
	Depreciation	–	£25,000
	Transfer to reserves	£193,000	

So much for the basic budgetary data (which could be either planned/projected or actual spending) and the existing resource allocation. From it managerial attention is drawn to questions of performance and effectiveness.

For example, the information services programme area requires the support of two person years' worth of time from the information analysis area; is this satisfactory given the target performance figures (the mean service times for requests have been based on past rates of performance)? Are the right levels and amounts of staff being used? Within the publication area has the right balance been achieved between intelligence bulletins and SDI profiles (whose production seems underresourced, and may not be allocated to the most appropriate programme (the information analysis area))?

Many questions can be raised by studying the basic data, and the answers to many will almost certainly involve cost calculations (standard costs, average costs and unit costs, historical cost analysis). The reader can use the basic data to explore the many questions posed and the implications of adopting different strategies (something which EBIC must inevitably do if it proposes to expand into Europe).

Any library and information organization can map out its activities in this way, and so consider the relationship between resources, costs and effective performance. In a large public library a divisional structure or team-based matrix could be treated as a potential programme area structure. In an academic library a similar process of analysis and systematic statement could be followed, and the fundamental questions asked: what is being produced for whom; what resources are needed to produce it in different amounts; what do those resources cost; and how do different combinations of resources and methods of production lead to variations in unit costs of intermediate and final output?

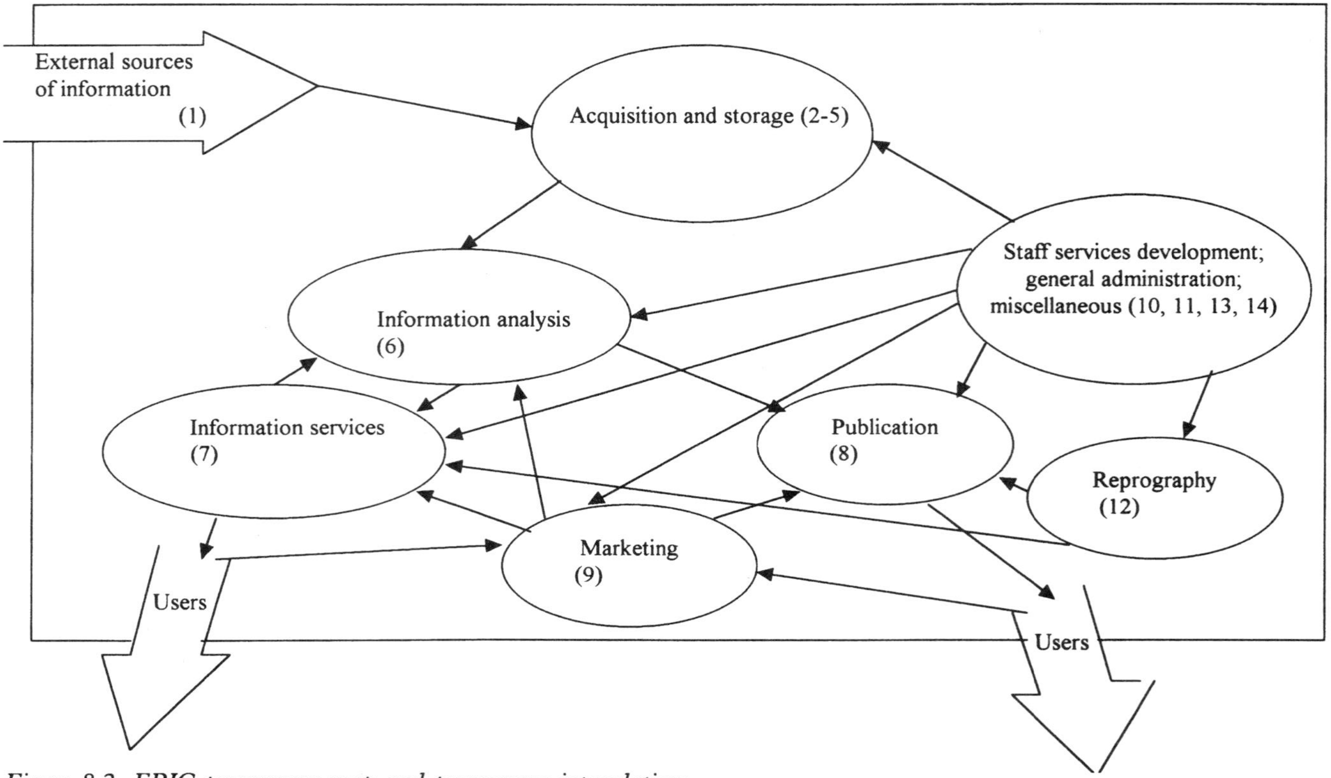

Figure 8.2. EBIC programme map and programme interrelations

8.1.3 Methods

Service cost structure

In developing a cost structure and cost data system for their company and its services EBIC management could be guided by the schema shown in Figure 5.10. The expenditure budget which summarizes gross expenses by programme area has already been presented (Table 8.1). Management would then go on to assess each programme in terms of its contribution to input, demand, throughput and output. Management would need a cost structure for each product and service line, cast in input, throughput and output terms, showing the share of costs borne by each programme as the work progresses through the system.

Acquisition and storage (2–5) and marketing (9) could be considered as input cost areas. Throughput would probably include all of programme 6 (information analysis) and elements of 7 (information services) and 8 (publication). The output cost areas would be defined in terms of the services and products and each unit of output would carry a full burden of total costs (derived from input and throughput and added to output). An appropriate distribution of expenses classified as overheads would be established based on programmes 1 (accommodation), 10 (staff services), 11 (staff development), 13 (general administration) and 14 (miscellaneous).

The input/throughput/output structure (or a product/service-based approach) should be regarded as an overlying structure for cost study and management information which is superimposed on the basic schema given in Figure 5.10 (which relates to any specific cost analysis task). This structure enables a costing system to provide a series of 'views' for management.

As a further illustration take one programme area – information analysis – and consider each stage. To start with the job and task description stage, that would require staff in that area/section to be examined. With work study methods and a general knowledge of activities in that area it is possible to develop a task categorization appropriate to the detail of cost data required. Higher levels of aggregation may be needed to provide the appropriate level of description for cost collection and cost accounting.

The exact task and levels chosen (e.g. definition of cost centres) depend very much on the problem or notion of costing the manager has in mind. For example, when an advanced office automation system was being introduced into the information analysis section, management was interested in specifying the cost structures for tasks done manually (indexing, abstracting, filing, document analysis) and comparing these to tasks done with files held in machine readable form with large amounts of keyboarding involved as production overhead. The initial investment was then examined with respect to cost-efficiency and cost-effectiveness, and longer term savings and productivity increases were identified. As in the procedure in Figure 5.10 the basic cost data were further processed according to needs (e.g. unit costs of operations, or more sophisticated opportunity cost, or cost-benefit calculations).

Cost study types and methods

The advanced office automation applications example covers all the significant stages of cost analysis from task definition to unit costing. From this basic analysis other cost measures can be constructed. The programme budget showing the distribution of expenses is very similar to a cost distribution. The expense burden of different programme areas (which could be cost centres or chosen as cost centres (or their components or aggregates)) can be manipulated to compute the costs of different operations. It would be useful for instance to highlight the share of cost borne by different grades of staff, and their contribution to the different service outputs. The main point to stress is the high degree of manipulability of costing and accounting data at this level. The manager has to learn to become familiar with the origins of and capability of those data, in the context of an appraisal of or decision about a part of the service.

Unit costs and unit times provide some of the most important management data, and can be produced at the level of final output (a bulletin issue or a telephone query handled) or prior to that (unit times of contributing suboperations, costed out for alternative grades of staff, in an effort to determine the most cost-effective solution). At EBIC 1,200 person hours per year are allocated to production of intelligence bulletins at a budgeted expenditure of £22,000. A cost analysis of bulletin production would begin with an examination of production methods and sources of expense, and go on to identify costs of each stage in the operation (using the methods outlined in Chapter Five).

The categorization of expenses (from which costs are subsequently derived) is a relatively straightforward operation provided that the conventions are observed. In Table 8.1 the broadest categories have been used, but it would also be possible (even desirable) to use much greater detail. For the EBIC costing and accounting system an accounts code based on the different programme area numbers could be used, expanded by use of task codes listed in Appendix 4. The EBIC accounts could be put on a microcomputer and managed with a standard accounting software package (although a specific programme with library capabilities would be better).

Current and capital accounts, expenditure and revenue
Treatment of the relationship between current and capital accounts has been kept to a minimum in this example. Capital budgeting is a specialized field of financial management. In EBIC the capital account is limited to the management of the bank loan, and maintenance of a reserve fund.

In budgetary terms EBIC has aimed to meet its planned expenditure through subscription revenue; this level of expenditure allows the provision of services adequate to meet the basic needs of its clients. It also allows EBIC to hold capacity to meet a certain level of additional demand, which generates an extra revenue of £243,500. The current financial strategy aims to service the debt and increase the reserves by means of this budgeted capacity to generate some extra revenue. It does not take much foresight to see that actual events may upset this strategy. The teaching value of the case method becomes clear when new events can be introduced to complicate matters and force managers to reconsider strategy. The relevance of budgetary control and cost control then becomes apparent.

In a given financial year much resource management is tactical with respect to the agreed budget strategy. Managers may propose options to meet circumstances such as an increase in demand from subscribers, or try to respond to additional demand from non-subscribers. If the costs of different tactical responses can be calculated (cost data being extracted or generated from different levels in the organization) the manager is in a stronger position to respond, and to re-allocate resources or control the flows between different activities.

This simple example should help the reader to discern the relationships between current and capital spending, between projected expenditure and revenue, and between the level of demand and the response in terms of goods and services produced. Levels of activity are associated with levels of cost, both as an absolute measure and as a relative indicator.

8.1.4 Implementation

A programme of organizational cost study rests initially on a knowledge of needs and requirements. How does the management checklist for needs and requirements (Section 6.2) relate to the circumstances of EBIC?

Prior to examining its budgetary procedures EBIC was not in a good position to collect cost information. Its line-item form of budget presentation was of limited use in assessing expenditure and cost distribution. The programme budget which has been cast as an alternative is a much more effective source of management information (Table 8.1). Given the general allocation of staff resources and the distribution of other expenses across the organization, it is possible to proceed and identify costs in different parts of the system; for example as the costs of final units of output or as throughput costs at certain key positions, and as costs associated with resource flows contributing to various activities (e.g. the cost of placing a document in the collection, the cost of maintaining a given file of information in the information analysis section).

The programme budget provides the necessary structure for cost reporting by being related to the major activities of the system; specific activities can be systematically analysed and elements within them coded for accounting purposes. Given a programme budget EBIC is in a strong position to create a cost gathering system in line with management needs.

The activity patterns of EBIC and some of the immediate problems and questions posed by them certainly suggest a need for cost data. There are strategic questions of product and service design (query answering vs. documentation), and of market and commercial development (subscribers vs. optional clients). Options can be prepared to solve these problems; each has resource implications and bears a different cost and price tag.

EBIC management needs regular cost data especially in unit cost and cost distribution form generated at key areas in the operations structure (by programme area, by product and activity, by grade of staff) and by user (differentiated by fixed revenue subscribers, and other clients, to whom a flexible pricing policy can be applied). EBIC management will probably work towards a strategy aimed at meeting its obligations to subscribers, minimizing total costs (at least staying within budgeted expenditure), and considering ways to expand its services to revenue earning clients, showing an awareness of marginal costs (see section 8.4.2), and thereby increasing its current level of profit.

In EBIC the manager and deputy manager (who provide the headship of marketing) are those most interested in the supply of cost data, since they are the two main business decision makers, as well as being the carriers of business risk. Regularly produced cost data will provide for cost control needs in the short run. When specific projects for medium and long-term development are undertaken, these will be costed as far as possible using standard unit times and costs for service activities (collected historically and validated for future use). The basic current cost reports would be tabulated and then aggregated to provide time series. EBIC would find weekly, monthly and quarterly reports useful.

If the reader has followed the discussion so far he or she will be in a good position to answer the remaining questions on the checklist (Section 6.2). Furthermore, the reader will want to apply those same questions not just to the EBIC case study but to the real world service to which they belong. The analogies will hopefully provide comfortable support, as well as a basis for further exploration.

The programme budget example of EBIC provides the basis for making a system description as a formal activity in cost study design, and it is a relatively straightforward matter to work through the stages of implementation. The reader should complete the 'imaginary' implementation by turning to the further checklists in Sections 6.10 and 6.11. By making decisions of one's choice and imaginatively developing the EBIC scenario the learner should be able to give satisfactory answers to most of the questions posed.

8.1.5 Managerial economics

This illustrative model has tried to show how budgeting, accounting, costing and performance measurement can be integrated as a natural response to resource management needs. The budget provides a structure for financial accounting and for managing resource allocations and flows. Cost data provide measures and indicators which are provided in different ways at different points in the system. Unit times and costs, and more basic accounts of the distributions of expenses (the source of costs) provide simple performance measures. More sophisticated studies and directed studies of a comparative nature such as cost-effectiveness and cost-benefit extend performance measurement within a framework of financial accounting and resource management.

The costing and accounting system is a statistical system, which when developed as a management information system becomes a means of appraisal and decision support. The discussion in Chapter Seven must serve to illustrate the possibilities and relevance of such developments to library and information services generally, and also to a case example like EBIC. Despite its limited detail the case study is adequate to reinforce the stated theoretical arguments. The idea of implementing a management information system must rest upon the lessons learnt and appreciated at that basic stage.

If there is a crucial idea to grasp from this case study it is that resource management often requires the manager to develop a feeling for abstract modelling from the real world of library and information services. In effect these are formal models for resource management, which can be calibrated with cost data and integrated within a management information system and a decision support system. The programme budget which has been developed for EBIC is a simple example of an abstract model; a further level of abstraction was introduced by drawing a programme map.

The model was then explored to suggest a range of questions about resource allocations and activities. Cost data are needed and can be generated at the beginning, during and at the end of the modelling process. The greater the capability of the managerial system to generate costs on a regular basis, the more success the manager is likely to have in developing economic models appropriate to practical circumstances, and then translating from model to real world. If this skill can be developed and practised the manager will have travelled a good way towards understanding the managerial economic aspects of the business organization, and the manager's response to it.

8.1.6 Practising with the EBIC model

Now some suggestions to help use the illustrative example. The following 12 issues can be addressed.

(1) Given the activities of EBIC and the market for its services is the present programme structure appropriate?
The structure is a great improvement on a simple line-item expenditure budget, but there is further scope for detailed breakdown of information analysis (6), information service (7), publication (8) and marketing (9). These are the main output programmes; breaking them down by individual product line or client would give useful information, which could be related to client-centred performance measures. This would help focus on the economic aspects of quality management and customer service, giving information useful for product pricing, pricing review and profit margins.

Any move to develop a continental European office would require programme elaboration, and would raise further issues relating to fixed costs and overhead burdens. The natural processes of change need to be reviewed for their budgetary consequences.

(2) What alternative allocation of staff to programme and section activities could be envisaged?
Staffing levels depend on job specifications and work rates and standards, as well as process reviews and performance appraisals. Programmes (6), (7), (8) and (13) have the highest staff expenditure/cost allocations, and would naturally be candidates for monitoring and review. More definitive answers clearly need output-related measures, which could also trace back staff contributions to profit making activities. Staff expenditure related matters in budgeting always have to be treated with care and sensitivity.

(3) What range of service performance could be expected if alternatives were implemented (e.g. the service time for queries; bulletin production schedules; level of servicing SDI profiles)?
There are no simple or single answers to any of these questions, and at the end the resolution is not just a matter of economics. But financial data are a positive contribution to measuring overall efficiency and performance. When decisions are taken in terms of the second question, any analysis has to employ some kind of modelling exercise. A 'what if . . .' question always leads to examination of processes both upstream and downstream of the activity. If fewer staff are allocated to a task and the same or better performance is required, upstream work will have to be done more rapidly or more efficiently and effectively (better retrieval methods in information searches), to keep within the personnel budget envelope.

(4) What range of market conditions could be expected, and what subsequent levels of demand might be envisaged?
Organizations have to engage in external environmental intelligence activities to determine the ultimate financial implications of market conditions. This can be a very open ended, time consuming and costly activity. Market trends need to be surveyed at all times. However, one relatively cost-effective way is through good customer service and quality management. The customer database is an exploitable and developable resource for promotion, feedback and evaluation: talking to the customers is a serious activity. When future product demand becomes known through market evaluation,

then service planning, budgetary planning and modelling become the essential activities.

(5) Should EBIC contract, maintain, or expand its current level of activity?
These are issues of business policy discussed in the early sections of Chapter Two which then lead on to financial management consequences, reviewed in later sections of Sections 3.7 to 3.9 (commercialization, income generation and growth). Such matters may lead to a resolution of issues raised in our fourth question. The nature of the question points to a consideration of market and demand issues as a policy issue first, then clarify the policy (strategically) and model the financial implications second. Nevertheless, the general financial condition of the organization will be known sufficiently to colour the first stage policy discussion.

(6) Attempt to compute unit costs from the expenditure and output data making reasonable assumptions about work load norms, activity flows etc.
Programmes (6) to (9) offer much scope for producing managerially useful unit costs. The unit cost of a bulletin or report is a vital measure to establish in calculating charges to clients and product prices.

For example, say that 11 per cent of the publication programme (8) annual workload was dedicated to producing an intelligence bulletin; the following calculation could apply.

(7) Given possible changes in demand, and therefore of marketing strategy, what alternative configurations of service and provision could EBIC provide?
This question addresses the operational and production consequences of the fourth and fifth questions. There are many possibilities; this is just one illustration. With new entrants to the European information services field one result will be greater competition, stable markets and lower margins. There may come a point when existing document publication activities are rationalized; for example, similar information could be delivered electronically through web publishing. This would lead to a closer relation between programmes (6) (information analysis), (7) (information service), and (8) (publication). Programmes could be redefined along product/service lines. There would be some retraining costs to bear, and in the short term increased information technology spending (capital account), financed by borrowing (with interest payments met from the reserves). The short answer to the question is that EBIC can

EXPENDITURE

Direct (annual) cost of bulletin @ 11% of programme (8) = £4,290

Indirect costs @ 5% of total costs (except programme (8)) = £38,150

[For the example an arbitrary calculation of 5% has been made which implies that the bulletin represents 1/20th part of the EBIC annual programme of activities]

Number of units produced 1200 (1000 subscribers + 200 sales) Number of copies @ 4 issues per year = 4,800 units (for sale) + 600 (150 each issue) for backfile, internal and promotion etc. (5,400 units)

unit cost = direct labour and consumables (£4,290) + reprographic labour and consumables (£2,720) [10% of all reprographic] plus indirect (£38,150) costs
―――――――――――――――――
number of units (5,400)

unit cost = £45,160 / £5,400

unit cost = £8.36/copy or £33.45 for four issues

unit price = unit cost + unit margin
£33.44 + £46.57 = £80.00

Note: Rationale for pricing. The volume of marginal revenue from subscribers depends on pricing and is sensitive to market conditions. The 200 sales subscribers consume 800 copy units per year. Allocating to these subscribers the full cost (£45,160 divided by 200) would give a unit price pf £225 per year. By covering the direct costs of all the bulletin output for the sales subscribers by marginal pricing alone (£7,010 divided by 200 = £35.05 which is above the total unit cost of the whole output) and setting the subscriber price at £80.00 (which is competitive) there is still a generous level of gross margin per subscriber (unit margin £46.57). The judgment made is that £225.00 per subscription is too high.

REVENUE

Projected subscriber revenue allocable to this bulletin (say 1/12th of the service package to a standard subscriber) = £67,000

+ income from additional sales = £16,000 (200 @ £80.00)

From these data and calculations an overall financial performance measure can be computed:

Total revenue	− total cost of bulletin (direct + indirect costs)	= total margin
£83,000	£45,160	£37,840
at 5,400 units (unit cost £8.36)		(unit copy margin £7.00)

reconfigure, and like most dynamic organizations does so progressively and flexibly.

(8) Attempt to provide in more detail a breakdown of the main blocks of expense
Essentially, this question is about the finer detail of budgeting. The exercise is carried out on the basis of a good knowledge of the system design, the operating procedures and processes and work study/work measurement knowledge. Procedural manuals are a useful repository of information and can be combined with work sampling and observational study. The question could begin with an audit of tasks done by the staff allocated under programme (13) (general administration). A workflow study might look into the cost of servicing a contract, preparing correspondence and even looking at work rates and 'downtime'. These questions reflect on the general knowledge of the organization and system required to manage effectively and to support budgetary planning (basic questions of 'what', 'how', 'when', 'where' and 'why').

(9) What scope is there for expenditure reduction and cost reduction?
Questions of this type are a natural consequence of the inquiries made in the eighth one. They are also implicit in those questions raised in the seventh too. There is almost always scope for expenditure reduction and cost reduction but the real secret lies in making the right judgment and decision at the right time. This should show awareness of the human and social consequences of those actions. Ideally precedent decisions should reflect a culture of efficiency and competence, so that erratic and hasty cost-cutting decision making can be avoided, because it always has negative consequences.

(10) Given that staff may claim salary increases, suggest how these might be funded: are staff reductions possible or can extra revenue be generated?
Given the tight commercial parameters within which the organization works, increased remuneration can only come as part of a productivity package focused on gaining extra sales. Additional product sales seem the best route to take implying that fixed costs (indirect costs) can be contained. This route has echoes of the issues raised in question seven; even increasing hard copy publication sales could be beneficial, although electronic web-based products would be even more effective, since pricing can be tied into licensing agreements.

Expanding publication sales could come through increasing regular subscriptions to the service, because if these are maintained the income flow is regular (but customers must be assured value for money). Non-subscription sales may also be attractive, provided that distribution costs can be kept low. One key issue surfaces here: the content of the subscription package; it includes some rights to querying answering services and other special services. All expansion, contraction and revenue/profit decisions will be determined by the balance of the package; more one-to-one customized services push up quasi-direct costs, reducing the proportion of service absorbed by indirect/overhead allocations.

(11) Consider the budgetary and cost implications of the proposed European expansion programme. What level of new demand is envisaged, and can some of it be satisfied by existing services? How could the expansion be funded, and what implications are there for future budgets and between current and capital budgets?

In this area EBIC faces a major strategic policy question. In some ways the expansion will at least replicate much of the activities of the UK-based centre. The main attraction of a continental office is direct access to a very competitive market, with the anticipation of significant growth prospects. In a future networked electronic environment the decision making is not as straightforward as it seems. Even so, much of the product and the service package can and will be produced and delivered electronically (unlike in the previous hard copy traditional environment where most stages of bulletin production were fixed in the London base). In theory EBIC could become a virtual networked organization with its productive facilities anchored in cyberspace. . . . but!

In reality the purpose of a continental base is less for production and more for marketing and promotional reasons; the rationale is a post-technological one, in that significant business is still conducted face-to-face in real time and real space. EBIC might consider Frankfurt or Berlin or Brussels (or two of these three) as the ideal place. The bases would likely be smaller (fewer staff, less accommodation, less fixed equipment and stock – so that London still remains the head office). Some economies of scale could be developed and central administrative functions remain concentrated on London.

This is only a taste of the answer to a very substantial problem. First of all local costs and prices would have to be investigated for staff, accommodation and services. The local legal, fiscal and social environment would have to be understood in all its implications. There would be fixed initial costs to cover of a semi-direct and indirect kind. The most serious financial concern would be that such significant expansion would have to be financed out of borrowing (essentially it is a capital account issue); this implies that market projections and the business plan have to be sound and secure enough to enable EBIC to see through the whole cycle without incurring losses; this expansion cannot be funded significantly from their reserves.

However these matters are resolved EBIC, like every other organization in the industry, must be aware that every decision has financial and cost consequences. The more care and exactitude given to financial planning the sounder the end results are likely to be: that indeed is the main mesage of this book.

(12) Consider the problems and costs of introducing a new mode of service or product within the existing service budget

This question is a reflection of many of the concerns of the previous questions, and an answer as such is not attempted. The purpose in posing the question is itself more to suggest a moral. It underlines the integration and circularity of much of the debate about business activities (in information service, library and documentation service and information management): the practitioner cannot take the financial decisions until the business and activities issues are resolved. Financial management, in the detail revealed in this and similar books, is in some ways no more than a selection of often very good and precise tools and techniques and their intelligent use in the right circumstances. Financial management alone will not tell the practitioner what the circumstances are, but when an understanding of those circumstances has been gained, the financial management skill and technique are very necessary indeed.

The remaining sections of this chapter are used to highlight a number of topics on which practitioner readers are likely to seek information and support from this book. Further references to the body of the text are made where possible, together with any useful reading.

8.2 Costing for budgetary planning

Costing for budgetary planning and its variants has become such an all purpose expression that to be useful it needs redefinition. Reference to Chapter Five provides what is needed.

The library and information service budget can be both a plan for resource allocation and expenditure, and a tool for predicting the target levels of cost to be achieved. In the introduction to Section 5.2 five types of cost study are listed, of which two are significant for budgeting. These are now highlighted below, and if more information is required Sections 5.2.1 to 5.5.5 can be consulted.

Cost analysis
This is the basic mode of study which provides information for the other descriptive and analytical methods. Cost analysis can be carried out and its data presented in a variety of ways (see notably Chapters Five and Six). Cost analysis requires the measurement of resources input to the system, an understanding of the nature and type of work carried out and, especially, an appreciation of the use of time by labour (through measurement or a substitute for it). Data from cost analyses can be fed into accounting, estimating, budgeting and performance measurement procedures.

Cost distribution and/or cost allocation studies
The terms are often used interchangeably and look at resource allocations, flows of resources and activities, especially in the throughput or transfer stage. These are useful descriptive procedures, providing a general view of the broad costs carried in different parts of the library system. These analyses help to understand the outcome of previous resource allocation and financial decisions, and corrections can be applied through the budgeting process.

In many practical cases the manager is developing the projected budget from a current budget, and the encounter with costing for budgeting will usually take the form of a cost distribution/cost allocation study. This is a form of retrospective analysis where the historical situation (based on the resources previously allocated) is used to make a first pass or estimate of current costs, which then form the basis for the projected future costs. Managers may expect change, therefore the future cost is of the form (current cost plus expected increase).

Various sources of information and intelligence are used to make best estimates of the expected increase: for example, a salary settlement might add four per cent to labour costs (expenditure projected on staff salaries), plus an increase in labour cost overhead. It is vital to remember that cost distribution/cost allocation studies yield costs based on aggregates of expenditure; the cost values cannot be considered as the measured costs of an operation or process. If measured costs are required then formal cost analysis has to be carried out (see the definition paragraph at the beginning of this section).

Cost analysis derived (measured costs) are prospective costs, as distinct from the historic cost allocation costs discussed in the general practical case in the preceding paragraphs. It is true that some of these historic costs may once have been derived as measured costs, but this serves only to emphasize the point being made.

Cost values generally have a high decay or obsolescence rate in the modern business environment, due to changes in inflation and exchange rates, the fluctuation in factor markets (accommodation and space rentals, equipment, labour and capital) and supplier prices. Old cost values (even relatively current historical costs of one year ago) are unreliable and volatile. Even a small change in values may be significant when multiplied across hundreds or thousands of transactions or units of output. In a dynamic business environment (which the contemporary information world definitely is) it is foolhardy to neglect cost studies; to do so must reduce the potency of financial management.

In the EBIC case the programme-by-programme cost allocation is made clear and simple in the programme budget matrix. Given more detail it could be made more complex, but it would still be manageable and intelligible because it is derived from systematic principles. On cost distribution/allocation principles the total cost of programme (8) is £39,000; six bulletins are currently produced. However, it is unlikely in practice that each bulletin consumes exactly the same resources and takes the same time to produce. A product cost derived from cost distribution/cost allocation averaging would be only a very rough guideline as to the true cost analysis for each bulletin; the variation between the bulletins could be quite wide.

How far the analysis is pursued depends on what you feel you want or need to know, and especially on what the consequences might be of not knowing (running a progressively less profitable bulletin, which is a cost burden and drain on profitability). A measured cost analysis would be the only way of getting at the cost truth. To be assured, the manager must have both the techniques and skill to measure (workstudy and workflow analysis, work measurement, time study, resource costs and consumption) and then to synthesize the data into a form useful for decision making. Sometimes business judgement relies on instinct, sometimes (often less) it relies on good measurement. It is exactly at these points that financial management skill in information and library service is tested.

8.3 Unit costing and service costing

Unit costing and timing uses cost analysis data with measures of output to give cost/unit indices; these are often used as performance measures. As a summarizing measurement technique unit costing and timing is attractive to managers, but it must be used with discretion, because of the sensitivity of unit costs to volume, the problems of variable to fixed costs, and the difficulties of the treatment of overheads.

This quotation from Section 5.2 (followed up in Section 5.2.3) clearly points to the value of unit cost measures for their summarizing function. Decision making invariably involves strong elements of comparison, so unit cost measures have a strong attraction; unit costs can be moved around the board until the endgame is reached. The chess analogy is appropriate since the move itself is only the artefact of a greater (business) strategy; the financial manager must think long, medium and short, so if a decision is finally taken on a unit cost criterion it should imply that other lines of thought have been exhausted.

The EBIC case has provided some instances of unit cost treatments, which can be reflected upon. Furthermore, the considerations relating to costing for budgeting have to be kept clearly in view. A cost distribution/cost allocation derived unit cost is both more general and less accurate than one derived from measured cost analysis. If the production process and its determinants (e.g. input prices) are held constant then the measured unit cost analysis value can be held good over a longer run; this is a valuable status if microunit costs (component parts of an operation) are being aggregated to a final cost centre.

8.4 Costing for market-orientated operations

The convergence on market-led and commercial operations in the information and library service business has been a constant theme of the book, and a recognition of long-term structural changes in business economics. On this basis all that has hitherto been written here about costing issues in the context of broader financial management is relevant and applicable.

The driving issue in any commercial activity in a market-oriented business environment is production for exchange. The market brings together sellers (suppliers, providers) and buyers (customers, clients, users). Pricing mechanisms come into play which reflect perceptions of value and needs on the part of sellers and buyers. The commercial activity is the result of the exchanges taking place between the parties in the market. Buyers have their perception of prices; they usually want them to be as low as possible, but consistent with the highest yield of consumer value. The producer/seller interest usually wants prices to be as high as possible, with the purpose of gaining maximum revenue from sales. In the context of costing this relationship is vital, because surplus (profit) is generated when revenue exceeds total costs.

Our perspective of costing study within financial management is directed to knowing the full extent of total costs, so that rates of return can be estimated and evaluated. The producer may not always be in control of the final outcome, because although the producer may use cost data to determine thresholds for prices (he must try to sell for more than it costs to produce) the commercial result is only obtained when the buyer enters the market and purchases at the price offered. Thus a combination of cost measurement and cost control and intelligent decisions over price setting (charging) in markets of varying competitiveness is the final test of the producer's financial managerial ability and business competence.

This argument is a highly simplified account of market economics, and the interested reader has many complementary texts to turn to for further intellectual support and advice. But this minimal statement, however crude, is necessary if the essentials of commercial activity, market behaviour, pricing and costing are to be understood and applied to information and library service business.

Once understood the practitioner sets out to deliver the performance within the organization (and ultimately the market) by deploying techniques of financial management: goal and objective setting, planning, budgeting, control and performance and evaluation study. The essentials of this operation can be seen in the step-by-step exploration of the EBIC case; they could be simulated and characterized in any of the applications discussed in Section 1.5.

8.4.1 Costing, charging and pricing

The evolution of the economic environment and the impact of this on the information and library community has been extensively discussed in Section 1.6 to 1.9. Over a period of 20 years the delivery of information and library service has become more strongly characterized by a market economic ethos and a growing commercial orientation.

There has never been a time when a significant public sector service organization was not concerned with its finances and at least some of their cost consequences, but even in this sector the shift in accent has accelerated significantly. There may still be delivery of service to the consumer 'free at the point of use' but behind the scenes concern over the financing and costs of this mode of delivery has never been more intense. In the public sector financial control and accountability have grown ever stronger. Out of the evolving public sector has come a growing mixed sector in which practitioners seek to maintain public service goals but within an increased market orientation.

Technological changes and new market opportunities have combined in the private market sector of the information economy to stimulate burgeoning growth (e.g. online bibliographic services, service automation providers, Internet gateways etc.); this growth has been stimulated by the 'new market economy' conditions as well as having to accept the discipline of the market. Financial and cost management was always at the heart of enterprise, but this central position has been re-emphasized.

Costing, charging and pricing has become a key relationship in this changing environment. In public service organizations it has amounted to a radical debate (and sometimes radical action) about social responsibilities, priorities and politics, as well as more straightforwardly professional issues (e.g. how do we incorporate cash handling and accounting in an organization culturally unfamiliar with it?). In the commercial sector (and in the new market-oriented public service organization or privatized/contracted out sector) costing, charging and pricing is at the cutting edge of commercial and organizational success (e.g. is the best Internet service provider the one with the lowest charge, or does a combination of price and service package yield the highest revenue?).

Where and when consumers are charged (i.e. made to pay at the point of use) and at what price the service is offered is strongly influenced by levels of service cost, as much as by the motivation to make a surplus/profit. Absolutely critical is the determination of total costs (absorbing all attributable expenditures, whether in money or time).

$$\text{(total revenue)} - \text{(total costs)} = \text{surplus (of revenue over costs)}$$

$$\text{surplus} = \begin{array}{l}\text{gross profit} \\ \text{(operating profit)}\end{array}$$

Total revenue and total cost are the mirror images of the revenue and expenditure budgets (discussed in Chapters Two and Three).

Total revenue is derived through this relationship.

(units sold) × (unit price) = gross revenue (turnover by time period)

It can be seen that cost factors and price are linked together through their impact on revenue. Simply, if cost levels are too high, charges cannot be set at a level low enough to attract the volume of custom; with prices perceived as too high (and not giving the consumer value for money) adequate revenue will not be generated through sales.

It must be appreciated that losses may be incurred when revenue fails to cover total costs, and a surplus is replaced by a deficit. In these discussions the illustration has been kept simple and basic: 'profit' generally means the gross operating profit.

In a working business accountants need to look at net profits as well.

(gross profit + other revenue incomes) − (revenue expenditure)

Interest, taxation and dividend payments are conventionally deducted from gross profits so net profits can be presented with differing deductions (profitability ratios). These data are final accounting presentations; what is emphaisized here is the cost beginning (of profits). The prudent financial manager is making profit calculations when budgets are laid down and cost analysis results are evaluated. So, if value added taxes or service taxes or local taxes (e.g. in the USA, Canada, Australia, New Zealand) have to be paid out of gross profits they must be identified as a source of expense (cost element) in budgetary and price planning (taxes must be costed into charges). Extensive treatments of these topics can be found in standard accounting textbooks; Dyson (1994) or its level equivalent is the type of work.

The EBIC case provides some example of these issues in practice: the bulletin example is one and the cost/revenue/profit implications of the service package to subscribers another. Library and information services face these issues in providing internal and external document delivery, implementing inhouse chargeback systems, providing photocopying and reprographic facilities, making equipment and facilities available on rental; in fact, in engaging in a growing range of commercial activities. Publishers are very familiar with cost/revenue/profit equations in editorial and production management. Information service, corporate information management and computing departments in organizations frequently operate in an internal market/chargeback environment where the same equation applies. The equation is part of the modern information services industry. Brindley (1993) and Webber (1989) have produced useful reviews of pricing strategies which capture the spirit of applications in this industry.

8.4.2 Marginal cost recovery

The concept of marginal cost is often applied to discussions of pricing, decision making and in the context of the reformed public sector (see Glossary for a definition of marginal costing). Dyson (1994) defines marginal costing as 'the accounting system in which variable costs are charged to cost units and fixed costs of the period are written off in full against the aggregate contribution. . .'. As such marginal costing methods are distinct from the absorption costing methods, which have generally been stressed in this book's discussions. Absorption costing disregards the fact that fixed costs will not be related to changes in activity, and by distinguishing fixed from variable cost elements goes on to charge the fixed element to the unit as an overhead.

What might appear inconsistent in theory is really flexibility of method and application; use of one method rather than the other depends on circumstances and what is sought to be shown. The values are relative: absorption costing tries to incorporate all the detail in the equation and then says 'make the decision'; the decision made tends to reflect the longer term. However, what may be needed in the financial strategy is positively to make a distinction between the short and the long term. This is acceptable provided the long term is not ultimately forgotten, because the financial past inevitably catches up with the financial future. If the business believes it can make a medium to long-term recovery (turn a loss into a profit), it makes sense to cost marginally (thus factoring out long-term fixed costs) from the short-term financial (cost/revenue/profit) equation. Dyson points out that marginal costing is a simple system to adopt, and instead of classifying (and absorbing) total cost into its direct and indirect elements, it is classified into its variable and fixed (costs that do not vary in direct proportion to units produced or sales revenue) elements.

A marginal cost statement can thus be characterized.

$$(\text{sales revenue}) - (\text{variable cost of sales}) = \text{contribution}$$

Contribution represents the difference between sales revenue and the variable cost of those sales; if the contribution has a positive value it can help to cover fixed costs.

(contribution) − (fixed costs) = profit (positive balance)/
loss (negative balance)

Dyson uses a simple example to illustrate the marginal cost concept in decision making. Owning a car can be costed on an absorption basis adding together all direct and indirect costs to get a total annual running cost which, divided by the annual kilometres travelled gives an average (absorbed) cost per kilometre; this is a historic cost. However, to calculate the cost of an additional journey (adding marginal kilometres) and to compare it with another means of transport to decide which is the best one to use, should not be done on the basis of the average (absorbed) cost per kilometre, but on the marginal variable cost per kilometre; this is a current cost (basically the cost of the fuel consumed). Real life cases are not always so simple as different decision makers bring different views to the problem. The green economist would prefer an absorption approach which costed in congestion, pollution and road (unsafety costs), thus giving a 'green' marginal cost.

EBIC's problem is less contentious, but the principle is the same. Once the fixed costs of the bulletin are calculated and stabilized (no further work is necessary to sustain that issue of the product) extra copies can be produced at marginal costs (material and print expense only). In the business environment of EBIC marginal costs of production are incurred, but the marginal copies of the bulletin are priced reflecting the absorbed average cost (profit is maximized). However, the green economist might challenge the low marginal costs of extra paper used by arguing that it does not reflect the future costs of planting trees or the ecological consequences of deforestation. People may say that one piece of paper does not matter, but the matter does lie in the fact that billions of pieces are used. Others may then assert that this a strong argument for paperless electronic communication. The moral is that marginal costing and pricing is a useful technique, but the message must be that it may not tell the whole story.

Marginal cost recovery was introduced into the discussion as one of the steps towards the commercial environment. When public service library and information organizations enter the commercial market they often adopt marginal cost recovery or marginal cost pricing. This approach allows the acknowledgement of public service and public subsidy, keeping charges as close to free at the point of service as can be achieved. It is the argument which underpins social welfare, where the fixed costs of the provision are borne by public support, financed by general taxation. Marginal cost pricing may therefore have to come into play, when demand exceeds critical levels which cannot be met by the publicly financed configuration.

EBIC's competitors might include information services supported by public funds (in the sense of a major public library (the British Library, the Corporation of London City Business Library) or the library and information service of a public higher education institution or business school), which can choose to operate under a marginal pricing regime or not (or even under a full cost recovery regime, as some trends argue is happening). In these circumstances EBIC managers might feel there are some uncompetitive practices in the market; they probably do not, preferring to get on with the job of competing and making maximum profits, secure in the knowledge that they can retain and even expand their customer base and provide it with high value cost-effectiveness.

3.4.3 Cost regimes for contracting out

Through the general discussion of Chapter 1 and in Sections 3.6 to 3.9 a picture emerges of an information and library sector which in some areas is becoming ever more market oriented and commercial in its outlook. Progressive implementation of the strategies and techniques advocated in this book will lead to the financial managerial regime best suited for contracting out and later for commercialization and full cost recovery.

The contracting out of formerly publicly funded and/or inhouse functions is often more than just a financial shock to the organizational system. Disturbance to existing organizational structures often leads to resistance from staff and the customer/public alike; existing social, cultural and political norms are being challenged, as well as economic and financial ones. Policy debates and decisions rationalize these factors and the least (or the best) is that majority support for the proposals can be gained.

Given the adoption of the financial managerial apparatus the way ahead is to proceed firmly with consideration. Planning and budgeting and a programme apparatus are essential so that control and management information mechanisms can be built up. Cost analysis will proceed parallel to planning and budgeting. A historic cost allocation/cost distribution can be made, with probes made via measured cost analysis; task analysis, work measurement and cost synthesis will follow for new activities and their programmes. It is essential to establish some historic cost level for the activity before tendering takes place and decisions made into contracting out.

Competitive tenders cannot be evaluated until internal cost regimes are known. Part of the contracting out process involves determining all critical performance standards (in both cost and service aspects) so they can be prescribed in contracts (with associated penalties for non-compliance). Cost and financial data are critical not just for technical calculations, but underlie the credibility of the decision to contract out and to select one supplier over another.

8.4.4 Commercialization and full cost recovery

A market-oriented information business sector is now well established, with examples ranging from the large global and international media, telecommunications, publishing and financial services information companies to their national equivalents, represented by large divisions of global companies and a widening range of small and medium enterprises of national origin. These organizations are commercial enterprises and the equal of any other business venture.

In the library community *per se* the number of global businesses is not large, but some of the examples are significant (the Library of Congress and the British Library which, although supported from public funds, have growing commercial activity, somewhere between marginal cost recovery and full commercialization), and to which can be added the more overtly commercial library networks and library automation companies (OCLC, BLCMP). These organizations in the library community have sometimes originated in the public sector, but became commercial when viable or when public funds could not support their expansion.

These library sector organizations can be offered as the examples of successful commercialization; this is a progressive process, which offers a number of advantages. Publicly funded organizations often find it difficult to finance not only expansion, but also maintenance of existing levels of activity. The move to the market (commercialization) has been offered as the way ahead often accompanied by privatization (selling off the public assets) or by injection of private sector funding in exchange for some commercial opportunities (private sector sponsorship is a very mild form of this); this introduction of private funds is similar to contracting out but more limited in its radical extent. The USA and latterly the UK (from 1979, and likely to be continued after 1997) have been laboratories for this private/public sector mixing.

This progression has introduced the notion of the social market into both the economic and the political debate. Commercialization is legitimized on economic grounds and some public opinion is placated by the maintenance of social criteria to provide acceptable levels of access and equality. Market economy gains are listed such as obtaining the benefits of competition, and with more suppliers entering the market, greater customer choice may result. Indeed, the theory asserts that prices should fall through competition (or at least remain stable). Customers are likely to derive greater value in the longer run as the more able drive out the less able performers, so the remaining suppliers are quality organizations competing with each other.

For one sector of the information industry the commercial market model is unproblematic; they face the problems that all businesses do. The real target of the commercialization process is the publicly funded sector, which is likely to develop in two streams.

One stream will remain reliant on public funds and will seek neither to recover any of its costs from the customer/user, nor feel any obligation to make a surplus of revenue over costs even through an underspend (it will spend all it is given). Yet this organization still needs good financial and cost management to retain the goodwill of its public funders.

The other stream will tend to adopt the social market model, while retaining an allegiance to social welfare activities. This is the likely model for the 'new' public library which will still have to compete with other public spending priorities, while developing commercialized activities and generating surplus revenue. The strength of argument for any public library service, as a social priority, will hopefully guarantee public funds for a basic service, and surplus revenue from market activities might be fed back to enhance the subsidy. Whether the ring fencing of the basic service is sustainable is both a socio-political issue and a library and information professional one. The public funding may serve the role of the fixed cost element in the marginal costing case discussed earlier and even keep services competitively priced. The late 1990s' review of the public library service in the UK will keep all these arguments under scrutiny for some time to come.

The market-oriented stream of public information organizations will need the full armoury of financial management and costing techniques. Cost recovery may not always be maximized in this model, but cost vigilance will be necessary to keep all costs to the lowest possible level. If managers wish to know these cost parameters (and they can hardly avoid needing to) they will have to implement the means to measure costs.

8.4.5 Further Reading: Pricing and Charging

Abels, E. G. and Lunn, L. F. (1996) Perspectives on . . . costs and pricing of library and information services in transition. *Journal of the American Society for Information Science*, **47**(3), 208–209

Akeroyd, J. (1991) Cost and pricing information: the bottom line. *Aslib Proceedings*, **43**(2/3), 87–92

Bailey, S. J. (1989) Charging for public library services. *Policy and Politics*, **17**(1), 59–74

Bawden, D. (1988) Value added information systems and services. In C. Oppenheim *et al.* (1991) (eds.) *Perspectives in Information Management*. Vol. 2. London: Bowker-Saur. pp.157–179

Brindley, L. J. (1993) Information service and information product pricing. *Aslib Proceedings*, **45**(11/12), 297–305

Cartmill, D. (1992) Charging for public library services. *Library Management*, **13**(6), 25–41

Norton, B. (1988) *Charging for library and information services*. London: Library Association

Olaisen, J. L. (1989) Pricing strategies for library and information services. *Libri*, **39**(4), 253–274

Pearson, D. and Yates-Mercer, P. A. (1992) Charging policies and practice in corporate information units in the UK: How to charge. *Journal of Information Science*, **18**(2), 127–137

Spigai, F. (1991) Information pricing. *Annual Review of Information Science and Technology*, **27**, 39–73

Taylor, R. S. (1986) *Value added processes in information systems*. Norwood, NJ: Ablex

Virgo, J. A. C. (1985) Costing and pricing information services. *Drexel Library Quarterly*, **21**(3), 75–98

Webber, S. (1989) *Priced business information services from the public sector: will they succeed?* 55th IFLA Council and General Conference, Paris, France 19–26.8.89. Contributed paper 107-CONTR-E,

Booklet 00, 23–28. (Also published in *IFLA Journal*, 1990, **16**(2), 220–230.)

Webber, S. (1993) Charging for library and information services in medical libraries: a review of the literature and a survey of current practice. *Health Libraries Review*, **10**(4), 202–223

Whitmell, V. (1994) Establishing long term relationships with your fee-based clients. Pt. two: costing issues. *Fee for Service*, **1**(2), 22–25

Yates-Mercer, P. A. and Pearson, D. (1992) Charging policies and practice in corporate information units in the UK: To charge or not to charge? *Journal of Information Science*, **18**(1), 11–25

8.5 Extending examples, applications and practice

At the conclusion of this chapter and indeed of this book, there is still more to be said, and perhaps more that the reader will wish to have read. However, an attempt has been made to lay down some of the principles and illuminate some of the practice on which financial and cost management in the information and library sector can be implemented.

This chapter has attempted to summarize the inter-connected themes of planning, budgeting, costing and performance measurement by linking the chosen example (EBIC) with the fuller discussion in the body of the text.

It has not been possible to provide other fully structured examples from all the information and library subsectors as outlined in Section 1.5. It is quite justified to ask why no example from public libraries, or from school or university libraries has been included or chosen as the case, because the matter at hand could be well illustrated by those organizations.

A justification for restricting the approach lies in the belief that the commercial example illustrated by EBIC defines a limiting case. In public and educational libraries the same structures and elements of the model would all apply. There are revenue and expenditure budgets, which ideally should be shown in programme form; the variety of services and products is all there too in actual or potential form.

The difference is that in the public service model the price of all services offered can legitimately be zero: zero is a valid price value in this model. On the cost side of the model the valid values are all greater than zero and should add up as expenditures to the total cost (which will be balanced with the grant income from the funding body; however in some circumstances they will exceed the grant income and the budget will show a deficit).

This book is therefore something of an invitation to practitioner readers to take matters into their own hands and look to their own service interests for examples and cases. They will find themselves surprisingly well informed (from a combination of their own experience and some stimulation it is to be hoped from this book). Such practitioners will be in the best position to make their service the laboratory for future budgetary and costing practice.

The student of the profession is not to be forgotten though, as the book has tried to present a logical and systematic narrative to what is a complex area. The first two chapters on context and resource management are freestanding introductions, but necessary foundations for Chapters Three and Four on the heart of financial management and the information needs of financial managers. Chapters Five and Six home in on cost measurement and analysis as core tools for the task. Chapter Seven looks at the integration of tools, structures and concepts in a framework of managerial economics, and culminates in the present chapter aimed at preparation for hands on practice.

For both practitioner and student the book is designed to be more than a practical manual; it has enough to start to practice, but its main purpose is to encourage thought and interest in financial management applied to information and library service. The book does not try to usurp the place of specialist texts on financial management, costing and accounting which can be mined for support and deeper detail. Its perspective is no less important for the financial managerial task than the work of the specialists just named; it regards the problem from the viewpoint of information and library managers, and urges them to gain the vital financial competence to meet the exciting future ahead.

8.5.1 Improving budgetary practices

Improving budgetary practice should be affirmed as a strategic goal of all information and library service managers. Budgetary planning and management and the budget is a microcosm of the managed organization and the health of the organization will be supported by the use of sound budgeting principles and practice. Budgetary planning can combine the strategic aspect with the detailed aspect, and internal and external factors. Good management (even better management) should follow from well executed budgetary practice.

Budgetary activities which lead to better co-ordination, less waste of time, effort and resource, result in reduced costs, give more accurate financial predictions, more responsive control and improved accountability could be described as improving. Managers in organizations need to audit their present positions and then take action towards these outcomes in the name of improving their budgetary practices.

8.5.2 Quality in financial management: the overall goal

The idea of continuous improvement is one of the vital ingredients of quality management. As a simple proposition greater quality in financial management can be achieved through improved budgetary practice. The results of this improved practice should feed through into the second vital area of quality management, which is improving customer satisfaction by meeting customer needs. The first beneficiaries of improved quality in financial management will be staff colleagues and other departments: the internal customers. External customers will be the beneficiaries of improved internal quality, in addition to any action taken specifically on their behalf.

When the precursor to this book was written (Roberts, 1985) the quality message was directed mainly towards costing practices in information and library services. More than a decade later, in the present work the general theme of cost management has been developed towards a broader base of financial management. As a result the quality message has been enlarged but is still of comparable strength. Cost measurement and cost management still remain at the heart and centre of financial management. There is still much room for improvement in the fields of application, and the need is as great given the expansion of traditional market sector activities, as well as the commercialization and movement into the social market of the publicly funded sector.

How much improvement has been achieved since the early 1980s? This is a difficult question and the answer given is only an educated guess. On the basis of volumes of professional literature as evidence, the progress in basic techniques and applications knowledge (costing, accounting, financial management) is still quite minimal, given the level of environmental change.

What the literature does show is a proportional increase in contributions on the general environmental changes, covering topics such as marketing, market activity, economics of new technologies, financing and funding, charging and pricing, government policy, information economics as an information policy issue, legal-economic issues such as copyright and intellectual property, and some discussion of social policy issues such as fee or free public library service, and the impact of changes on disadvantaged groups.

One conclusion could be that there is still a knowledge gap in some areas of information and library service financial management, indicating that there are some textbooks to be written to bridge theory and practice. One practitioner view (or even the views of a group) might deny this, and as opinions of individual experience they might be valid views. So another conclusion might be made around the suspected knowledge gap as follows: collective sharing of experience, expressed in the literature and the professional debate is still necessary and given the urgencies of the times it can be considered a priority. If nothing else, this would be one more positive step towards ensuring quality in financial management. It would enhance any stride that may be gained by the contribution of the present work.

8.5.3 Making progress: a selection of readings

This collection of readings is an attempt to highlight some of the most useful references, which can be used to make progress towards broader and deeper studies of both the theory and practice of financial management. It is offered as a stimulus rather than as a substitute for accessing the wider range referred to elsewhere in the book. Inevitably, there may be some bias in the choices made so as to keep the list short, and omission in no way signifies lack of merit or relevance in the contributions of other authors. The other 'further readings' given should still receive proper attention and scrutiny.

Alley, B. and Cargill, J. (1986) *Keeping track of what you spend: the librarians guide to simple bookkeeping*. Phoenix, Ariz: Oryx Press

Brindley, L. J. (1993) Information service and information product pricing. *Aslib Proceedings*, **45**(11/12), 297–305

Clements, D. W. G., (1975) The costing of library systems. *Aslib Proceedings*, **27**(3), 98–111

Brophy, P. (1986) *Management information and decision support systems in libraries*. Aldershot: Gower

Foggo, T. and Bartlett, T. (1993) *Financial management for librarians*. Newcastle upon Tyne: NTG/SCET. (Open Learning package)

Harris, C. (1987) (ed.) *Management information systems in libraries and information service: proceedings of a conference held at the University of Salford, July 1986*. London: Taylor Graham

Jones, L. and Nicholas, D. (1993) Costing medical libraries: the feasibility of functional cost analysis. *Health Libraries Review*, **10**(4), 169–201

Kantor, (1989) Library cost analysis. *Library Trends*, **38**(2), 171–188

Kingma, B. R. (1996) *The economics of information: a guide to economic and cost-benefit analysis for information professionals*. Littleton, Colo: Libraries Unlimited

Lancaster, F. W. (1993) *If you want to evaluate your library...* London: Library Association

Line, M. B. (1986) The survival of academic libraries in hard times: reaction to pressures, rational and irrational. *British Journal of Academic Librarianship*, **1**(1), 1–12

Martin, M. S. (1994) Library finance: new needs, new models. *Library Trends*, **42**(3), 369–584 (Special issue on library finance)

McKay, D. (1995) *Effective financial management in library and information services*. London: Aslib

Mitchell, B. J., Tanis, N. E. and Jaffe, J. (1978) *Cost analysis of library functions: a total system approach*. Greenwich, Conn.: JAI Press

O'Donovan, K. (1991) Costing library services – towards a model for the NHS. Proceedings of a seminar and workshop held at the University of Newcastle upon Tyne 13 December 1990. *Health Libraries Review*, **8**(2), 120–141

Office of Arts and Libraries (1990) *Keys to success: performance indicators for public libraries*. London: Office of Arts and Libraries. (Library and Information Series no. 18)

Prentice, A. (1983) *Financial planning for libraries*. Metuchen, NJ: Scarecrow Press

Prentice, A. E. (1985a) (ed.) Budgeting and accounting. Special issue of *Drexel Library Quarterly*, **21**(3)

Roberts, S. A. (1984a) (ed.) *Costing and the economics of library and information services*. London: Aslib. (Aslib Reader Series Volume 5)

Robinson, B. M. and Robinson, S. (1994) Strategic planning and program budgeting for libraries. *Library Trends*, **42**(3), 420–447

Schauer, B. P. (1986) *The economics of managing library service*. Chicago: American Library Association

Smith, G. S. (1989) Managerial accounting and charging models of administrative behavior. *Library Trends*, **38**(3), 189–203

Smith, G. S. (1991) *Managerial accounting for libraries and other not-for-profit organizations*. Chicago: American Library Association

Snyder, H. and Davenport, E. (1997) *Costing and pricing in the digital age: a practical guide for information services*. London: Library Association

Webber, S. (1993) Charging for library and information services in medical libraries: a review of the literature and a survey of current practice. *Health Libraries Review*, **10**(4), 202–223

References

Adams, R. J. *et al.* (1991) *Decision support systems and performance assessment in academic libraries*. London: Bowker Saur. (British Library Research, Information Policy Issues)

Adams, R. J., Collier, M. and Meldrum, M. (1991) *Decision support systems in academic libraries*. Leicester: Leicester Polytechnic. (British Library Library and Information Report LIR 83)

Allen, L. (1989) Strategic planning for libraries: a convergence of library management theory and research. *International Journal of Information and Library Research*, **1**(3), 197–212

Alley, B. and Cargill, J. (1986) *Keeping track of what you spend: the librarians guide to simple book keeping*. Phoenix, Ariz.: Oryx Press

Allred, J. (1979) Measurement of library services: an appraisal of current problems and possibilities. *Library Management*, **1**(2), 1–46

American Library Association (1966) *Library statistics: a handbook of concepts, definitions, terminology, prepared by the staff of the Statistics Coordinating Project*. Chicago: American Library Association

Association of Research Libraries (1981) *The economic and financial management of research libraries: resource notebook*. Washington, DC: ARL/RLG (Papers of an exploratory meeting sponsored by ARL and Research Libraries Group (RLG))

Aren, L. J., Webreck, S. J. and Mark, P. (1987) Costing library operations – a bibliography. *Collection Building*, **8**(3), 23–28

Axford, H. W. (1972) (ed.) *Proceedings of the LARC Computer-based Unit Cost Studies Institute, September 16–17, 1971*. Library Automation Research and Consulting Association

Baggott, J. (1977) *Cost and management accounting made simple*. London: W. H. Allen

Bailey, S. J. (1989) Charging for public library services. *Policy and Politics*, **17**(1), 59–74

Baker, D. (1992) Resource allocation in university libraries. *Journal of Documentation*, **48**(1), 1–19

Bannock, G., Baxter, R. E. and Rees, R. (1972) *The Penguin dictionary of economics*. Harmondsworth: Penguin Books

Barnes, R. M. (1968) *Motion and time study: design and measurement of work* 6th edn. New York: John Wiley

Batty, J. (1968) (ed.), *Cost and management accountancy for students*. London: Heinemann

Bawden, D. (1988) *Value added information systems and services*. In C. Oppenheim *et al.* (1991) (eds.) *Perspectives in Information Management Vol 2*. London: Bowker-Saur. pp.157–179

Bawden, D. and Blakeman, K. (1990) *IT strategies for information management*. London: Butterworth

Blagden, J. (1980) *Do we really need libraries?* London: Bingley/Saur

Blagden, J. (1982) *Financial management*. In *Aslib handbook of special librarianship and information work* 5th edn. London: Aslib. 53–73

Bloor, I. G. (1991) *Performance indicators and decision support systems for libraries: a practical application of 'Keys to success'*. Leicester: Leicester Polytechnic Library. (British Library Research Paper No.93)

Bommer, M., and Chorba, R. (1981) *Academic library decision support systems*. Washington, DC: Association of Research Libraries

Botten, D. (1982) Implementation: the effects upon management. In *Centre for Library and Information Management* (1982). *The impact of new technology*, pp.59–67

Braunstein, Y. M. (1989) Library funding and economics: a framework for research. *IFLA Journal*, **15**(4), 289–298

Brindley, L. J. (1993) Information service and information product pricing. *Aslib Proceedings*, **45**(11/12), 297–305

Brockman, J. R., (1982) Australian college library management, the AARL statistics and inter-library comparison. *Australian Academic and Research Libraries*, **13**(3), 163–168

Brockman, J. R. and Klobas, J. E. (1979) Contemporary issues in the economics of Australian academic libraries. *Australian Academic and Research Libraries*, **10**(4), 230–236

British Library. (1989) *Gateway to knowledge: strategic plan 1989–1994.* London: British Library

Brittain, J. M. and Abbott, W. (1993) (eds.) *Information management and technology in healthcare: a guide to education and training.* London: Taylor Graham

Brophy, P. (1986) *Management information and decision support systems in libraries.* Aldershot: Gower

Brophy, P. and Coulling, C. (1996) *Quality management for information and library managers.* Aldershot: Gower

Buckland, M. K. (1975) *Book availability and the library user.* Oxford: Pergamon

Buckland, M. K. (1988) *Library services in theory and context.* Oxford: Pergamon (also 1st edition 1983)

Buckland, M. K. *et al.* (1970) *Systems analysis of a university library: final report on research project.* Lancaster: University of Lancaster Library (Occasional Paper No. 4)

Buckley, B. J. (1993) *Survey of library and information plans.* London: South West London Information Network (SWIFT) (BLR&D Report 6128)

Campbell, J. D. (1994) Getting comfortable with change: a new budget model for libraries in transition. *Library Trends*, **42**(3) 448–459

Carbone, P. (1995) The committee draft of international standard ISO CD 11620 on library performance indicators. *IFLA Journal*, **21**(4), 274–277

Carson, J. (1988) *Desktop publishing and libraries.* London: Taylor Graham

Centre for Library and Information Management (1980) *Administrative effectiveness.* Loughborough: Centre for Library and Information Management (Aids to Library Administration Series (ATLAS) No. 1)

Centre for Library and Information Management (1982) *The impact of new technology on the management of libraries: papers presented at a course organised by the Library Association and CLAIM.* Loughborough: Centre for Library and Information Management (CLAIM Report No. 14)

Clark, P. M. (1985) Accounting as evaluation as reporting: the uses of online accounting systems. *Drexel Library Quarterly*, **21**(3), 61–74

Clements, D. W. G. (1975) The costing of library systems. *Aslib Proceedings*, **27**(3), 98–111

Computers in Teaching Initiative (1996) *Resources guide* 6th edn. Loughbrough: CTILIS

Cooper, A. (1980) *Financial aspects of library and information services: a bibliography*. Loughborough: Centre for Library and Information Management (CLAIM Report No. 5)

Cooper, A. and Hart, M. (1981) *Average prices of British academic books January-June 1981*. Loughborough: Centre for Library and Information Management (CLAIM Report No. 11)

Cronin, B. and Gudim, M. (1987) *Anatomy of innovation: an analysis of innovation in the information services sector*. Glasgow: Strathclyde University (British Library Research Paper No. 31)

Cronin, B. (1994) *Marketing of library and information services 2*. London: Aslib

Cummings, M. M. (1986) *The economics of research libraries*. Washington, DC: Council on Library Resources

Currie, R. M. (1972) *Work study* 3rd edn. London: Pitman

Dainton Report. (1969) *Report of the National Libraries Committee*. London: HMSO

Daniel, F. H. (1976) Performance measures for school libraries: complexities and potential. In *Advances in Librarianship*, **6**, 1–51

Department of National Heritage (1995) *Public libraries: assets to the community: final report of the DNH review of the public library service*. London: Department of National Heritage

De Prospo, E. R., Altman, E. and Beasley, K. E. (1973) *Performance measures for public libraries*. Chicago: Public Libraries Association

Dewey, P. R. (1992) 202 + software packages to use in your library. . . . Chicago: ALA

Dossett, P. (1992) (ed.) *Handbook of special librarianship and information work*. 6th edn. London: Aslib

Dudley, E. *et al.* (1991) (eds.) *The economics of library and information services: an Anglo-German perspective*. London: Anglo-German Foundation for the Study of Industrial Society

Du Mont, R. R. and Du Mont, P. F. (1979) Measuring library effectiveness: a review and assessment. *Advances in Librarianship*, **9**, 104–141

Dyson, J. R. (1994) *Accounting for non-accounting students* 3rd edn. London: Pitman

Earl, M. J. (1989) *Management strategies for information technology*. London: Prentice Hall

Farnham, D. and Horton, S. (1993) *Managing the new public services.* London: Macmillan

Financing our public library services: four subjects for debate. (1988) London: HMSO (Cm324)

Finer, R. (1982) The human side of change. In *Centre for Library and Information Management, The Impact of New Technology.* pp.31–50

Ford, G. (1973) *Library automation: guidelines to costing.* Lancaster: Library Research Unit

Ford, G. (1991) Finance and budgeting. In C. Jenkins and M. Morley (eds.) *Collection management in academic libraries.* Aldershot: Gower. pp.21–56

Gilder, L. and Schofield, J. L. (1976) *Work measurement techniques and library management: methods of data collection.* Cambridge: University of Cambridge, Library Management Research Unit (LMRU Report No. 2)

Gimbel, H., (1969) *Work simplification in Danish public libraries: the report of the Work Simplification Committee of the Danish Library Association.* Chicago: American Library Association

Gorman, G. E. and Howes, B. R. (1989) *Collection development for libraries.* London: Bowker-Saur

Gurnsey, J. and White, M. S. (1989) *Information consultancy.* London: Bingley

Hamburg, M. *et al.* (1974) *Library planning and decision making systems.* Cambridge, Mass: MIT Press

Harrington, L. T., Carruthers, R. M. L. and Moffat, M. (1981) Inter-library comparisons: a report on progress with particular reference to public libraries. *Journal of Information Science,* **3**(6), 271–281

Harris, C. (1987) (ed.) *Management information systems in libraries and information services: proceedings of a conference held at the University of Salford, July 1986.* London: Taylor Graham

Hawgood, I. and Morley, R., (1969) *Project for evaluating the benefits from university libraries: final report.* Durham: Durham University (OSTI Report 5056) ED 051 824

Hayes, R. M. and Becker, J. (1974) *Handbook of data processing for libraries* 2nd edn. New York: Wiley-Becker-Hayes

Hayes, S. and Brown, D. (1994) The library as a business: mapping the pervasiveness of financial relationships in today's library. *Library Trends,* **42**(3), 404–419

Herner, S. and Vellucci, M. J. (1972) *National inventory of library statistics practice*. Washington, D.C.: Herner & Co

Hill, M. W. (1994) *National information policies and strategies: an overview and bibliographic survey*. London: Bowker-Saur.

Humphreys, K. (1974) Costing in university libraries. *Liber Bulletin*, (5/6), 8–32

Hutton, W. (1995) *The state we're in*. London: Cape. (Revised edn. (1996) published by Vintage Books)

International Labour Office (1958) *Introduction to work study*. Geneva: International Labour Office

Jenkins, C. and Morley, M. (1991) (eds.) *Collection management in academic libraries*. Aldershot: Gower

Jenkins, C. and Morley, M. (1993) Collections. In M. B. Line (1993) (ed.) *Librarianship and Information Work Worldwide 1992*. London: Bowker-Saur. pp.71–104

Joint Funding Council's Libraries Review Group (1993) *A Report for the HEFCE, SHEFC, HEFCW and DENI*. Bristol: HEFCE (also known as the Follett Report)

Jones, G. (1981) Inter-library comparisons and the CIFC. *Library Review*, **30**(3), 133–142

Jones, D. (1988) (ed.) *The impact of charges on the public library service: proceedings of a seminar organised by the Federation of Local Authority Chief Librarians and the Library Association*. London: Library Association

Jones, L. and Nicholas, D. (1993) Costing medical libraries: the feasibility of functional cost analysis. *Health Libraries Review*, **10**(4), 169–201

Jurow, S. and Barnard, S. B. (1993) (eds.) *Integrating Total Quality Management in a library setting*. New York: Haworth Press

Kantor, (1989) Library cost analysis. *Library Trends*, **38**(2), 171–188

Kennington, D. (1990) *The planning process and library and information services: a manual for preparing Library and Information Plans*. Stamford: Capital Planning Information. (British Library Research Paper No. 88)

Khoo, G. *et al.* (1991) Serials fiscal control using a flat file database management system on a microcomputer. *Serials Librarian*, **20**(1), 91–105

King, D. W. and Bryant, E. C. (1971) *The evaluation of information services and products*. Washington, DC.: Information Resources Press

King, D. W., Roderer, N. K. and Olsen, H. A. (1983) (eds.) *Key papers in the economics of information*. White Plains, NY: Knowledge Industry Publications for ASIS

Kinnell, M. (1989) (ed.) *Planned public relations for libraries: a PPRG handbook*. London: Taylor Graham

Kinnell, M. (1992) (ed.) *Learning resources in schools: Library Association guidelines for school libraries*. London: Library Association

Kinnell, M. (1993) (ed.) *Managing library resources in schools*. London: Library Association

Koenig, M. E. D. (1981) *Budgeting techniques for library and information centers*. New York: Special Libraries Association

Koenig, M. E. D. and Stam, D. C. (1986) Budgeting and financial planning for libraries. *Advances in Library Administration and Organization*, **4**, 77–110

Knott, G. (1983) *Practical cost and management accounting: a fresh approach*. London: Pan Books

Lancaster, F. W. (1977) *The measurement and evaluation of library services*. Washington, DC.: Information Resources Press

Lancaster, F. W. (1993) *If you want to evaluate your library...* 2nd edn. London: Library Association Publishing

Leimkuhler, F. F. (1972) Library operations research: a process of discovery and justification. *Library Quarterly*, **42**(1), 84–96

Leonard, L. F. *et al.* (1969) *Centralized book processing: a feasibility study based on Colorado academic libraries*. Metuchen, NJ: Scarecrow Press

Library and Information Services Council (1988). *Financing our public library service: LISC's response*. London: Whitaker's for LISC and OAL

Library Association (1974) *Professional and non-professional duties in libraries* 2nd edn. London: Library Association

Library Association (1988) *The Library Association's response to Financing our public library service: four subjects for debate, cm324*. London: Library Association

Line, M. B. (1986) The survival of academic libraries in hard times: reaction to pressures, rational and irrational. *British Journal of Academic Librarianship*, **1**(1), 1–12

Line, M. B. and Line, J. (1987) *National libraries*. London: Aslib

Line, M. B. (1990) (ed.) *Academic library management*. London: Library Association

Lynch, M. J. and Eckard, H. M., (1981) *Library data collection handbook.* Chicago: American Library Association–Office for Research

MacDougall, A. F. (1985) *Statistical series in library and information services: current provision and future potential.* Loughborough: Loughborough University. (Elsevier International Bulletins, EIB Report Series No. 9)

Martin, M. S. (1978) *Budgetary control in academic libraries.* Greenwich, Conn.: JAI Press (Foundations in Library and Information Science Volume 5)

Martin, J., Vickers, P. and Feeney, M. (1991) *Information UK 2000.* London: Bowker-Saur

Midwinter, A. and McVicar, M. (1991) The public librarian as budget manager. *Journal of Librarianship and Information Science,* **23**(1), 9–20

Midwinter, A. and McVicar, M. (1994) *The size and efficiency debate: public library authorities in a time of change.* London: Library Association. (BLR&D Report No. 6143)

Miles, I. *et al.* (1990) *Mapping and measuring the information economy: a report produced for the Economic and Social Research Council's Programme on Information and Communication Technologies.* London: British Library. (Library and Information Report No. 77)

Mitchell, B. J., Tanis, N. E. and Jaffe, J. (1978) *Cost analysis of library functions: a total system approach.* Greenwich Conn.: JAI Press

Mohr, M. (1979) Review of: Mitchell, B. J. *et al.* (1978) *Cost analysis of library functions: a total system approach.* Greenwich, Conn.: JAI Press In *Journal of Information Science,* **1**(4), 241–242

Moore, N. (1976) *Statistical series relevant to libraries.* London: British Library (BLR&D Report No. 5300)

Moore, N. (1977a) The need for library statistics. *Liber Bulletin,* (7/8), 24–29

Moore, N. (1977b) *Statistics concerning academic libraries.* London: British Library (BLR&D Report No. 5355)

Morgan, S. (1995) *Performance assessment in academic libraries.* London: Mansell

Morse, P. M. (1968) *Library effectiveness.* Cambridge, Mass.: MIT Press

Murison, W. J. (1988) *Public library: its origins, purpose and significance* 3rd edn. London: Bingley

National Center for Higher Education Management Systems (1979) *Library information handbook: handbook of standard terminology for reporting and recording information about libraries*. Boulder, Colo: NCHEMS

Nicholson, H. (1992) Uncomfortable bedfellows: enterprise and academic libraries. *Journal of Librarianship and Information Science*, **24**(1), 9–12

Norton, B. (1988) *Charging for library and information service*. London: Library Association

Oakeshott, P. and White, B. (1987) *Publishing and information services in the public and private sectors*. Plato Publishing and Brenda White Associates (British Library Research Paper No. 15)

Oakeshott, P. and White, B. (1991) *Joint ventures in publishing and information services: public libraries and the private sector*. Plato Publishing (British Library Research Paper No. 96)

Office of Arts and Libraries (1987) *Joint enterprise: the roles and relationships of the public and private sectors in the provision of library and information services*. London: OAL (No. 16 Library and Information Series)

Office of Arts and Libraries (1990) *Keys to success: performance indicators for public libraries*. London: Office of Arts and Libraries. (Library and Information Series No. 18)

Orr, R. H. (1973) Measuring the goodness of library services: a general framework for considering quantitative measures. *Journal of Documentation*, **29**(3), 315–332

Pack, P. J. and Pack, F. M. (1988) *Colleges, learning and libraries: the future*. London: Bingley

Pantry, S. (1994) (Personal communication)

Parry Report (1963) *The Report of the Committee on Libraries*. London: HMSO

Pearson, D. and Yates–Mercer, P. A. (1992) Charging policies and practice in corporate information units in the UK: How to charge. *Journal of Information Science*, **18**(2), 127–137

Poll, R. (1993) Quality and performance measurement – a German view. *British Journal of Academic Librarianship*, **8**(1), 35–47

Prentice, A. E. (1983) *Financial planning for libraries*. Metuchen, NJ: Scarecrow Press

Prentice, A. E. (1985a) (ed.) Budgeting and accounting. Special issue of *Drexel Library Quarterly*, **21**(3)

Prentice, A. E. (1985b) Budgeting and accounting: a selected bibliography. *Drexel Library Quarterly*, **21**(3), 106–112

Raddon, R. (1997) (ed.) *Information dynamics*. Aldershot: Gower

Raffel, J. A. and Shishko, R. (1969) *Systematic analysis of university libraries: an application of cost-benefit analysis to the MIT libraries.* Cambridge, Mass.: MIT Press

Risk, J. M. S. (1956) *The classification and coding of accounts.* London: Institute of Cost and Works Accountants (Occasional Paper No. 2)

Roberts, S. A., (1981) Internal costs of inter-library lending in British university libraries. *Interlending Review*, **9**(3), 101–103

Roberts, S. A. (1982a) Planning for change – impacts on structures and procedures. In *Centre for Library and Information Management, The Impact of New Technology*, pp.9–30

Roberts, S. A. (1982b) *Current developments in library economics and related issues: report on a study visit to the United States of America.* Loughborough: Centre for Library and Information Management (CLAIM Report No. 19)

Roberts, S. A. (1982c) Review of: The Centre for Interfirm Comparison Interlibrary comparisons, pilot comparison with public libraries. London: British Library (BLR&D Report No. 5638). In *CRUS News*, (15), 16–17

Roberts, S. A. (1984a) (ed.) *Costing and the economics of library and information services.* London: Aslib. (Aslib Reader Series Vol. 5)

Roberts, S. A. (1984b) (comp.) *Unit times for library and information operations: a working list extracted from the literature. (Unpublished report. Contact author for further details)*

Roberts, S. A. (1984c) The management and development of information and library provision in the social sciences. *Journal of Documentation*, **40**(2), 94–119

Roberts, S. A. (1985) *Cost management for library and information services.* London: Butterworths

Roberts, S. A. (1989) Budgeting and costing promotional activities – paying the price and value for money. In M. Kinnell (1989) (ed.) *Planned public relations for libraries: a PPRG handbook.* London: Taylor Graham. pp.46–58

Roberts, S. A. (1993) Economics of information. In C. Oppenheim (1993) (ed.) *Perspectives in Information Management*, **3**(1), 19–41

Roberts, S. A. (1993) Editorial in *Health Libraries Review*, **10**(4), 165–168. (Introduction to an issue of papers on costing and charging)

Roberts, S. A. (1997) The contribution of librarianship to information management. In J. M. Brittain (1997) (ed.) *Introduction to information management.* Wagga Wagga (NSW): Centre for Information

Studies, Charles Stuart University-Riverina, 23–49 (CIS Occasional Monographs, Number 16)

Robinson, B. M. and Robinson, S. (1994) Strategic planning and program budgeting for libraries. *Library Trends*, **42**(3), 420–447

Schwuchow, W. (1977) The economic analysis and evaluation of information and documentation systems. *Information Processing and Management*, **13**(5), 267–272

Smith, C. (1988) (ed.) *Towards a policy for charging: proceedings of a seminar held in London on 26th May 1988*. Hitchin: Effective Technology Marketing Ltd

Smith, G. S. (1983) *Accounting for libraries and other not-for-profit managers*. Chicago: American Library Association

Smith, G. S. (1991) *Managerial accounting for libraries and other not-for-profit organizations*. Chicago: American Library Association

Smith, G. C. K. and Schofield, J. L. (1971) Administrative effectiveness: times and costs of library operations. *Journal of Librarianship*, **3**(4), 245–266

Stephens, A. (1988) The application of life cycle costing in libraries. *British Journal of Academic Librarianship*, **3**(2), 82–88

Stirling, J. F. (1981) *University librarianship*. London: Library Association

Stroetmann, K. A. (1991) Management economic issues of library and information services: a review of the German literature. *Journal of Information Science*, **17**(3), 161–173

Sumsion, J., Pickering, H. V. and Berridge, P. J. (1993) *LISU annual library statistics 1993: featuring trend analysis of UK public and academic libraries 1982–92*. Loughborough: LISU (LISU Public Library Statistics Unit Report No. 7)

Te Boekhorst, P. (1995) Measuring quality: the IFLA guidelines for performance measurement in academic libraries. *IFLA Journal*, **21**(4), 278–281

Thomas, P. A. (1971) *Task analysis of library operations*. London: Aslib (Aslib Publication No. 8)

Thompson, J. (1991) *Redirection in academic library management*. London: Library Association

Thompson, J. and Carr, R. (1987) *An introduction to university library administration*. London: Bingley. 4th edn.

Totterdell, B. and Bird, J. (1976) *The effective library: report of the Hillingdon project on public library effectiveness*. London: Library Association

University Grants Committee (1975) *Capital funding for university libraries.* London: University Grants Committee (Atkinson Report)

Usherwood, B. (1988) *The public library as public knowledge.* London: Library Association

Virgo, J. A. C. (1985) Costing and pricing information services. *Drexel Library Quarterly*, **21**(3), 75–98

Von Busse, G. and Ernestus, H. (1972) *Libraries in the Federal Republic of Germany.* Wiesbaden: Otto Harrassowitz. (Dated, but still a useful source of background information in English)

Ward, J. Griffiths, P. and Whitemore, P. (1990) *Strategic planning for information systems.* Chichester: John Wiley

Ward, P. L. (1982) (ed.) *Performance measures: a bibliography.* Loughborough: Centre for Information Management and Public Libraries Research Group, Loughborough, Centre for Library and Information Management (CLAIM Report No. 15)

Webb, S. (1995) *Creating an information service* 3rd edn. London: Aslib. [1st edition 1988]

Webber, S. (1989) *Priced business information services from the public sector: will they succeed?* 55th IFLA Council and General Conference, Paris, France 19–26.8.89. Contributed paper 107-CONTR-E, Booklet 00, 23–28

Webber, S. (1993) Charging for library and information services in medical libraries: a review of the literature and a survey of current practice. *Health Libraries Review*, **10**(4), 202–223

Webster, D. E. (1981) *The economics and financial management of research libraries: an overview of the issues.* Association of Research Libraries (1981)

West, A. (1988) *A business plan.* London: Pitman. (NatWest Small Business Bookshelf)

White, B. (1987) *Striking a balance: external services in academic libraries.* Brenda White Associates. (British Library Research Paper No. 30)

White, B. (1992) *Maintaining the balance: external activities in academic libraries.* Brenda White Associates. (British Library Research Paper No. 100)

Yates-Mercer, P. A. and Pearson, D. Charging policies and practice in corporate information units in the UK: To charge or not to charge? *Journal of Information Science*, **18**(1), 11–25

Glossary

Many readers of this book are unlikely to be fully cognisant with the specialized terminology of costing and accounting. Rather than break the flow of discussion in the text with formal definition of terms as they are introduced, a glossary of the main concepts and terms has been prepared, as a supplement to the text. A number of sources have been used to provide formal definitions, which in many cases have then been expanded and/or adapted to fit the context of library and information service costing. This is not a comprehensive or exhaustive glossary; for this extension the reader is referred back to the primary sources.

The main sources used are as follows:

Bannock, G., Baxter, R. E., and Rees, R. (1972) *The Penguin dictionary of economics*. Harmondsworth: Penguin Books

Batty, J. (1968) *Cost and management accounting for students*. London: Heinemann. (This reproduces as an appendix the *Terminology of Cost Accountancy*, prepared by the Institute of Cost and Works Accountants in 1966)

Glossary of management terms. (1981) Loughborough: Centre for Library and Information Management. (British Library R and D Report no. 5662)

Kempner, T. (1976) (ed.) *A handbook of management*. Harmondsworth: Penguin Books

Absorption costing

See also **Overheads** Ultimately all overheads that have been apportioned to cost centres have to be absorbed by cost units. Overhead absorption is usually achieved by the use of one or a combination of overhead cost rates; for example, labour hour rate, machine hour rate, direct material cost percentage. Absorption costing would be used to calculate the annual storage cost/volume in a library collection or the annual cost per maintained reader place in a library building.

Accounting More fully cost accounting, which is primarily concerned with meeting the cost information requirements of management. The cost accountant classifies, records, allocates, summarizes and reports to management on current and future costs.

This involves the following responsibilities: (1) design and operation of cost systems and procedures; (2) determination of costs by departments, functions, responsibilities, activities, periods and other cost centres and cost units; (3) comparison of costs of different periods, of actual costs with estimated costs, and costs of different alternatives; (4) the presentation and interpretation of costing information as an aid to management in controlling current and future operations.

Cost accounting is an area within management accounting, and nowadays the two are often synonymous. Cost accounting can be viewed in practical terms as decision accounting. Other types of accounting (subsumed within management accounting) are stewardship (traditional tax accounting (e.g. profit and loss accounts and balance sheets)) and control accounting (concerned with managerial efficiency).

Few libraries recognize the cost and managerial accounting functions in the same way as business enterprise does. But each library shares the same financial responsibilities as outlined above. Clearly library managers have an interest in becoming more conscious of their role as managerial accountants and need the appropriate tools for the task.

Activity sampling A method for collecting data about task and job operations based on random sampling (by time or frequency interval). Subjects or observers record activities at times or points selected on logging sheets or in work diaries. A random sample should generate sufficient observations of the elements to enable a general picture of times and costs to be built up, which is statistically reliable.

Average costs Average cost is calculated by dividing total costs of a given number of units of output by that number of units. The average cost is sometimes referred to as unit cost. In general short run average costs will be above long run average costs. The assumption is that in the long run all inputs have been adjusted to minimum cost levels for a given level of output, whereas in the short run, only some will be at the most efficient level for a given level of output. In most library cost studies average costs and unit costs have been taken to refer to the short run.

Avoidable costs These are costs of production which would not be incurred if a given output were not produced. They are closely related to variable costs or prime costs, which are the direct result of producing additional units. Avoidable costs can be either direct or indirect. Total avoidable costs need not equal total variable costs, since if an enterprise ceased production of a good or service, it may 'avoid' costs, which must be incurred if any output is to be produced, but which do not vary with output.

Break-even analysis

See also **Marginal costing** Break-even analysis is the study of how costs and profits vary with the volume of production, using accounting methods of analysis. A break-even chart can be used as a simple budgeting tool. The chart method does make a number of simplifying assumptions, but used with care the model can provide and relate output and sales targets. In a break-even chart total cost in relation to (sales) volume is shown as a straight line relationship from zero production to a point indicating 100% production capacity.

Break-even analysis can be applied to a number of library operations, usually of a finite nature, and provided surrogate measures can be constructed for sales volume and profit. Library bindery and reprographic operations are an example.

Budget A financial and/or quantitative statement, prepared and approved prior to a defined period of time, of the policy to be pursued during that period for the purpose of obtaining a given objective. It may include income, expenditure and the employment of capital. Two main types of budget presentation have been discussed in this book: the line-item budget and the programme budget.

Budgetary cycle Budgetary development and planning in an organization is essentially a cyclical process. Budget estimates are drafted for one or more years ahead prior to implementation, and post-budget period reviews initiate a fresh cycle. The process is cyclical i.e. repetitive and cumulative. Cyclical and systematic approaches incorporating feedback from previous periods should improve organizational and service performance.

Business strategy A combination of managed policy, planning and implementation which serves to link corporate vision and mission with the achievement of productive and corporate objectives.

Capital appraisal

See also **Discounted cashflow** A set of methods and techniques within capital budgeting. It is concerned with the analysis of prospective costs and benefits of possible new investments, and the evaluation of the desirability of committing resources to them. Its special value is in helping decision makers assess the consequences of capital projects for enterprise finances.

Classification of costs The classification of costs is the basis of all cost accounting systems. It is the identification of each item of cost, and the systematic placement of like items of cost together according to their common characteristics. The process is an essential step in the summarization of detailed costs.

Costs are classified by functions, and within functions costs are collected by cost centres and cost units. Within cost centres and cost units, costs are further classified into cost elements (basically material costs, labour costs, expenses). Cost elements are treated as direct costs (allocated) or indirect costs (apportioned). Direct costs are referred to as prime expenses (directly traceable to the production of a cost unit or activity of a cost centre). Indirect costs are called overheads, and ultimately have to be absorbed by all cost units.

Cost Broadly speaking cost is the measure of what has to be given up in order to achieve something.

Two concepts of cost can be distinguished which may, but need not, be equivalent: (1) opportunity cost, defined in terms of the value of the alternatives or other opportunities foregone in order to achieve a particular objective. This will amount to the same thing as outlays, if and only if the prices with which the outlays are calculated currently reflect the value of alternative uses of the resources. If they do not, the two concepts diverge, and, since opportunity cost is concerned with the real sacrifice involved in achieving something, it is the measurement of costs as 'outlays' which is incorrect; (2) outlays: accountants define cost as the money expenditure or total outlays to achieve something.

The principle of opportunity cost involves asking what is actually foregone by choosing a particular alternative. This concept is preferred by economists, because it leads to a more rational process of decision-taking, in which the returns from an alternative are compared to the real costs involved in undertaking it.

The difference in an approach to the meaning of cost between the economist and the accountant is that the former is primarily interested in optimal decision-taking whereas the latter is more traditionally concerned with ex-post recording and presentation of money flows.

Cost allocation Cost allocation is defined as the allotment of whole items of cost to cost centres or cost units. Cost allocation refers to direct expenditure which can be directly identified with a cost centre or unit, as distinct from indirect expenditures which are apportioned.

Cost analysis Cost analysis is often used as a generic term for cost study, but its preferred use in this text is to describe the primary stage in assessing basic costs for a task, cost centre, cost unit, cost element or other appropriate level of description. Basic data from cost analysis can then be used to calculate other higher order management costs.

Cost-benefit analysis Cost-benefit analysis is a technique which attempts to set out and evaluate the social costs and social benefits of investment projects to help decide whether or not a project should be undertaken. The essential difference between cost-benefit analysis and ordinary investment appraisal is the stress on social costs and benefits. The aim is to identify and measure the losses and gains in economic welfare which are incurred by society as a whole if a particular project is undertaken. In library and information service management and research the concept has been used rather more widely to connote assessments of effectiveness and performance, in addition to general social benefit (and disbenefit). Nevertheless, this wider role for the technique draws heavily on the methods of the more specialized approach.

Cost centre A cost centre is a location, person or item of equipment (or group of these) for which costs may be ascertained for the purposes of cost control. A cost centre consists of an aggregate of lower order functions, known individually as cost units.

Cost: controllable and non-controllable Costs can be divided into controllable and non-controllable categories for a given department or cost centre. It is a means of indicating responsibility for costs within sections of an enterprise.

Cost data Cost data is a generic term for cost statistics generated from cost analysis using specific and rigorous methods or more generalized methods, such as estimation and allocation. The term is used loosely in practice, but should at the very least indicate properly collected usable data, which is managerially useful for decision purposes.

Cost-effectiveness Cost-effectiveness can be simply defined as a method of finding either (a) the cheapest means of accomplishing a defined objective or (b) the maximum value from a given expenditure. Cost-effectiveness can also be considered to be a measure of the efficacy with which various means will achieve a given goal or level of performance judged to be satisfactory.

Cost-efficiency Cost-efficiency has to be distinguished from cost-effectiveness; it refers to the maximizing of the effectiveness of spending, regardless of effectiveness in terms of stated project objectives or performance criteria. It implies the elimination of wasteful operations to achieve a given level of output at minimum cost; it does not necessarily maximize performance.

Cost element Within cost centres and cost units, costs are further classified into cost elements or categories of expense (basically material costs, labour costs, other expenses). Cost elements are treated as direct costs (allocated) or indirect costs (apportioned).

Cost in accounting systems An accountant usually measures the resources acquired by a business in terms of acquisition cost, and an accounting system will generally be a record in terms of the historical costs of resources, and the costings of outputs and finished goods will generally be fully allocated unit costs.

In contrast, the economist thinks of costs in terms of opportunity costs. Since the accounting system is the primary source of cost information for an enterprise, it is essential to appreciate the significance of the differences and similarities of the approaches of the accountant and economist for economic decision-making purposes.

Cost measure A cost measure is cost data, often in summary form (e.g. a unit cost), which relates to some purposive need of the manager for information, comparison or decision. A cost measure implies that some objective need and purpose for the data has been identified e.g. to distinguish between the internal and external costs of handling an inter-library loan.

Cost studies An all embracing term for the different kinds of cost study ranging from basic cost analysis to the development of management costs and specialized cost measures.

Cost unit A cost unit is a product, service or time (or combination of these in relation to which costs may be ascertained for the purpose of cost control. The cost unit may be a job, batch, contract or product group depending upon the nature of the production (of goods or services) on which the enterprise is engaged. Ultimately all cost centre costs are allocated to, or apportioned to, or absorbed by unit costs. During technical processing of acquisitions in a library, an individual title can be regarded as a cost unit at each stage of the process. A certain cost is incurred as each sub-process is completed, and these can be aggregated to give the process cost for the technical processing cost centre (i.e. the cataloguing and acquisition sections combined in this example).

Costing The 'active' context of cost study, which is used to describe the technical aspects of implementing a cost study to derive cost data. The term has procedural implications, emphasizing the fact that a specific method or technique is being followed.

Costing systems The principal types of costing systems are absorption, differential, direct, historical, job, marginal, process and standard. Brief descriptions of the costing system/type of cost are given elsewhere in the glossary.

Differential costing Differential costing is concerned with the effect on costs and revenue if a certain course of action is taken. The term differential cost is generally used by accountants to describe the same costs that economists refer to as incremental costs. Differential costs may be defined as the increases or decreases in total cost that result from any variation in operations. Differential costing eliminates the residual costs which are the same under each alternative and therefore irrelevant to the analysis. Differential cost is a simple yet essential concept in decision making.

Direct costing Direct costing was developed to overcome the distortion caused by fluctuations in the level of stocks, and to eliminate the problem of the volume variance where there are large seasonal variations in the level of sales. Under direct costing only variable components of cost are charged to products for inventory and accounting purposes, and fixed costs are not included in standard product costs. Marginal costing became the term used in Britain to describe the direct costing approach developed in the USA.

Direct costs *See* ***Variable costs***

Discounted cashflow Discounted cashflow is a method of appraising investments based essentially on the idea that the value, to an individual or firm, of a specific sum of money depends on precisely when it is to be received. Given the existence of interest rates it is always better to receive money earlier than later, and to pay money later rather than earlier.

Since the value of a sum of money depends on when it is received, it follows that in appraising investments, which typically yield profits over future time, the profits accruing at different points in time cannot simply be added up. It is necessary to discount for the time value of money by *discounting* (dividing by a suitable factor to find what the present worth or *present value* of a future sum really is). The result of this procedure is a discounted cashflow, on the basis of which the true profitability of an investment can be appraised. Discounted present value (DPV) can be expressed in a generalized formula: $\mathrm{P}n = \mathrm{Po}\ (1 + i)^n$ for any number of periods to show the equivalent of any sum of money as between any two dates. The present value of a sum of money to be received in periods hence is:

$$\mathrm{PO} = \frac{\mathrm{P}n}{(1 + i)^n}$$

By reducing sums received at different points in time to equivalent terms, by the above procedures they can be added together to give meaningful total sums.

Effectiveness criteria

See also **Performance** Effectiveness criteria define the parameters (the limits or boundaries) of performance which are needed to guide management decision and/or control. For example, specified levels of unit cost for producing a service are a criterion which indicates a standard of performance.

Enterprise culture A term used to describe an economic and social policy environment in which a commercial culture of market capitalism and economics is positively encouraged; the benefits of growth, competition and primacy of the individual consumer are stressed; some commentators suggest that valuable redistributive, egalitarian and welfare goals may not be achieved under this regime.

Estimation of costs and times A term used to describe costing and cost analysis studies in which estimates of values are used rather than measured ones (obtained by full work measurement, activity sampling, or other precise means). Estimating may be the only convenient way of obtaining data in some circumstances, but obviously caution is required to control for under- and over-estimation and the continuation of errors in values.

Evaluation A generic term used to describe the many different kinds of process relating to performance measurement and effectiveness analysis. It is a term which is often used with a much wider connotation, embracing quantitative as well as qualitative approaches to study.

Expenses *See* **Primary expenses**

Financial accounting A term often used in contrast to the decision-oriented management accounting. Basically the process and techniques of collecting, analysing, summarizing and presenting financial data in any organization. It covers bookkeeping, general and stewardship accounting, and the presentation of organizational and company accounts. Financial accounts data forms the basis for constructing management accounting data.

Fixed costs

See also **Absorption costing; Overheads** Costs which in the short run do not vary with output. These costs are borne even if no output is produced, and are consequently called overheads, e.g. payment of rent on a building, and interest payments on past borrowing. In the long run, by definition, there are no fixed costs; that is, all costs are variable.

Fixed expenses *See* **Indirect costs**

Historical costing/Historical cost The job costs and process costs calculated may be either historical or standard costs. With a historical costing system actual unit costs are accumulated after operations have taken place. Historical costs are ascertained after the costs have been incurred, standard costs are calculated before the costs are incurred. Historical costs are of limited value themselves, but are an essential part of a standard costing system. The historical costs are compared with the predetermined standard costs, and the differences analysed for control purposes. The principal disadvantages of using historical costs in isolation are: doubtful accuracy; impossibilty of sound interpretation, because of many unknowns; no yardstick to measure efficiency against; delays in taking action are inevitable.

Imputed cost Imputed cost is the opportunity cost of inputs owned by an enterprise, which it supplies to itself, and which have alternative uses. In practice the owner may not be paid a 'price' for these inputs, but will take the residual revenues after all cost payments have been made to factors of production bought in. Any input supplied by the owner may have an alternative use, with a corresponding price, and this represents the effective cost of using that input in the enterprise. A price or cost could be attributed to each input supplied by the owner, even if no explicit price is paid – this is called the imputed cost of the input.

There are many occasions when the library manager should try and consider the opportunity costs (imputed costs) of capital equipment and stock, in determining optimal decisions and resource allocations.

Indirect costs

See also **Overheads** Indirect costs are usually called overheads and ultimately have to be absorbed by all cost units. Conversely, overheads can be defined as the aggregate of indirect costs. In contrast to direct costs, indirect costs are not directly traceable to the production of a cost unit or the activity of a cost centre.

Investment appraisal *See* **Capital appraisal**

Line-item budget A basic form of budget presentation in an organization which uses organizational sections and expense categories as the main principle of division and display; it is input orientated, and contrasts with the output orientated programme budget presentation, which stresses categories of expense by product, service, activity centre. Programme budgets are sometimes referred to as performance budgets.

Management accounting The presentation of accounting information in such a way as to assist management in the creation of policy and in the day to day operation of an enterprise. The emphasis is on using financial accounting and cost data for control and decision making.

Management costs Cost measures devised principally for informing decisions; they could equally well be called decision costs. The term includes a wide range of specific and specialized costs e.g. unit costs, marginal costs, fixed/variable cost differentiation.

Management information system The idea of a management information system implies and suggests the formalization of all sources and types of information and intelligence from the point of view of collection, storage, analysis and dissemination. A management accounting system is one part of a total management information system; cost data files would form a specific part of it.

Managerial economics A hybrid development of applied economics in the context of the management of business enterprises. The traditional aspects of the economic study of the firm and its markets (e.g. demand, price, profits etc.) are supplemented by operational research and accounting. The goal of managerial economics is the improvement of business decision making. Modelling is frequently used to assist an understanding of the real world of the business enterprise.

Managerially useful costs

See also **Management costs** A concept chosen in this text to draw attention to the need to produce useful cost data, especially for output and performance measurement. The concept is related to the more specific idea of management costs.

Marginal cost The change in total costs of production which results when output is varied by one unit, or the avoidable costs of producing an additional unit of output. A distinction is usually made between short run marginal costs – the increase in costs which results from an increase in production, when not all the inputs used by an enterprise can be varied, and long run marginal costs – a change in costs resulting from a change in output, when all inputs, and in particular capital, can be varied. Marginal costs refer to a single kind of increment only, i.e. the addition of another unit to fixed plant. Marginal cost is essentially a short run concept, and differential and incremental costing deal with short run and long run problems.

Marginal costing Marginal costing is essentially a study of the effect of cost/volume/profit relationships based on a classification of costs as fixed or variable. It is an accounting technique which ascertains marginal cost by differentiating between fixed and variable costs. It is primarily concerned with providing management with information on the effects on costs and revenues of changes in the volume and type of output in the short run, although it does have long run applications. Marginal costing can be used as an analytical tool to study cost/volume/profit relationships, or it can be incorporated into a system for recording and collecting costs.

Market Traditionally, the place where buyers and sellers meet to exchange commodities. The term is now also used more generically and broadly to encompass all buyers and sellers, actual and potential and/or all aspects of the commodity environment from production to consumption. The term is used in compound words such as market research, market planning, market growth, information market etc.

Method study Method study is the principal technique for reducing work content, which is primarily a matter of eliminating unnecessary movement on the part of material or operatives and of substituting good methods for poor ones.

Objective accounts An alternative form of presentation of accounts which takes a responsibility (line) and/or programme approach. It is contrasted with the subjective form of accounts, where expenditure is listed according to the totals of each kind of primary expense (see Chapter Three for further discussion).

On cost The contribution of the cost of overheads added to the direct cost of production.

Operating cost A term used in the USA for prime variable cost.

Opportunity cost

See also **Cost; Imputed cost** Opportunity cost is a cost concept, which can be employed in decision making. It is concerned with the best alternative foregone, and is usually measured by the profit foregone under the best available alternative. It is frequently difficult to measure, but remains an important managerial and accounting concept associated with decision making.

Overheads

See also **Fixed costs** Overhead as an accounting term is generally defined as the sum of all business costs which cannot be traced to specific units of output, or are not traced, because it is too costly or inconvenient to do so. Traceability in this context refers to identification with the unit of output in the physical sense of being embodied in that output. In an overhead cost classification, such costs are regarded as common costs with respect to specific units or batches of output, and they contain both fixed and variable elements.

Sometimes overheads are defined as synonymous with indirect costs to distinguish them from the three categories of direct costs (raw materials, wages, expenses). Overheads are usually classified into categories, reflecting the organization of the enterprise.

Overhead costs consist of three broad groups: fixed costs, which tend to be unaffected by variations in volume of output in the short run; variable costs, which tend to vary directly with variations in volume of output; semi-variable costs, which are partly fixed and partly variable.

The most important aspect of overhead cost accounting is the question of attribution of overheads to the costs of units of output, and to the costs of alternative courses of action in decision making. In absorption costing the emphasis is on the need to allocate all costs, and to do this for optimal decision making. In marginal costing there is a belief that trying to allocate the unallocable is responsible for misinforming the decision maker, and that only costs which vary with the volume of output or the implementation of a particular decision alternative can be (or should be) attributed to that output or alternative. The accountant's and economist's usages of the term should be distinguished. The latter generally defines overhead costs as fixed costs and prefers marginal costing procedures.

Performance Performance is a generic concept applied to the means of rating the processes of activity in an organization, and implies constructing appropriate measures to realize this in practice. The idea of performance should be related to the higher order concept of evaluation.

Performance measure A quantitative statement (or sometimes a qualitative indicator) of the actual performance achieved. A performance measure should include adequate means of specifying its range and limits (parameters); this is done partly by defining effectiveness criteria, but it also relates to an understanding of the underlying aims and objectives of the process or activity in question.

Plan An agreed course of action designed to facilitate the implementation of a policy and the achievement of associated objectives. A plan embodies systematic, sequential and logical aspects designed to optimize achievement; for example through the most efficient deployment of resources. Plans also allow greater scope for monitoring, control, feedback and evaluation.

Policy Generally used to describe a broad statement of specific direction and action which an organization uses as a basis for its actions and activities. Ideally, it should be as a result of rational consideration of alternatives and should command a high degree of acceptance in the organization.

Primary expenses A primary expense is defined as one which cannot be divided into two or more distinct types of expenditure; that is, a primary expense account holds one type of expenditure only. Primary expenses may be direct (variable) expenses or indirect (non-variable) overhead expenses.

Prime costs Strictly, variable costs plus administrative and other fixed costs that can be avoided in the short or long term if there is no output, even while the enterprise remains in business. Often used loosely as a synonym for variable costs.

Process costing Process costing (as opposed to job costing) is used in enterprises where large quantities of homogeneous or similar units of product are produced by continuous methods. In such enterprises it is not possible to identify the successive jobs as batches of output for cost accounting purposes. The emphasis in process costing is on the accumulation of costs for all work units over a given period of time. At the end of each period the cost per unit of goods produced is determined as the average unit cost for the period. The conditions for the use of process costing are continuous or mass production, loss of identity of individual items or lots and complete standardization of product or process.

The great majority of library and information service operations costing is treated as process costing. One off costings, e.g. for a new circulation system, or other capital projects, are treated as job costings.

Profit Economists and accountants have different notions of profit, which correspond in some ways to their different ideas of cost. Precise definitions all include the common idea of a surplus after commitments and liabilities have been met. Profit is residual after money to meet expenses has been expended.

Programme A programme can be generally defined as an area of resource allocation and management structure, which can be individually identified and sustained. Any element which can be operationally defined can be regarded actually or potentially as a programme, but in practice most programmes are frequently product and/or service orientated, and have a strong activity bias.

Programme budget

See also **Line–item budget** A method of budget presentation which uses a programme structure of contributing activities and final outputs (products and services) as the main principle for division and the display of expenses. It is output orientated, can assist the study of performance and can help the review and clarification of objectives.

Programme structure A programme structure is a helpfully complete statement of the activities of an organization and their interrelationships, in a form which can be used in budgetary planning and management. It can be represented in tabular form with programme descriptions, and can usefully be mapped diagrammatically. (See the EBIC example in Chapter Eight).

Programming Programming is used in this text in the context of developing a programme structure for an organization. The process will begin with an examination of organizational aims and objectives, and may involve review and systems analysis. The programme structure becomes the basis for budgetary planning and development.

Resource management A generic term for the area of managerial activity concerned with obtaining, deploying and using resources for given ends in an organization. Resource management covers strategic, tactical and operational phases, and lays emphasis on efficiency, effectiveness and the achievement of performance goals.

Revenue The term is used in this text in the limited sense of income earnt by or accruing from the activities of an organization. However, on a broader level revenue is used to refer to all sources of finance available to an organization e.g. as in revenue contrasted with expenditure, both used in the wider sense.

Standard costing In a standard costing system predetermined costs are carefully computed and later contrasted with actual costs to aid in cost control. The differences between the actual costs and the predetermined standard costs are called variances. Cost accountants analyse the variances by causes. The principal cost variances calculated by comparing actual and standard costs are illustrated.

In principle there is no difference between standard costs and budgeted costs; both are based on the principle of predetermination of cost, but there is a difference in scope between a budget system, and a system of standard costs. Budgeting includes objectives for all activities during a certain period, whereas standard costs relate to detailed costs of operation. Standard costs are scientifically predetermined costs of materials, labour and overheads chargeable to a product or service. In this system the standard costs are usually entered into the books of account for comparison with actual costs. Standard costing

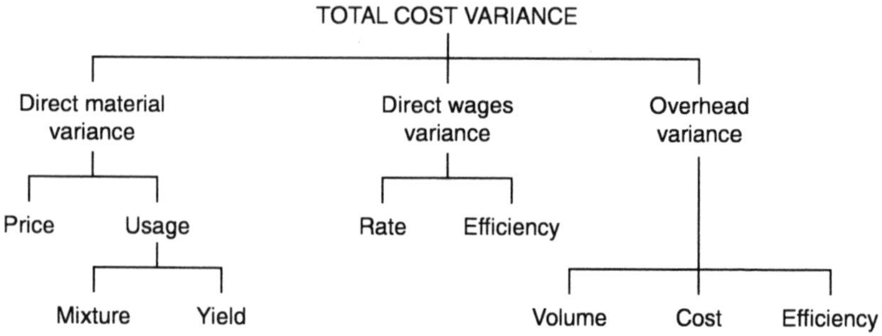

permits a system of 'exception reporting', whereby attention is given principally to the cost variances. In an enterprise operating this system costs are accumulated by departments and cost centres.

Subjective account An accounting statement is in subjective form when the expenditure is listed according to the totals of each kind of primary expense. The concept is related to, and can be contrasted with an objective form of accounting, which traces expenditure according to the purpose or object for which it has been made (see Section 5.3.6 for further discussion).

Time accounting conventions In work measurement procedures it has been found useful to determine standards for relaxation time, available working time, and other time divisions to assist in consistency and comparability of data and studies.

Time study Time study is a technique for determining as accurately as possible from a limited number of observations the time necessary to carry out an activity at a defined standard of performance.

Total costs Total costs can be defined as the sum of prime costs (broadly the direct or variable costs incurred) and overheads (indirect costs).

Unit costs *See* **Average costs**

Unit times A unit time for an activity will normally be derived by work measurement techniques; the unit time may refer to any suitable entity (e.g. a whole or part operation or a series or set of operations). It is desirable to have unit time standards (e.g. validated times) if these are to be used for costing, and especially for the synthesis and estimation of unit costs.

Value for money A concept used to denote the scale and impact of return provided to or received by the consumer when a commodity exchange within the price mechanism takes place. The return may have a direct monetary element, but also includes subjective valuations e.g. dependent on quality management aspects (e.g. fitness for purpose), level of user need or perception of changes that may ensue once information is obtained.

Variable costs

See also **Avoidable costs; Operating cost** Variable costs are costs which vary directly with the rate of output; principally labour costs, raw material costs and energy. These are also known as operating costs, prime costs or direct costs.

Variable expenses

See also **Avoidable costs; Operating costs; Prime costs; Variable costs** Difficulties of definition sometimes arise when cost and expense are used synonymously. In practice costs are derived from or relate to expenditures made. Thus, variable expenses are expenses which vary directly with the rate of output.

Variance (cost) analysis

See also **Standard costing** The analysis of cost variances; that is the difference between a standard cost and the comparable actual cost incurred during a period. The total cost variance is made up of a number of constituent elements: e.g. direct materials cost variance, direct wages variance, overhead variance; these can be further subdivided (e.g. materials variance depending on price and usage).

Work measurement Work measurement is concerned with investigating, reducing and subsequently eliminating ineffective time (time during which no effective work is being produced, whatever its cause). The techniques of work measurement are important in practice for establishing work and time standards for specific activities; hence its usefulness for calculating unit times, as the basis of unit costs.

Work sampling *See* **Activity sampling**

Work study Work study is a collective term used to describe the combination of techniques involved in method study and work measurement. Awareness of unfavourable cost patterns may lead to managerial action in the form of instituting work studies, in an effort to improve physical efficiency and ultimately cost-effectiveness.

Zero-base budget The use of Zero-Base Budgeting (ZBB) is designed to focus the manager's attention on evaluating activities and making decisions. ZBB is a method of budgetary planning and presentation which includes objective setting, programme evaluation and operational decision making involving managers and staff. Decision units (similar to programmes) are identified and analysed in 'decision packages', which are evaluated and valued, before making an appropriation request. The operating budget reflects the 'packages' in its structure. In each fresh budgetary cycle the previous sums appropriated are 'set to zero', and each proposal is justified afresh.

Appendix 1

Specimen information file contents

Note for 2nd edition: a number of functions listed are no longer current practice (e.g. tasks related to manual card catalogues); the original text has been left unaltered on the premise that readers will see how to update with their own contemporary examples.

A1.1 (Source: Clements 1975)

Units of measurement

Data collected regularly	Data collected as required
A. New inputs to the library	
1. Items ordered 1.1. Number of titles ordered (If possible count under the following headings) (i) by purchase (ii) by exchange (iii) by donation (iv) by legal deposit	(1) Proportion selected but not ordered (2) Amount of second-hand material ordered (3) Proportion of orders needing to be chased or hastened (4) Performance of various sources of supply
2. Items received 2.1. Current serial titles (excluding monograph series) Count the number of current serial titles received, counting each title once only (i.e. exclude duplicate copies) – this means counting bibliographic titles and not parts 2.2. Number of patents received (i) UK patents (ii) Non-UK patents	(1) Number of new titles taken (2) Number of titles ceasing publication (3) Number of separate parts to be registered/recorded (4) Number of modifications required to existing records, e.g. change of title, change of price, etc.
2.3. Printed materials (monographs, etc. excluding current serial titles, patents, printed maps, musical scores) (If possible count under the following headings) (count by volumes or units) (i) by purchase (ii) by exchange (iii) by donation (iv) by legal deposit 2.4. Printed maps (Count by number of sheets) 2.5. Music (Count by number of separate scores)	*Applicable to all types of items received* (1) Number and type of items ordered but not received (2) If appropriate, other types of material received should also be broken down by (i) purchase, (ii) exchange, (iii) donation and (iv) legal deposit

Data collected regularly	Data collected as required

2.6. Manuscript material
(Includes full-size copies if not commercially published but excludes microform copies)
(Count by number of units to be catalogued)

2.7. Microforms
(i) Microfilms by number of rolls
(A standard roll is 30 metres long, approx. 100 ft; 60 metre lengths count as 2 rolls, etc.)
(ii) Other microforms
(Count by the number of physical units, e.g. sheets of microfiche, number of microcards)

B. Processing outputs of the library

1. *Stamping*
(Stamping of newly acquired material with appropriate library ownership and/or date-stamp)

(1) Number of items stamped
(2) Delay between receipt of item by library and shelving (and date-stamping if appropriate)

2. *Item streaming*
(Sorting newly acquired material and routing according to processing steps required, e.g. type and level of cataloguing, need for classification, need for binding, etc.)

(1) Proportion of items received undergoing each of the processing steps available
(2) Delays between receipt of items, completion of each processing step and final shelving

3. *Cataloguing and subject work*

3.1 Number of separate titles catalogued; and number of catalogue entries prepared.
(If possible count under the following headings)
(i) monographs
(ii) new serial titles
(iii) individual serial articles
(iv) other material

(1) Level of cataloguing used and amount and type of material going to each level
(2) Number of entries revised
(3) Number of existing entries in the catalogue altered/amended
(4) Amount of modification and revision needed to the authority files
(5) Amount of time required for authority checking during preparation of catalogue entries

3.2. Number of separate titles subject analysed and/or indexed; number of separate titles classified; and number of subject entries prepared

(1) Type and level of subject work and amount and type of material going to each
(2) Number of entries revised
(3) Number of existing entries altered/amended

4. *Production of catalogue and other bibliographic tools*
4.1. Number of records typed and/or keyboarded
4.2. Number of entries proof-read prior to final production
4.3. Number of catalogue cards produced
4.4. Number of catalogue entries printed or produced (excluding catalogue cards). Please indicate whether produced in printed form, microfilm, COM, etc.

(1) Delays between receipt of final entries and production of finished products
(2) Proportion of entries produced by each of the processes used
(3) Amount of machine time lost

Data collected regularly	Data collected as required
4.5. Number of other bibliographic tools produced (please specify)	
5. *Binding, labelling, boxing, etc.*	
5.1. Binding control (Scheduling, etc. of items to be sent to the binders) (Count by number of physical units bound)	(1) Amount and type of material to be bound and rebound (2) Delays in binding (3) Proportion of items received from binders requiring further binding work
5.2. Shelf location system	(1) Type of shelf location system used, number of units dealt with
5.3. Labelling	(1) Type of labelling system used, number of physical units labelled
5.4. Boxing (Preparation of boxes for serial parts, loose material, etc.)	(1) Number of boxes prepared (2) Number of physical units boxed
5.5. Covering (Covering of books, etc. with protective jackets, etc.)	(1) Methods used and quantities dealt with
5.6. Filing and shelving	(1) Number of physical units of new acquisitions shelved (2) Number of units of stock withdrawn for discarding (3) Number of units of stock replaced due to wear, outdated editions, etc. (4) Amount of tidying of material on open shelves in wrong position (5) Number of catalogue cards filed (6) Number of existing catalogue entries replaced due to wear, damage, etc. (7) Number of existing catalogue entries withdrawn

C. Service functions of the library

Data collected regularly	Data collected as required
1. *Reception/screening of readers*	(1) Number of applications for readers' tickets dealt with
2. *Book application and reservation* (Concerned with readers' applications for books stored in closed access) 2.1. Number of applications received 2.2. Number of volumes or units reserved 2.3. Number of requests not satisfied	(1) Analysis of distribution of numbers of applications made during each day and of seasonal fluctuations (2) Analysis of number of volumes reserved per reader and periods of reservation (3) Analysis of requests not satisfied and reasons (4) Analysis of reader failure in locating material in the catalogue
3. *Book supply* (Location and retrieval of material stored in closed access) 3.1. Number of volumes or units requested 3.2. Number of volumes or units supplied 3.3. Number of requests not supplied 3.4. Number of requests taking longer than than '*x*' minutes to supply	(1) Analysis of length of delays in delivery and their causes (2) Analysis of type, age of publication and subject of items requested (3) Analysis of reasons for requests not being satisfied (4) Analysis of number and size of volumes requested per reader

Data collected regularly	Data collected as required
4. *Loan services*	
4.1. Loans to readers for use outside the library (i) Number of volumes lent (ii) Number of items reserved	(1) Analysis of loan requests by type, age of publication and subject (2) Number of volumes overdue (3) Number of reservations satisfied and length of delays (4) Distribution of issues during the day showing peaks of use
4.2. Lending to other libraries (i) Number of requests received (ii) Number of requests satisfied (iii) Delays in supply	(1) Original items lent to libraries in UK and overseas (2) Number of photo- or other copies issued to libraries in UK and overseas (3) Analysis of type, age of publication and subject of requests received and sources of requests and analysis of unsatisfied requests
4.3. Circulation of literature to members of own organization	(1) Number of titles circulated and number of people on lists for each title
4.4. Borrowing from other libraries (i) Number of items requested (ii) Number of items received	(1) Analysis of items requested (2) Analysis of sources of supply (3) Analysis of speed of supply
4.5. Location services (Supply of location of items not held in stock) (i) Number of requests received (ii) Number of requests satisfied (iii) Delays in supply	(1) Source of requests and source of supply (2) Analysis of type, age of publication and subject of requests received, satisfied and unsatisfied
5. *Information services*	
5.1 Number of enquiries received and number satisfied broken down by (i) readers' enquiries (ii) telephone enquiries (iii) postal enquiries (iv) telex enquiries	(1) Analysis of number and type of requests received and satisfied (2) Analysis of requests unsatisfied (3) Amount of time required to answer requests and material used to supply answer
5.2. Compilation of bibliographies, reading lists, etc.	(1) Number of bibliographies, reading lists, etc. compiled. Frequency of duplicate requests. Amount of time required to prepare these items.
5.3 Other services (e.g. translations, exhibitions, educational services, etc.)	(1) Analysis of requests for each type of service against demand, costs and charges
6. *Reprographic services*	
6.1 Photocopying (see also 4.2. above under loan services) (i) Number of requests received and satisfied and whether requests received by post or from readers in the library (ii) Number of sheets produced	(1) Analysis of type, age of publication and subject of requests received, satisfied and unsatisfied (2) Analysis of size of orders (3) Analysis of speed of supply (4) Analysis of costs and charges

Data collected regularly	Data collected as required
6.2. Microfilming (i) Number of requests received and satisfied (ii) Number of frames produced	(1) Analysis of type, age of publication and subject of requests received, satisfied and unsatisfied (2) Analysis of size of orders (3) Analysis of speed of supply (4) Analysis of costs and charges
6.3 Other copying and photographic services (i) Number of requests received and satisfied (ii) Number of units produced (e.g. frames, prints, etc.)	(1) Analysis of type, age of publication and subject of requests received, satisfied and unsatisfied (2) Analysis of size of orders (3) Analysis of speed of supply (4) Analysis of costs and charges

TABLE A1.2 Selected cost measures by Library Function (Source: Hamburg *et al.*, 1974)

Function	*Total cost*	*Units of output*	*Other divisor*	*Data element*	*Subtotals*
Provision of building area	User area		Population	Cost of user area per capita	Library unit
	Staff area		Staff man-years	Cost of staff area per full-time staff member	Library unit
	Document storage area		Document volumes	Cost of document storage area per volume	Library unit, document form
	Function total	Square feet		Cost of providing building area per square foot	Library unit
Provision of user furnishings	Function total		Population	Cost of user furnishings per capita	Library unit
Selection of documents	Act of selecting	Titles selected		Selection cost per title selected	Document subset
	Act of selecting		Population	Selection cost per capita	Document subset
	Document expenditure	Volumes selected		Document expenditure per volume selected	Document subset
	Document expenditure		Population	Document expenditure per capita	Document subset
Acquisition of documents	Function total	Volumes added		Acquisition cost per volume added	
Processing of documents	All processing, except binding	Volumes added		Non-binding processing cost per volume added	
	Binding of new documents	Volumes added needing binding		Binding cost per new volume bound	

TABLE A1.2 continued

Function	*Total cost*	*Units of output*	*Other divisor*	*Data element*	*Subtotals*
Control of document location and use	Function total	Exposures		Cost of control of document location and use per exposure	Library unit
Facilitation of document use	Function total		Population	Cost for facilitating document use per capita	Library unit
Maintenance and weeding of documents	Binding	Volumes bound		Binding cost per old volume bound	Document form
	Weeding	Volumes weeded		Weeding cost per volume weeded	Library unit
Access to documents in other libraries	Incoming documents or photocopies	User requests satisfied from other libraries		Cost of obtaining documents per satisfied request	
	Outgoing documents or photocopies	Documents or photocopies sent to other libraries		Cost of satisfying requests by other libraries per outgoing document or photocopy	
Provision of aids to locate documents within the library concern	Classification without preprinted card	Titles classified without preprinted card		Cost of classifying without preprinted cards per title	Document subset
	Classification with preprinted card	Titles classified with preprinted card		Cost of classifying with preprinted cards per title	
	Cataloguing	Titles added		Cataloguing cost per title added	Document subset

TABLE A1.2 continued

Function	*Total cost*	*Units of output*	*Other divisor*	*Data element*	*Subtotals*
	Function total	Titles added		Cost of providing aids to locate documents within the library of concern per title added	
	Function total		Population	Cost of providing aids to locate documents within the library of concern per capita	
Provision of aids either to identify existing documents or to locate them in other libraries	Expenditure for indexes	Indexes added		Index expenditure per index added	Document subset
	Processing of indexes	Indexes added		Cost of index processing per index added	Document subset
	Function total		Population	Cost per capita of providing aids either to identify existing documents or to locate them in other libraries	
Personal assistance for document identification and for providing information	Function total	Questions answered		Cost of personal assistance per question answered	Library unit; Population subset
	Function total		Population	Cost of personal assistance per capita	Library unit; Population subset
Publications, advertising, and exhibits	Publications	Publications		Cost per publication	
	Advertising	Advertising campaigns		Cost per advertising campaign	

TABLE A1.2 continued

Function	*Total cost*	*Units of output*	*Other divisor*	*Data element*	*Subtotals*
	Exhibits	Exhibits		Cost per exhibit	Library unit
	Function total		Population	Cost of publications, advertising, and exhibits per capita	Population subset
Personal communication with members of the population being served	Function total	Personal communication		Cost per personal communication	Population subset
	Function total		Population	Cost of personal communication per capita	Population subset
Planning and administration	Function total		Population	Cost of planning and administration per capita	
Support	Function total		Population	Cost of support per capita	Library unit
ALL FUNCTIONS	Grand total	Exposure		Total cost per exposure	Library unit; Population subset
	Grand total	Visit		Total cost per visit	Library unit; Population subset
	Grand total		Population	Total cost per capita	Library unit; Population subset

Appendix 2

The description of library systems (After Humphreys, 1974)

Note for 2nd edition: a number of functions listed are no longer current practice (e.g. tasks related to manual card catalogues); the original text has been left unaltered on the premise that readers will see how to update with their own contemporary examples.

A2.1 Levels and terms

A2.1.1 Levels

Sub-system: Primary area within a system, not necessarily corresponding to any single traditional library department.

Procedure: The level concerned with information flow. Information movement and processing grouped as consecutive or related activities are identified. The components of processing are functions, elements and steps.

Function: A function is an identifiable activity within processing designated by a verb. Functions must refer to similar levels of activity within a procedure. A function can consist of a single element of a sequence of related elements.

Element: This specifies a discrete part of the processing involved in an individual function. An element can consist of a single or a sequence of steps. There are two types of element:

(1) Elements that do not contain decision, i.e. sequential steps;
(2) Elements which comprise decision(s).

Step: A single action within an element and the smallest part of any processing. It is specified by a statement containing a single verb. Steps can be common to all elements.

TABLE A2.1.2 Terms to define the library system

Sub-system	*Procedures*	*Functions*
Acquisition: The total acquisition system covering the initiation, checking, effecting, receipt and clearing of orders for items added to the library's holdings.	**Select:** The stage relating to suggestion and initiation of orders.	**Originate:** The source and initiation of an order.
		Check: The check on a suggestion for the presence of existing records for the same item in the library files, and for the correct publishing details.
		Transcribe: The transcription of suggestion details into standard form.
	Order: The activities producing and despatching orders and of maintaining a record of them.	**Produce:** Production of the library's standard order form, its checking and confirmation.
		Despatch: Despatch of the order.
		File: Filing of a copy of the order and related records.
	Receive: Report on orders placed, arrival of items and checking.	**Unpack:** Dealing with correspondence; opening of parcels and batching of items.
		Check: Check of items received against the order file; any annotation; check on physical condition of items received, together with fund and financial accounting.
Processing: The area of work following the receipt of items to produce	**Input:** Initial incorporation of an item into the library stock.	**Accession:** Process of incorporating items into library stock.

TABLE A2.1.2 continued

Sub-system	*Procedures*	*Functions*
bibliographic records for for incorporation into the library's files and to release items for preparation.		**Allocate:** Placing of items for processing, batching and streaming.
	Process: The creation of bibliographic records and their replication.	**Catalogue:** Provisional choice of heading and entry; check to establish these; writing out bibliographic record in standard form which is then checked.
		Classify: Establishment of subject content; check of schedules and previous use of classmark or subject term; adding of classmark and library location on standard catalogue form.
		Reproduce entry: The generation of records for incorporation into the library's files.
	Output: The stage of releasing the items and bibliographic records.	**Distribute:** The placing of items for preparation.
		File: The batching and filing of records for the library's files.
Use: The area of actual library service available to users being the regulation of stock, the enquiry services, other services and library-user education.	**Search:** The process for satisfaction of customer enquiries other than those classified under Inform.	**Resolve internal:** Dealing with customer enquiries by using internal facilities.
		Resolve external: Dealing with customer enquiries by means of external facilities.

TABLE A2.1.2 continued

Sub-system	*Procedures*	*Functions*
	Control: The constraints governing the use of stock.	**Control access:** Regulation of the use of stock and registration of of user categories. **Issue:** Provision of facility for borrowing and reserving items.
	Reproduce: The provision of facilities for use of alternatives to the traditional physical stock of the library and provision of appliances for their use.	**Provide photo-services:** Provision of equipment to copy library and other materials. **Provide non-book equipment:** Provision of appliances.
	Inform: Information and training in the use of the library.	**Lecture:** Tours, instruction and answer to enquiries about use of library. **Provide literature:** Written guides to the use of the library. **Disseminate:** Information service, bulletins, bibliographic services, abstracting service, etc.
Maintenance: The areas of service in the physical sense, being the stock on the shelves, the upkeeping of records and control of the environment.	**Stock:** The physical makeready and repairs to items; review of stock and shelf supervision.	**Prepare:** Preparation for shelving and use. **Bind:** Bind and repair. **Update:** Review of stock use and of the condition of stock. **Shelve:** Shelf supervision.
	Catalogue: Revision and physical maintenance of the catalogue file.	**Revise:** Correction of entries, withdrawal.

TABLE A2.1.2 continued

Sub-system	*Procedures*	*Functions*
		Maintain: Replacement of worn cards, alteration of cabinet guides, etc.
	Environment: The maintenance of the fabric and equipment.	**Clean:** Dusting, polishing, etc.
		Equip: Lights, machinery, etc.
		Furnish: Tables, shelves, cabinets, etc.
		Control: Temperature, humidity, heating, etc.
Administration: The notional area of service to the library that enables the other sub-systems to operate.	**Services:** Operational services.	**Provide:** Secretarial, Clerical, Porterage } Service
	Management: Planning and control of the library sub-systems.	**Plan:** Research and development, etc.
		Control: Personnel staffing, accounting, etc.
		Train: Training staff, Library School students, etc.
		Liaise: Relations with larger entity – university, corporation, etc.

An industrial accounts classification (After Risk)

(The following table is an extract from a full accounts classification)

TABLE A3.1 Overhead section of accounts code

Indirect labour (200)

		0	*1*	*2*	*3*	*4*	*5*	*6*	*7*	*8*	*9*
	200										
'Manual' (excluding setters)	210		Related to specific cost centres				Not related to specific cost centres				
Non-manual	220		Supervision (weekly)		Technical (including setters)	Inspection (weekly)	Clerical (weekly)			Training and learning (weekly)	
On repairs and maintenance	230		of land	of buildings	of roads etc.	of plant and machinery	of vehicles			of fixtures etc.	
(Additional analysis of repairs if needed)	240										

TABLE A3.1 continued

Indirect labour (200)

		0	*1*	*2*	*3*	*4*	*5*	*6*	*7*	*8*	*9*
Lost time	250		Due to material	Due to machinery	Due to management e.g. lack of work					Time spent attending meetings	Other types of lost time
Extra payments	260		Bonus related to output	Overtime premium	Shift premium		Merit awards not directly related to output				Extra payments not elsewhere classified
Monthly paid employees	270		Supervisory staff (monthly)		Technical staff not primarily on supervisory work	Inspection (monthly)	Clerical staff (monthly)			Training and learning (monthly)	Other monthly paid staff including general management
Employee benefits: 1. Paid directly	280		Holiday pay	Sick pay	Supplementary pensions	Lump sum or ex gratia payments	Co-partnership payments			Make-up pay for staff in H.M. forces	Other direct benefits
2. Not paid directly	290		National insurance		Pension contribution by employer					Tuition fees etc. paid by employer	Other indirect benefits

TABLE A3.1 continued

Indirect materials (300)

		0	*1*	*2*	*3*	*4*	*5*	*6*	*7*	*8*	*9*
	300										
	310				Lubricants		Petrol			Stationery etc.	
	320										
On repairs and maintenance	330		of land	of buildings	of roads etc.	of plant and machinery	of vehicles			of fixtures etc.	
	340										
Water, heat, light and power	350		Water	Coal etc.	Fuel oil etc.	Electricity purchased	Gas purchased				Other types
	360										
	370										
	380										
	390										

Note (1) There will usually be a separate code for indirect materials, and the 300 Group of the Accounts Code can be adapted to hold the first two stages of division of the code for indirect materials. If that is done, it will be necessary to rearrange the position of the code numbers for indirect materials used on repairs and maintenance.

(2) The items given above are, of course, far from being exhaustive.

TABLE A3.1 continued

General charges Group 1 (400)

		0	*1*	*2*	*3*	*4*	*5*	*6*	*7*	*8*	*9*
	400										
Payment to contractors: (1) Repair work	410		of land	of buildings	of roads etc.	of plant and machinery	of vehicles			of fixtures etc.	
(2) Other work	420		Carriage inwards	Hired transport (excluding passenger cars)	Demurrage		Carriage outwards			Warehousing charges	Other contracting work
Travelling etc. expenses	430		Rail, road, air, water travel	Car expenses (excluding petrol)	Car and cycle allowance	Entertainment	Road licences				Other travel
Communications	440		Telephone (external)	Telegrams and cables	Telephone (internal) and recording or amplifying instruments	Postages					Other communication expenses
Information and knowledge	450		Periodicals, books, etc.		Conference fees		Trade association subscriptions			Research associations	Patent fees and other payments for information

TABLE A3.1 continued

		0	*1*	*2*	*3*	*4*	*5*	*6*	*7*	*8*	*9*
Advertising and publicity	460		Sales literature	Press adver-tising	Samples and presents	Photo-graphs, blocks, etc.	Advertising agents			Public relations advisers	
Professional fees (excluding advertising)	470			Rating surveyors		Tax advisers	Audit fees			Legal fees	Business consultants etc.
Charges relating to money	480		Bank charges								Other charges e.g. night safes; paper and canvas bags etc.
Sundry general charges	490				Subscriptions and donations (excluding employees)						Other general charges

General charges: Group 2 (500)

	500										
Insurance	510		Fidelity guarantee; cash; insurance stamps	Employer's liability	Third Party	Fire (excluding cars, vans, etc.)	Cars, vans, etc.			Consequential loss	Goods in transit and other charges

TABLE A3.1 continued

		0	*1*	*2*	*3*	*4*	*5*	*6*	*7*	*8*	*9*
General charges: Group 2 (500)											
Taxation	520			Rates			Taxes on profits				Tithes, way-leaves, etc.
Interest payable	530		Bank interest			Hire purchase charges				Interest on debentures	Other interest
Rent and hiring charges	540			Rent payable		Hire of machines					Other rent etc. charges
Depreciation	550		of land	of buildings	of roads etc.	of plant and machinery	of vehicles			of fixtures etc.	
	560										
	570										
	580										
	590										

Appendix 4

Summary task description listing

The main heading categories of a preliminary Task Description Schedule together with suggested task codes for accounting purposes are outlined.

In this scheme the first and second order categories (e.g. B Personnel Management; BA Recruitment and Selection) could form a basis for defining programmes and cost centres. The third and fourth categories (functions and elements/steps) are procedural and functional, representing tasks and cost units (if these need to be defined for a high level of detail in costing).

Items in each of the four orders are coded for the practical purposes of manual data collection, processing, and analysis of time and cost data. Where machine or computer assistance is used to collect, process and analyse time and cost data such identifiers are essential.

The coding scheme proposed has four levels:

1 the major systems and programmes found in library and information service, described by a short mnemonic phrase which is used as the first element in a complete coding

2 sub-systems and sub-programmes, described by a single letter A/Z and forming the second element in the task code citation

3 functional elements of the main library and information procedures, each described by a unique number, allowing a maximum of 999 separate task functions to be identified

4 elements of functions and steps of processes of the main library and information procedures, described by a three number code

allowing a maximum of 999 separate elements or steps to be enumerated per function.

Such a coding would be capable of more than ample coverage of all likely elements required for time and cost studies. The enumeration and selection of the major system and programme areas is broadly derived from the Library Association scheme (*Professional and Non-professional Duties in Libraries*, 2nd ed. (1974) London: Library Association), with the addition of a category for lending activities, and one for attributes (for example of the kind enumerated in the British Library Planning Secretariat scheme). Items in orders 3 and 4 are not enumerated in this summary, neither are sections (H), (J) and (K) in the first and second levels.

The tables follow on the next page.

Programmes and cost centres				*Procedures*		
System/ programme			Sub-system/ sub-programme	Functions		Element/step
Phrase	*Letter*		*Letter*	*Number*		*Number*
(A)	GEN	/	(A/Z)	001/099	/	001/999
(B)	PER	/	(A/Z)	100/199	/	001/999
(C)	PUB	/	(A/Z)	200/299	/	001/999
(D)	SEL	/	(A/Z)	300/399	/	001/999
(E)	ACQ	/	(A/Z)	400/499	/	001/999
(F)	CAT	/	(A/Z)	500/599	/	001/999
(G)	PRO	/	(A/Z)	600/699	/	001/999
(H)	INF	/	(A/Z)	700/799	/	001/999
(J)	LEN	/	(A/Z)	800/899	/	001/999
(K)	ATT	/	(A/Z)	900/999	/	001/999

Key
(A) General administration and management
(B) Personnel management
(C) Public relations
(D) Selection/acquisition and withdrawal/disposal
(E) (as one section or divided)
(F) Catalogue, classify and index
(G) Production, preparation, conservation, housing and handling of material and associated equipment
(H) Information
(J) Lending
(K) Attributes

A4.1 Summary of task description schedule

A. *General administration and management*

(A) Accounts work
001 General
002 Acquisition and relegation procedures
003 Budgeting
(B) Administration
004 General
(C) Computers and ancillary equipment
005 General
(D) Data processing
006 General
(E) Equipment
007 General
008 Maintenance and repair
(F) Library building
009 General
010 Cleaning
(G) Personnel services
011 General
(H) Professional communication
012 General
(I) Reprographic
013 General
(J) Research and development
014 General
(K) Security and portering
015 General
(L) Secretarial and clerical
016 General
(M) Miscellaneous
017 General

B. *Personnel management*

(A) Recruitment and selection
001 General
(B) Remuneration
002 General

(C) Staff management
  003 General
(D) Staff and manpower planning
  004 General
(E) Staff training
  005 General
(F) Staff welfare
  006 General

C. *Public relations*

(A) Information files
  001 General
(B) Mailing lists
  002 General
(C) Professional activities
  003 General
(D) Publications
  004 General
(E) Publicity activities
  005 General
(F) Retail sales
  006 General
(G) User relations
  007 General

D/E. *Selection/acquisition and withdrawal/disposal*

(A) Selection
  001 General
  002 Approval selection
(B) Accessioning
  003 General
(C) Acquisition
  004 General
  005 Archives processing
  006 Bibliographic searching and checking
  007 Periodicals
(D) Gifts and exchanges
  008 General
(E) Input processing
  009 Intellectual
  010 Mechanical
(F) Stock management
  011 General
(G) Deselection
  012 General
(H) Discarding
  013 General
(I) Accounting
  014 General
(J) Other
  015 A/V items
  016 Special materials processing
  017 User education materials
  018 Microform
  019 Reference selection
  020 Reference inventory and
  006 weeding
  021 Reserve book room

F. *Catalogue, classify and index*

(A) Adaptive cataloguing
  001 General
(B) ADP/mechanized production
  002 General
(C) Approval processing
  003 General
(D) Archives processing
  004 General
(E) Auxiliary functions
  005 General
(F) Bibliography
  006 General
(G) Book processing
  007 General
(H) Cardstocks
  008 Preparation
  009 Procurement
(I) Catalogue maintenance
  010 General
(J) Cataloguing
  011 General
(K) Clerical support
  012 General
(L) Distribution of copy
  013 General
(M) Documentation processing
  014 General
(N) Filing
  015 General
(O) Indexing
  016 General
(P) Management
  017 General
(Q) Policies
  018 General
(R) Post-cataloguing
  019 General
(S) Pre-cataloguing
  020 General
(T) Proofing and checking
  021 General
(U) Recataloguing
  022 General

(V) Reclassification
023 General
(W) Selective cataloguing
024 General
(X) Serials
025 General
(Y) Special materials
026 Indexes
027 Special collections
028 Media
029 Vertical file
(Z) Subject work/classification
030 General

G. *Production, preparation, conservation, housing and handling of material and associated equipment*

(A) Archives processing
001 General
(B) Binding
002 General
003 Post-binding
004 Pre-binding
(C) Book distribution
005 General
(D) Book fetching
006 General
(E) Book processing
007 General
(F) Boxing (periodicals)
008 General
(G) Cleaning
009 General
(H) Conservation
010 General
(I) Data input and processing (mechanized)
011 General
(J) Document processing
012 General
(K) Equipment
013 General
(L) File storage
014 General
(M) Special materials processing
015 General
(N) Guiding materials
016 General
(O) Inhouse materials production
017 General
(P) Inventory and shelf reading
018 General
(Q) Packing/unpacking
019 General
(R) Paperback books
020 General
(S) Photographic and reprographic services
021 General
022 Duplicate, photocopy, print
(T) Postal work and mailing
023 General
(U) Publishing
024 General
(V) Reference collection
025 General
(W) Relocation of stock
026 General
(X) Repairs to library materials
027 General
(Y) Reserve books
028 General
(Z) Searching for items
029 General
(AA) Secondary publications
030 General
(AB) Security
031 General
(AC) Serials work
032 General
(AD) Shelf and stack maintenance
033 General
(AE) Shelf tidying
034 General
(AF) Special collections processing
035 General
(AG) Stock maintenance
036 General
(AH) Storage and shelving (physical)
037 General
(AI) Transport
038 General
(AJ) User education materials
039 General

Appendix 5

Data recording forms

A number of examples of data recording forms are reproduced in order to illustrate typical layouts, and to provide a source for the reader to develop similar examples for individual circumstances.

The first forms come from the Library Management Research Unit, and are taken from Gilder, L. and Schofield, J. L., *Work Measurement Techniques and Library Management: Methods of Data Collection* (1976) Loughborough: Library Management Research Unit. Form 2a (not reproduced) is a procedure narrative form. The fifth example is a very basic recording sheet (diary form) also used by the Library Management Research Unit.

Form 1a

LIBRARY MANAGEMENT RESEARCH UNIT SURVEY

NAME .... DEPARTMENT ....

(Details of work performed on tasks not directly connected with your department. Please include details of sickness, leave etc.)

DATE	TASK	HOURS	DATE	TASK	HOURS

Form 1b

LIBRARY ACTIVITY FORM
LIBRARY MANAGEMENT UNIT INFORMATION SYSTEM

NAME .... LIBRARY ....

PERIOD FROM .... TO .... GRADE ....

Please record details of all tasks carried out except those of ....
If the process is in connection with periodicals prefix data with 'P'. In addition please record leave, sickness, compensatory time off etc.

DATE	DETAILS	UNITS	HRS. MINS	DATE	DETAILS	UNITS	HRS. MINS
				TIME WORKED OUTSIDE NORMAL HOURS			
				DATE	DETAILS	UNITS	HRS. MINS

FORM 2b

LIBRARY MANAGEMENT UNIT INFORMATION SYSTEM

NAME: .... LIBRARY: ....

PERIOD FROM: .... TO: .... GRADE: ....

Please record details of tasks carried out in connection with the processes shown below. Work in respect of periodicals prefix data with 'P'.

Process	Date	Time Taken	Number of units
Book selection		Hrs. Mins.	Number of Recommendations
Selection	28/9	2.00	32
	29/9	1.20	49
	30/9	1.00	14
	1/10	0.50	14
	2/10	0.50	10
Final selection	2/10	0.30	
Selection	5/10	0.45	19
Selection	6/10	0.15	6
Selection	7/10	0.15	5
Processing Selections Until Arrival of Book		Hrs. Mins.	Number of Orders Placed (Titles)
Checking and signing orders	28/9	0.30	
Checking and signing orders	29/9	0.10	
Correspondence	29/9	0.30	
Orders	1/10	0.10	
Processing from arrival of books to passing on for catalogue process		Hrs. Mins.	Number of Items Received
Accounts	29/9	0.15	
Selection of Donations	30/9	0.20	10
Acknowledgements	30/9	0.05	20
Accounts	5/10	0.15	
Accounts	6/10	0.20	

Process (State if checking)			Date	Time Taken	Number of units
Cat. and Clnes	Cat.	Class		Hrs. Mins.	Number of Main Entries for Typing/ Checked
✓	(checking)		30/9	1.00	11
✓			1/10	2.45	21
✓			2/10	2.30	18
✓	(checking)		5/10	1.00	11
✓			5/10	2.00	13
✓		✓	7/10	5.15	39
Catalogue Typing/ Check Typing				Hrs. Mins	Number of Main and Added Entries
Check typing			29/9	0.45	102
Check typing			30/9	0.20	51
Other Processes Prior to Shelving Labelling, etc.				Hrs. Mins	Number of Items Forwarded
Processing			7/10		15
Filing New Entries				Hrs. Mins.	Number of Entries Filed

Form 2c

SUMMARY SHEET

LIBRARY: ______________________________ PERIOD: __________

MATERIAL: ______________________________

Activity	Work Unit	Total elapsed time	No. of Work Units completed	Hourly Rate	Average	
					Time	Cost
Selection	No. of Recommendations					
Processing selections until arrival of item	No. of orders placed					
Processing selections on arrival of item to passing on for cataloguing	No. of items received					
Cataloguing	No. of main entries ready for typing					
Catalogue process-checking	No. of entries checked					
Catalogue typing	No. of main entries typed No. of added entries typed					
Catalogue typing checking	No. of cards checked					
Other processes prior to shelving	No. of items forwarded					
Filing new entries	No. of entries files					

Appendix 6

A library management information system (after Hamburg)

A6.1 Library information system structures

For purposes of classification and design, a general library information system can be conceptually broken down into a number of separate subsystems. Each subsystem can then be considered separately. It is often easier to design an information subsystem for a separate function, such as circulation control, than to try to design one information system for the entire library. However, interdependencies between the subsystems will exist, and these need to be taken into account in a total system design.

Two alternative breakdowns of a general library information system are given. *Figure A6.1* depicts an information system hierarchy based on a design by Robert M. Hayes and Joseph Becker (1970). They identify six major subsystems, each of which is composed of a number of separate files.

Figure A6.2 depicts an information system design which differs from the Hayes-Becker design in fundamental ways. It identifies four sources of library data: the population to be served, library service and operations, user-library interaction, and the rest of society. Without recommending any particular system design for all libraries, a crosswalk is presented between the Hayes-Becker information system and the alternative system.

The purpose of a crosswalk between the two information system designs is to indicate how library personnel might translate any data file from one system into the other system. *Table A6.1* depicts the crosswalk from the list of seventeen functions to the six Hayes-

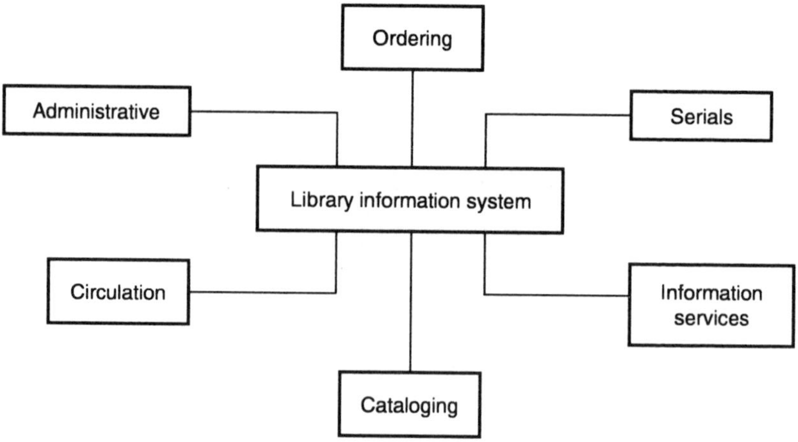

Figure A6.1. Hayes-Becker library information system

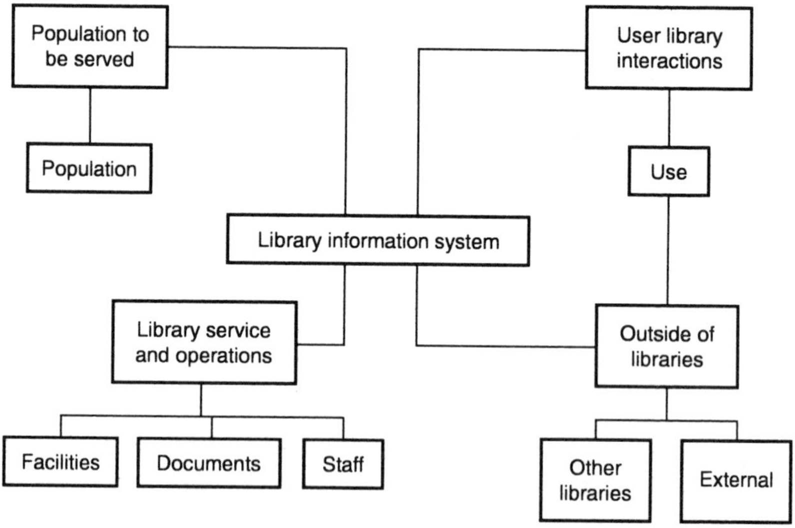

Figure A6.2.

Becker subsystems. A 'question mark' indicates that there is no clear correspondence or else no counterpart in the other system. *Table A6.2* depicts the crosswalk from the Hayes-Becker subsystems to the list of function numbers.

The content of the Hayes-Becker system design is outlined now. The six information subsystems are broken down into files, and the

TABLE A6.1 Crosswalk between seventeen functions and Hayes-Becker subsystems

Function	*Hayes and Becker Subsystem*
Providing physical facilities	
(1) Provision of building area	Administrative
(2) Provision of user furnishings	Administrative
(3) Maintenance of facilities	?
Providing access to documents and indexes within the library	
(4) Selection	Ordering; serials
(5) Acquisition	Ordering; serials
(6) Processing	Ordering; serials
(7) Classification and cataloguing	Cataloguing; serials
(8) Control of location and use	Circulation; serials
(9) Facilitation of use	Circulation; serials
(10) Maintenance and weeding	?; serials
Providing access to documents in other libraries	
(11) Provision of aids primarily to locate documents in other libraries	?
(12) Facilitation of access to documents in other libraries	?
Promoting library use	
(13) Personal assistance for document identification and location and for conveying information	Information services
(14) Publications, advertisements, and exhibits	?
(15) Personal communication at the initiative of the library with members of the population being served	?
Planning, administration and support	
(16) Planning and administration	Administrative
(17) Support	Administrative

TABLE A6.2 Crosswalk between Hayes-Becker subsystems and appropriate function numbers*

Hayes and Becker subsystem	*Function numbers*
Administrative	1. 2. 16. 17
Circulation	8. 9
Ordering	4. 5. 6
Cataloguing	7
Serials	4. 5. 6. 7. 8. 9. 10
Information services	13
?	3. 10. 11. 12. 14. 15

* See Table A6.1 for functions associated with each function number.

files can be further subdivided into accounts, records and data elements. Their system design is organized in the following way:

I. Administrative subsystem

A. Financial files

1. Balance sheet accounts file (by account number within department)
   a. Salary-related accounts (salary; payroll taxes; pension fund; insurance; social security)
   b. Supplies accounts (office supplies; book preparation supplies; automotive supplies; building maintenance supplies)
   c. Printing and reproduction accounts (office copying equipment; printed forms; reports)
   d. Office expense accounts (postage; telephone and communication; office services; office equipment, purchase; office equipment, rental)
   e. Facility accounts (rent; utilities; construction materials; motor vehicles)
   f. Book accounts
   g. Financial accounts (cash; accounts payable; accounts receivable; depreciation)
2. Purchase order file (by purchase order number)
3. Accounts payable file (by vendor number)

B. Personnel files

1. Personnel file (by employee number) (application forms; interviews and references; appointments, transfers and promotions; performance ratings)
2. Payroll records file (by employee number) (time records: checks issued to employees; payroll change records)

C. Management files-cost accounting

1. Direct cost accounts (by process and job) (historical costs; standard costs; time, amount of work performed; material used; administrative unit; level of complexity)
2. Overhead cost accounts (by type of expense)

II. Circulation subsystem

1. Transaction file (by call number) (documents charged to borrower-user or other library; documents charged to

internal library function; documents returned but not purged)

2. Call card file (by transaction number) (when book card or borrower card is missing)
3. Hold call card file (by call number)
4. Borrower registration file (by borrower identification number)
5. Scheduling file (by call number) (deliveries and pick ups)
6. Security file (by call number) (for military classified records)
7. Overdue file (by call number)
8. History file (by call number) (analysis of prior circulation records)

III. Ordering subsystem

1. In process file (by author and title) (shows vendor and order status-edited; purchase order written; I.D. card written; encumbered; order received; invoice received; order paid; overdue; back ordered; partial order received; wrong material; defective material; cancelled; waiting to be catalogued; clear from in-process file; copied to standing order file)
2. Order file (by order number) (shows vendor and documents of outstanding orders, without bibliographic information)
3. Vendor file (by vendor number) (shows orders)
4. Fund file (by fund code number) (status of each fund)
5. Invoice file (by invoice number within vendor number) (for each invoice received, shows items received, cancelled and outstanding)

IV. Cataloguing subsystem

1. The catalogue or index (by author, title and subject) (for bibliographic description, intellectual access, intellectual organization, physical access, alerting and administration)

V. Serials subsystem

1. Master serial records file (by serial identification number) cataloguing data – name changes; alternative titles; analytical entries for separately titled issues;

a unique identifier; a limited set of subject headings; reference to abstracting and indexing journals by which the serial is or is likely to be covered

Ordering data – renewal dates; names and addresses of publisher, society or association; vendor number; fund number; reference to associated publications

Receiving data – frequency of publication; volume and issue numbering practice; expected irregularities; check-in points; claiming criteria

Binding data – style and colour; number of issues per binding volume; binding dates; special instructions for binding

Holdings data – bound volumes and separate issues; gaps and missing issues; wants; locations of holdings

Distribution data – names and addresses of individuals and organizations, and locations for distribution

2. Receiving file (by serial, by receipt or by issue expected)

VI. Information services subsystem

1. Database for users (by subject key word)

The Hayes-Becker library information system design not only specifies the content of the system in an extensive fashion, but it also indicates the type of reports and analyses that the system facilitates. The following list indicates the major reports that result from their system. No special purpose programs are required to obtain these reports for the most part. Analyses that do require special programmes are indicated in parentheses.

I. Administrative subsystem

A. Financial
   1. Expenditure reports
   2. Analyses of variances
   3. Budgetary plan
   4. Reports by vendor
   5. Checks to vendors
   6. Cash status reports
   7. History (bookkeeping; vendors)

B. Personnel
   1. Service reports
   2. Performance evaluations

3. Checks to employees
4. Payroll reports

C. Management-cost accounting
1. Labour efficiency reports
2. Labour distribution reports
3. Actual versus standard comparisons

D. Management-production control
1. Production schedules
2. Future work-load forecasts

II. Circulation subsystem
1. Recall notices
2. Overdue notices
3. Long-term circulation list
4. Hold list
5. Replacement borrower cards
6. Replacement book cards
7. Registered borrower list
8. Fines
9. Document distribution schedule
(10. Analysis of document use by user)
(11. Analysis of document use by document)
(12. Analysis of document use by user and document)

III. Ordering subsystem
1. Status of items on order by author/title
2. Estimates of cataloguing work loads
3. Notices to requesters
4. Claims notices
5. Orders printed
6. State of library funds, including danger signals
7. Invoice payment authorization
8. List of cancelled and out-of-print items
9. Vendor report of number of items ordered; average delivery time and number cancelled due to inefficiency

IV. Cataloguing subsystem
1. Frequency of use of material
2. Frequency of assignment of subject terms and of co-occurrence

V. Serials subsystem

1. Expected arrival list
2. Current information list
3. Invoice charges approved and disapproved for payment
4. Bindery control list
5. Claims and renewal requests
6. Error list
7. New acquisitions list
8. Current expenditure characteristics
9. Subject heading list
10. Master shelf list
11. Routing lists
12. Membership lists

VI. Information services subsystem

1. Information retrieval

With respect to the specific content of this information system, important design considerations are degree of detail and level of aggregation. Library data elements may be defined according to one or more of the following eight categories:

1 **Time period** If time period is not indicated for a data element, it is assumed that it is associated with a year and is aggregated not more frequently than annually. Time period is indicated if less than annual subtotals, by hour, day, week, month, season, semester and so forth. For instance, time period is indicated for attendance, which may be tabulated with respect to any time frame.

2 **Population subset** For public libraries, the population to be served may be subdivided into population subsets with respect to age, reading or educational level, occupation, geographical area or other special characteristics. For university libraries, they may be defined with respect to status (undergraduate, graduate-master's, graduate-PhD, faculty, staff, other) and subject area of interest. For example, for the number of persons in the population served by the library, it may be useful to tabulate by population subset. The term 'per capita' is used to refer to each person in the population to be served or to each person in a population subset; actually, it indicates a division by the appropriate number of persons.

3 **Document subset** Document subsets may be defined with respect to form, subject matter and other characteristics. An example of a data element for which document subset subtotals may be relevant is number of documents added.

4 **Library unit** Each separate physical location of a library may be considered a different library unit. Also, larger units may be segmented even further: for example, departmental libraries or subject departments in the same building. An example of a data element for which library unit subtotals may be relevant is the number of microform readers.

5 **Exposure type** Various types of document exposure have been identified, including circulation, direct in-library exposure, indirect exposure (where a library employee communicates to an individual as a substitute for direct exposure), photocopy use and interlibrary loans. An example of a data element for which exposure-type subtotals may be useful is the number of document exposures.

6 **Staff type** The library staff may be delineated by extent and type of education and experience. This delineation may be accomplished with respect to degree attained or primary function performed. Ordinarily, there is a distinction between professional and non-professional personnel, with possible additional categories of semi-professional and student assistant. Staff type is a useful tabulation for full-time equivalent personnel, particularly if delineated further into library functions. Alternatively, separate counts may be made of full-time and part-time staff.

7 **Storage locations** Documents are stored in various library units and, within library units, in various locations. Each relatively distinct location may be identified for certain data. For example, it may be helpful to delineate the number of linear feet of shelving by storage location.

8 **Use period** In addition to being placed in a storage location, every library document is assigned a specific use period. The period may range from a one hour in-library reserve charge to an unlimited circulation use. An example of a data element for which use period subtotals may be beneficial is the mean time between the withdrawal and return of a document.

The eight dimensions just listed are the major categories for defining most library data elements. However, for a particular decision, there may be other dimensions that might also be relevant. Significant indicators of input, output and performance of each library function are formulated by taking ratios of appropriate data elements. The ratios of quantitative data elements must be examined in conjunction with whatever descriptive or qualitative information may be available to a library decision maker. Analysis of descriptive information may yield additional relevant quantitative data elements.

Index

Note: Page numbers in bold denote glossary.